American Subcultures

A BEDFORD SPOTLIGHT READER

American Subcultures

A BEDFORD SPOTLIGHT READER

Eric Rawson
University of Southern California

bedford/st.martin's
Macmillan Learning
Boston | New York

For Bedford/St. Martin's

Vice President, Editorial, Macmillan Learning Humanities: Edwin Hill
Senior Program Director for English: Leasa Burton
Program Manager: John E. Sullivan III
Executive Marketing Manager: Joy Fisher Williams
Director of Content Development: Jane Knetzger
Developmental Editor: Jennifer Prince, Lexi DeConti
Content Project Manager: Louis C. Bruno Jr.
Senior Workflow Manager: Lisa McDowell
Production Supervisor: Robert Cherry
Media Project Manager: Rand Thomas
Manager of Publishing Services: Andrea Cava
Project Management: Lumina Datamatics, Inc.
Composition: Lumina Datamatics, Inc.
Photo Editor: Hilary Newman
Photo Researcher: Angela Boehler
Permissions Editor: Kalina Ingham
Permissions Researcher: Eve Lehmann
Senior Art Director: Anna Palchik
Text Design: Castle Design; Janis Owens, Books By Design, Inc.; Claire
    Seng-Niemoeller
Cover Design: John Callahan
Cover Photo: Carsten Koall/Getty Images
Printing and Binding: LSC Communications, Harrisonburg

Manufactured in the United States of America.

2   1   0   9   8   7

f   e   d   c   b   a

For information, write: Bedford/St. Martin's, 75 Arlington Street, Boston,
    MA 02116

ISBN 978-1-319-06203-3

Acknowledgments

*Text acknowledgments and copyrights appear at the back of the book on
pages 337–39, which constitute an extension of the copyright page. Art
acknowledgments and copyrights appear on the same page as the art selections
they cover.*

The Bedford Spotlight Reader Series is a g
readers, each featuring Bedford's tradem.
readers in the series collect thoughtfully chose.
an entire writing course—about thirty-five selecti.
tors to provide carefully developed, high-quality inst.
able price. Bedford Spotlight Readers are designed to h.
inquiries from multiple perspectives, opening up topics.
food, gender, happiness, humor, money, monsters, and su.
critical analysis. An Editorial Board of more than a dozen con.
whose programs focus on specific themes have assisted in the
ment of the series.

Bedford Spotlight Readers offer plenty of material for a compo.
course while keeping the price low. Each volume in the series offers n.
tiple perspectives on the topic and its effects on individuals and society
Chapters are built around central questions such as "What Is Life Like on
the Margins?" and "What Values Do Subcultures Share with Mainstream
America?" and so offer numerous entry points for inquiry and discussion. High-interest readings, chosen for their suitability in the classroom,
represent a mix of genres and disciplines, as well as a choice of accessible
and challenging selections to allow instructors to tailor their approach.
Each chapter thus brings to light related—even surprising—questions
and ideas.

A rich editorial apparatus provides a sound pedagogical foundation.
A general introduction, chapter introductions, and headnotes provide
context. Following each selection, writing prompts provide avenues of
inquiry tuned to different levels of engagement, from reading comprehension ("Understanding the Text"), to critical analysis ("Reflection and
Response"), to the kind of integrative analysis appropriate to the research
paper ("Making Connections"). An appendix, "Sentence Guides for Academic Writers," helps students with the most basic academic scenario:
having to understand and respond to the ideas of others. This is a practical module that helps students develop an academic writing voice by giving them sentence guides, or templates, to follow in a variety of rhetorical situations and types of research conversations. A website for the series
offers support for teaching, with a sample syllabus, additional readings,
video links, and more; visit **macmillanlearning.com/spotlight**.

American Subcultures is a resource for the first-year college writing class. Today's students are navigating an American cultural landscape that often seems divided into competing camps defined by rigid politics, tastes, economic interests, and ethnic, racial, and gender identities. Investigating what constitutes a subculture and how marginalized communities affect our shared experience is a topic of natural interest.

Not surprisingly, students arriving on campus for the first time bring a wide range of perspectives on the multifarious American experience. Many identify with particular subcultures. Family, friends, and fellow citizens, as members of subcultures, influence students, helping to define what it means to be an American in the twenty-first century. Almost everyone has a notion of what "mainstream" culture has traditionally valued: democracy, free-market capitalism, individual effort and opportunity, equal treatment under the law, and the freedoms of speech, thought, religion, and association.

Whatever their backgrounds and values, in pursuing their education, students continue to cherish elements of the American Dream. *American Subcultures* explores how the mainstream culture represented by this Dream is constructed through drawing boundaries and defining norms. This process, at various levels of society, can often be intolerant and unforgiving, but it can also be life-affirming and liberating for those who identify with a particular subculture. Futhermore, understanding the myriad ways in which those around us position themselves in society generates empathy and leads us to question our own ways of life.

In the Chapter 1 reading from *The Stranger Next Door*, an analysis of a conflict over gay rights in a small Oregon town, sociologist Arlene Stein demonstrates that for norms to exist, deviancy or "otherness" must also exist. In fact, social order is established through a process by which "deviants are created and punished" so that "a community's boundaries remain a meaningful point of reference for its members only as long as they are repeatedly tested by people who are on the fringes of the group and repeatedly defended by those within it." We often think of these deviant or marginalized groups as locations of powerlessness, but this is not always the case. By occupying alternative roles, subcultures can become places of radical possibility within which we can identify and understand larger cultural identities, as well as expand our vision of personal expression.

This is not to say that subcultures always promote goodness and light. In fact, like American culture as a whole, subcultures can be violent, racist, and sexist. Understanding the shadowy side of the American mainstream helps to define our personal and shared beliefs and practices.

Although *American Subcultures* deals with the many and varied ways by which people are defined socially, it is not intended as a sociology primer but as a collection of texts that will stimulate critical thinking and discussion in the composition classroom. In addition, the book is meant to foster reading skills, to encourage investigation and expression of personal values, and to introduce multidisciplinary forms of writing.

The ability to engage a text—their own or that of others—is a life skill, as is the attention students give to their own thinking and written expression. Voices from a number of disciplines—cultural studies, journalism, psychology, political science, history, media studies, the arts—make *American Subcultures* suitable for writing-across-the-curriculum courses.

Drawing from a wide range of essays, articles, personal narratives, news reports, blogs, and academic studies, this reader raises significant questions about the role of subcultures in American life: What is life like in a marginalized group? To what degree does the subculture choose marginalization? What elements define a subculture? By what means does a subculture challenge authority? What kinds of freedom does the subculture open up within the larger culture? How do resistance and deviance help define norms? How do subcultures reproduce the values of mainstream culture? In what ways have subcultures been subsumed by the larger culture, and how have the subcultures responded? For an extended introduction to these topics, please see the Introduction for Students on page 1.

In selecting this material, I have tried to remain open to both historical and contemporary communities from across a spectrum of ideologies, demographics, and practices. The readings present diverse perspectives on race, class, gender, sexuality, and geography, ranging from Idaho survivalists to Brooklyn hipsters, from California skaters to rodeo queens. My aim is to provide texts that resonate with one another, as well as with the reader's experience. For example, "Growing Up Amish" and "A Life Apart: A Brief Introduction to Hasidim" in chapter one both examine communities that embrace marginalization. Read together, these essays prompt students to make new connections. Many of the selections are short enough to be read and discussed in class. Others are better suited to deeper reading and reflection. All can generate meaningful analysis and arguments, personal essays, or research papers, as students respond to the questions following each selection. For alternate pairings, I have included tables of contents organized by theme, discipline, and rhetorical purpose. These can be found on pages xix–xxx and gives instructors greater flexibility for using the topic of subcultures in their writing courses.

Over the past several years, my colleagues and I have been redesigning our first-year writing course around the kinds of thematics represented in the Bedford Spotlight Reader series. We wanted to develop a range of topics that would appeal to students and generate thoughtful discourse. Most of us were not experts in the core material of the thematics we settled on. Fortunately, such a thematic organization is not intended to promote subject seminars per se but to provide occasions for writing. In fact, teaching writing in the context of thematic material about which we were not specialists turned out to be a very good thing. It meant that we entertained many of the same questions and concerns as our students. We were compelled to engage with provocative material we might not have otherwise, and we were inspired to develop semester-long arcs of connected assignments. Even better, the thematic model allows students to bring their own interests — even obsessions — to the course. Most of all, focusing on themes drawn from contemporary culture means that we can engage with the kind of reading and writing students will encounter not just in their academic careers but in their lives as working professionals and productive citizens.

Acknowledgments

I owe a thousand thanks to the many good people who contributed to this book. I particularly want to acknowledge Jennifer Prince for her inestimable editorial skills. This book would have been a poorer endeavor without her keen insights and assiduous attention to detail. She reminds me, once again, that the writing is never done until it has been scrutinized by "second eyes." I also extend my gratitude to John Sullivan, program manager for readers and literature. From start to finish, he has guided me with the utmost professionalism. I would also like to thank Edwin Hill, vice president of editorial humanities at Macmillan Learning; Leasa Burton, senior program director for Bedford/St. Martin's English; Lexi DeConti, Associate Editor; Andrea Cava, publishing services manager; Lou Bruno, content project manager; Lisa McDowell, workflow manager and Angela Boehler and Eve Lehmann, permissions researchers.

I am also grateful to the many reviewers who provided early feedback on this book: Craig Bartholomaus, Metropolitan Community College-Penn Valley; Erica Bertero, Del Mar College; Terri Chung, North Seattle College; Kenneth Culton, Niagara University; Lynée Gaillet, Georgia

State University; Karen Gardiner, University of Alabama; Stacie Hanes, Kent State University; Jim Hayes, Grand Rapids Community College; Cari Keebaugh, North Shore Community College; Megan O'Neill, Stetson University; Christina Scheuer, North Seattle College; Michelle Sidler, Auburn University. Their comments proved invaluable as I sorted through masses of material on American subcultures.

Perhaps most important, I acknowledge the debt I owe my students at the University of Southern California who indulged my enthusiasms and critiqued my frequent excursions into esoteric reading material. These admirable individuals have helped me to understand what they need—and want—in the writing classroom. As I assembled the readings and supporting material for this book, I did so with the familiar faces of my students in my mind's eye. In particular, my General Education Seminar showed me new ways of thinking about American subcultures, particularly those they themselves were invested in. As we say, repeatedly, on this campus, "Fight on!" Finally, I thank my wife, Callie Cardamon, for giving me the space to put this whole thing together and for providing superb critiques of the manuscript at all stages of development. *Grazie.*

Eric Rawson

Bedford/St. Martin's is as passionately committed to the discipline of English as ever, working hard to provide support and services that make it easier for you to teach your course your way.

Find **community support** at the Bedford/St. Martin's English Community (**community.macmillan.com**), where you can follow our *Bits* blog for new teaching ideas, download titles from our professional resource series, and review projects in the pipeline.

Choose **curriculum solutions** that offer flexible custom options, combining our carefully developed print and digital resources, acclaimed works from Macmillan's trade imprints, and your own course or program materials to provide the exact resources your students need.

Rely on **outstanding service** from your Bedford/St. Martin's sales representative and editorial team. Contact us or visit macmillanlearning.com to learn more about any of the options below.

Choose from Alternative Formats of *American Subcultures*

Bedford/St. Martin's offers a range of formats. Choose what works best for you and your students. *Popular e-book formats* For details of our e-book partners, visit **macmillanlearning.com/ebooks**.

Select Value Packages

Add value to your text by packaging one of the following resources with *American Subcultures*.

LaunchPad Solo for Readers and Writers allows students to work on what they need help with the most. At home or in class, students learn at their own pace, with instruction tailored to each student's unique needs. *LaunchPad Solo for Readers and Writers* features:

- **Pre-built units that support a learning arc.** Each easy-to-assign unit is comprised of a pre-test check, multimedia instruction and assessment, and a post-test that assesses what students have learned about critical reading, writing process, using sources, grammar, style, and mechanics. Dedicated units also offer help for multilingual writers.

- **Diagnostics that help establish a baseline for instruction.** Assign diagnostics to identify areas of strength and for improvement and to help students plan a course of study. Use visual reports to track performance by topic, class, and student as well as improvement over time.

- **A video introduction to many topics.** Introductions offer an overview of the unit's topic, and many include a brief, accessible video to illustrate the concepts at hand.

- **Twenty-five reading selections with comprehension quizzes.** Assign a range of classic and contemporary essays each of which includes a label indicating Lexile level to help you scaffold instruction in critical reading.

- **Adaptive quizzing for targeted learning.** Most units include LearningCurve, game-like adaptive quizzing that focuses on the areas in which each student needs the most help.

Order ISBN 978-1-319-06203-3 to package *LaunchPad Solo for Readers and Writers* with *American Subcultures* at a significant discount. Students who rent or buy a used book can purchase access and instructors may request free access at **macmillanlearning.com/readwrite**.

Instructor Resources

You have a lot to do in your course. We want to make it easy for you to find the support you need—and to get it quickly. Instructor resources can be downloaded from **macmillanlearning.com**. Visit the instructor resources tab for *American Subcultures* for additional resources, including supplementary online links and sample syllabi.

Contents

the Angels are such good copy is that they are acting out the day-dreams of millions of losers who don't wear any defiant insignia and who don't know how to be outlaws."

Chapter 3 How Do Subcultures Challenge Authority? 143

Chapter 4 What Values Do Subcultures Share with Mainstream America? 207

Chapter 5   What Happens When Subcultures Go Mainstream?   267

Contents by Discipline

Gender and Sexuality Studies

History

Journalism

Contents by Theme

Pop Culture

Race and Ethnicity

Sexuality

Contents by Rhetorical Purpose

Argument

Autobiography

Classification and Division

Definition

Description

Evaluation

Narration

Observation

Reflection

American Subcultures

A BEDFORD SPOTLIGHT READER

Introduction for Students

Although its subject is American society, this book offers a collection of texts that will stimulate critical thinking and frame opportunities for meaningful writing in general. *American Subcultures* provides you with several exciting opportunities: to develop a sound writing process appropriate to the argumentative and analytical nature of academic writing; to learn critical thinking and reading skills; to investigate and express personal values; and to master interdisciplinary and versatile forms of written communication.

The design of this book is predicated on the notion that good writers, like good students, are made, not born. There is nothing innate about the ability to write well.

Strong writing — or academic success in general — results from dedication, curiosity, engagement, and effort. Writing can — and should — be a means of discovery, of generating knowledge, rather than merely an instrument for repackaging and disseminating information. We write to learn rather than merely learn to write.

Why Subcultures?

By focusing on a single theme, *American Subcultures* encourages you to explore a topic on many levels. The texts in this reader address notions of identity, family, home, success, education, and the body politic, delving into the history and changing definitions of the "alternative cultures" that have evolved in the U.S. since the late 1940s.

We all belong to some community of like-minded individuals — including the collegiate community, which has practices and values that are as distinct as those of the more radical subcultures featured in this book. We also all share the experience of American life, broadly defined. In our sprawling, pluralistic society, it is often difficult to identify what constitutes the American "mainstream." Nonetheless, we have a notion of what American culture has traditionally valued: representative democracy, free-market capitalism, individual effort and opportunity, equal treatment under the law, and freedoms of speech, thought, religion, and association.

In addition, we might include elements of the American Dream, such as the nuclear family, home ownership, economic advancement, and education. Within the mainstream, individuals disagree about the relative value of these elements; but for a subculture to have a meaningful existence, a coherent mainstream culture must at least be imagined. *American Subcultures* explores how the mainstream culture represented by this Dream is constructed and maintained through a process of drawing boundaries and defining norms.

So what exactly is a subculture? Sociologists debate whether a particular group — say, the ravers of the 1990s — counts as a subculture, a scene, a counter-culture, or a special-interest group. With the aim of understanding the complexities of contemporary life, it is perhaps best to leave the question of what constitutes a subculture as open as possible. Nonetheless, a good working definition might read: "Subculture: a self-identified social network that recognizes shared values and practices which differ significantly from mainstream society." This self-identified social network needs a critical mass of members; three dudes in a basement do not constitute a subculture. In addition, the members of a subculture must *know* that they are members. They must also know who does *not* belong to the group, so that a distinction between the group and the larger culture is maintained.

Responding to Reading

We read for many reasons: to gather information, to learn procedures, to be entertained, to gain enlightenment. We also write for many reasons: to instruct, to report, to argue, to amuse, to clarify, to discover. These two activities — reading and writing — are closely bound. We read in order to write; we write in order to be read. To write clear analysis and argument at a college level, you need to read carefully, giving thoughtful attention to the perspectives of others.

In thinking critically about the topics of this book, you will engage a number of questions: To what degree does a subculture choose marginalization?

Why does participation in subcultures appeal so strongly to youth? Are there "good" subcultures and "bad" subcultures? How should we respond to subcultures that turn criminally violent? What kind of freedom does a subculture open up within the larger culture? In what ways has a particular subculture been subsumed by the larger culture, and how has that subculture responded?

American Subcultures does not ask you to adopt a particular response to any of the communities presented here. Rather, you are encouraged to approach the readings critically, annotating the text, identifying places where you agree and disagree, judging the quality of the evidence and the effectiveness of the prose. In some cases, you might find yourself harshly judging the values and practices of a particular community; in others, you might discover that you share core beliefs with an unfamiliar subcultural group. In any case, you are encouraged to think deeply about the material, analyzing it with an open mind and forming arguments based on clear reasoning and evidence.

Organization of the Book

American Subcultures is organized around five main themes. These themes are intended to stimulate thinking but should not limit what you have to say. The texts are drawn from a wide range of sources, including magazine and newspaper articles, scholarly journals, personal memoirs, blogs, and online publications. As you read, you will discover a multiplicity of perspectives based on gender, race, ethnicity, sexual orientation, geography, and other factors that contribute to our individual identities.

Each chapter begins with a short summary of themes and a synopsis of the readings you will encounter. After each selection, three sets of questions ask you to demonstrate an active understanding of the text, to reflect deeply on the implications of what you have read, and to make connections between the readings and outside research sources. Whether personal or scholarly, your responses can lead to significant analytical and argumentative writing. In any case, you should not treat the questions as addressing the point of the reading, but as rich and meaningful occasions for writing, research, and discussion.

The first chapter, "What Is Life Like on the Margins?," asks you to think about what it is like to be cast, often not by choice, as a member of a marginalized subculture. Each of the communities discussed has either removed itself or been excluded from mainstream American life. In some cases, this situation suits the members of the group, but in other cases, their subcultural status results in a great deal of suffering. In all cases, it is worth considering how the existence of these groups challenges American social and political systems.

The second chapter, "How Do Subcultures Define Themselves?," examines the ways marginalized communities police their boundaries and impose particular definitions of membership. The selections in this chapter derive their authority from adopting the perspectives of the subcultures' members, often with surprising results.

The third chapter, "How Do Subcultures Challenge Authority?," revolves around terms we usually associate with the marginalized: rebellion, resistance, anti-authoritarianism. Each of the readings features people who consciously challenge the dominant, or hegemonic, culture. In most cases, these communities face a vanishingly small chance of being embraced by the mainstream. Rather, they serve as cultural border towns, marking the boundaries of acceptable values and practices.

The fourth chapter, "What Values Do Subcultures Share with Mainstream America?," takes a different view of outlier communities. These communities may not represent a normal cross-section of American life, but they explicitly share many of the values and practices we associate with mainstream culture, particularly a commitment to personal autonomy and political liberty.

The final chapter, "What Happens When Subcultures Go Mainstream?," examines a problem faced by all successful alternative communities: assimilation by the mainstream culture. In this case, the margins move to the center, the subculture is reimagined and reconfigured by media and commercial interests, and the energy and freshness of the subculture is absorbed into popular culture. On the one hand, this process is not necessarily bad, since the boundaries of the mainstream are expanded. On the other hand, many of the attractions of the subculture are neutralized as the mainstream devours them.

You are not meant to read the chapters in isolation. Rather, you should seek resonances among the various readings and accompanying study questions. You should also use the readings as jumping-off points for further research and exploration. What do others have to say about a particular subculture? Are there alternative points of view? What is the historical context of a particular community's genesis? How has the community evolved over time? What larger issues of American social and political life are implicated in the study of a particular group? Writing effectively means putting yourself in an ongoing conversation about a topic, listening to other voices, and contributing your own discoveries and interpretations. Don't hesitate to let your research take you in new directions.

Getting Started

Consider how you position yourself in the cultural landscape. To what community do you belong? It's okay if you don't identify with a specifically marginalized group — that is, a subculture. You still belong to some kind of community, even if that community is the dominant culture.

You should endeavor to look beyond the obvious. For this mini-assignment you are not writing a report or an extended diary entry but developing an argument about how to understand a person — *you* — in terms of his or her social group. Strive to find ideas and examples that challenge your thinking about what we assume is the natural way of living. In two to three pages respond to the following: What community do you belong to, and how does your position in this group help define who you are and what you value?

Since you cannot be wrong about who you are and where you belong, go ahead and take some risks in your writing. Say something that's meaningful to you. Say something about your topic that hasn't already been said a hundred times. Say something that you believe will interest your audience. If you can work at these goals, you will have begun to write at a college level.

1

What Is Life Like on the Margins?

The readings in this first chapter argue that without marginalized communities to define the boundaries of the dominant culture, it is difficult to maintain and understand our identities as Americans. We often take it for granted that the way we live is simply the "American way." Yet as the writers in this collection contend, there are many, many American ways. Sociologist Arlene Stein's excerpt from *The Stranger Next Door* offers an overview, both theoretical and practical, of how certain groups become marginalized, either by choice or by circumstance. Chapter One provides a glimpse into life in marginalized subcultures. In some cases, the picture is one of misery; in others, living outside the mainstream seems meaningful and satisfying. Either way, excluding these communities from mainstream life serves not only to reinforce cultural norms but also to shape those norms as alternative social groups engage with the dominant culture.

In "The Lords of Dogtown," G. Beato traces the rise of a 1970s working-class subculture that has long since gone mainstream: skateboarders. Beato has a particular interest in how these teenaged skaters appropriated public and private space for their own use, and quickly rose to national prominence.

In contrast to the public presence of the skater kids, Nina Stochlic describes efforts to bring the largely unknown community of American gypsies out of the shadows. Tristan Ahtone investigates the youth gangs of another extensive subculture: Native Americans, historically the most marginalized ethnic community in the United States. Finally, an excerpt from Teresa Gowan's book *Hobos, Hustlers, and Backsliders* shines a light on the homeless men of San Francisco, whose lives stand in stark contrast to the affluence of the city.

Two of the readings, "Growing Up Amish" and "A Life Apart: A Brief Introduction to Hasidim," deal with communities whose identities are primarily religious and who vigorously maintain their separation from mainstream society. As you read this chapter, consider the ways that these multifarious groups help us to shape our sense of what it means to be members of a diverse and dynamic American culture.

photo: Carsten Koall/Getty Images

from *The Stranger Next Door*

Arlene Stein

In 1994, sociologist Arlene Stein spent several months in a place she calls "Timbertown," Oregon, a community caught up in a battle to change the town's charter to prohibit "special status" for homosexuals. During her time there, Stein came to realize that gay rights was only a proxy issue through which different groups of residents fought to conserve or expand various definitions of "community." This reading is excerpted from her book-length analysis of how the townspeople defined themselves and "others." Stein is a professor of sociology who studies gender, sexuality, and American culture. She has received the Ruth Benedict Book Award and the Simon and Gagnon Award for career contributions to the study of sexualities.

Why do some social differences that are submerged and unremarkable become sources of division? In the United States, few have taken up guns to defend their version of what is right and true, but Americans have frequently responded violently to such perceived social problems as drug use, abortion, and satanic ritual abuse, to name a few. Stanley Cohen coined the term "moral panic" to describe how some issues — such as pornography, homosexuality, and pedophilia — engage the passion and focus of people in ways that seem to far outweigh the real threat.

• • •

Throughout American history, moral crusades against drinking, campaigns against pedophilia, child abuse, and satanism identified deviant social categories and dramatized and normalized identities and institutions such as the traditional family and Christianity. A wave of religious revivals in 1831 converted large numbers of middle-class Americans to millennial beliefs. The decade that followed saw a massive "protest cycle" in temperance, abolition, and moral-reform movements, each based on a sense that sudden, dramatic change was possible in this world, a view impossible under older Calvinist fatalism.[10]

In the 1920s, cultural clashes about the teaching of evolution in the public schools rippled through the United States, culminating in the Scopes trial, in which a biology teacher was charged with challenging state and biblical law. The clash between Clarence Darrow and William Jennings Bryant was a battle over values — a culture war that pitted

Calvinist fatalism: belief, originating with theologian John Calvin (1509–1564), that a person's salvation is predetermined by God.

9

modernists against fundamentalists. As liberal critic Horace Kallen put it, "The Great War with tanks and planes and poison gas has been followed by a battle of values, or norms and standards; a struggle of theories of life."[2] Fundamentalists retreated after the Scopes trial, in which creationism was roundly condemned, and for fifty years occupied themselves with building their own culture and institutions, breaking out into public life only occasionally in momentary spurts of activity.

• • •

In a recent book about Yugoslavia's disintegration into warring ethnic factions, author Michael Ignatieff tells a story about a Serbian militiaman who is asked what he has against his former Croatian neighbors.[3] The man looks scornful and takes a cigarette packet out of his jacket. "See this? These are Serbian cigarettes." Over there, he says, gesturing out of the window, "they smoke Croatian cigarettes." In other words, we are Serbians because we are not Croatians. A sense of similarity among *us* rests upon a sense of difference from *them*.

What this story suggests is that in their everyday lives individuals 5 make countless decisions about who is a friend and who is an enemy, about who should be included in a particular community and who should not. People do things because they wish to protect an image of who they are in relation to the group of which they believe they are a part. We conceptualize the world into those who deserve inclusion and those who do not. Boundaries mark the social territories of human relations, signaling who ought to be admitted and who excluded. The desire to root out others in order to consolidate a sense of self seems universal. How do human beings perceive one another as belonging to the same group while at the same time rejecting human beings whom they perceive as belonging to another group? Why must we affirm ourselves by excluding others?

> "A community's boundaries remain a meaningful point of reference for its members only as long as they are repeatedly tested by people who are on the fringes of the group and repeatedly defended by those within it."

A community's boundaries remain a meaningful point of reference for its members only as long as they are repeatedly tested by people who are on the fringes of the group and repeatedly defended by those within it. Sociologists tell us that in order to create a sense of social order, which all societies must establish, deviants are created and punished. "Whenever a boundary line becomes blurred," writes Kai Erikson, "the group members may single out a label as deviant someone whose behavior had previously gone unnoticed."[4] The act of naming things that are dangerous demonstrates to those in the community "just how awesome its powers really are."[5] This clarifies what is acceptable and what is not, who belongs in the community and who does not. Identities that had no political or even existential significance can acquire a genuine hold as badges of group identity overnight. Though the making of collective identities and boundaries is always inherently political, at certain moments such processes become explicitly politicized.

Symbolic boundaries become more important during periods of rapid social change — when geopolitical boundaries become less central. In colonial America, as communities grew and changed, some individuals who were previously accepted as part of the group found themselves run out of it as heretics — witches. In Yugoslavia, as national unity collapsed, ethnic boundary drawing came to the fore. The more pressure there is on communities to change, it seems, the more vigorously boundaries are symbolized and conformity demanded. Clearly, the world is changing in many different ways, and at a rapid pace. In this country, during the past few decades, an unprecedented number of women have entered the workforce; the globalization of the economy has made us less and less dependent upon a sense of place, economically and culturally. Even residents of small-town Oregon, who consume media beamed from satellite dishes and work for companies whose manufacturing operations are located in far-flung parts of the world, are subject to these and other modernizing processes.

During the past decade, huge geopolitical shifts have shaped U.S. political culture. The collapse of Communism destroyed the faceless enemy upon which our national identity had been based, and had an enormous, largely unacknowledged impact upon the nation's sense of itself. The issue of "who is American" became more and more unclear. It used to be that Americans defined themselves as not-Communists. But once Communists no longer posed a threat, the drive to figure out the meaning of America became even more urgent. Communism was no longer a threat. What would replace the "other" against which American identity was defined? "A symbolically contrived sense of local similarity," writes Richard Jenkins, is sometimes "the only available defense."

Historically, the right has drawn much of its strength, collective identity, and legitimacy from its ability to construct a coherent, visible enemy, and to demonize the "enemies within" in the name of the imagined nation.[6] As the old devils — Communists, working women, the counterculture — lost their power, a new devil was needed — preferably one that embodied the worst excesses of the permissive society, that transgressed sexual respectability, that seemed sufficiently outside the community to be alien, but that simultaneously represented familiar (and therefore doubly scary) urges that were accessible to anyone. How better to construct a sense of identity, the *we*, than by articulating a clear sense of what one abhorred? How better to affirm one's purity than by getting rid of the dirt?

Sigmund Freud° has noted that the compulsion to name and exclude   10 dangerous "others" may be more virulent the more similar those others are to you; all likeness must be denied and difference exaggerated. He called this the "narcissism of small differences." Freud noticed the ease with which larger cultural groups latch on to smaller groups or groups seen as social intruders, leading the English and the Scots, North and South Germans, to turn against one another, venting their aggressive impulses. He recognized how Jews have, historically, "rendered most useful services" throughout European history by being a favorite target of violent aggression.[7] For many centuries they were the "strangers" against which Europeans defined themselves. Familiar and yet unfamiliar, visible and yet faceless—they did not fit easily into any of the established categories through which people made sense of their world. These "others" who were not quite "other" caused confusion and anxiety, which made them particularly susceptible to hateful passions and efforts to clearly delimit "us" and "them."

Do lesbians and gays play a similar role in the contemporary United States? I wondered. For many centuries, the philosopher Michel Foucault tells us, the boundaries separating the homosexual and heterosexual worlds were either weak or nonexistent; homosexual and heterosexual behavior existed side by side. There was not yet an understanding of homosexuals as a recognizable, definable category of people. With the emergence of sociosexual medical categories, this changed: homosexuals became understood as a distinct group of individuals, radically different from heterosexuals. The construction of a "homosexual role," Mary McIntosh argues, "kept the bulk of society pure."[8]

It's no wonder that a series of anti-gay campaigns rippled through the United States in the 1990s, when lesbians and gay men were becoming more and more fully integrated into American life and the boundaries separating the homosexual and heterosexual worlds were blurring.

Twenty years ago, I graduated from college, packed my bags, and moved to the West Coast, fleeing from watchful parental eyes and hoping deep down to meet the girl of my dreams. I was certainly not alone. Tens of thousands of young people had migrated there before me in search of the great gay metropolis, that "imagined community" where people could act on their same-sex desires and receive support for doing so.[9]

Sigmund Freud: Austrian neurologist and founder of psychoanalysis (1856–1930).

But only a couple of decades before, same-sex behavior was confined to the margins of society, in shadowy bars in major cities, or to secret, forbidden desires. Men and women possessing attractions for members of their sex were forced to keep them under wraps lest they lose their jobs and their families.

But after years of living with the "culture of suspicion," which defined clear boundaries between straight and gay worlds, and cast homosexuals into secretive double lives, in the 1960s and 1970s some activists vowed to overturn the prevailing notion of "homosexuality as pollution." Gay liberationists attempted to "smash the categories": the boundaries separating heterosexuality and homosexuality were, they pro-claimed, social illusions. For a brief moment, these ideas caught fire. Many people, influenced by the movement, were faced with a *choice* about whether to be with women or with men. Those who had never entertained the idea of homosexuality were forced to scrutinize the nature of their attractions. The heterosexual imperative was profoundly shaken.

References

1. James Jasper, *The Art of Moral Protest: Culture, Biography, and Creativity in Social Movements* (Chicago: University of Chicago Press, 1998), 94.

2. Horace M. Kallen, *Culture and Democracy in the United States: Studies in the Group Psychology of the American Peoples* (New York: Boni & Liveright, 1924), 13.

3. Michael Ignatieff, *Ethnic War and the Modern Conscience* (New York: Metropolitan Books, 1998).

4. Kai Erikson, *Wayward Puritans: A Study in the Sociology of Deviance* (New York: John Wiley and Sons, 1966), 8–19.

5. Robert Scott, and Jack Douglas, *Theoretical Perspectives on Deviance* (New York: Basic Books, 1972), 29.

6. Anna Marie Smith, "A Symptomology of an Authoritarian Discourse," in *Cultural Remix: Theories of Politics and the Popular*, ed. Erica Carter et al. (London: Lawrence & Wishart, 1995), 224; Michael Paul Rogin, "The Countersubversive Tradition in American Politics," *Berkeley Journal of Sociology* 31 (1986): I–33. But the right does not have exclusive claims to boundary making. See my *Sex and Sensibility: Stories of a Lesbian Generation* (Berkeley: University of California Press, 1997); and Joshua Gamson, "Must Identity Movements Self-Destruct? A Queer Dilemma," in *Queer Theory/Sociology*, ed. Steven Seidman (Cambridge: Blackwell, 1996).

7. Quoted in Nancy Chodorow "The Enemy Outside: Thoughts on the Psychodynamics of Extreme Violence with Special Attention to Men and Masculinity," *Journal for the Psychoanalysis of Culture and Society* 3, no. 1 (1998): 26.

8. Mary McIntosh, "The Homosexual Role," *Social Problems* 16 (1968): 262–70.

9. John D'Emilio, *Sexual Politics, Sexual Communities: The Making of Homosexual a Minority in the United States* (Chicago: University of Chicago Press, 1983); Kath Weston, "Get Thee to a Big City: Sexual Imaginary and the Great Gay Migration," *GLQ* 2 (1995): 253–77.

Understanding the Text

1. According to Stein, how does a conception of "us" depend upon a conception of "them"? Who is a deviant, and how is deviance recognized?

2. Why do "symbolic boundaries become more important during periods of rapid social change" (par. 7)? What types of social changes does Stein identify as particularly pronounced at the turn of the twenty-first century?

3. What does Sigmund Freud mean by the "narcissism of small differences" (par. 10)?

Reflection and Response

4. To which subculture, if any, do you belong? Do you identify as a member of mainstream culture? What defines your membership in this social group?

5. Is there a way of defining who we are without positioning our identities against "others"? Discuss several alternatives.

Making Connections

6. As gay culture is increasingly integrated into mainstream culture, what new "massive protest cycles" loom on the horizon? Which groups currently face demonization? Why? How might their battles play out?

7. Considering Sinclair Bolden's claims in "The Real Real: The Five Ways Subcultures Police Themselves Online" (p. 78), how does the internet enforce the "symbolic boundaries" between social groups?

The Lords of Dogtown

G. Beato

G. Beato is widely known for his engaged and engaging articles on popular culture. He writes for a number of publications, including *Mother Jones*, *The Baffler*, and *Suck*. In "The Lords of Dogtown" (1999), Beato traces the genesis of the skater subculture to a group of kids who in the early 1970s left the waves they surfed under the Pacific Park pier and began riding their homemade skateboards on the school playgrounds and in the empty swimming pools of the Westside of Los Angeles. The rebellious, even arrogant, attitude they brought to skating revolutionized the sport and launched a hardy subculture that still flourishes today.

Twenty years ago, you did not drop in on Tony Alva.

Twenty years ago, if you found yourself standing next to the volatile, gravity-defying Alva at some crowded backyard pool in the Valley, and he was planning to take the next run—even though he'd just taken the last one—it was best to not even look at him.

Tonight, however, such ancient protocols are no longer in effect. Alva, 41 now, bearded and dreadlocked, has come to The Block, a theme-park-size mall in Orange, California, to skate the new Vans Skatepark, an indoor, 46,000-square-foot skateboarding Oz located between a Virgin Megastore and a brewpub. Hundreds of skaters and spectators are here celebrating the park's opening. As a dozen or so mostly teenage skaters stand in an informal line, waiting for their chance to try out the smaller one of the park's two cement pools, they seem wholly oblivious to Alva. To them he's just another skateboarder in baggy jeans and a scuffed yellow helmet. Somewhat older, perhaps, but of no readily apparent significance.

True, a handful of old-school types approach Alva as he waits, tapping his shoulder, talking briefly, paying their respects. But the younger skaters don't really notice these exchanges. They're checking out the pools and the vert ramp° and the two areas designed to look like streets in the real world.

As Alva stands poised at the edge of the drop, rocking slightly, his ⁵ left foot planted on the board that bears his name, a wispy blond-haired nine-year-old, completely unaware of him, stands in the same position just a few feet away. And when the guy in the pool blows a backside grind at its far end, the nine-year-old pushes off with his right foot.

It's a moment of minor blasphemy—a nine-year-old, a kid who can barely even skate, dropping in on Alva! Alva, the leader of the Dogtown

---

vert ramp: skateboarding ramp that transitions from a horizontal surface to a vertical one.

boys, the former World Champion, the godfather of urban skate-punks who transformed skateboarding from a sport of short little muscular dudes doing nose wheelies into the minor religion that it is today. Does the kid have any clue what he's doing? Any clue at all?

Twenty years ago, "Mad Dog" Alva would have fired his board at the tiny kid's head. But today, he simply claps twice, like a Little League coach, and smiles at all the shorties in line.

"Hey, Is This Your Carburetor?"

Tony Alva grew up in Santa Monica, a few blocks from the beach and a failed amusement park called Pacific Ocean Park. In 1958, CBS spent $10 million renovating the 28-acre park, which was built on a huge concrete-and-steel pier. By 1967, however, the park had been shut down due to poor attendance and soon fell into a state of slow deterioration.

While much of the original SoCal surf culture sprang up around affluent enclaves like Malibu and La Jolla, the Venice/Santa Monica area that Pacific Ocean Park bridged was run-down and gritty. Dogtown, the locals called it. The streets were lined with boarded-up storefronts, liquor stores, and ratty dives, like an underground coke-snorting emporium known as the Mirror-Go-Round. The area beneath the pier was even seedier. Junkies shot up there, gay men used it as an anonymous trysting spot, bums established long-term subterranean encampments. But the pier served another function as well: 275 feet wide, extending hundreds of feet into the ocean, it created three separate breaks for the Dogtown locals to surf.

The danger inherent in surfing the P.O.P. pier, with its numerous con- 10 crete pilings and crowded conditions, led to a tradition of intense clannishness: You had to have confidence in your fellow surfers. Sometimes outsiders were discouraged via an abrupt punch in the face, no questions asked. On other occasions, a local might paddle out to an alien surfer, clutching a carburetor in his free hand. "Is this yours?" he would ask the trespasser, then drop the carburetor into the ocean. It was here, in P.O.P. surf culture, that Alva was introduced to the principles that would later inform the Dogtown skate scene.

The same year that Pacific Ocean Park closed, Alva's mother divorced his father. Alva's sister and brother went with their mom; nine-year-old Tony remained with his dad. "My dad worked a lot, so I didn't really see him that much," says Alva. And while his father coached him in Little League and bought him his first surfboard at the age of ten, there was also a darker side to their relationship. "He was angry at a lot of different things," Alva recalls. "When he drank, he could be kind of brutal."

As a consequence, Alva spent as much time as possible at the beach, where he used to hang with another local kid named Jay Adams. Four years younger than Alva, Adams had practically grown up on the beach. His stepdad was a surfer who owned a rental concession on the pier's northside, and Adams was always underfoot, a skinny, hyperactive board-sports prodigy with a malicious grin and a spontaneous approach to life—Huck Finn by way of the Pacific Coast Highway. He started surfing almost as soon as he had learned to swim; by the time he was eight, he was already an accomplished surfer and a fixture at P.O.P.

"Me and Jay were like the only younger kids allowed to surf there," says Alva. "But we had to earn it first. The older guys would go, 'Okay, you can come out for a while, but first you have to do Rat Patrol.' We'd sit up on the pier with these wrist rockets and this pile of polished stones, and just bombard anyone who was from outside our territory with whatever was available. Rocks, bottles, rotten fruit. Jay was a notoriously good shot."

Paul Revere's Wild Ride

In 1970, Alva and a couple of friends decided to ride their bikes to Brentwood to check out Paul Revere Junior High. Some of the older P.O.P. surfers had been talking about the school's playground. Revere was built on a hillside, and for whatever reasons of economy or aesthetics, the flat playground was edged with sharply sloping, 15-foot-high banks instead

Jay Adams, the youngest member of the Zephyr Competition Skateboarding Team, was renowned for his fluid, surf-inspired skating style. He was nicknamed "The Chosen One" by his peers. Archive Photos/Getty Images

of retaining walls. "To a 12-year-old kid it was awesome," Alva says. "The asphalt had just been repaved, so the banks were really smooth and pristine—just these huge, glassy waves."

Throughout the '60s, surfing had always taken precedence over skate-   15 boarding in Dogtown. Skating was mostly just a means of transportation, or something to do if the waves weren't breaking. By 1970, the sport had reached a particularly desultory stage. "No one was skateboarding back then. You couldn't even buy a skateboard in the store," says Stacy Peralta, another Dogtown local. Kids would often have to construct their own from spare pieces of household furniture and repurposed roller skate parts.

But after the Dogtown kids discovered Paul Revere and other school-yard skate spots like Bellagio and Kenter Canyon, the inadequacies of their equipment seemed incidental. The schoolyards' asphalt "waves" broke beautifully every single day, all year round, creating entirely new possibilities for the sport. The Dogtown kids started applying their surf-ing techniques to concrete, riding low to the ground with their arms outstretched for balance, skating with such intensity that they often destroyed their homemade boards in a single session.

"We were just trying to emulate our favorite Australian surfers," Alva says, explaining the genesis of their new low-slung, super-aggressive style. "They were doing all this crazy stuff that we were still trying to fig-ure out in the water—but on skateboards, we could do it."

Three years later, the introduction of urethane wheels resurrected interest in skateboarding. By then, the Dogtown kids had developed an approach to skating that was far more evolved than what anyone was doing at the time. "No one else had that same surf-skate style, because they didn't have banks like that anywhere else," Alva says. "We had this tradition that was unique to our area."

The Importance of Customer Service

Outside the Jeff Ho & Zephyr Productions Surf Shop, in front of a wall-size mural of co-owner Jeff Ho surfing a wave that was almost pornographic in its perfect, arcing glassiness, Alva and Adams and a few other Dogtown kids were skateboarding back and forth, cutting off cars, catcalling pass-ing girls, staring down all the pedestrians who failed to avoid them—like the two guys who had just rolled in from Van Nuys or wherever, more jock than surfer (but trying hard with their Vans and Hang Ten shirts), who tried to enter the shop's front door. It was locked. They looked at their watches. It was 3 p.m.

Inside, Skip Engblom, one of the shop's owners, sat in a rocking chair, 20
drinking vodka and papaya juice and watching the scene play out. This
was one of his favorite pastimes. "Hey!" cried one of the Van Nuys guys,
finally noticing him. "Open up. This door's locked."

"What the fuck do you want?" Engblom yelled back.

"I want to look around."

"If you want to come in here, you've got to give me some money
first," Engblom said. "If you just want to look around, go to the fucking
library."

"I've got fucking money," the guy said, pulling a twenty out of his
wallet and waving it in front of the window. "Let me in and I'll spend it!"

• • •

For the local Dogtown kids, the shop served as a second home. They 25
used to help Ho shape and repair boards in the shop's backrooms in
exchange for discounts or free merchandise. At night, the place turned
into a kind of speakeasy, over which the charismatic Ho — wearing
rainbow-tinted glasses, four-inch platform shoes, and striped velveteen
pants — presided. Local bands performed, and drugs were dispensed with
typical '70s largesse.

With his shop, Ho tried to provide the same sense of family and community that he'd found at the beach as a kid growing up. "I was a loner,
this geeky little Chinese runt kid who couldn't play sports until I discovered surfing. And then I saw these other kids, growing up the same way. I
mean, who's going to be hanging out all day at the beach?

The kids who don't want to be hanging out at home. So, to them, I
would say, 'Check it out, this is surfing. If you use your talents, you can
make something of yourself.'"

To this end, Ho sponsored two surf teams: one for the area's best
surfers, guys who were in their late teens and early 20s, and, in a move
that was fairly unusual at the time, one for the younger kids, who were
destined to become the next wave of stars. As skateboarding's popularity increased, the junior surf team, which had included Tony Alva, Jay
Adams, Shogo Kubo, and Stacy Peralta, evolved into the Zephyr Competition Skate Team — a 12-member group of the best skaters in Dogtown.
Ho gave them team T-shirts. "We wanted to give them colors, something
to be a part of."

"To wear the team shirt was just unreal," says Peralta. "We were all
middle- and lower-class kids, and it wasn't like we had a lot of opportunities. We weren't the kids who were going to graduate as valedictorians

or the guys from Palisades driving BMWs to the beach. So to be chosen to be a part of something like that was just the hottest thing that could happen to a kid in that area."

A Funky, Funky Look

The Bahne-Cadillac Skateboard Championship, held in the summer of 30
1975, was the largest competition that skating's revival had yet inspired. The two-day event featured downhill, slalom, and freestyle competitions. The organizers had built a 150-foot-long wooden ramp especially for the competition. More than 400 enthusiasts traveled to Del Mar, California, to attend the championship. "It was the first major contest where skaters from all over county came together," says Peralta. "We came in not knowing anything about the outside world—who else was skating, what their style was like. It was as if we'd evolved in this Galapagos Island vacuum."

The Zephyr team wore uniforms, sort of—matching Vans deck shoes and blue T-shirts emblazoned with their team name. Even so, the Z-Boys, as they would come to be known, seemed wild-looking compared to the other competitors. Their shoes were torn and scuffed, and their jeans were missing back pockets, the inevitable result of low-altitude power-slides. "Our hair was so long and fluffy that we'd all chopped our bangs off two inches over our eyebrows," says Alva. "It was just a funky, funky look." In addition, they carried themselves with an aggressive, streetwise swagger. "We were pretty hard-core when it came to anybody trying to compete with us," he says. "We kind of psyched out everyone there before we even started skating against them."

• • •

In the competition's first event, the freestyle preliminaries, contestants had two minutes in which to impress a panel of judges with their most creative skateboard skills. At that time, state-of-the-art freestyle was a static, tricks-oriented endeavor: competitors performed nose wheelies while rolling in perfect circles, popped handstands on their boards, or did as many consecutive 360s as they could manage.

The Z-Boys thought that kind of stick-man, tick-tack style was pathetic. And Jay Adams, the team's first member to ride, immediately demonstrated their contempt.

Pushing hard across the platform that had been set up for the event, Adams picked up speed quickly, carving back and forth to generate more forward momentum. As he neared the platform's far end, he crouched low, lower than most of the people who were sitting in the bleachers had ever seen anyone get on a skateboard.

The crowd started shouting as Adams pushed closer to the platform's 35 edge—he looked as if he were about to shoot right off. But then he lowered his body even more and pulled a hard, extremely fast turn. The maneuver left his body fully extended, hovering just inches above the platform, with his right arm thrust out for balance and his left hand, palm down, planted on the platform, serving as his pivot. In an instant, he spun 180 degrees and began rolling in the opposite direction, even faster than he was before launching into the turn. The bleachers erupted with enthusiastic, disbelieving cheers. "All the kids just went ballistic, completely out of their minds," says Peralta. "They'd never seen that kind of speed and aggressive style before."

In slightly under two minutes, Adams's explosive performance was over. He hadn't done a single handstand or kickflip. For the rest of the day, while their competitors rolled around the platform like ridiculous, slo-motion, runaway gymnasts, every other Z-Boy proceeded to dazzle the audience. "It was like Ferraris versus Model-T's," says team member Nathan Pratt.

And it wasn't just the crowd that sensed the discrepancy. For the first time, the Z-Boys themselves began to realize that what had become commonplace to them was actually a revelation to everyone else. "After competing against other skaters, we knew straight out we were a step above," Alva says. "Our whole approach to the deal was different."

The Zephyr team's routines were so unprecedented the judges didn't even know how to score them.

A Gunfight Every Afternoon

News traveled fast. Within a week of the contest, kids from all over the state were showing up at the shop to see if they could best the Z-Boys. "It was like a gunfight every afternoon of the week," says Engblom. "And the more guys that Tony and Jay and Stacy blew out, the more would show up. One bunch of guys came all the way from Arizona."

Around town, the team's blue Zephyr Competition jerseys turned 40 to gold. Team members called them their "get-laid" shirts. Other kids tried to buy them, and when that didn't work, they tried to steal them. *Skateboarder* magazine started publishing articles about the Z-Boys and Dogtown; photographers became a standard feature of even their most informal skate sessions. Competitions were proliferating, thousands of kids all over the country were buying boards, and suddenly people who weren't particularly interested in skateboarding itself were interested in skateboarders....

Flying Lessons

"Skaters by their very nature are urban guerrillas," wrote Craig Stecyk, an artist friend of Ho's and Engblom's, who maintained a small art studio at the shop. Stecyk documented and, in large part, defined the emerging Dogtown ethos via the photographs and articles he submitted to *Skateboarder* magazine. "The skater makes everyday use of the useless artifacts of the technological burden. The skating urban anarchist employs [structures] in a thousand ways that the original architects could never dream of." This was a radical notion: Before the Z-Boys, few people had ever thought to skate anything but pavement. The useless artifact that the Dogtown boys employed most often could be found in the bone-dry backyards of rich SoCal homeowners. In the mid-'70s, the state was in the midst of one of its worst droughts in recorded history, and all over Los Angeles there were empty pools—in Brentwood backyards, at the secluded outer reaches of Malibu estates, and in the hills of Bel Air, where recent fires had leveled million-dollar houses but left the pools intact.

> "Skaters by their very nature are urban guerrillas. The skater makes everyday use of the useless artifacts of the technological burden."

"Almost immediately after we discovered that you could skate these things, a network of kids developed," says Peralta. "It was like how people will use drugs to attract famous people. These kids would call up the shop and say, 'Hey, we got a pool,' because they wanted us to come out there and skate with them."

In the summer of 1976, every week brought a new pool. There was O.J. Simpson's football-shaped pool in Pacific Palisades, a magician's rabbit shaped pool in Santa Monica. When a pool grew too crowded or the neighbors started calling the cops too often, they simply found another. Hunting for pools was almost as important as skating them, and the Dogtown boys became obsessed with finding new ones.

"I would drive my VW Squareback° really slowly down these alleys in Beverly Hills, and Jay would be standing on the roof, looking over fences," says Peralta. They consulted the local real estate listings in the hope of finding unoccupied homes with pools in the back. Out in the Valley, they staked out a fireman's house until they learned his schedule; when he left one night for his 24-hour shift they used gas-powered pumps to drain his pool, then returned the next morning to skate it. Once, Adams and Shogo Kubo paid $40 to a pilot at the Santa Monica airport for a one-hour ride.

VW Squareback: compact automobile manufactured by Volkswagen from 1961–1973.

"You were supposed to be listening to this guy's pitch for flying lessons, but we spent the whole time looking for pools," he says.

"It became this big, secret, cat-and-mouse-type deal," says Jim Muir, 45 one of the most avid Dogtown pool-skaters. "You'd be sneaking around from your friends, because you didn't want them to know about a new pool because then it'd get too crowded. You'd be sneaking around from the property owners, sneaking around from the cops." They kept look-outs posted at strategic vantage points. If the cops rolled up in front of the house, they simply ran out the back. If the cops came from the back as well, then the Dogtowners went sideways, over fences. Soon, as many as four or five police cars were responding to calls. "The one place where we did get harassed constantly was this abandoned estate in Santa Monica Canyon across the street from [*Mission Impossible* star] Peter Graves's place," says Peralta. "He'd call the cops on us and we'd climb up into the trees and hide—and they'd be right below us, searching, not seeing us while we were up there. As soon as they left, we'd climb down and start skating again."

When the cops did catch them, they were usually let off with a warning. On occasion, they were arrested for trespassing. That only made them more determined. "The adrenaline rush of jumping over a fence and actually skating in someone's backyard and getting out of there before they came home—that was totally crazy," Alva says. "You can't jump over people's fences in Beverly Hills nowadays. You'd get eaten by a Doberman, shot by a security guy."

Like the schoolyard banks, pools offered a controlled vertical environment that led to rapid innovation; most skateboarders believe that Dogtown is the birthplace of aerials (others claim it was San Diego). "Aerials came from surviving, from being very aggressive and hitting the lip until eventually we were just popping out and grabbing the board in the air," says Alva. "It was something instinctive. Either you made it or you ended up on the bottom of pool, a bloody mess. It happened by total spontaneous combustion. Then we realized that there was an endless array of things we could do."

Photographers like Stecyk and Glen E. Friedman (who was 13 at the time) started capturing these revolutionary moves on film. Suddenly, all across America, kids were ripping out the pages of *Skateboarder* magazine and hanging photos of the Dogtowners on their walls: Tony Alva, flipping off the camera while hanging sideways in mid-air; Jay Adams, his face twisted into a look of the most primal juvenile-delinquent disdain, grinding the edge of a pool so hard he actually knocks its coping out of place.

● ● ●

"Everyone Wanted to Make Their Millions"

In the beginning, free equipment and the get-laid utility of the Zephyr Competition T-shirts had been reward enough for the team's members. By 1976, however, skateboarding was on the verge of becoming a $400 million industry. The Z-Boys were getting older; they were graduating from high school and starting to wonder about what bigger, better deals might be out there for them.

• • •

Introducing Tony Bluetile

One day, the Dogtown boys were sneaking into movie star pools; the next, they were appearing in movies. Tony Alva landed a role in the film *Skateboard* as "Tony Bluetile," a farting, beer-drinking, *Playboy*-reading skate-thug who ends up losing the big race to Leif Garrett. Stacy Peralta, who at 17 was suddenly earning $5,000 a month from his sponsorship deal with G & S, starred in *Freewheelin'*, a low-budget, cheesy skateboarder romance released in 1976. "I was so embarrassed at the premiere," says Peralta, "that I hid behind a curtain the whole time."

While the executive director of the International Skateboard Association primly told *People* magazine that Tony Alva represented "everything that is vile in the sport," the new Dogtown style was in high demand all across the country. For kids who couldn't quite match Alva's radical athleticism or Jay Adams's spontaneous irreverence, a skateboard or helmet bearing their signatures was the next best thing.

But could you really package the ungovernable energy of a guy like Jay Adams? Could you really turn a kid who barreled down the streets of West Los Angeles plucking wigs from the heads of old ladies into your corporate spokesdude? Often you couldn't. In Mexico, where Adams, Alva, and several other Dogtowners had traveled to attend the opening of a new skatepark, the kids who had once emulated their favorite Australian surf heroes now began to resemble rock stars.

"When we got there, this guy told us that if we wanted to score any pot or anything, that they would set us up," says Alva. "It ended up being the cops who brought it to us, this big trash bag full of weed." In the daytime they skated, and at night they partied with groupies and trashed their hotel rooms. At a local brothel, a fat, lactating prostitute ardently pursued the 16-year-old Adams. "She just kept chasing him around the room, shooting milk out of her tits at him," says Alva. "We were these full-on little rats in surf trunks who got wild and raised hell, and [skate promoters] just fed off our energy. It was almost like being on tour with Metallica."

As Alva's notoriety increased, he started hanging out with rock stars and wearing white suits and wide-brimmed, pimp-style fedoras. When he and his new friend Bunker Spreckels, a playboy millionaire heir to a sugar fortune and the stepson of Clark Gable, went in search of new pools to skate in Beverly Hills, they hired limousines to chauffeur them.

By 1977, all of the Dogtown boys were prospering. Alva won the 55 World Pro Championship that year. Soon after, he left Logan Earth Ski, and, with the help of an entrepreneur named Pete Zehnder, created his own line of skateboards. (The company's slogan: "No matter how big your ego, my boards will blow your mind.") Peralta left his sponsor to become a partner in Powell Skateboards, which subsequently became known as Powell-Peralta. Jim Muir and another Dogtown local, Wes Humpston—who used to draw on his homemade boards to pass the time while traveling to various skate spots—trademarked the Dogtown name and produced the first line of skateboards to feature elaborate graphics on the underside of their decks. Jay Adams had his signature Z-Flex board and a helmet called the Flyaway. "I made good money off that for a while," he says. "But that only lasted about a year."

If the history of Dogtown is largely forgotten today, its influence is inescapable. "They were revolutionary style-setters," says Kevin Thatcher, publisher of Thrasher. "I mean, snowboarding, rollerboarding, skysurfing, even surfing now—it all comes from what Jay and Tony were doing.... So many people are trying to be hard-core now, but those guys didn't even have to try. It just came to them naturally."

Understanding the Text

1. Where is Dogtown? How would you describe the neighborhood? What kind of kids lived there in the early 1970s?
2. How did the Z-Boys adapt the values and practices of surfing to skating?
3. When former Z-Boy Nathan Pratt says that his skate team compared to others was "like Ferraris versus Model-Ts" (par. 36), what does he mean?

Reflection and Response

4. Like many subcultures, the Z-Boys challenged the status quo, adopting new aggressive skating postures and a rebellious, iconoclastic attitude. Discuss how these qualities were first on display at the Bahne-Cadillac Skateboard Championship, held in Del Mar, California, in 1975. Why do you think that the other competitors, fans, and judges were so shocked by the Z-Boys?
5. To what extent did accident, coincidence, and luck contribute to the formation of the new skating subculture? Use specific examples from the reading to support your discussion.

6. In the end, why were the Z-Boys unable to maintain their status as an aggressive, rebellious outsider community? What are some possible responses for a subculture when their values and practices suddenly become wildly popular? How does the original skater ethos continue to influence the large skater community today?

Making Connections

7. The Z-Boys community that congregated at Jeff Ho's and Skip Engblom's surf shop in Ocean Park found a substitute for their own broken families. What other subcultures featured in this book provide a family for members? How does the concept of "family" help shape the behavior of these subcultures? How might we connect the skyrocketing divorce rate, stubborn poverty, and increased drug-addiction of the mid-twentieth century to the rise of youth subcultures?

8. The photographer Craig Stecyk comments that "the skater makes everyday use of the useless artifacts of the technological burden," reconfiguring stairways, playgrounds, railings, swimming pools, and other public and private spaces for their own use (par. 41). What other subcultures challenge the use of spaces in similar ways? What questions does the repurposing of technology and architecture by subcultural "urban guerillas" raise?

American Gypsies Are a Persecuted Minority That Is Starting to Fight Back

Nina Strochlic

The Romani people, more commonly known as gypsies, originated in northern India. About a thousand years ago, they migrated to Europe, where they faced centuries of enslavement, persecution, and ethnic cleansing. Since the mid-nineteenth century, Romani from central and eastern Europe have immigrated to the United States, establishing a significant presence in Southern California, Texas, Chicago, St. Louis, Seattle, and the Northeast. Despite a large population, the American Roma community remains largely invisible to mainstream society. Nina Strochlic, a former reporter and researcher for *The Daily Beast*, examines recent efforts to claim Romani heritage and correct misconceptions. Strochlic lives in Washington, D.C., and is currently a staff writer at *National Geographic*.

In October, a young blond girl was taken by Greek police in a sweep of a Roma camp near the central town of Farsala, and the couple she was found with were charged with abducting a minor. Her picture was plastered in news outlets across the world: hair in braids, dirty fingers clenched, a fearful look in her blue eyes. Dubbed the "Blond Angel" in headlines, four-year-old Maria was assumed to be a victim of kidnapping or child trafficking until it was discovered she was, in fact, Romani. Her moniker in headlines quickly transformed to "Mystery Gypsy."

Just days after Maria made headlines, a similar situation occurred in Ireland when two blond-haired, blue-eyed children were taken from their dark-skinned families. DNA tests proved both children belonged to their parents.

Across the Atlantic, the approximately one million American Roma lay low, fearful of the bigotry, marginalization and violence that have plagued their European counterparts and ancestors for a thousand years (the discrimination extends even to what they're called by outsiders—"Gypsy" is a frowned-upon term among Roma activists). As soon as she saw the news, Seattle resident Shon Paramush called her friend Morgan Ahern, a Romani activist. "If I were in Europe, they would take Savina," said the distressed dark-haired, dark-skinned Romani mother of a blond-haired, blue-eyed 2-year-old daughter. "Yes, they would," Ahern replied.

"Every Roma was outraged by [the Maria story]. That's why we try to be invisible in this country," says Ahern, who also lives in Washington. She notes that many American Roma try to "pass" for other ethnicities when they're outside their families. "That's a real privilege we have in this country, being invisible, but it's a double-edged sword because when you're invisible it's hard to unite people for political action."

Assimilation makes sense to American Roma who don't wish to suf- 5 fer the same persecution their European counterparts face daily. There, an estimated 10 to 12 million Roma compose the largest and poorest minority group in the world, with a recent survey showing 90 percent subsisting under the poverty line.

In the U.S., they're scattered: coming from a multitude of countries, speaking many dialects, practicing disparate traditions, and observing various levels of traditionalism. But few Americans realize that there are Roma living in their midst, or that they've been here since the beginning—three Roma are said to have accompanied Columbus on his second voyage to the New World. And the Roma count a number of high-profile figures in their ranks. Guitarist Django Reinhardt was Romani, and some theorize such disparate icons as Charlie Chaplin, Michael Caine, Elvis Presley, and even former President Bill Clinton come from Roma roots.

Undocumented by the U.S. Census, American Roma may keep their heritage under wraps, but when it does emerge, they've faced discrimination from friends, landlords, waiters, classmates, strangers, cops, store clerks, and professors. Many were raised with warnings not to tell others of their ethnic identity, and so they remain a hidden ingredient in America's melting pot.

> "Many were raised with warnings not to tell others of their ethnic identity, and so they remain a hidden ingredient in America's melting pot."

"American Roma come from many different sub-groups, so it is hard for them to organize when they may have little culturally in common," says Dr. Carol Silverman, head of the anthropology department at the University of Oregon. But in the past decade, a new crop of activists has emerged, and they're forming advocacy organizations and school programs to aid their underserved communities, determined to set the record straight on their cultural identity. But each headline-making event or raid can set their work back. Dr. Silverman calls the recent news from Europe "devastating for American Roma."

Maria's story hit especially close to home for Morgan Ahern, who says she was seven years old when she and all Romani children her age and older were taken from their Brooklyn community by authorities of the State of New York and put into institutions and foster homes. It was 1955, and her parents—Roma who had escaped the Holocaust in Europe—were accused of child abuse because of their itinerant lifestyle. It was a program she likens to the forced assimilation of Native Americans through government-run boarding schools. She lost her native Romani dialect, she says, after it was beaten out of her at Catholic institutions.

In the early 80s, while teaching women's studies at the University of 10
Colorado at Boulder, Ahern bumped into a woman crossing the street. "I
think I'm your mother," the woman said. She was right.

In 1985, Ahern launched her Roma-heritage organization, Lolo Diklo,
which is now a roving educational museum based on Vashon, an island
off Seattle. Not long after she settled there, a friend proposed she rent the
cottage on her property. But the offer was rescinded just before Ahern
was due to move in. The friend's husband refused to "let a dirty gypsy on
his property," Ahern says she was told.

Since then, the islanders have come to know that derogatory remarks
won't fly with the now-retired 66-year-old Ahern, who gives anyone who
uses the term "gypped" a talking to. "No one says anything insulting to
me," Ahern says. But the Maria incident was a reminder of the pervasive discrimination. "It's as if people were gleeful finally they could prove
gypsies could steal babies, when, in all the centuries of that stereotype,
there's not one recorded proof it has happened once," she says.

"Should you need to have a lighter-skinned person vouch for you?
Does that have to be the standard?" asks Kristin Raeesi, a 34-year-old
Romani activist and grant writer at the University of Alaska. Though
Raeesi has a dark complexion, her newborn son, with his blue eyes and
light brown hair, and Raeesi's younger sister, who sports light hair and
bright green eyes, are proof of the diversity found in Roma populations
and even within families. "The blond angel foundling must have been
snatched by horrible dark people," Raeesi says scathingly.

Growing up in a Wyoming town of 600 people, Raeesi was instructed
to hide her Romani background and claim a more "acceptable," as she
puts it, heritage. This lesson was solidified the only time she ever heard
her culture mentioned in school, when a grade school teacher read Shel
Silverstein's poem, "The Gypsies Are Coming" to the class. It begins:

> The gypsies are coming, the old people say,
> To buy little children and take them away.

After that she kept her mouth shut. "When you don't see yourself 15
represented in the school and you don't see yourself even in dominant
society, TV shows, or movies—maybe one reference here or there and it
was always something negative—you hide," she remembers. Today, she
is out of the closet. "I know it sounds corny but I feel like I'm OK with
myself—finally—it's only taken me 30-plus years to get there."

In college, Raeesi took a Balkan music class at the University of Wyoming and spoke publicly about her heritage for the first time. But shortly
into the term, an anthropologist guest lecturer called the Roma a dirty
and culture-less people. Raeesi couldn't contain herself. "Stop talking,"
she yelled, standing up in front of the class, near tears, and berating the

woman for using her standing to discriminate. "If I hadn't been in the class, people would have said, 'I guess they really are dirty,'" Raeesi says.

The clichés of gold-draped gypsies in caravans reading fortunes and swindling outsiders have dogged Roma since they arrived in Europe as refugees from India in the Middle Ages. Considered heretics for their practice of fortune telling and palm reading, they adopted a nomadic lifestyle to avoid persecution, and practiced trades they could take on the go. A thousand years later, millions still live across Europe in shanty towns, often targeted by police, denied social services, and even segregated within schools.

Though many no longer practice traditional occupations or travel nomadically, the stereotypes persist.

A reputation of thievery and crime brings with it closer monitoring and sometimes direct targeting of Roma communities, even in the U.S., where the profiling is not nearly as harsh as in Europe. The 2001 *Police* magazine article titled "Gypsies: Kings of Con" asserts that Gypsies "look upon the rest of society simply as their 'prey'," and "there is no sin in stealing if you are a Gypsy." Five years later, a *Los Angeles Times* investigation revealed a group of 800 or so detectives across the U.S. who call themselves "The National Association of Bunco Investigators" and who specifically patrol neighborhoods for "Gypsy crime," mainly described as scams and fraud.

Activists' allegations about racial profiling are an issue of semantics, says 20 Dennis Marlock, special investigator with the Milwaukee Police Department, who created a stir with his book *License To Steal: Traveling Con Artists: Their Games, Their Rules—Your Money.* The crimes are not inherent to Roma as a whole, Marlock says, but the work of an organized criminal group of Roma who call themselves Gypsies. He equates them to the Sicilian Mafia, a criminal group within the population of Sicilians. "It's not law enforcement that created negative connotations. If we're guilty of bringing that to the public, then I'm guilty," he says. He later addresses the Roma activists who have come out against him: "It's not me causing you problems, it's your criminal element." He recalls calling a meeting when "American Gypsies were flooding in by the carload" to Milwaukee. "This is America. If you claim fortune telling as what you do, fine, but if you're gonna be ripping [people] off . . . you're going to see a lot of me," he told them, and then asked for volunteers who submitted to being fingerprinted and photographed.

Raeesi knows the stereotypes she's up against each time her heritage comes up. "When you identify yourself, you may not be starting from zero—you're starting back from zero. First of all, we don't live in wagons, we don't all travel, we don't all tell fortunes. Some do, but a lot of us have university and college educations." These aren't the stories people are used to, she says.

And mainstream media and entertainment depictions offer little diversity. "Americans tend to have a fantasy view of 'Gypsies' from popular culture that is both romantic and criminal," says Dr. Silverman, noting that the depictions have been on the rise since the 70s. Representations of Roma as promiscuous, untrustworthy, and uneducated on shows like TLC's *My Big, Fat American Gypsy Wedding*, which has aired for the past two years, followed by *Gypsy Sisters*, and National Geographic's *American Gypsies* in 2012, have infuriated activists.

The issue, Raeesi says, is the narrow segment chosen for mainstream representation. It's something that would never fly with another minority group, she points out, noting that for any one negative depiction of others, many successful, educated public figures serve as counterweights. Not so for the Roma. "For Romani people you have these reputations, but what is the counter?" Raeesi asks "What would make people say, 'They're not all like that'?"

The lack of diversity in pop culture portrayals can have real-world consequences. When TLC's show first aired, Glenda Bailey-Mershon, a North Carolina Romani writer who tutors young Romani students, says they told her they were widely harassed. "That is a factor in young people not wanting to go to school," she says. The entertainment industry may say depictions are harmless, but she says they don't understand what power they hold. "Remembering that American TV is broadcast all over the world—and this show began in Great Britain—in places where our people have more problems, it can be the difference between getting beaten up and even losing your life."

When 39-year-old author Oksana Marafioti first heard about the upcoming TLC show, she was excited enough about the opportunity to change mainstream perceptions that she auditioned. Meeting producers in Los Angeles, Marafioti, who used to work as a cinematographer in the movie business, told them she and her Romani peers were college educated. "They were like, 'Yeah, but do you have gypsy weddings or get togethers where people wear traditional clothes or play violins?'" 25

Growing up in California, Marafioti had similar misconceptions about her culture. Her parents had been part of a traveling multi-generational variety show in the Soviet Union, but her father, more inclined to play Jimi Hendrix than traditional Romani music, ended up bringing the family to America. "My parents didn't want to always be careful—they wanted to forget who they were and live how they wanted." They arrived in Hollywood when she was 15, and she found that being Gypsy made her cool. Kids would say things like, "I thought you guys all lived in caravans," and not knowing much about her heritage, she believed it. "I was almost living the stereotype and thinking it was the truth because that's what I was hearing."

Negating those stereotypes is why, Marafioti says, she chose being Romani as the subject of her 2012 book, *American Gypsy: A Memoir*. It was a nerve-wracking undertaking for someone who rarely revealed her ethnicity beforehand, but she hoped to just change one mind into thinking, "Well look, they're just like everyone else," Marafioti says. "I want for people to understand behind the word Gypsy there's an actual human being and there's a diversity in human life."

Her effort is apparently contagious. When she recently told her oldest son to be careful about letting people know his Romani roots, the 14-year-old struck back: "He says, 'No, Mom, this is who I am, this is what I'm going to say.' He's very convinced that he deserves to be able to be what he wants to be," she says, bemused and then pauses. "Maybe he's too young and just doesn't understand."

Some of Marafioti's fears came true. In 2012, when she was on tour for her memoir in California, a couple began to follow her. At two or three of her readings, she says, they heckled her. They believed, she says, that she belonged to "a subhuman category" and that "we're prone to criminal activity, early pregnancy, and a lack of education is due to our inability to learn properly." Not long after, Marafioti had another follower: a man who sent her threatening notes. "Gypsies must die," she said he wrote in one.

"People are actually not thinking of us like we're human beings, and when you consider someone less than you, you can justify anything," says Marafioti. 30

At a recent cocktail party, a woman stuck out her hand and asked Glenda Bailey-Mershon if she would read her fortune. For Bailey-Mershon, who grew up in Appalachia as a descendant of Romani slaves brought to America in the 1700s, her light hair and complexion didn't raise many eyebrows. But for anyone curious enough to ask, she cited a mixed Native American ancestry. Today, the 64-year-old writer takes any opportunity to answer questions about the Roma.

Over the past two decades, Roma activism has been on the rise. Women especially have been claiming leadership roles. Bailey-Mershon and Raeesi are founding members of the Foundation for Roma Education and Equality (FREE), a new organization that plans to form a free school program, both online and in physical locations, for Romani teens looking to get their GED. It will tie in classes on history and culture, and maybe even a language program. "We've never been taught our own history," Raeesi says. They're also advocating for Roma inclusion in Holocaust remembrance programs, where they're often ignored, even though the Nazis exterminated an estimated half a million European Roma.

FREE has completed a three-student test program which began in January 2012, and plans to launch another version next fall in the neighborhood of FREE's president, Sonya Jasaroska, who lives in a tight-knit community of more than 300 Macedonian Roma in the Bronx that formed in the early 70s.

● ● ●

Today Jasaroska, who said she once "hid and hated" her heritage, is eager to tell people about her background if they ask. "I wait for them to

A Life Apart

Immy Humes

New York native Immy Humes is a television producer and Oscar-nominated documentary filmmaker. The essay that follows is one of several that Humes wrote for Menachem Daum's and Oren Rudavsky's PBS documentary series *A Life Apart: Hasidim in America* (1997). She has worked on several media projects for Independent Lens, the National Geographic Channel, and Michael Moore's *TV Nation*. Her six-part video series on unemployment among the "99 percenters" appeared on the website *Salon* in 2012. As a documentarian, she brings to her study of New York's Hasidim an eye for telling detail and a drive to explore American ways of life that have remained largely unknown. Daum and Rudavsky are documentary filmmakers who have also collaborated in the making of *Hiding and Seeking* (2004) and *The Ruins of Lifta* (2016).

A Brief Introduction to Hasidism

The Hasidic ideal is to live a hallowed life, in which even the most mundane action is sanctified. Hasidim live in tightly-knit communities (known as "courts") that are spiritually centered around a dynastic leader known as a *rebbe*, who combines political and religious authority. The many different courts and their rebbes are known by the name of the town where they originated: thus the Bobov came the town of Bobova in Poland (Galicia), the Satmar from Satu Mar in present-day Hungary, the Belz from Poland, and the Lubavitch from Russia. In Brooklyn today, there are over sixty courts represented, but most of these are very small, with some comprising only a handful of families. The great majority of American Hasidim belong to one of a dozen or so principal surviving courts. Hasidism is not a denomination but an all-embracing religious lifestyle and ideology, which is expressed somewhat differently by adherents of the diverse courts (also called "sects").

The Hasidic way of life is visually and musically arresting, with rich textures, unusual customs, and strong traditions of music and dance. Hasidic tales, intriguing and memorable doorways into a complex world of Hasidic thought, religious themes, and humor are fruits of a long and continuing oral tradition. Popularized in the non-Hasidic world by writers such as Martin Buber, Isaac Bashevis Singer, and Elie Wiesel, they are famous for their particular wisdom and wit.

Yet this world is virtually unknown to most Americans, who are apt to confuse Hasidic men, who wear beards, side-locks,° black hats, and long coats, with the similarly-dressed Amish. This shared style of dress does

---

side-lock: lock of hair falling at the side of the face and worn as a distinguishing mark.

make a stereotypical comment and then I school them," she says
it rarely fails: "They say, 'Are you a fortune teller? Are you a musi
Do you steal kids?'" Then she explains the role of discrimination in
these stereotypes came to be. She hopes speaking out will give the
in her community a sense of pride she never had growing up. "We're
learning the ropes," Jasaroska says. "When you're not educated and do
know what your options are, you're going to sit back and be quiet."

Now the population of educated Roma is bigger than ever, and they
ready to speak up when cases like Maria's make the news. It's time, Jas
roska says, that Roma make a fuss. "This is the land of the free, home o
the brave, where you have equality, and if we keep quiet as American
and Roma, then shame on us."

Understanding the Text

1. Why does the author begin and end her discussion of the Roma with the
   story of Maria, the "Blond Angel"?

2. List a few of the many Romani stereotypes Strochlic mentions. In what ways
   are these stereotypes related?

3. What are some of the ways by which American Gypsies are "starting to fight
   back"?

Reflection and Response

4. Why might the Roma prefer to remain undocumented — "invisible" to the
   mainstream culture? What are the advantages and disadvantages of social
   invisibility?

5. As Strochlic points out, law-enforcement agencies across the U.S. routinely
   characterize the Roma as liars, thieves, and con artists. What are the
   practical effects of this kind of ethnic profiling? What other subcultural
   communities are similarly profiled?

Making Connections

6. In her essay, Strochlic objects to the way in which mainstream media depict
   American Gypsy culture. Which other subcultures are also narrowly represented
   in contemporary media? Are there any subcultures that are afforded a more
   nuanced portrayal? Why? Give specific examples to support your discussion.

7. Although the Roma are widely demonized, their culture is also often romanti-
   cized. Discuss how the portrayal of the "gypsy" functions in a particular work
   of literature, art, music, or film.

indeed reflect similar values of piety, extreme traditionalism, and separatism. But where the Amish are farmers in rural communities, the great majority of the approximately two-hundred thousand American Hasidim live and work in enclaves in the heart of New York City, amid a number of vital contemporary cultures very different from their own.

Most of the approximately 165,000 Hasidim in the New York City area live in three neighborhoods in Brooklyn: Crown Heights, Williamsburg, and Boro Park. Each of the three neighborhoods is home to Hasidim of different courts, although there is overlap and movement between them. There are approximately forty-five thousand Satmar Hasidim in Williamsburg, over fifty thousand Bobover Hasidim in Boro Park, and at least fifteen thousand Lubavitch in Crown Heights. The population of each of these groups has increased dramatically since the first American Hasidic communities were formed in the late 1940s and 1950s, with especially rapid growth in the last two decades.

Boundaries and Separation

Concerned with keeping themselves spiritually clean, the Hasidim are   5
preoccupied with ideas of biblical concepts of purity and contamination. In this ordering of values, separation from outsiders is inevitable and understandable: it is a mode of self-protection, as well as a keeping straight of categories. As the anthropologist Mary Douglas notes in *Purity and Danger*, the Hebrew language itself recognizes this affinity between apartness and hallowedness: the Hebrew words for separate and for holy share the same root.

Orthodox neighborhoods in some cities are demarcated by an *eyruv*, a wire strung high above the streets, outlining the boundaries of the community. Eyruv means blending: the border serves to "blend" the neighborhood into one ritual space, while erecting a ritual boundary between it and the world. Within the delineated space, special liberties—such as carrying objects, or pushing a stroller—that would otherwise violate the ritual laws of keeping the Sabbath are allowed. Just as this border marks the boundaries of the sacred community, so distinctions in language, dress, hairstyle, and demeanor serve Hasidim as personal boundaries, protecting the separation of an individual Hasid from the secular world.

Hasidim also maintain a language barrier against the non-Hasidic world. Just as Hasidic dress serves as a visual marker of separation, so the sound of Yiddish serves as an aural one. A favorite Hasidic saying states, "A Jew speaks Jewish," and a prominent Yiddish sign at the Bobover girls' school reads "A proud girl speaks Yiddish." Most American Hasidim have little use for modern spoken Hebrew, which they consider debased by its

Visiting Hasidic Jews at the tomb of Rabbi Elimelech, one of the founding rebbes of the Hasidic movement, in an annual event marking his death. Janek Skarsynsk/ Getty Images

divorce from the holy context of prayer and study. They reserve Hebrew for textual study and use Yiddish for much of their daily speech. The rebbe communicates with his Hasidim in Yiddish, Yiddish is taught in school, and used for explication and study of Hebrew sacred texts. The Hasidic home is bilingual, with English and Yiddish sometimes mixing together (many English words have found their way into Brooklyn Hasidic Yiddish, and a Hasid speaking English will often lapse into Yiddish). The stricter sects, Satmar, for instance, place little value on the study of English. . . .

Hasidim also preserve their separation through a separate school system. One of the very first things the Hasidim did upon settling in America was to found schools and yeshivas. Although the Hasidic schools fulfill minimum requirements set by state authorities such as the New York State Board of Regents, they do not teach basic scientific knowledge such as the theory of evolution, for example.

Boys and girls receive separate and quite different educations, beginning with pre-school. Girls attend all-girls schools through the age of seventeen or eighteen, normally from eight in the morning to around three in the afternoon. Boys, on the other hand, usually extend their school hours at the age of eleven until six in the evening, and after bar mitzvah, the coming-of-age ceremony at age thirteen, return to school after supper for another few hours of study. (Sunday is a regular school day for both sexes, while Friday is a half day to allow preparation for the Sabbath, which arrives at sunset.) There is a current trend towards extending the years of schooling, including more religious education for girls. Some see this as an attempt to further shore up the cultural bulwarks of separation.

While the girls learn more English and history than the boys, as well 10 as practical religious knowledge such as the laws of *kashrut*,° the boys focus on the Talmud, the great 63-volume compendium of Jewish law and commentary. Early arranged marriages, usually around age twenty, are encouraged, and birth control is generally frowned upon as it is seen as contradicting the biblical commandment to "be fruitful and multiply." After marriage, nearly all young men continue to study for at least a year or two. This study is paid for by parents, in-laws, wives, and grants from benefactors in and outside of the community.

College and graduate education is now almost totally discouraged, as it is seen as a source of cultural contamination. The generation now reaching college age is in general stricter than its parents; it is common to see children of Hasidic college graduates who would never consider higher education. Most secular education is eschewed in favor of minimal technical training for jobs that keep Hasidim within or close to the community. As a result, in sharp contrast to the case in virtually any other Jewish community, among the Hasidim there is a shortage of professionals: Hasidim have to turn outside for doctors, lawyers, and even sometimes for musicians to play at weddings. It is a matter of some concern and controversy whether this dearth of professionals presages economic trouble for the community.

Although some Hasidic men work independently, as self-employed computer consultants, electricians, contractors, or estate appraisers . . . most work together with other Hasidim. Concentrated mostly in small retail, import/export, and manufacturing businesses in Brooklyn and the Lower East Side of Manhattan, many are involved with providing goods and services to the community, such as teaching, or the manufacture and distribution of kosher food items, religious articles, publications, or Hasidic clothing.

Hasidim are also involved in the diamond, garment, and discount retail electronics industries.

> "The experience of close community, united around religious purpose, can provide a profound sense of well-being and identity, of belonging and rootedness."

kashrut: set of Jewish dietary laws.

Most Hasidic women who work outside the home (usually after their children are grown) are employed by close relatives in their small businesses, or by the community as teachers, administrators, community social workers, or other functionaries. There are also women who run small businesses, usually services or small manufacturers, themselves.

Community

Whereas in mainstream American culture the ego is at the center of the 15 universe, for the Hasidim it is the group that counts. The experience of close community, united around religious purpose, can provide a profound sense of well-being and identity, of belonging and rootedness.... Humanities advisor Samuel Heilman points out the "palpable sense of community" in Hasidic life:

What all Hasidim are always conscious of is: "How many we are." The purpose of a tish° is ostensibly to gather at the rebbe's table, but really it is to look at "How many we are," to feel the press of flesh, to celebrate the group itself. The worst thing for a Hasidic group is to build a building which is too big. You have to be able to feel the body politic—if you can't feel it and smell it and touch it, it would be a failure. You will never hear a Hasid walking through a crowd of other Hasidim saying "Excuse me" or "Pardon me," he walks through pushing and shoving. The whole thing at a Hasidic gathering is, you get pushed and shoved, and you can feel it and smell it in the most intimate way. Not only do they share food, they literally share their bodies. And this is an extraordinary thing when you think about it, because here are people who elsewhere go out of their way not to touch anyone else, not a woman, not a stranger.

• • •

A Niche within Modernity

While at first glance Hasidim appear analogous to the Amish or other groups in America who actively defend themselves against all encroachments of contemporary life, it is more correct, as Barbara Kirschenblatt-Gimblett has pointed out, that the Hasidim have found "a niche within modernity." Their ethos of sacralization allows Hasidim to use aspects of modernity towards ends compatible with their world view.

tish: joyous public celebration.

Technology, shunned by groups such as the Amish, is embraced by many Hasidim and used to enhance, intensify, and strengthen their own culture and economic life. The Lubavitchers, for example, use state-of-the-art television technology to broadcast live and around the world the rebbe's audiences with his followers, although they are opposed to television viewing of all secular programs. Hasidim have dominated New York City's discount retail electronics market. They sell radios, televisions, computers, and cameras, although they won't buy televisions themselves. They videotape weddings and other events and view them on monitors that cannot receive incoming programs. There is a lively recording business for Hasidic music, but most tapes only have the voices of Hasidic men.

Some long-standing differences and tensions between certain Hasidic courts have only been exacerbated during their years in America. The most famous feud is between the Hungarian Satmar and the Russian/Polish Lubavitch, who divide over issues of outreach, openness to modern and secular custom and technology, and Zionism. The Satmar vehemently oppose the state of Israel, viewing it as a blasphemous arrogance—since it is only the Messiah who is supposed to bring the Jewish nation back from exile to Israel. The Lubavitch, on the other hand, have accommodated themselves to Israel's existence and are now very involved in attempts to influence Israeli politics and social policies towards stricter religious observance. The division between the two courts has sometimes resulted in serious violence.

The Satmar are one of the most separatist sects, resisting almost all behaviors, activities, styles, and contacts that would lead them to accommodation with the surrounding American mainstream culture. Other Hasidim see all daily behavior as sanctifiable, and go to some lengths to elevate potentially assimilative activities, or just plain neutral ones, to the status of sanctified acts. An interviewee reports conflicting views about the great American pastime: "Baseball is not only a Gentile habit, it is a waste of time, a clear violation since it replaces an opportunity to study the Torah." Yet he also approvingly recalls an incident at a Hasidic summer camp when the rabbi reminded the boys that their ball playing was also mitzvah, a sanctified action, because it improved their physical condition so they could better pursue religious study.

In a radical departure from tradition, Lubavitch Hasidim (the largest 20 sect worldwide) have extended the notion of sanctification of the profane to proselytizing. Judaism generally discourages converting Gentiles as a threat to the integrity of Jewish life. While the Lubavitch do not seek to convert non-Jews, they do actively reach out to Jews. Their "mitzvah mobiles" work the streets of many American cities with significant Jewish populations. Young Hasidim buttonhole passers-by, asking "Are you a Jew?" They try to persuade Jewish men to put on *tefillin* (the ritual prayer straps of Orthodox and Conservative Judaism) and give women Sabbath candles to light at home. The widespread Lubavitch campaign includes sending proselytizing Hasidim to college campuses, as well as extensive missionary efforts abroad.

The Lubavitch are distinctive in other ways. They have paid greater attention to the special needs of women within their community, and have extended religious and secular educational opportunities to women as they absorb outsiders and have increased contact with the world outside.

Intersections with the Outside World

The picture of the Hasidim as members of a homogeneous closed community, people of one mind who turn their backs on the modern world, is inaccurate. There are deep differences between different groups of Hasidim, and great individual variety within each group. In addition, the doctrine of separation, of self-protection from contamination from the outside society, exists side by side with the Jewish, yet particularly Hasidic, notion of sanctifying the profane. This creates the possibility of "elevating" and absorbing outside influence, adopting and adapting everything from a secular love tune to "beepers" and baseball into the service of piety.

Also, American Hasidim have been Americanized in their particular way. As our advisor, Professor George Kranzler points out:

Hasidic life in the United States is not totally "A Life Apart." To some degree it has assumed characteristics that qualify it as "American." In contrast to the Amish, for example, the isolation of the Satmar Hasidim is only "sociocultural," but the spirit of the younger American-born Hasidim, their economic adjustment, particularly their "entrepreneurship," is quintessentially American.

Understanding the Text

1. What does Humes mean when she writes that the Hasidim have an "ethos of sacralization" (par. 16)?

2. List some of the ways in which the Hasidim literally separate themselves from the society around them.

3. Samuel Heilman talks about the "palpable sense of community" in Hasidic life (par. 15). How is this sense of community made physical? Why is this close physicality important to the Hasidic community?

Reflection and Response

4. Why do you think that the children of college-educated Hasids are now those most opposed to higher education? What impact has this trend away from higher education had on the Hasidic community? Include specific textual evidence to support your speculation.

5. How do religious or spiritual commitments shape your own life? Even if you are not personally religious, consider the ways the society in which you live is influenced by religious beliefs and practices.

6. How is the Hasidic relationship with technology paradoxical? Do you see the practice of selling goods one would not use oneself hypocritical or principled? Draw an example from mainstream culture to support your answer.

Making Connections

7. What other subcultures make literal and figurative separation from mainstream society a condition of their existence? What characteristics do these subcultures share with the Hasidim? Discuss in depth.

8. Research the history of the Hasidim, tracing their roots back to Eastern Europe. How does their past help explain their continued commitment to separateness? How do their European antecedents inform their communities in America? Which aspects of their society have not translated well to the New World?

...ng Up Amish: Building an Amish Identity

Richard A. Stevick

Old Order Amish constitute one of the best-known American subcultures, instantly recognizable for their old-time clothing, horse-and-buggies, beards and bonnets, agricultural economy, and rejection of the American political system. Psychologist Richard Stevick spent decades working with Amish adolescents, establishing close relationships with communities across the United States. In this selection, Stevick provides insight into what it means to come of age in a religious collectivist society in which personal identity is subordinated to group goals and values. Stevick shows how powerful norms provide both safety and restrictions for Amish youth as they make the transition to adulthood. A professor emeritus at Messiah College, he currently serves as a consultant for the National Institute of Mental Health's long-term study of Amish children.

In a collectivist° society like that of the Amish, the young people's task is not to distinguish themselves from others by their uniqueness and achievement, but rather by their willingness to support and strengthen the group. This happens by "giving yourself up," as they call it. Despite their unique personal preferences, tastes, and personalities, they are expected to accept their church's collective *Ordnung,*° with its explicit rules for dress and behavior. An Amish person's identity is achieved through tempering much of his or her personal autonomy. Because the Amish know that humans are weak and that sacrifices are difficult, they believe that forming an Amish identity is too important to be left solely to the individual and his or her family. Ideally, all members—individually and collectively—share the responsibility of helping each child and youth form a firm identity as a member of their Amish community.

In mainstream society, young people may flounder for years as they seek to know who they are and where their niche is in a complex, individualistic world. Many modern youth find the struggle long, lonely, and too often unsuccessful. At puberty, they may begin both their movement toward independence from parents and their growing involvement with peers, but they might not gain financial independence and intimate relationships until their midtwenties or later. In contrast, Amish young

collectivist: relating to prioritizing the good of the group over the welfare of the individual.
Ordnung: German word for *order* or *discipline,* referring to the set of rules governing Amish life.

people almost never begin to seriously socialize with their peers until they are sixteen or seventeen. By this age most are working full time as adults, and by the time they are twenty-one or twenty-two, most have joined the church, are married, and are starting families. Instead of an exploratory period of a decade or more on their way to full-fledged adulthood, most Amish youth typically spend no more than five years in this pursuit: from the time they enter their *Rumspringa°* until they reach full Amish adult status.[1] Everyone, young and old, knows exactly what their society expects of them.

Unlike mainstream youth, who are confronted with a multitude of vocational, value, and lifestyle choices, the ultimate task of an Amish young person is deciding whether or not to accept an Amish identity. This culminates either in being baptized and joining the church, or in assuming a non-Amish identity that results in leaving one's community. This is the most critical decision an Amish youth will ever make. Becoming a church member means embracing the expectations of one's community. Not joining the church, or joining but then leaving, almost never occurs without great pain and existential struggle. An Amish identity takes root deeply into one's psyche, or soul.

Components of an Amish Identity

A teenager's family is an important source in forming his or her identity. Children and youth from loving Amish families begin to effortlessly assume an Amish identity.

Those children from highly regarded families are also likely to form 5
positive self-identities, since they benefit directly from the accomplishments and status of their parents and grandparents. "Everyone knows that Klines are bright and that Smuckers are exceptionally hard workers." Young people whose parents fail to meet community ideals may struggle more with attaining a positive identity, both personally and socially, because of their familial liabilities.

In Amish society, a family's success is usually measured, among other things, by hard work, thrift, good management, and the outcome of their children. Consequently, a major component of one's identity is influenced by how industrious and intelligent a worker he or she is. Since most Amish children learn to work early in their lives, and thus develop a sense of their own efficacy and competence, by their midteens almost all are able to transition smoothly into adult work responsibilities. For example, a fifteen-year-old girl in Franklin County, Pennsylvania, taught

Rumpringa: period when adolescents are given personal freedom, usually ending with the choice of baptism into the church or leaving the community.

twenty-five children in grades one through eight. When she started, she was scarcely a year older than her oldest students.

During the girl's second year of teaching, her twelve-year-old sister transferred into her one-room school to help the older girl by teaching the school's eight first-graders how to read. Parents of the schoolchildren reported that the sisters did well. If Amish youth are not supposed to be proud of their work, they are certainly permitted to feel satisfaction in applying themselves diligently and accomplishing tasks like these. Since these young hard workers are esteemed by both their peers and adults, they have a good foundation on which to develop a positive and robust sense of self-worth.

Another major identity component for Amish youth, whether positive or negative, is shaped by their choice of peers, especially in the large settlements. In Lancaster County, peer groups (youth groups) are called "gangs," and in northern Indiana, similar groups are called "crowds." In both places, these gatherings of cohorts provide an important arena for shaping one's identity, especially through one's age-mates and best friends. In a Lancaster County daughter settlement, a father observed, "Youth from farm families tend to hang out with each other, and those whose dads work away find their friends in that group." As in mainstream society, Amish young people tend to gravitate toward those who are like themselves, a situation that further reinforces their identities. "I hang out with the rowdy boys," explained an eighteen-year-old from Montour County, Pennsylvania, who lived in a small, conservative daughter (offshoot) settlement from the Lancaster County settlement. "Almost all the Youngie do what they are supposed to do, but my friends and me like to have fun together. Sometimes it gets us in trouble." Despite the increased impact of peers, especially during the rumspringa years, the power of their community and their families exerts a constant counterbalance to the excesses of the young, tacitly and intentionally reminding them of adult values and expected behavior.

Identity and Dressing Amish

The symbolic aspects of their attire promote and reinforce the desired Amish identity. The majority of Americans, from children to grandparents, distinguish themselves through their dress. What a person wears often reveals his or her personal or family income, social class, extravagances, love of adventure, travel history, political or sexual preferences, or non-conformity. Amish clothing, on the other hand, is designed to minimize individual tastes and differences. It demonstrates one's willingness to squelch personal preferences and uniqueness by accepting the group's attire and the community's expected standards of decency. By reducing individual or economic differences, an Amish person's garments symbolize his or her membership in the group, rather than being apart from or above it. Whether one is a teenager or a grandparent, conformity in dress reinforces a person's identity as an obedient and yielding member of the community.

* * *

Parents need not tell their growing children that their apparel will 10 immediately mark them as different. As they mature, the young people implicitly recognize the contrasts between themselves and the tourists or the community's English neighbors, with their jewelry, shorts, slacks, and ostentatious colors and patterns. Fancy clothing, with buttons and bows or neckties and belts, has always belonged to the worldly minded, not to the plain people of God.[2] The Amish also believe that any apparel that is form fitting or revealing, whether it is shorts, short skirts, or sleeveless or low-cut blouses, indicates a worldly and wayward heart. Because children and youth are immersed from infancy in these communal clothing expectations and examples, the formation of their Amish identity is constantly strengthened and reinforced.

Despite community standards and parental reminders, a significant minority of youth, especially in the large settlements, express their independence by departing from the plain and simple dress standards during their transitional Rumspringa period. These independent-minded youth are generally invisible to mainstream society, since they often mimic the currently popular styles in the rest of the country. These fashion statements may be directed toward parents and other adults, to demonstrate the young people's independence, however temporary. It is more likely, though, that such deviance in dress may be designed to make a similar show of independence to their peers, or perhaps to seek acceptance by conforming to the standards of their more daring peers. In this case, the medium most likely is the message: "Look how cool I am. I'm not afraid to defy my parents or the ministers. And I can certainly pass for English if I want to." A desire to be well accepted, admired, and cool is certainly not confined to English adolescents.

A Healthy Sense of Self

Non-Amish observers, accustomed to the autonomy and choice inherent in an individualistic culture, might wonder if communal restrictions result in stunted or cookie-cutter personalities and impaired self-esteem. If such is the case, most outsiders who have face-to-face or extended contact with Amish children and youth fail to detect such outcomes. Instead, observers often comment that Amish young people appear to have high levels of maturity and confidence. They also note the poise with which the youngsters and teens relate to peers and adults, both friends and strangers. Little formal research has focused on the social skills and psychological well-being of Amish youth, but relatively few of them appear to be depressed, sad, lonely, or hostile.[3] If anything, their sense of who they are seems to be both clear and positive.[4]

Not surprisingly, Amish parents, teachers, or ministers rarely talk about building their children's self-esteem. That idea, with its self-focus, is contrary to their way of thinking. They believe that children will learn to feel good about themselves by finding and fulfilling their God-given roles within the Amish community. If the majority of Amish youth are, in fact, psychologically robust, this should not come as a surprise. Compared with the complex and often vague demands placed on youth in competitive mainstream society, those faced by Amish youth are clear and within reach of most. As Donald B. Kraybill° has observed, "Achieving the Amish dream is much more attainable for the typical Amish individual than achieving the American dream is for the average mainstream individual."[5] Work competence is both within reach and acquired by virtually all Amish youth, and this sense of confidence and agency undoubtedly contributes positively to their self-esteem and the formation of their Amish identity.[6]

> "Achieving the Amish dream is much more attainable for the typical Amish individual than achieving the American dream is for the average mainstream individual."

• • •

Autonomy: Independence within a Communal Society

Perhaps because of their Anabaptist° emphasis on an adult decision to join the church and follow Christ, most Amish allow their youth more latitude and independence for exploration and experimentation than one might expect, especially in the larger communities. Many parents make an abrupt shift in their treatment of their teenagers when the young people reach sixteen or seventeen and begin their rumspringa period. Throughout their children's formative years, the most common Amish parenting approach would be labeled authoritarian or traditional, according to family specialist Diana Baumrind. Parents are the

---

Donald B. Kraybill: American author and scholar of the Old Order Amish (b. 1946).
Anabaptist: Protestant movement that arose in the 16th century to advocate the baptism of adult believers only.

undisputed authorities, and they expect immediate obedience. Until their children are ten or eleven, most parents will not hesitate to spank them for disobedience or defiance. After their children begin going with the young folks, however, most parents tend to be more permissive as they recognize the new status of their sixteen- or seventeen-year-olds.

The most tangible way in which parents acknowledge their children's 15 newfound status is to allow them the freedom to socialize with their friends without being dependent on their parents or older siblings for transportation. Normally this freedom is demonstrated by parents giving a horse and carriage to each son when he begins going to the singings. Unless their parents cannot afford it, almost all males over sixteen may lay claim to this traditional form of transportation. Those youth running in the fastest circles may reject their parents' offer and opt to buy a motor vehicle of some sort as soon as they have the money and can legally do so. Whether traveling by 1 or by 200 horsepower, these teenagers have increased privacy and freedom with their new mobility.

Girls rarely have their own carriages, at least in the early stages of Rumspringa, so they are dependent on their brothers or male relatives for rides to singings and other events until the girls begin courting.[7] Nonetheless, females, along with their male cohorts, are granted the freedom to fully enter social life and attend singings. With their newly gained freedom, males are much more likely than females to deviate from adult and community expectations in the areas of dress, car ownership, alcohol

Two Amish carriages pass one other on a rural highway.
Education Images/Getty Images

consumption, friendship with outsiders, and church membership. The tendency for disproportionately more single males to leave the Amish than females probably reflects the males' greater need for independence and autonomy.[8]

Exerting One's Independence

Besides having new opportunities to travel with their peers, youth have other realms in which to express their autonomy. Because attire and appearance are such central components of Amish life and expectations, some youth find this a convenient target for expressing their independence, especially in the larger communities. In many settlements, many teenage boys trade their plain clothes for what they believe to be the English look: in some cases, knit shirts, black jeans, and sneakers; in other cases, stylish polo shirts, khaki cargo pants, and sandals or expensive athletic footwear, depending on their peer group. To the embarrassment of their parents, a few young men have even sprouted forbidden moustaches.

Teenage girls, who tend to dress more conventionally, may still hitch up or lengthen their skirts, shave their legs, sport gold pins on their sweaters or jackets, and wear flip-flops or sandals, even in some of the conservative circles. Also, if females dress in English attire, it happens most often when they are out with their peers. One girl related how she told her date to wait for her at the end of the lane. Before she met him, she quickly changed into English clothes and stored her Amish garments in a bag in the carriage or car....

Parents and church leaders are well aware that the youth are in a sometimes unpredictable borderland where the scrutiny of parents is diminished and control by the church has not yet taken over. The young person who wishes to become a member of the Amish church, however, will ultimately yield to that control. What helps in that final transformation is that during their formative childhood years, most youth have learned unquestioned obedience to their parents. This childhood training undoubtedly prepares the young people to later submit to the demands of the community. Sometimes rules will be bent, such as while traveling or visiting other Amish affiliations with different standards, but within an individual Amish community, the Ordnung can be changed only by the consensus of the group. Until that happens, the expectation is that the rules are to be binding on all members, old and young alike.

Accepting the Boundaries

Consequently, young people aspiring to church membership rarely struggle 20 about whether they should go to high school or college, become physicians or lawyers, marry outsiders, move away from the Amish community, or postpone having children until after they have been married for a while. One reason is that their primary reference group almost always consists of other Amish youths and adults. Therefore most do not feel deprived because they must work so hard, end their formal education at age fourteen or fifteen, or drastically restrict their vocational choices.

Having a group of serious-minded peers also helps diminish the impact of mainstream values and influences. For most youth, "joining church" is a natural choice that indicates a willingness to curtail one's autonomy and accept the community's strictures. All other choices naturally flow out of this ultimate decision—whether or not to become a baptized Amish member. When an individual joins the church, there is to be no turning back from that covenant, and no exceptions are allowed. As one elder stated, "Joining church is a spiritual marriage, and just as in an earthly marriage, we cannot divorce the church and still be Amish."

The Balancing Act

Given the limited range of choices in this collectivist society, is identity development as important for Amish youth as it is for mainstream teenagers? Certainly everyone, English or Amish, needs to know how he or she is different from everybody else, so in that sense, forming one's identity is a universal task. But are identity issues equally important for all cultures? Undoubtedly, in traditions that stress uniformity and conformity, the task of developing one's identity differs from what happens in mainstream society, with its emphasis on individualism and independence. For the majority of youth who choose to remain Amish, it would appear that acquiring a clear identity would be a relatively easy task, because of limited choices and well-defined expectations.

Once again, though, things are rarely as simple as they seem. Sociologist Denise Reiling studied Amish life and culture for nearly ten years in a settlement that bordered northern Indiana and southern Michigan. During that time, she devoted more than 300 hours interviewing a randomly selected group of sixty Amish-reared youth and adults about their Rumspringa. She reported that in her sample, "identity during this decision-making period [of whether to be baptized or leave the community] was reported to be highly ambiguous. Almost every participant's description depicted this decision-making period as one of limbo, wherein the child does not identify as Amish, even though continuing to live in an Amish home and to engage in Amish cultural practices.... Virtually every participant reported that they experienced social isolation during this time, which generated a high level of depression and anxiety." Reiling concluded that these participants experienced strong levels of "negative affective response" and "angst." She attributed these effects, at least in part, to the length and seriousness of the deviant activities of the youth of that particular group, and to the conflict between the Amish cultural expectation of obedience to God and the church and what Reiling regarded as the unspoken parental expectations that their teens should experience a sow-their-oats Rumspringa to weed out the unworthy and strengthen those who choose to eventually join.

Even in settlements where most youth do not participate in deviant activities or feel conflicted about adult expectations, those Amish young people with a strong need for personal independence or those who are dissatisfied with their way of life have a much more complex task, fraught with the potential for psychological and emotional distress or damage.... Despite the fact that one can find many ex-Amish who express satisfaction with their having left, almost none leave the culture without serious struggles and difficult adjustments to mainstream society.

One indication of how deeply the Amish identity runs may be found   25 in the way that even those youth who are flaunting their community's rules react to outsiders seeking to learn about the inner workings of Amish life.... This non-cooperation on the part of these rowdy youth reflects an instinctive loyalty acquired in their separatist community. Despite youthful dalliance or deviance, in a relatively short time most of them abandon their worldly ways and return to their Amish roots. This fundamental sense of who they are, now and in the future, is both pervasive and powerful enough to maintain their primary identity as Amish. This identity provides the core that allows them to give up their autonomy, the right to do anything they please, and to accept the restrictions and proscriptions of the community. This relinquishment is necessary if they are going to be contented, committed members of this communal subculture.

Notes

1. Developmental psychologists Marcia (1980, 1994) and Erikson (1968, 1980) described this period of exploration as a moratorium, a byproduct of a complex society that temporarily relaxes expectations for mature performance and behavior.

2. An exception to this utilitarian attire is that boys in the conservative horse-and-buggy Amish groups in Lancaster County wear bow ties when they dress up.

3. An informal survey was taken among Amish attending a county fair and then discussed on an ABC special, *Mystery of Happiness* (aired 15 Apr. 1996).

4. On reading this section, a convert to the Amish wrote: "I agree. The children are *so* loved and accepted."

5. Presentation at Young Center, Elizabethtown College (May 1991).

6. Biswas-Diener et al. (2005) administered several self-reporting surveys on various components of happiness (SWB = Sense of Well-Being) to both Old Order and New Order volunteers in Illinois. The authors concluded that, as a group, the Amish scored significantly higher than "neutral" in their sense of happiness, their memory of positive over negative events, and their perceived happiness, as judged by their friends.

7. An Amish father wrote: "This sets the pattern of a male being dominant, because girls must get rides from boys to go to gangs and singings. Girls are dependent on the boys."

8. This parallels Batson and Ventis's (1982) findings, which indicated that in North America, women typically outnumber men in religious expression and church attendance.

Understanding the Text

1. Explain the term *Rumspringa*. Why is Rumspringa of central importance to the Amish teenager?

2. In what ways do the Amish purposely distinguish themselves from the rest of society? List specific examples from the reading and discuss how these physical details or subcultural practices serve to construct Amish identity.

Reflection and Response

3. Stevick writes that the Amish "believe that forming an Amish identity is too important to be left solely to the individual and his or her family" (par. 1). In other words, the entire community should shape an individual's identity. To what extent is this also the case in mainstream American life? In your own life?

4. To remain in the Amish community is "the most critical decision an Amish youth will ever make" (par. 3). What are the most critical decisions that you will make? Explain.

Making Connections

5. How is the Amish subculture similar to the Hasidic subculture described earlier in this chapter? In what ways do they differ? Why is choosing marginalization from the mainstream culture necessary for these communities to survive?

6. How do Amish values and practices directly challenge the mainstream commitment to the "American Dream"?

7. In recent years, many Amish communities have been pressured by drug abuse, incursions of new technologies, and as the amount of available farmland declines, the need to seek employment in the English world. Research how the Amish are responding to these challenges and compose a short argument about the future of the group.

Native American Gangs

Tristan Ahtone

Tristan Ahtone is an award-winning journalist and member of the Kiowa Tribe of Oklahoma. Born in Arizona and educated at the Institute of American Indian Arts and the Columbia School of Journalism, he has reported for *The Newshour with Jim Lehrer*, *National Native News*, *Frontline*, Wyoming Public Radio, *Vice*, *Fronteras Desk*, and *NPR*. He serves as an officer for the Native American Journalists Association, and currently lives in Albuquerque, New Mexico. The series of articles from which the following selection is drawn was originally written for *Al Jazeera America* and published in 2015.

A Cross to Bear

MINNEAPOLIS — It was Sunday, game day, and James Cross turned down the television volume, rose from his armchair and lifted his purple Vikings windbreaker to show off his tattoos.

"This is a drive-by scene," he said as he pointed to the image on his stomach. "I never finished it, though. I was going to put 'Do another drive-by to make another mother cry.'"

He turned around and pulled the purple windbreaker up to show off his shoulders.

"I got forks on the back, which represents the Disciples," said Cross, referring to a tattoo of two hands making the sign of the Latin Gangster Disciples. "Then I've got tattoos on my face. I had a teardrop, but we covered it up with a feather just so everybody wouldn't be intimidated and I could get a job. Everybody knows a teardrop is for murder."

When they were around the age of 7, he and his twin brother first 5 hooked up with the Latin Gangster Disciples. One day, he said, they were hanging around with the older guys and someone said, "Hey, go get that cash register," referring to a nearby convenience store.

"We went and got that cash register," Cross said. "There was an old man working there, couldn't do nothing, couldn't hardly move, so it was an easy hit."

Not that easy. They got caught and he began a long string of encounters with the law. Now 48, he has spent almost half his life in prison. That time has taken a very serious toll on his life.

"My kids, they've been on drive-by shootings with me when they were babies and little kids," said Cross. "I wish I'd never showed them that — how to live, how to be a gang member."

His youngest son, Jerome Cross, decided not to become a Latin Gangster Disciple like his father. Instead, he joined up with the Shotgun Crips and is now serving a 33-year sentence for murder.

"He went from innocent to fucking gangster," said James Cross "He's 10 probably the smartest one of all of us, but he just wanted to be like Dad. He won't be out till 2029 or 2030."

Compared with their African-American or white counterparts, Native American gangs and gang members are a relatively new phenomenon, tracing their roots back to the 1980s and '90s, when city gangs introduced themselves to Indian Country and began recruiting.

The young men and women joining these gangs come from myriad backgrounds, some involved with Native American cultural and spiritual practices, others from broken homes and some even from supportive, two-parent, middle-class homes.

The growing threat of Native gangs is not a retelling of cowboys and Indians set against the backdrop of a modern black market. It's a story about how historical trauma, federal policy, and tribal pride have created a new Indian problem: organized crime.

The question remains: Why do the youths of Indian Country join gangs?

James Cross and his twin brother, Gerald Cross, sat outside smoking 15 cigarettes and drinking coffee. A pair of pit bulls wrestled for a stick at their feet, and old minivans and sedans rolled through the streets, the boom and beat of hip-hop music occasionally rattling trash cans and the plastic side paneling of houses.

"When he goes to jail, I can feel it," said James as he pointed to his brother. "We never fought one on one. We made sure that people knew if you messed with one Cross, the other one was coming. That's how we grew up. To this day, it's still like that."

Both of them were taken from their Anishinaabe and Dakota° parents at the age of 4 because of alcoholism and were adopted by a white family. Gerald says the home was safe, clean and a loving environment, but James says he knew he didn't belong. The two joined the Latin Gangster Disciples primarily because it was something to do and seemed cool.

"Just being able to count on people, not feeling like you were rolling alone — just seemed like it was a good thing," said Gerald. "We were part of something. We were clicking. We had things."

If it weren't for the tattoos, it would be hard to tell the two apart. James has the gang signs for the Latin Gangster Disciples on his back,

Anishinaabe and Dakota: Native American tribal affiliations concentrated on the Northern Plains.

while Gerald has them on his chest. Whereas James has a drive-by scene on his stomach, Gerald's is tattoo-free; instead, he has a city scene down his arm with "Most hated 612"—612 being the Minneapolis area code.

While James has elected to take the straight life, Gerald still dabbles 20 in drugs and occasionally runs the streets. "You know right from wrong," said Gerald. "But you're going to do what you're going to have to do. If you can accept the consequence of getting caught, then do what you've got to do."

The growling pit bulls grew tired of the stick, and one waddled into the shade to yawn, snort and nap while the other sat between the Cross brothers, hung its tongue out and drooled into the grass.

Minnesota has nine criteria, and individuals have to meet three of them to be considered a gang member. They include being arrested with a gang member, wearing clothing identified with a gang, appearing in a photo with a gang member engaging in gang activity, being identified as a gang member by a reliable source and being regularly observed with gang members.

"There is a problem around the definition of a gang," said Katie Johnston-Goodstar, an assistant professor at the University of Minnesota School of Social Work. "It starts to become a spectrum of ideas rather than a single entity."

According to her, there are good gangs, and there are bad gangs. Good gangs could be viewed as a natural, almost necessary reaction to hostile environments, providing structures for young people to have appropriate identity development—and in Indian Country, where history has had serious effects on people's sense of identity, to cultivate a healthy conception of being Native.

"We need to talk about all the disruption of community that hap- 25 pened through continual policies and practices over the last 200 years," said Johnston-Goodstar. "We're still feeling those effects and impacts and that trauma and ongoing trauma."

For instance, in 1862, President Abraham Lincoln ordered the hanging of 38 Santee Sioux men in the largest mass execution in American history, 80 miles south of Minneapolis in the town of Mankato. The hanging came in the aftermath of the Minnesota Uprising, in which Dakota tribal members attempted to drive white settlers from their territory after being robbed, cheated and starved by local, state and federal officials. Those who weren't hanged were removed to Nebraska, and over the next 100 years, the area's remaining tribes and bands underwent brutal changes—moving to reservations, sending culture and tradition underground and migrating from their homelands to cities like Minneapolis.

Between 1992 and 2002, Native Americans came into contact with violent crime at double the rate of the rest of the nation; around

60 percent of victims described their attackers as white. And between 2005 and 2009, over half of all violent crimes that took place in Indian Country were declined by authorities for prosecution.

"A lot of times, we just want to say, 'Oh, this kid is bad,'" said Johnston-Goodstar. "But if we look at the community history, if we look at their personal history, if we look at chemical dependency in the home, it's all these other environmental impacts that are really giving them little to no choice."

According to the Minnesota Department of Human Services, Native American children in Minnesota are six times more likely to make contact with child protective services than white children, eight times as likely to experience neglect and 12 times as likely to spend time in out-of-home care.

"From the inside, it's about protection, it's about positive identity 30 development around a cultural-historical presence and possibly some criminal activity on a misdemeanor kind of level," said Ross Roholt, a member of the gang assessment team at the University of Minnesota. "The bigger piece is that these groups come together to protect themselves and to create a space to see themselves as Native."

In 1993 two Minneapolis police officers found two Native American men who were passed out drunk, handcuffed them, threw them in the trunk of their car and drove around town before delivering them to a hospital. According to Human Rights Watch, the officers claimed that they were worried about the men and wanted to get them to a hospital quickly. One of the officers had been repeatedly accused of arresting and driving people to the Mississippi River to beat and interrogate them. In the 1960s, the American Indian Movement was founded in Minneapolis to protect Native people from police brutality.

"I don't think that the gangs are all that different than the American Indian Movement in a lot of ways," said Eric Buffalohead, chairman of the American Indian studies department at Augsburg College in Minneapolis. "It's about protecting yourself in a culture of violence."

Today new, international pressures affect many cities with Native communities. Somali refugees have begun making the South Side of Minneapolis home and now live in the same neighborhoods as Natives, sometimes displacing families.

"It's created some interesting territorial skirmishes and problems with the Somali gangs versus the Native gangs," said Buffalohead. "It's created this really interesting, supermulticultural situation but also troubling because everyone wants their piece of the pie, and when you're at the bottom of the barrel, fighting for scraps, things can be tough."

According to data from 2007, fewer than half of Native Americans 35 over age 25 had earned a college or graduate degree. A 2014 report asserted that Native American teens experience the highest suicide rate in the country.

"It's easy to sensationalize gang violence. It's easy to sensationalize crime," said Oliviah Walker, a member of the gang assessment team. "It's easy to put 'Native Mob' in a handful of newspapers and just have it blow up because it takes the focus away from systemic and structural violence that occurs in our communities."

James Cross ended his career on the streets in prison and in tears.

"I wanted to be the toughest, scariest known dude," he said. "But last time I got locked up, all my sons and my wife came to see me, and it just broke me down."

They had a message for him: Come home, stop with the drugs, stop the gang activities, and stop the violence. Most important, they told him they loved him.

"Man, that was the hardest thing," he said. "When it comes to people 40 telling you they love you and you know deep down they love you for real? I couldn't stop crying. And crying in jail? Was that hard to cover up."

Today Cross works as a dishwasher at a Native community center in Minneapolis. His wife has health problems, and he cares for his granddaughter and his sons. Because of his tattoos, most jobs turn him away. Because of his arrest history, others won't hire him.

On the weekends, he helps run sweat lodges for anyone who wants to participate, including current and former gang members. He also runs a motivational speaking program, Real Talk Native, in which he talks to high school students about the dangers of joining gangs.

"I tell kids, 'If you're really into changing and getting out of the gang, it's possible,'" said Cross. "I try to get these kids to find a better life."

Seated in an armchair in his purple Vikings windbreaker with tattoos on his face, neck and arms, he settled in to watch the game. The front door to his home was open, a breeze blew through the screen, and outside the sun was shining.

"It's hard to be good, you know?" said Cross. "When you're so used to 45 just dealing with everything with violence? That's why everybody can't even believe I'm doing this."

Boys in the Woods

PONSFORD, Minn.—The boys passed a one-gallon bottle of spiced rum from person to person, waiting for Saturday night on the White Earth Reservation to begin. Cigarette and marijuana smoke curled slowly around the low-hanging light fixtures as caps were twisted off beer bottles and tossed onto counters or into an overflowing trash can.

Senister—who agreed to be interviewed only if he could use a pseudonym—lit a menthol cigarette, took a pull from the rum, and cleared his throat.

"We got members scattered everywhere, but there's going to be a point when we need everyone in the field," said Senister to the boys in the room.

Born 33 years ago in Oklahoma, the Ponca tribal member is a leader of the Minneapolis street gang known as the Native Disciples. He had traveled to the reservation to meet new members of the White Earth chapter, encourage morale and conduct something comparable to a military inspection.

"We're trying to start a chapter in Oklahoma; hopefully we can get 50 that started," continued Senister. "We're just trying to get bigger. I want you brothers to understand that."

Compared to Senister, the Native Disciples of White Earth were children. The twins were the youngest at 16, while Dell, the regional capo for the gang, was the oldest at 19.

"I haven't met most of you brothers, and there's other brothers and sisters I haven't met, but I'm going to make my rounds," said Senister. "Salute!"

"Salute!" answered the room in unison as beer cans and bottles clinked together in approval.

> "Native people have endured cultural alienation, the loss of their language and their land, the destruction of family and social structures. They've weathered the resulting social dysfunction."

Native people have endured cultural alienation, the loss of their language and their land, the destruction of family and social structures. They've weathered the resulting social dysfunction. For some youth, gangs offer a shelter from those realities.

The largest, most best-known gang in Indian country, Native Mob, has 55 gone quiet after a massive shutdown of the organization in 2013, and while both old and new Native gangs are hoping to take its place, the Native Disciples are likely the only group with the ability to do so.

Instead of feathers and leathers, today's Indian renegades wear baseball caps and baggy pants. But unlike previous outlaws, they're as big a threat to their own people as they are to the realities they push back against.

Dell dusted snow off Travis Buckanaga's tombstone while Gordy straightened a plastic wreath and replanted a wooden cross with a blue bandanna tied to it.

"That's how we got to know Senister," said Dell as he stood back to admire his cemetery maintenance work. "Because this guy right here died."

In January of 2013, Native Disciple Travis Buckanaga was shot and killed at a house party near the White Earth Reservation, and Senister, along with other Native Disciples, traveled to the reservation to attend the funeral. By the end of their visit on White Earth, they had recruited half a dozen new members to the Native Disciples and left Dell in charge.

"In the city there's a lot of action; out here there's nothing," said 60 Gordy. "It's way different from Minneapolis."

Leading up to the early 1990s, gangs in Minneapolis' Native American neighborhoods primarily existed for protection. Gangs from Chicago, Detroit and other major cities had begun moving into the area, and Native kids often banded together to resist the growing number of threats. There were groups like the Clubsters, the Naturals and the Death Warriors—small, all-Native gangs going up against larger, primarily African-American, outfits.

Minnesota's two most prominent Native American gangs—Native Mob and the Native Disciples—began with the killing of Randy Pacheco.

Randy Pacheco was a Native member of the Vice Lords, a Chicago-based gang that had moved to the Twin Cities, and was shot in 1994 after an altercation with the Bercier brothers.

The Bercier brothers, Joe and Terry, were members of the Shinob-Mob, a small Native gang formed in East Phillips. Terry Bercier was convicted for the murder, while Joe Bercier went free.

With Joe out on the street, Pacheco's fellow Vice Lords wanted revenge 65 for his death. As per Vice Lord rules, they went to leadership for permission, but when the gang's all-African-American leaders told them no, Pacheco's Native compatriots did it anyway and were excommunicated. They formed their own gang: Native Mob.

Of course, the killing of Joe Bercier meant someone would have to pay, and the Gangster Disciples—another Chicago-based gang that had moved to Minneapolis—had ties to the Bercier family.

Tit for tat escalated, and Native members of the Gangster Disciples soon found themselves at war with Native Mob and the Vice Lords. Again, following Gangster Disciple rules, Native members went to their leadership to ask for help as violence intensified. The gang's African-American bosses turned them down, and the East Phillips Gangster Disciples had to fend for themselves. They eventually split to form the Native Disciples.

Nearly 20 years later, in 2013, local, state and federal officials launched a takedown of Native Mob resulting in dozens of arrests and convictions under the Racketeer Influenced Corrupt Organizations Act (RICO). The gang's membership was estimated at more than 200 members across cities and reservations in Minnesota, Wisconsin and North and South Dakota, and Native Mob's crimes included drug trafficking, weapons sales, assault, witness intimidation, murder, human trafficking, sexual assault and racketeering.

Currently, the Native Disciples are working to catch up.

At a snow-covered, Y-shaped intersection on the White Earth Reser- 70
vation, the twins' beastly Chevy Caprice turned left, jerked right, then
banked left again before missing its turn and gliding up a hill, narrowly
avoiding a head-on collision with a thicket of trees. The car bounced
and jerked, then jackknifed into the air, its headlights illuminating the
ice-covered treetops for a moment before returning to earth with a crash,
blowing out its two front tires and careening into a ditch.

The engine died and the entire car steamed in the snow. The car's occu-
pants spilled out, wide-eyed and confused and screaming with laughter.

Senister looked on in disbelief: Almost half of the White Earth chapter of
the Native Disciples was now stuck on the side of a snow-covered reservation
back road in the middle of the woods. Some of the boys laughed and giggled
while others opened fresh beers or walked to the side of the road to pee.

"Dell, where the hell are we right now?" demanded Senister.

"I don't know, bro," replied Dell as he took a swig of beer.

"We're in your neck of the woods, dude, and you got us messed up out 75
here!" yelled Senister. "This is not how capos operate!"

"Yeah," replied Dell as he finished his beer and tossed it toward the woods.

"You take orders, and if you don't, we have something for you when
you don't want to listen to us," said Senister. "You might not know, but
we're a part of something. What do you call that in college?"

Everyone thought about it for a moment.

"A sorority," someone answered.

"It's like a sorority, you know what I mean? You gotta keep your peo- 80
ple in line," yelled Senister. "If we have to come up here and show you
brothers what to do, we can do that."

About 45 minutes later a beat-up old minivan skidded up at the scene and
opened its doors. The boys scrambled in, then took off toward the liquor store
to buy another gallon of spiced rum and meet up with the rest of the crew.

Detailed information about gang activity in Indian country is hard to
come by. In 2000, the National Youth Gang Center found that 80 percent
of Native gang members were male, and that around three-quarters of
them were under the age of 18, but its findings were inconclusive as to how
many gangs there are in Indian Country. No studies have been done since.

"There's no one-size-fits-all for Indian country," said Walter Lamar, a former deputy director of the Bureau of Indian Affairs' Office of Law Enforcement who now runs his own law enforcement consulting firm. "Gangs are
sucking the lifeblood out of some of our communities; then in others, you
basically have a group of young people that are engaged in vandalism."

Native Disciples gang chapters can be thought of a bit like corporate
franchises. On the White Earth Reservation, for example, members get to
represent the organization and can ask for assistance if war breaks out,

but mostly they sell drugs and send a portion of the profits back to the head office in Minneapolis. On White Earth, Dell serves as the gang's regional capo, but he answers to capos in the city—people like Senister.

In Minneapolis, the Native Disciples rely on three capos to make deci- 85
sions instead of one boss, so that if disagreements arise there will always be a majority vote on the course of action.

"Most gangs, especially in Indian country, are loose-knit groups of 20, 30, 40 individuals, and one or two people will emerge as the leaders," said Mike Martin, president of the Minnesota chapter of the Midwest Gangs Investigators Association. "That's different than having a hierarchical structure like Native Mob has, like the Native Disciples have."

In 2011, the FBI concluded that most Native American gangs were disorganized, lacked structure, had scarce ties to national-level gangs and could not control large geographic areas or populations. However, gangs like the Native Disciples and Native Mob demonstrate that there are growing exceptions to the rule.

"These kids are not Cosa Nostra; these are not Medellin or Cali cartels,° but they are seriously influential and dangerous elements in the community," said Bryan Kastellic, task force commander of the Wisconsin-based Native American Drug and Gang Initiative. "These are not groups that we ever underestimate."

Senister pulled one of the twins into the living room and leaned in close.

"Take care of that," he said quietly. "You ain't got to go overboard, just 90
take care of it."

"I'll take care of that," replied the boy.

"No," said Senister. "I want to see it. You boys can say you're going to do it, but whatever."

The boy nodded dutifully, then looked nervously around the room and out the window to where a small cadre of the boys had gathered in the yard.

"We gotta hold each other accountable, because if we don't, nobody else will," said Senister to the boy. "Nobody cares about us Natives. How we eat. How we live. They don't care. We gotta look out for each other. Now let's take care of that. You ready?"

"Yeah," replied the boy.   95

Senister bent his knees just enough so his eyes were level with the boy's and looked into his face.

"You ready?"

The boy nodded.

A few minutes later the Native Disciples had made a circle in the yard around one of the boys, who lay on his back in the snow.

"Why are you doing this?" screamed the boy. "I didn't do nothin'!"   100

Cosa Nostra, Medellin, Cali: large, highly-organized criminal organizations.

The Native Disciples moved in closer, tightening the circle. The boy wailed.

"Hit him," someone yelled.

With arrests and indictments having resulted in the temporary absence of Native Mob, a power vacuum exists in Minnesota's Indian gang world. And while both new and old gangs are eager to fill it, the Native Disciples may be the only group with the organization and manpower to do so.

What the state's Native gang landscape will look like by the end of the year, or 10 years from now, is hard to predict. Native Mob could return stronger than it was before, it could split into factions, or it could disappear. The Native Disciples might be prosecuted on RICO charges, or expand into chapters as far south as Oklahoma, or be at war again with larger outfits moving into their territory, as they were in the 1990s. Right now, they're just settling into Indian country, and waiting.

"You can do anything in life, but you have to work for it. Take it. There's no free lunch," said Senister. "Anything we're going to do, we're going to have to fight for it, or we're going to have to kill for it." 105

Understanding the Text

1. What does Ahtone mean when he refers to "Indian Country"?

2. How does the author use history to explain the trauma and violence currently afflicting Native American communities?

Reflection and Response

3. Why do you think that the author dedicates so much space to the stories of gang members? What is the rhetorical effect of this appeal to pathos?

4. Most of the Native American gangs mentioned in the article are offshoots of African American gangs. In what ways are the experiences of Native American and African American urban youth similar? In what ways do they differ?

5. The author, citing chilling statistics, implies that Native American youth gangs are an inevitable outcome of systemic social dysfunction in the larger Native American community. To what degree do you believe that antisocial, even criminal, behavior is a result of social structures? To what degree does it result from individual choices? Explain your answer in detail.

Making Connections

6. Research current conditions on Native American reservations. How is "rez" life distinct from the experience of urban Native Americans? How is it distinct from mainstream culture? Do the tribes constitute subcultures?

7. One of the authorities cited in the text mentions "good gangs" as a useful and understandable reaction to hostile environments. Develop an argument in support of this position, citing at least one specific example of a good gang and exploring its genesis, development, and persistence.

from *Hobos, Hustlers, and Backsliders: Homeless in San Francisco*

Teresa Gowan

Teresa Gowan is a professor of sociology at the University of Minnesota, specializing in urban studies, addiction, poverty, and marginality. Her 2010 book on homeless men in San Francisco, from which this selection was taken, examines the medicalization and criminalization of homelessness, and is a result of years of up-close-and-personal ethnographic research on the streets. Her recent research deals with the place of addiction treatment in social policy. She won the Mary Douglas Prize for Best Book in 2011.

"When I was first homeless, I stayed around the TL,° you know, because that's where the food was, the shelters was. I was kinda knocked out, you know, stunned. I would just go where the homeless people were supposed to go. I mean, now I know other places, but it seemed like everything was there. I just lined up for St. Anthony's, the shelters, MSC, Hospitality House, like there wasn't nothing better to do." Ray, a bearded African American in a black leather jacket, stopped to examine one of the garbage bags tied on his shopping cart, which seemed to be leaking valuable aluminum cans onto the road.

"They say you go here for this, you go there for that," Ray continued, yanking a new garbage bag from a clump inside the cart. "Seems kind of convenient, like it's a supermarket, a supermarket for being homeless. Except you be waiting all day here, all day there. Wasting your life away. Getting pushed around. Getting ripped off, hustled, beat up, beat down. I hate the damn Tenderloin."

The hard-drinking sailors and wintering miners are long gone, but San Francisco's Tenderloin still holds the ghostly memory of old Barbary Coast San Francisco, the busiest port in the United States and the West Coast capital of prostitution, dope, gambling, and crimping.° Over the last thirty years the city's other remaining strands of institutions catering to poor single people—the hotels and diners on Kearny, Broadway, Divisadero, Folsom, even the city's primary heroin market around Sixteenth and Mission—have steadily shrunk into smaller pockets and strips. To the northwest, the seamy blocks of Polk Gulch are still

---

TL: the Tenderloin, an historically crime-ridden district in downtown San Francisco.
crimping: kidnapping men into service as sailors, a practice prevalent in the nineteenth century on the West Coast and elsewhere.

gentrifying, while on the other side of Market Street only the tenacious finger of Sixth Street remains of the old South-of-Market "foreign quarter," which once held 40,000 units of cheap housing for single men.

The Tenderloin, though, still digs its heels into downtown San Francisco, a teeming ghetto of the dispossessed, home to thousands of poor whites, African Americans, Latinos, Southeast Asians, refugees and bohemians, swindlers and prophets. By concentrating many of the city's most disreputable poor, it stands as a bulwark against the engine of gentrification north and south, its rambling slum hotels, liquor stores, sex shops, low-income housing developments, and poverty agencies covering a good fifteen city blocks between Union Square and City Hall.

• • •

The majority of the thousands of homeless people moving through 5 the Tenderloin streets in any given week are there to eat, to obtain other services provided in the neighborhood, or to buy crack, speed, or other drugs. Some of them are sleeping in one of the large shelters that border the neighborhood, others coming in from other parts of the city. Everywhere there are tired or ragged-looking people, lining around the block for the soup kitchens or making their way fast along the sidewalks. They are given away by their backpacks and blankets, their shaggy 'fros, beards, and torn, dirty clothes.

As Ray said, the Tenderloin is where homeless people are supposed to go. The aggressive policing of its border streets and spaces, of Powell Street, Civic Center Plaza, and the adjacent stretch of Market Street, gives a clear enough message that ragged loiterers should stay within the Tenderloin's "rabble zone." While many homeless people resist this corral, fearing and disliking the streets of the TL, not everybody feels that way. There are often hundreds of homeless men and women on the teeming sidewalks of Eddy or Ellis, Hyde or Leavenworth, many of them addicted to crack, most of them African American, who wander up and down, engage in desultory conversations, and generally pass time around the neighborhood. It is these individuals, the archetypical and often self-identified street people, who have come to define the character of the neighborhood in the eyes of other homeless people, and, indeed, in the eyes of many San Franciscans.

• • •

Some of the street's most scurrilous reprobates had only drifted into an outlaw identification as adults, but many more were like Sammy and Del,

"The decision to move beyond fantasy and actually live outside the law is always going to be stronger among those who have the least to gain from playing the 'straight' game."

just continuing on a path set much earlier in life. The high proportion of African Americans among the latter group will surprise no one familiar with the history and current conditions of black America. Flirting with the dark side may run deep within American popular culture, but the decision to move beyond fantasy and actually live outside the law is always going to be stronger among those who have the least to gain from playing the "straight" game—namely, among those trapped in economic and social marginality. The humiliating job restrictions for black men historically pushed generation after generation of ambitious young men to try their hand in the illicit economy, and this black male valence of the street hustler's game has only become stronger over the last century. While other groups previously connected with illicit economies—Jewish Americans, Italian Americans, Chinese Americans, for example—gained increasing respectability and some degree of success in the legitimate economy in the post-WWII period, large numbers of African Americans were left behind. In the great immigrant cities, new groups of hard-up incomers—Dominicans, Colombians, Russians—stepped on those underwater treads of ethnic succession, but across the nation as a whole, vice became more tightly racialized, with new generations of impoverished African Americans moving to fill the niches left behind by their upwardly mobile compatriots.

The gap between the black poor and the rest of America has worsened since the great deindustrialization of the 1970s and 1980s, which devastated the black working class even more than their white peers. Faced with a growing surplus labor force, the politicians of the new right turned to crudely punitive forms of social control: workfare, school exclusions, proliferating techniques of surveillance, and, above all, incarceration, nearly quadrupling the population behind bars between 1975 and 2000 and continuing to grow rapidly through the 2000s. Often directly pushing the media to focus on crack dealing and other street crimes already coded black, they were able to mobilize the weight of American's racialized symbology in support of fierce new sentencing policies. As John Edgar Wideman,° Loic Wacquant,° and more have compellingly elaborated, the criminal has become "coded" African American and imprisonment

John Edgar Wideman: American novelist (b. 1941).
Loic Wacquant: French sociologist (b. 1960).

one of the most important ways of "marking race," a bizarrely normalized rite of passage for ordinary black men.

This carceral° bent to social policy has not only warped the lives of several million individuals and their families, but further degraded the spaces where poor people are concentrated, especially the ghetto neighborhoods and skid row zones of the deprived central city that endlessly trade their population with the mushrooming satellite ghettos of the prison-industrial complex. Men and women often come out penniless and practically friendless. When I met Fox, for example, he was riding a night bus in nothing but hospital pajamas and sneakers way too small for his feet. After fourteen months in jail for crack possession he had been released at 11 o'clock at night with six dollars and twenty cents. The grandmother who had raised him was long dead, his brother was in prison himself, and the rest of his family had given up on him years earlier. He had absolutely nowhere to go and had defaulted to riding the bus all night.

On the Tenderloin streets, the workings of the carceral society were easy enough to excavate. The streets may have beckoned, but just as important, the men had known little but castigation and violence in other spaces. With fierce punishments at home, suspensions and expulsions from school, endless frisks and frequent arrests, low-paid work punctuated by firings, their behavior had consistently been found wanting and they had failed to prosper. Time inside had only reinforced tenfold their sense of a world split into two hostile camps: cops and robbers, screws and cons, those who went to church and those who ran the streets. 10

After the high point of sympathy in the mid-1980s, representations of the homeless veered back in the direction of the racialized moral judgment dominant in most public conversations about crime and urban poverty. Though there was certainly still room for "deserving" categories such as veterans and the mentally ill, the urban African American homeless—the majority in most large cities—became increasingly defined as street people (fueled, in the case of New York City, by middle-class hostility toward "squeegee men").° This definition brought together two symbolic binaries: the foundational American division between black and white, converging on to the equally ancient polarity between the dangerous vagrants outside and the decent within.

In this respect too the Tenderloin hustlers mobilized the same symbolic oppositions as the authoritarian pundits and politicians who wanted to clear them out of public space. Blackness and the street converged. Never mind the cold; staying outside all night was a badge of

carceral: relating to prison.
squeegee men: individuals who wipe the windshields of cars stopped in traffic, then solicit payment.

black pride. "We the people of the night," Sammy told me with a half-smile. "Takes a black man to run the streets, night and day."

• • •

The suspicious, aggressive disposition of street hustlers and wolves was germinated in deprivation and alienation, articulated in a language that constructed each and every stranger as a hostile force. The hustlers' ways, learned in youthful gang-banging, then fixed and amplified by their experiences of incarceration, returned prison culture to the streets, reproducing a climate of fear and distrust across not only the skid row but also the shelters and soup kitchens. Their competitive, dog-eat-dog worldview cemented its own reality, not just for the true believers, but for thousands more who were forced into the corral.

"You have to get wise, living on the street," said Mikey, a prematurely aged white man with mental health problems. We were standing in line on the Tenderloin's Turk Street, waiting to get into St. Anthony's soup kitchen. "I used to be a lot of a nicer person. But you learn you can't trust no one in this place. Not in the shelter, not here. There's too many people looking to rip you off. Mean, cheating, low-down kinds of people. And I'm not being racial. It's just a fact: this neighborhood is not safe, and I keep my head down, and keep my own company, and that is how I stay alive. For real."

Many talked of "keeping their heads down," and indeed eye contact 15 was an area of constant tension. If a homeless man always avoided the eyes of other men, he came across as weak or scared and set himself up for later attacks. If he met their eyes in a nonhostile way he might be taken for a fool and fall victim to some hustle. But then again, if he held another man's eyes too assertively, this might well be taken for a challenge. People developed their own ways of negotiating this treacherous path. James Moss, a six-foot-two, street-smart African American and a former Turk Street crack dealer, felt far more vulnerable on the streets after his crippling stroke. As he walked toward another black man on the sidewalk he would fix him with a fiat, imposing stare for about two seconds, then acknowledge him with a reserved, formalistic, "How're you doing?" Finally he would end the interaction by firmly dropping his eyes.

The actions of the "wolves" directly countered the city's attempt to corral the homeless and very poor into the Tenderloin and the smaller skid row pockets of the city, instead fueling a steady centrifugal movement out to other spaces on the street. The exodus was just as much about the shelters and hotels themselves, which not only concentrated contact with other people on the street, but frequently added their own contribution of petty domination and symbolic violence. For many residents, the shelters are an unpleasant reminder of time behind bars. "I don't know what they're thinking, some of these shelters," said recycler Morris, who had done two spells in jail for drug possession. "You can't expect to put a load of people together and have them all respect each other, respect each other's personal shit. The few assholes will mess it up for everyone. And they do. Every night there is some bullshit. It's impossible to really sleep. You know, I have my earplugs, but all the same it always wakes me up, someone going off, something missing. And it stinks. Man, does its stink. Close your eyes, you're in jail again. Worse even.

"But I could stand the stink if they would put in some kinds of cages, you know like the old cage hotels. For security. Even some of the jails, they understand this. Like over in Contra Costa County, they give you the key in your cell. It's the only way to make it safe. So you don't have to fight, you don't have to get all your personal items lifted. But the last thing they seem to care about is keeping people safe. Instead it's rules and constant—I mean *everlasting*—disrespect. It knocks you down."

[Ray's] migration away from the Tenderloin was driven by a similar mixture of alienation with the services and dislike of the wolves. "I soon got real sick of it all. It drives you crazy, man." Ray shook his head. At the time of this conversation he had been on the street for more than a year and joined the city's army of homeless recyclers. In the interim he had grown a jutting beard and large Afro. With his long, ropy arms tightly gripping a train of two large carts, he made an imposing figure. After collecting bottles since two in the morning, Ray and his companion, Clarence, decided to share a late-morning joint. Clarence, always a little foggy, was smoking a lot at that time, hoping that marijuana would help him cut down on his crack use. While Clarence tipped the last scraps into his pipe, Ray continued his complaints about the downtown homeless scene. (He had to go to the Tenderloin the next day to reapply for General Assistance, which he had not received in eight months.)

"Like with the shelter. I like to keep on the move. I've always been that way. But they have you standing, standing, standing—then having to deal with some nasty little crackheads hustling you every second you don't pay attention. One guy gets you talking, the other is in your bag, in your pocket, taking your shit. You stand in line forever, and when you do get in, those people do not treat you with respect. They let you know you are dirt. Dirt! Especially the monitors. You get some of the worst people in there and what do they do? They give them special jobs, special privileges, you know, 'cause they work it, they talk the talk. It makes you sick to your stomach. And outside it's worse. I'm not a straight kind of guy. I've been around. But I can't stomach the endless, endless BS. Nobody talks to you without they are trying to play you for a fool; somebody is always trying to fuck with you.

"So I go up Van Ness a few blocks, set me up in the bushes on one of 20
those streets up there—what do I get, second night I'm there, a damn
ticket." ...

Where else did the shelter exodus trickle? Many stayed nearby, hanging in limbo in the downtown area. Despite the great police clearances
of the 1990s, people continued to feel that this was the part of the city
in which they had most right to be, where there were few residents to
offend. Some found strength in numbers. Every night a scattered shanty
village would assemble behind the San Francisco shopping center downtown, to be quickly disassembled in the early morning. Hundreds of
frightened and lonely souls adopted a night shift, sleeping fitfully on
benches and walls during the day and wandering at night. Sammy, whose
ghoulish "jack rolling"° made him an expert on the sleeping homeless
man, called such people "ghosts," and it is true that they could look eerie
to those around them. They had to sit, rather than lie, to avoid trouble
with the police, but would rest motionless, their head and upper bodies
covered entirely with a blanket.

Thousands more dispersed themselves throughout the city. Certain
areas, such as tourist destination Fisherman's Wharf or the elegant sidewalks of Pacific Heights, were hard places to sleep unmolested by police
or security guards. But everywhere else homeless people slept on the
sidewalk, in alleys, doorways, cars, parks, beside and underneath freeways, on patches of waste ground, or in one of the city's rare abandoned
buildings. Some put up tents on the sidewalk, mans' earned around
sleeping bags and cardboard, others just crashed out on the ground, their
clothes their only protection.

• • •

Morris was a rare man on the street, a book reader and a true organic
intellectual. [S]ome of the homeless recyclers were very engaged by
the idea that they were heirs to the honorable lineage of the American
hobo. Morris spent hours trying to flesh out this idea, trawling the San
Francisco public library system and the Internet for hobo arcana. In the
evenings, he would read by torchlight from a box full of printouts and
photocopies he kept stashed in his encampment.

In his own little corner of Dogpatch, Morris made strenuous attempts
to create and maintain community. One evening a shouting fight broke
out when black loner Tom tried to stop two newcomers from building a
camp in his vicinity.

jack rolling: robbing drunks.

"Be cool, brother," Morris urged him, walking over to stand between 25
Tom and the newcomers. "We have to respect each other. We are not
d-dogs! We are men." He nodded earnestly at both parties in turn.

"That's right! And a man needs a bit of his own damn space," flashed
Tom.

"We don't want nothing to do with your mangy crackhead ass,"
retorted one of the newcomers.

"D-D-D-Don't be talking like that!" thundered Morris, his anger
inflaming his stutter. "We're not about that kind of b-b-bullshit, not
round here. You want to beat each other down, there's plenty of places
you can d-do that. We've been b-beat down enough."

Mustachioed Carlos, who had wandered over to see what was going
on, nodded his agreement. "Yeah, come on now, keep it cool."

Morris brokered a compromise, whereby Carlos, who had only a small 30
tent to move, would shift nearer to Tom, giving up his own space for the
newcomers to pitch their shanty. (In return, one of the newcomers gave
Carlos a small amount of marijuana, one of skeet San Francisco's primary
currencies.)

The way that Morris and Carlos successfully mediated this conflict
was, just as much as Sammy's brutal "jack rolling" of his fellow homeless,
an example of discourse in action. Morris refused to believe that people
on the street had to behave like "dogs" and, with the help of Carlos,
accomplished a moment of community organization, which made his
claim a reality....

Jaz's journey from the Heroin Central west of the Tenderloin to the
Dogpatch dumpster divers exemplifies the men's desire for a coherent
map of the world, for some sense of authenticity that could save their
embattled self-respect and make sense of their difficult ways of life. His
story is particularly enlightening about how different micro-cultures
developed distinctive ways of using drugs. I imagine many readers to
be skeptical that street addicts can exercise any control whatsoever over
their drug use. As Darin Weinberg has described in rich detail, drug reha-
bilitation facilities and the twelve-step movement have combined with
other cultural strands to produce a popular construction of the street
addict that stands for utter chaos, loss of all regulation, and a constant
threat of quite heinous criminality. In Jaz's case, though, you can see how
a new relationship of trust enabled him to move into what he considered
a much less degrading form of drug-addicted homelessness.

Jaz was not trying to pretend he was not an addict. In fact, he was
unusual in that he often wore a T-shirt that revealed his tracks and burns
to all and sundry, only slipping on a long-sleeved shirt when leaving the
neighborhood. What he wanted was not denial but other people with

whom he could get by on the street in a way where he could still feel cool rather than a "fucking lowlife." Around people like Morris and Carlos, as well as his own crew, this had become possible. Most, though not all, of the Dogpatch street homeless were drug users, but underlying their ethic of cool and respect was an agreement that they were not dogs but men, and that they did not have to give themselves up completely to the dark side of sin-talk by subordinating every element of their existence to getting high. Surely this project of balance also gave extra intensity to the elements of play, the appreciation of nature, and the passionate friendships among Quentin's crew.

Jaz's camp companion, Ray was another restless drifter. He had moved within all the street microcultures ... ultimately joining the more laid-back scene of Quentin, Billy, and Jaz. Ray had never known much of a settled home. As a kid is the late 1960s he had drifted with his mother and sister through a couple of Oakland Black Power collectives, learning to question the extent to which a black man should tangle with the white man's world. The family also wandered through Los Angeles, the Bronx, Philadelphia, and Tucson, leaving Ray with vague memories of hundreds of housemates and no idea of the number of schools he had attended. What stayed clear in his mind was the high school in South Philly where he got into heroin. His mother dragged him hack to a clean house in Oakland, but Ray could never quit for long.

In his twenties he spent a couple of years in Morocco, Senegal, and 35 Liberia, where he sold hashish to white travelers. Ray's dream, though, was to trade African crafts. He brought a few boxes of carvings hack to the United States and tried to set himself up with a market stall, but he never kept enough money to return to Africa. He reluctantly worked on and off in parking or security, staying with girlfriends here and there. In his thirties he did two stretches for heroin possession, which did not help him improve his position in the labor market. While serving a third stretch, this time for a minor marijuana offense, his mother died. His sister was somewhere in Philly, and his ex-girlfriends were sick to death of bailing him out. For the first time, he had absolutely nowhere to go.

Ray's broad life experience helped him to ease through the varied ecology of the San Francisco street, slowly gravitating toward a way of life that felt, if not exactly acceptable, at least less painful or difficult than other choices and toward companions of the street to whom he felt better suited.

Since joining Quentin's crew, Ray had become uncomfortable with the idea of being classed as a victim of homelessness. "I don't really think of myself as homeless," he said earnestly. "OK, I know I am officially, and it's not like I could afford to live inside in this city. All the same, homeless doesn't sound right for me. It was different when I was in the Tenderloin, you know. Even in the Haight. But now I'm camping out—that's more what it feels like. Like if they drove us off of here again, you wouldn't see us in the shelters. Billy and me, we're thinking we might go up to the Sierras, see the mountains. But the others don't wanna go."

• • •

Already we have seen some very different responses to the stigma of being homeless. While the hustlers tended to deny that they were homeless at all, Morris and his companions deflected the shame of homelessness back onto the cruelties of the system. The Dogpatch dumpster divers developed a different response, hence the claim that they were to some extent intentionally homeless, or at least "not really homeless," as Ray put it. In Quentin's case there was probably something to this. With the others, though, intentional homelessness seemed better understood as a perspective developed on the street. Like the hustlers, they were trying to wrest back some sense of agency, of having a say in the shape of their own lives. Yet their notion of the street was a very different one, defined in terms of a quite different grammar of action—an intimate and trusting collectivism unusual in the "TL."

• • •

Ray still spent time with Morris and Clarence, but he had never really adopted their strong work ethic, and he now seemed profoundly relieved to find others who were cool—distanced from the "crazy" death quests and Hobbesian war of the street—yet still fiercely critical of straight life. He appreciated the playful, less morally laden perspective of Quentin's crew, their refusal to pity themselves or to be ashamed of their heroin addictions. Neither the "wolves" of sin-talk, the enslaved addicts of sick-talk, nor the noble victims of systemic injury, his new friends gave him a space to revisit the radical critique of his youth in the 1960s, albeit in a very different key. His long ambivalence about the entanglements of marriage, work, and materialism had come together with his desire to keep steering his own destiny. "Homeless doesn't sound right for me," he said.

• • •

As we have moved from the hustlers of the Tenderloin to the Dogpatch 40 recyclers and dumpster divers, we have seen how specific city spaces— become discursively "charged" within the homeless scene, concentrating, nurturing, and symbolizing different forms of street existence. This intimate dialectic between spatialized practices and discourses on homelessness became particularly noticeable when men from the Tenderloin and Dogpatch moved into each other's orbit.

The vignette preceding this chapter, "Watch Out, San Francisco!," shows something of the hostility between hustler Del and the black recyclers who pushed their loads through the Tenderloin. From the perspective of Del, leaning nonchalantly against a wall for much of the day, the pro recyclers were suckers in that they worked harder than they needed to. Worse, they were suckers with attitude. They deluded themselves by thinking they were like real workers when in fact they were "dope fiends and bums." In Del's world, homelessness happened only to sinners, by definition. This meant that he himself was ultimately far more honest than Morris, for example, because he knew that he was fundamentally on the street side of the street-straight line rather than trying to pretend that he was "working for the city or something."

Del's ridicule of the earnest efforts of the black pros was incisive in its own way. He was certainly right that the honor of their dirty work lay mostly in their own eyes. But at the same time, what Del did not seem to see was how his defiant orientation to the street represented a twisted form of consent to his own social exclusion. Del, Fox, and Linc's San Francisco was tiny compared with the city of the recyclers or Quentin's crew. Sammy roamed a slightly wider circle, but rarely ventured more than fifteen minutes' walk away from the central Tenderloin. All of them carried the ghetto walls with them, feeling little desire and no sense of entitlement to move outside of what for them was a safety zone. Just as their discourse of sin reproduced their socialization in carceral institutions of punitive neoliberalism, their attachment to the Tenderloin tidily reproduced the city's attempts to corral the indigent away from tourist zones and middle-class neighborhoods.

In the meantime, while Del was wandering back and forth around the drug market of Boedeker Park, Morris and Clarence were out on what Clarence called their "patrols," pushing through not only the Tenderloin but Pacific Heights, Russian Hill, Chinatown, or North Beach, passing the time of day with regular acquaintances among the broad variety of bar staff and city residents who saved them bottles. Their home turf, Dogpatch, was not an island so much as a relatively safe base for more expansive activities. What Del saw as slavish behavior brought them not only some spatial freedom but a degree of social integration, even a sense of citizenship.

The Dogpatch community did not last. First South Beach, then the entire eastern shore of the city exploded in a millennial development frenzy. Quiet dead-ends, stagnant basins, and ancient bars and restaurants disappeared under new townhouse and "live-work" villages, the 3Com Stadium, a college campus, and enterprises from golf drives to biotech start-ups. The area of Morris's first camp became an Esprit outlet store, and successive ticketing and towing campaigns drove out the van livers.

They swiftly stripped them of their shiny aluminum rims and trim, 45 which they hauled away for scrap. The city was quick to retaliate, razing much of the undergrowth that had sheltered the nearby camps and changing the relatively hands-off policy toward the area.

Like the homeless shanty dwellers in Dordick's New York study, the Dogpatch campers had "something left to lose": safety, human connection, place. Clarence, for one, returned to sleeping without a camp, crashed out on the sidewalks around Division Street. A few months later, he had taken to talking to himself.

"What would you say? Yeah, that's seven pounds, that's right, seven pounds," he was muttering as I pulled up on my bike.

"Yeah, I can't say I don't miss making a camp," he said when I asked him about Dogpatch. "Over there, you could have something to come back to. Most people would look out for you, you know."

"You haven't found anywhere else decent lately?" I asked.

"Not really. I get sick of trying to get myself together. I am out work- 50 ing and then, shit, my place is trashed! Like by the freeway, they come by every couple weeks and just break everything down, like it's not already trashed out enough. It's not worth it, making anything.

And it was cool to be around other guys, around other recyclers."

"You lonesome?"

"I'd say I'm just about as lonesome as a man can be before he goes crazy."

Understanding the Text

1. What connections does Gowan make between prison culture and homeless culture?

2. Summarize the reasons Gowan gives for the high number of African Americans in the homeless community.

3. According to the text, what parts of cities are particularly attractive for those who are homeless? Why?

Reflection and Response

4. How does Gowan's training as a sociologist influence the way in which she presents homeless subculture? Are her ethnographic methods of street interviews and in-person observation effective? How well do they mesh with her more factual, reportorial material?

5. In what ways are the homeless literally on the margins of society? How does this status affect mainstream judgments of the homeless subculture? How does this physical marginalization differ from that of, for example, the Hasidim or the Amish?

6. It is clear from the individual stories that Gowan records that the divide between productive membership in the mainstream culture and the trauma of homelessness can be very, very thin. In reflecting on your own life, what are the elements that determine your status in your community, your safety, your future possibilities, your economic security, and your personal associations?

Making Connections

7. Referring to at least one other subculture featured in this book, show how membership in a particular social group results less from personal choice than from chance or impersonal social pressures.

8. Investigate homelessness in your own community. Offer a brief analysis of the situation and of the official governmental response to the subculture.

2 | How Do Subcultures Define Themselves?

Although they are often purposely marginalized by the dominant culture, subcultures themselves also draw boundaries, determine who belongs, stamp out dissent, and enforce both explicit rules and implicit social standards. As they emerged in the second half of the twentieth century, American subcultures often faced either outright discrimination or less-than-well-meaning attempts to subsume them into the mainstream. In either case, members have had to find ways to maintain the values and practices of the community, as the readings in Chapter Two demonstrate.

In "The Real Real," Sinclair Bolden provides a guide for thinking about issues of authenticity and membership in self-identified communities. He discusses the many ways by which groups police their boundaries and exclude outsiders, particularly in our digital era. Bolden's essay can be applied to all the readings that follow.

Members of specific subcultures wrote most of the selections in this chapter, providing an insider's perspective. Hunter S. Thompson travels with the Hell's Angels to find out what motivates their antisocial, even criminal, behavior; Elisa Melendez defends her cosplay enthusiasms against an outside critic; Sue-Ellen Case offers her memoir of the San Francisco lesbian scene in the early 1970s; and former "military brat" BJ Gallagher enthusiastically endorses the social values of the offspring of military personnel.

As close observers, Edward Dolnick and William Finnegan comment on Deaf subculture and skinhead subculture, respectively. Their outsider status allows these writers to objectively assess how members of these communities police their own behavior. While we might object to the values they cherish or the means they take to protect them, these subcultures feel empowered, paradoxically, to exercise their freedoms of expression and association.

Finally, Anatole Broyard, in a seminal essay from the late 1940s, portrays an emerging subcultural individual — the hipster. Many who knew Broyard have recognized him in his meditation on this alienated urban character, who through the decades has morphed into a new type but retained a core commitment to the special knowledge available only to those who belong. Although the boundaries of communities evolve over the years, like the hipsters, many subcultures have maintained commitments to traditional values and practices.

The Real Real: The Five Ways Subcultures Self-Police Themselves Online

Sinclair Bolden

As a production coordinator, Sinclair Bolden has long been at the center of the New York (sub) cultural scene. At the time that he wrote the following article, Bolden was a freelance "cultural strategist" for Sylvain Labs. In this role, he was able to "engage in field research to observe cultural and lifestyle events and experiences to identify emerging trends." This position gave him a bird's-eye view of contemporary culture and lends his essay authority. As you read, consider how your experiences with online communities mesh with or differ from the "self-policing" that Bolden describes.

For as long as there have been groups, there have been insiders fighting to protect the cultural values of their group, and outsiders trying to join, borrow, or steal what it is that makes those groups special. While every subculture has different ways of doing this, the practice of establishing systems to measure the "Realness" of subculture members is a universal social self-defense mechanism. But this idea of "realness" is a complicated one; it's an abstract concept that at its core is about both being honest and transparent but also about being accepted by others as legitimate for group membership. It's a way of pleading your identity in the court of public opinion, hoping that you're found "Real."

At the advent of the internet, it would have been conceivable to imagine a future where these subcultures slowly broke down thanks to the level of interconnectivity being offered us — social network fluidity was being dramatically increased. It was easy to find these sorts of utopian° pontifications about what our future held in the '90s. But as we learned, from commerce to content, more than anything, the internet enabled the long tail. This meant that subcultures flourished in the digital age. This growth came with a whole slew of new issues, because the free and open nature of the internet makes it difficult to protect and control the values of a subculture — groups are perpetually susceptible to interlopers and charlatans. However, as is often the case with systems under pressure, subcultures have evolved several behaviors in the digital world that help keep them alive and strong, and keep group members connected.

---

utopian: idealistic; aiming for a state of perfection.

First, let's look at how subcultures have been maintained in the real world.

Punk and Hip-Hop

The punk subculture created an identity system as tough as the second-hand leather that defined much of its style. Central to punk's identity were DIY, anti-establishment, anti-commercial, pro-individual, and artistically expressive values. As it rose to prominence in the late '70s and early '80s, Punk's fashion, music and "attitude" would become a target of commercial appropriation and infiltration. However, punk was obsessed with the concept of "realness." The complex codes of speech, art, humor and gender roles that punk informally developed were aggressively, even violently, enforced. This allowed the identification and shaming of posers, those who were purely interested in punk to be cool, and not for its idealistic virtues. This obsession with "realness" as a core value of punk protected it against the attempts at appropriation by outsiders, allowing it to survive and eventually splinter into sub-groups like metal and grunge.

Hip Hop went through many of the same challenges that punk did. 5 Self-proclaimed status, calling out rivals, socio-political activism, and straight up partying were all authorized subjects of exploration and expression in hip-hop. What was unique and special about the idea of "Realness" in hip-hop was that the idea became an integral and articulated part of the art form itself. This was particularly evident as hip-hop grew increasingly aware that its stylings, identity, and creative direction were being devoured by mainstream cultural and corporate interests. "Realness," through the ideal of "Real Hip Hop," became a resistance movement by MCs and rappers to preserve the autonomy of their culture and its heritage. Realness was a device, albeit somewhat intangible, to share and preserve the oral history of the experience that shaped their identity and the values of the culture.

At some point the idea of realness hit an almost paranoid level; the fear of losing it, the anxiety of being accused of fakeness, the need to keep it despite often dramatic changes in life or circumstance. We see this with Jennifer Lopez and her ascension to a Pop Culture icon status while claiming to still ferociously asserting her "realness." In 2002, JLo released "Jenny from the Block," in which she demanded that she was still "Real" despite all of her success.

This song, and many of JLo's songs, are fundamentally declarations to the people of the communities that she grew up in that she is still a member. She is recursively stating the values of her neighborhood, her friends, and showing she still has not exchanged that identity for any other—that she hasn't sold out. Her songs, and even album titles, have deep context to remind her people that she's still "from the block." She was doing this because those seminal experiences from the Bronx were still a huge part of her identity, and she refused to have that identity taken away by success.

This need to prove membership isn't new. From handshakes to coded language, people have been able to demonstrate "realness" and membership in the real world for millennia. The question became, how could you prove this in the online world where the "eye test" might not be an option?

The Digital Transition

Historically a shared physical space—a literal common ground—was at the heart of the genesis, establishment, and diffusion of any subculture. Neighborhoods and cities served as a foundation for contextual inspiration. Corners, nightclubs, and speakeasies were protected "turf" where coded aesthetics took shape. CBGB was the Mecca of Punks. Attendance was mandatory, commitment was tested, and newbies were distinguished from posers. Underground dens acted as "hush hubs," granting anonymity and shelter for the most subversive values and behaviors, protecting members from potential reprisals by uncompromising and closed-minded mainstreamers.

Without such reefs to guard their shores, exposure of subcultures and   10 their micro-genres, memes, and lifestyles became almost inevitable. Without protection of their cultural and intellectual capital, a sort of cultural imperialism loomed. Thus, establishing "realness" amongst participants may possess even greater import in the digital landscape than the real world.

Users translate tips and tricks from the pre-digital age to hide in plain sight online.

Deep contextual cues, code words, and other seemingly innocuous symbols enable members to find each other online without alerting outsiders. Coincidentally the flat topography of the internet that leaves subcultures more exposed also allows them to find and recognize like-minded peers with the help of some of the following clever tricks.

"For as long as there have been groups, there have been insiders fighting to protect the cultural values of their group, and outsiders trying to join, borrow, or steal what it is that makes those groups special."

At its core expression of group membership is a deep form of intimacy. It's only logical that people are protective of this information, and that they would find creative ways to protect these intimate moments. Group identity is a powerful thing, and questioning someone's realness is at its core an indictment of their perceived personal identity. This is serious stuff.

Taking Realness Online

The following five behaviors are forms of self-policing and protecting subcultural values, as well as their members' sense of identity. It's easy to write off the simple twitter behaviors and online banalities, but in a modern world deeply interwoven with the digital world, these behaviors are the scaffolding of our sense of self.

1. Rep Check

Everyone tends to get brave on the internet, because an online beat down tends to come with a lot fewer consequences than IRL; it doesn't break bones, it just bruises pride. As such, the "Rep Check" is a common

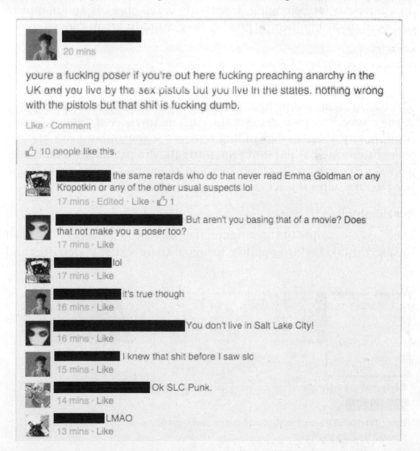

The act of calling into question the merits and credentials of someone who is speaking about a subject the person "rep checking" believes is outside of their reach, permission, or expertise.

sheatheman 1 year ago
The video creator(s) made the BASIC mistake of thinking vaporwave and seapunk are the
same thing. The difference is seapunk is specifically oceanic imagery. The Greek columns
and arches, which represent virtual gateways, i.e. the Internet, is much more of a vaporwave
attribute. There are many similarities though, and I suppose we can forgive this very amateur
amalgamation of imagery.

The act of publicly and sometimes aggressively sharing, demonstrating, or co-opting
credibility and status within a subgroup.

practice. A "Rep Check" consists of questioning another's status as a
group member, participatory voice, or authoritative position within the
culture. "Time in," taste, and cultural capital are examples of benchmarks
driving these checks, and they often lead to a much larger conversation
on guideposts for belonging. Essentially, a rep check is an attempt to
silence or discredit others by proving they're not in-group enough.

2. #NetFlex

The #NetFlex has historically had any number of names—see "pissing
contest" and "chest thumping." You'll find the #NetFlex in a number
of different forms online from gratuitous overshares and name dropping
to the classic "I've been doing X since before it was cool." Status staking
is ultimately a way of demanding respect for the amount of time and
energy someone has put into something they're passionate about. People want recognition, this is obvious, but sometimes on the internet you
need to take status if you're not getting it freely.

3. #Humbleflag

The classic example of the #humbleflag IRL is the "hanky code" used
by queer individuals to publicly to signal their sexual preferences and

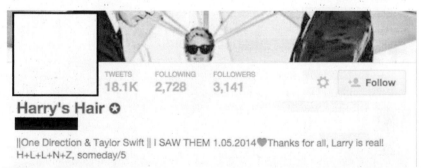

||One Direction & Taylor Swift || I SAW THEM 1.05.2014♥Thanks for all, Larry is real!
H+L+L+N+Z, someday/5

A #humbleflag is an overt and public message that is obscured through deep context
or coded language so as to only be meaningful to other in-group members, therefore
waving membership like an invisible flag.

proclivities in a time before it was ok to be out. In the real world Hanky Codes, different styles of daps, the number of studs on your jacket, etc., are all examples of Badging. Online there are symbols, hashtags, avatars, and memes that let others know that an individual is "in the know" and should be considered part of the in-group. For the unindoctrinated, these often innocuous badges likely won't merit a second glance, but for those on the inside of a subculture they are beacons connecting like-minded people to their peers.

4. Co-Signing

When someone is trying to establish their credibility in a subculture, any sort of bump from other credible sources helps. The result of this is a sort of publicity given to interactions with the most elite members of any group, a sort of co-opting of the credibility of others to establish one-self. Whether it's through placing the date of a meaningful interaction in the bio on a twitter account or using a screen capture of the interaction somewhere, it serves the purpose to advance membership

Co-signing is the act of publicizing recognition received from other members – Likes, Retweets, Reposts, Shares, Follows, @ mentions – in order to affirm and elevate one's own status within a group.

5. Swarming

One amazing aspect of insect hives is that they do incredible things with a small set of rules—instincts that they act on automatically, but in large numbers produce strange and complex responses. If we think about the specific set of values shared by any online group or subculture like the instincts of insects, you can see strange and coordinated complex responses when those values are violated. #Gamergate was the collective outcry of gamers coming together about journalistic ethics. Though #Gamergate has recently taken a somewhat anti-feminist bent, for better or worse, it is a complicated example of people uniting about a perceived threat to a subculture. Don't give Justin Bieber the Grammy? If you're the winner, get ready for the #Beliebers to swarm. Put out a

Schultz   2m
If the #HasJustineLandedYet outrage has taught all of us one thing
it's Social media works.
Expand   ← Reply   ↻ Retweet   ★ Favorite   ••• More

Lisa   2m
#HasJustineLandedYet? Gosh, what a dumb person.
Expand   ← Reply   ↻ Retweet   ★ Favorite   ••• More

Scott   2m
On the bright side, Justine is free to pursue her true of love stand-up
comedy now! #HasJustineLandedYet
Expand   ← Reply   ↻ Retweet   ★ Favorite   ••• More

Randts   2m
#HasJustineLandedYet if not please tweet me @justinesacco will
pick you up
Expand   ← Reply   ↻ Retweet   ★ Favorite   ••• More

Alice   2m
GO TO google.as/url?sa=t&rct=j...
AND★RT★FOR★NEW★FOLLOWERS★✔Utah,Target,#HasJustin
eLandedYet,#2013TaughtMe,#ScottPilgrim,#internationalcarrotda
Expand   ← Reply   ↻ Retweet   ★ Favorite   ••• More

The Dude Dean   2m
Why can't a message of love or peace go viral?
#HasJustineLandedYet
Expand   ← Reply   ↻ Retweet   ★ Favorite   ••• More

The simultaneous, and seemingly uncoordinated, collective response of group members to come to the defense of a group's culture or leaders by attacking or discrediting the perceived threat.

terrible reality show about Black Sorority Sisters? Heels and earrings are coming off, and thousands are almost instantly calling for a boycott. And make a joke about AIDS in Africa on Twitter? Well, #justinehaslanded & #needsanewjob.

Understanding the Text

1. How does Bolden define "realness"?
2. According to Bolden, why do groups such as the punk subculture develop "complex codes of speech, art, humor, and gender roles" (par. 4)? How are they enforced?

Reflection and Response

3. Considering the many ways that we experience other people in an online context, do you believe that it is possible to achieve what the author refers to as "a deep form of intimacy" in internet communities? Draw examples from your own experience.
4. Bolden uses Jennifer Lopez's 2002 hit, "Jenny from the Block," as an example of an artist's proving her "realness." Listen carefully to the song, then analyze the ways that JLo purposefully asserts her membership in a particular community. Consider lyrics, music, and performance.
5. Offer an example from your own online experience of each of the five behaviors Bolden claims that people use to establish their "realness" in cyberspace: rep check, NetFlex, humbleflag, co-signing, swarming.

Making Connections

6. As Bolden points out, subcultures historically required an actual shared space in order to form meaningful identities. Using specific examples, discuss how new kinds of communities have formed online, thereby bypassing the need to be together in one time and place.
7. Choose one of the subcultures discussed in this book and investigate how it makes use of the internet to promote itself, encourage group unity, or share news. Consider how the values of the particular subculture influence the design of its online sites and the kind of material shared online, as well as the disadvantages of promoting an online presence.

A Portrait of the Hipster

Anatole Broyard

Anatole Broyard's famous portrait of the hipster appeared in *Partisan Review* in 1948. In his essay, he identifies one of the first American subcultures to arise after World War II. Significantly, the hipster he portrays is African American, a member of a historically marginalized community to which Broyard himself belonged — and which he rejected.. Born in New Orleans to a mixed-race Creole family, Broyard "passed" as white for most of his life, rising through the ranks of the New York intelligentsia to become one of the premiere essayists of his generation. The ironic double stance adopted by the urban hipster could very well describe the author himself, perhaps the original hipster.

As he was the illegitimate son of the Lost Generation, the hipster was really *nowhere*. And, just as amputees often seem to localize their strongest sensations in the *missing* limb, so the hipster longed, from the very beginning, to be *somewhere*. He was like a beetle on its back; his life was a struggle to get *straight*. But the law of human gravity kept him overthrown, because he was always of the minority—opposed in race or feeling to those who owned the machinery of recognition.

The hipster began his inevitable quest for self-definition by sulking in a kind of inchoate delinquency. But this delinquency was merely a negative expression of his needs, and, since it led only into the waiting arms of the ubiquitous law, he was finally forced to *formalize* his resentment and express it *symbolically*. This was the birth of a philosophy—a philosophy of *somewhereness* called *jive*, from *jibe*: to agree or harmonize. By discharging his would-be aggressions *symbolically*, the hipster harmonized or reconciled himself with society.

At the natural stage in its growth, jive began to talk. It had been content at first with merely making sounds—physiognomic° talk—but then it developed language. And, appropriately enough, this language described the world as seen through the hipster's eyes. In fact, that was its function: to re-edit the world with new definitions . . . jive definitions.

Since articulateness is a condition for, if not actually a cause of, anxiety, the hipster relieved his anxiety by disarticulating himself. He cut the world down to size—reduced it to a small stage with a few props and a curtain of jive. In a vocabulary of a dozen verbs, adjectives, and nouns he could describe every-thing that happened in it. It was poker with no joker, nothing wild.

physiognomic: relating to the belief that one's outer features reveal inner character.

There were no neutral words in this vocabulary; it was put up or shut up, 5
a purely polemical language in which every word had a job of *evaluation* as
well as designation. These evaluations were absolute; the hipster banished
all comparatives, qualifiers, and other syntactical uncertainties. Everything
was dichotomously *solid, gone, out of this world,* or *nowhere, sad, beat,* a *drag.*

In there was, of course, somewhereness. *Nowhere,* the hipster's favorite
pejorative, was an *abracadabra* to make things disappear. *Solid* connoted
the stuff, the reality, of existence; it meant concreteness in a bewilder-
ingly abstract world. A *drag* was something which "dragged" implications
with it, something which was embedded in an inseparable, complex,
ambiguous—and thus, possibly threatening—context.

Because of its polemical° character, the language of jive was rich in
aggressiveness, much of it couched in sexual metaphors. Since the hipster never did anything as an end in itself, and since he only gave of
himself in aggression of one kind or another, sex was subsumed under
aggression, and it supplied a vocabulary for the mechanics of aggression.
The use of the sexual metaphor was also a form of irony, like certain
primitive peoples' habit of parodying civilized modes of intercourse. The
person on the tail end of a sexual metaphor was conceived of as lugubri-
ously victimized; i.e., expecting but not receiving.

One of the basic ingredients of jive language was *a priorism.°* The a
priori assumption was a short cut to somewhereness. It arose out of a
desperate, unquenchable need to know the score; it was a great protection, a primary self-preserving postulate.° It meant "it is given to us to
understand." The indefinable authority it provided was like a powerful
primordial or instinctual orientation in a threatening chaos of complex
interrelations. The hipster's frequent use of metonymy° and metony-
mous gestures (e.g., brushing palms for handshaking, extending an index
finger, without raising an arm, as a form of greeting, etc.) also connoted
prior understanding, there is no need to elaborate, I dig you, man, etc.

Carrying his language and his new philosophy like concealed weapons, the hipster set out to conquer the world. He took his stand on the
corner and began to direct human traffic. His significance was unmis-
takable. His face—"the cross-section of a motion"—was frozen in the
"physiognomy of astuteness." Eyes shrewdly narrowed, mouth slackened
in the extremity of perspicuous° sentience, he kept tabs, like a suspicious

---

polemical: strongly critical or controversial in speech or writing.
a priorism: doctrine that knowledge rests upon principles that are self-evident to reason.
postulate: a claim about the existence or truth of something.
metonymy: figure of speech in which a thing is named by an associated attribute.
perspicuous: clearly expressed and easily understood.

proprietor, on his environment. He stood always a little apart from the group. His feet solidly planted, his shoulders drawn up, his elbows in, hands pressed to sides, he was a pylon around whose implacability the world obsequiously careered.

Occasionally he brandished his padded shoulders, warning humanity 10 to clear him a space. He flourished his thirty-one-inch pegs like banners. His two-and-seven-eighths-inch brim was snapped with absolute symmetry. Its exactness was a symbol of his control, his domination of contingency. From time to time he turned to the candy store window, and with an esoteric gesture, reshaped his roll collar, which came up very high on his neck. He was, indeed, up to the neck in somewhereness.

Jazz musicians Thelonious Monk, Howard McGhee, Roy Eldridge, and Teddy Hill outside Minton's Playhouse circa 1940. Hipsters—known as hepcats until the rise of swing—adopted the dress, slang, and attitude of jazz musicians. William Gottlieb/ Getty Images

He affected a white streak, made with powder, in his hair. This was the outer sign of a significant, prophetic mutation. And he always wore dark glasses, because normal light offended his eyes. He was an underground man, requiring especial adjustment to ordinary conditions; he was a lucifugous° creature of the darkness, where sex, gambling, crime, and other bold acts of consequence occurred.

At intervals he made an inspection tour of the neighborhood to see that everything was in order. The importance of this round was implicit in the portentous° trochees° of his stride, which, being unnaturally accentual, or discontinuous, expressed his particularity, lifted him, so to speak, out of the ordinary rhythm of normal cosmic pulsation. He was a discrete entity—separate, critical, and defining.

Jive music and *tea*° were the two most important components of the hipster's life. Music was not, as has often been supposed, a stimulus to dancing. For the hipster rarely danced, he was beyond the reach of stimuli. If he did dance, it was half parody—"second removism"—and he danced only to the off-beat, in a morganatic° one to two ratio with the music.

> "By discharging his would-be aggressions symbolically, the hipster harmonized or reconciled himself with society."

Actually, jive music was the hipster's autobiography, a score to which his life was the text. The first intimations of jive could be heard in the Blues. Jive's Blue Period was very much like Picasso's: it dealt with lives that were sad, stark, and isolated. It represented a relatively realistic or naturalistic stage of development.

Blues turned to jazz. In jazz, as in early, analytical cubism, things were 15 sharpened and accentuated, thrown into bolder relief. Words were used somewhat less frequently than in Blues; the instruments talked instead. The solo instrument became the narrator.

Sometimes (e.g., Cootie Williams) it came very close to literally talking. Usually it spoke passionately, violently, complainingly, against a background of excitedly pulsating drums and guitar, ruminating bass, and assenting orchestration. But, in spite of its passion, jazz was almost always coherent and its intent clear and unequivocal.

---

lucifugous: avoiding light.
portentous: overly solemn, meant to impress.
trochee: stressed syllable followed by an unstressed syllable; here used metaphorically to describe an uneven way of walking.
***tea*:** marijuana.
morganatic: referring to the marriage of people of unequal social rank.

Bebop, the third stage in jive music, was analogous in some respects to synthetic cubism. Specific situations, or referents, had largely disappeared; only their "essences" remained. By this time the hipster was no longer willing to be regarded as a primitive; bebop, therefore, was "cerebral" music, expressing the hipster's pretensions, his desire for an imposing, full-dress body of doctrine.

Surprise, "second removism" and extended virtuosity were the chief characteristics of the bebopper's style. He often achieved surprise by using a tried and true tactic of his favorite comic strip heroes:

The "enemy" is waiting in a room with drawn gun. The hero kicks open the door and bursts in—not upright, in the line of fire—*but cleverly lying on the floor, from which position he triumphantly blasts away, while the enemy still aims, ineffectually, at his own expectations.*

Borrowing this stratagem, the bebop soloist often entered at an unexpected altitude, came in on an unexpected note, thereby catching the listener off guard and conquering him before he recovered from his surprise.

"Second removism"—*capping the squares*—was the dogma of initia- 20 tion. It established the hipster as keeper of enigmas, ironical pedagogue, a self-appointed exegete. Using his *shrewd* Socratic method, he discovered the world to the naive, who still tilted with the windmills of one-level meaning. That which you heard in bebop was always *something else, not* the thing you expected; it was always negatively derived, abstraction *from*, not *to.*

The virtuosity of the bebopper resembled that of the street-corner evangelist who revels in his unbroken delivery. The remarkable run-on quality of bebop solos suggested the infinite resources of the hipster, who could improvise indefinitely, whose invention knew no end, who was, in fact, omniscient.

All the best qualities of jazz—tension, élan,° sincerity, violence, immediacy—were toned down in bebop. Bebop's style seemed to consist, to a great extent, in *evading* tension, in connecting, by extreme dexterity, each phrase with another, so that nothing remained, everything was lost in a shuffle of decapitated cadences. This corresponded to the hipster's social behavior as jester, jongleur,° or prestidigitator.° But it was his own fate he had caused to disappear for the audience, and now the only trick he had left was the monotonous gag of pulling himself—by his own ears, grinning and gratuitous—up out of the hat.

élan: vigorous enthusiasm, energy, or style.
jongleur: travelling minstrel.
prestidigitator: one who has skill performing magic with the hands.

The élan of jazz was weeded out of bebop because all enthusiasm was naive, nowhere, too simple. Bebop was the hipster's seven types of ambiguity, his Laocoön,° illustrating his struggle with his own defensive deviousness. It was the disintegrated symbol, the shards, of his attitude toward himself and the world. It presented the hipster as performer, retreated to an abstract stage of *tea* and pretension, losing himself in the multiple mirrors of his fugitive chords. This conception was borne out by the surprising mediocrity of bebop orchestrations, which often had the perfunctory quality of vaudeville music, played only to announce the coming spectacle, the soloist, the great Houdini.

Bebop rarely used words, and, when it did, they were only nonsense syllables, significantly paralleling a contemporaneous loss of vitality in jive language itself. Blues and jazz were documentary in a social sense; bebop was the hipster's Emancipation Proclamation in double talk. It showed the hipster as the victim of his own system, volubly tongue-tied, spitting out his own teeth, running between the raindrops of his spattering chords, never getting wet, washed clean, baptized, or quenching his thirst. He no longer had anything relevant to himself to say—in both his musical and linguistic expression he had finally abstracted himself from his real position in society.

His next step was to abstract himself in action. *Tea* made this possi- 25 ble. Tea (marijuana) and other drugs supplied the hipster with an indispensable outlet. His situation was too extreme, too tense, to be satisfied with mere fantasy or animistic domination of the environment. Tea provided him with a free world to expatiate in. It had the same function as trance in Bali, where the unbearable flatness and de-emotionalization of "waking" life is compensated for by trance ecstasy. The hipster's life, like the Balinese's, became schizoid; whenever possible, he escaped into the richer world of tea, where, for the helpless and humiliating image of a black beetle on its back, he could substitute one of himself floating or flying, "high" in spirits, dreamily dissociated, in contrast to the ceaseless pressure exerted on him in real life. Getting high was a form of artificially induced dream catharsis. It differed from *lush* (whisky) in that it didn't encourage aggression. It fostered, rather, the sentimental values so deeply lacking in the hipster's life. It became a *raison d'être*,° a calling, an experience shared with fellow believers, a respite, a heaven or haven.

Under jive the external world was greatly simplified for the hipster, but his own role in it grew considerably more complicated. The function of his simplification had been to reduce the world to schematic

---

Laocoön: in Greek mythology, a seer and priest of Apollo.
***raison d'être*:** reason for existence.

proportions which could easily be manipulated in actual, symbolical, or ritual relationships; to provide him with a manageable mythology. Now, moving in this mythology, this tense fantasy of somewhereness, the hipster supported a completely solipsistic system. His every word and gesture now had a history and a burden of implication.

Sometimes he took his own solipsism too seriously and slipped into criminal assertions of his will. Unconsciously, he still wanted terribly to take part in the cause and effect that determined the real world. Because he had not been allowed to conceive of himself functionally or socially, he had conceived of himself *dramatically*, and, taken in by his own art, he had often enacted it in actual defense, self-assertion, impulse, or crime.

That he was a direct expression of his culture was immediately apparent in its reaction to him. The less sensitive elements dismissed him as they dismissed everything. The intellectual *manqués*,° however, the desperate barometers of society, took him into their bosom. Ransacking everything for meaning, admiring insurgence, they attributed every heroism to the hipster. He became their "there but for the grip of my superego go I." He was received in the Village as an oracle; his language was *the revolution of the world, the personal idiom*. He was the great instinctual man, an ambassador from the Id. He was asked to read things, look at things, feel things, taste things, and report. What was it? Was it *in there?* Was it *gone?* Was it *fine?* He was an interpreter for the blind, the deaf, the dumb, the insensible, the impotent.

With such an audience, nothing was too much. The hipster promptly became, in his own eyes, a poet, a seer, a hero. He laid claims to apocalyptic visions and heuristic discoveries when he *picked up*; he was Lazarus,° come back from the dead, come back to tell them all, he would tell them all. He conspicuously consumed himself in a high flame. He cared nothing for catabolic° consequences; he was so prodigal as to be invulnerable.

And here he was ruined. The frantic praise of the impotent meant 30 recognition — *actual somewhereness* — to the hipster. He got what he wanted; he stopped protesting, reacting. He began to bureaucratize jive as a machinery for securing the actual — really the *false* — somewhereness. Jive, which had originally been a critical system, a kind of Surrealism,° a personal revision of existing disparities, now grew moribundly self-conscious, smug, encapsulated, isolated from its source, from the sickness which spawned it. It grew more rigid than the institutions it had

---

manqué: referring to a person who has failed to live up to expectations.
Lazarus: man who was raised from the dead by Jesus.
catabolic: referring to breaking down into simpler parts.
Surrealism: cultural movement of the 1920s known for dream-like art and literature.

set out to defy. It became a boring routine. The hipster—once an unregenerate individualist, an underground poet, a guerilla—had become a pretentious poet laureate. His old subversiveness, his ferocity, was now so manifestly rhetorical as to be obviously harmless. He was bought and placed in the zoo. He was *somewhere* at last—comfortably ensconced in the 52nd Street clip joints, in Carnegie Hall, and *Life*. He was *in there* . . . he was back in the American womb. And it was just as hygienic as ever.

Understanding the Text

1. Broyard portrays the hipster as someone who approaches society from a position of "second removism" (par. 13). How does this attitude toward the world give the hipster a kind of authority?

2. Broyard identifies one of the features of the hipster as his "solipsism" (par. 27). What does he mean?

3. What is *jive*?

Reflection and Response

4. Although Broyard alludes to historical roots, he doesn't investigate the social and historical conditions that gave rise to the hipster. In a short essay, historicize this subculture by exploring how the African American experience in the first half of the twentieth century provides the conditions for the hipster's existence.

5. Broyard writes in a fairly high style, using precise but unusual vocabulary and sophisticated sentence structures. Why do you think he casts his discussion in such poetic language? What is the effect of using such language? How would his writing have been different if he had been a sociologist instead of a public intellectual?

6. What became of this version of hipster subculture? Has it reasserted itself since the late 1940s?

Making Connections

7. Investigate the history and style of bebop. How does this kind of music "correspond to the hipster's social behavior"? In other words, how is the hipster's style and attitude toward the world influenced by bebop?

8. Referring to Douglas Haddow's "Hipsters: The Dead End of Western Civilization" (p. 260), describe the contrast between the 1940s hipster and the twenty-first century hipster. Are there any common characteristics beyond the shared name "hipster"? Explore in depth.

Cosplay: Two Views

Linda Stasi and Elisa Melendez

In 2013 Linda Stasi published a review in *The New York Post* of the SyFy channel program *Heroes of Cosplay*. Stasi's review struck a sour note with many members of the cosplay community, prompting Elisa Melendez to write an open letter piece to the *Post*, in which she defends the cosplay subculture. "Cosplay," a contraction of the words "costume" and "play," refers to the practice of dressing as a specific character from film, television, comics, or other media. After a dozen years as the television critic for the *Post*, Long Island-native Stasi currently writes for the *Daily News*. Melendez is a lifelong gaming enthusiast and contributor to the *Miami New Times*, *Slate*, and *Fusion*.

Linda Stasi: Syfy Looks at World of Make-Believe Reality in *Heroes of Cosplay*

I'm so confused—or maybe *they* are.

In case you don't know (and I sure didn't), there are hundreds of thousands of people around the world who spend millions upon millions of dollars on intricately constructed costumes for their personal use.

No—not just gowns or nutty Civil War costumes that people wear for reenactments. Nor is it the job description of the costume designer at a local theater group.

That's all mere child's play, or should I say "cosplay," compared to real thing—cosplay. What the hell *is* that?

It's competitive costume-making and costume-wearing at comic con- 5 ventions—events at which competitors spend thousands of dollars and hundreds of hours on outfits to look like characters in animated movies, comic books, graphic novels, and video games.

It's not enough to go to a costume store and rent a Demon Hunter outfit? I mean, seriously. Renting is so last decade!

Syfy, which loves all things comic, cosmic, and costume has a new series, *Heroes of Cosplay*, devoted to these very folks who are devoted to competing around the country at comic conventions.

Competitive cosplayers make giant molds, sew elaborate outer space outfits, spray-paint their bodies, and create armor from plastic molds they build themselves.

We learn that if the cosplay industry has a legend, it's the one-and-only Yaya Han—a woman who is such a remarkable designer/wearer of the wild, hugely expensive costumes she and her boyfriend create that she's now the go-to authority.

She is, in fact, a cosplay mogul with lines of accessories and God 10
knows what else. Then there are the competitors themselves, some fairly
new to cosplay and some who've been doing it years.

We aren't given any in-depth knowledge about what these folks do to earn
a living in the real world that enables them to spend every waking hour and
dime on making costumes. Several of them seem to be involved in the industry.

No one seems rich, but there are big cash prizes for winners, which
helps defer the cost of the elaborate costumes.

The weird thing (well, all of it is weird) is that these folks really want
to *be* the fictional characters they portray.

If you like cosplay yourself, you'll love *Cosplay*.

Elisa Melendez: Cosplay Is Creative, Not Crazy

Yesterday's *New York Post* review of upcoming SyFy reality show, *Heroes* 15
of Cosplay, angered quite a few of us in the geek community. The article
portrays the cosplay community as "confused" and "weird," all while
looking down its nose at those who might enjoy the creative pursuit.

Yes, cosplay is insanely time-consuming. Yes, cosplay is expensive. Yes,
cosplay represents a subset of fandom that not everyone is into, and that
can be jarring to an outsider. I haven't
seen *Heroes of Cosplay*; maybe it wrongly
portrays the subculture. But it's your
job as a journalist to educate yourself
about your subject matter before jumping to conclusions based on a reality TV
show. Cosplayers shouldn't be scoffed
at, lumped in with "nutty Civil War
reenactors," because you were too cool
for school to inform yourself an extra
smidge about the industry.

> "Yes, cosplay is insanely time-consuming. Yes, cosplay is expensive. Yes, cosplay represents a subset of fandom that not everyone is into, and that can be jarring to an outsider."

We here at Cultist° love ourselves some cosplay, so we felt we needed
to set the record straight, just in time for any future cosplay articles and
reviews you might try to run.

1. Cosplayers come from all walks of life, from full-time employees to students

No need to wonder anymore "what these folks do to earn a living";
anyone from your dentist to that adjunct professor/freelance writer over
there (cough) can be a potential cosplayer. I spoke with one Miami-area

Cultist: arts and culture section of *The Miami New Times* newspaper.

cosplayer, Jonathan Stryker, who is a marketing personal assistant for an author, videographer, and photographer but manages to find time for his favorite hobby. Another cosplayer, Alexa, happens to be a full-time writer for gaming journalism juggernaut Polygon. Ryan, a Miami lawyer, attended his first ever con (Florida Supercon 2012) in full *Doctor Who* regalia, fez and all.

2. Cosplay can range from store-bought pieces with handmade accents to full-fledged custom creations

This writer's *Game of Thrones*-inspired get-up . . . took just a couple of days. I bought the dress, and made everything else — only half that hair is actually mine. Sure, some people will spend a ton of money on construction or commissioning custom creations. Many others are just starting out and don't necessarily abide by hard and fast rules regarding construction. They just want to express their love for these characters and show off some artistic skill. Which brings me to my next point . . .

3. Cosplay's not all about the competition or the cash, but it's nice if and when you get it

Stryker says, "It all becomes worth it when you walk up on stage and   20 people cheer for your hard work; or when you're walking around and hundreds of flashes follow you to capture a beautiful moment in time."

A cosplayer attends Comic-Con International: San Diego dressed as Storm, a character from the X-Men comics. Matt Cowan/Getty Images

South Carolina cosplayer Jessica says it's a great way to connect with other fans. For Alexa, it's just something to do with her friends.

4. Not all of us want to be the characters we're portraying—but performing can be part of the fun!

It's the challenge of creating an homage to beloved characters. For Jonathan, cosplay is "the ultimate art form. It combines make-up, sewing, painting, sculpting, crafting, designing, acting, etc." But you don't have to be a method actor to cosplay—you just have to like something enough to dress up as it and have fun.

If you can pull a character off completely, though, it becomes a more impressive feat. . . .

5. You, at some point in time, may have been a cosplayer and not even known it

Next time you think about disparaging a cosplayer, you might as well curse yourself for any time you've ever dressed up and performed a character for yucks on Halloween. If you cared one iota about the authenticity of your costume and your ability to do them justice; if you ever had a glimmer of worry about being recognized—then the joy of seeing someone's face light up when you walked into a room because they got it; if you have ever been crowned the winner of your office Halloween party for absolutely nailing it, then congrats! You've actually walked a mile in our finely crafted shoes. And that makes you just as "weird" as the rest of us.

Understanding the Text

1. What are Stasi's main criticisms of cosplay subculture as represented by SyFy's *Heroes of Cosplay*?

2. What, specifically, angers Melendez about Stasi's review of *Heroes of Cosplay*?

Reflection and Response

3. What does the open letter form allow Melendez to say that she could not say in a formal essay?

4. Characterize the tone of both Stasi's and Melendez's writing. Is the tone appropriate in each? Is it effective? What limitations does the tone of the writing impose?

5. Do you feel that Melendez is justified in her critique of Stasi's review? Explain.

6. Journalistic writing is often limited by word counts. Does this limitation prevent either Stasi or Melendez from offering sufficient supporting evidence for their claims? If so, what kind of evidence do they need?

Making Connections

7. Watch an episode of *Heroes of Cosplay* online. Is Stasi's *New York Post* review accurate in fact and in spirit?

8. Locate a current review of a television show or movie and respond to it in a short essay. (Note: you do not have to disagree with the reviewer's claims.)

9. How might Patton Oswalt ("Wake Up, Geek Culture. Time to Die," p. 305) respond to Stasi's review as well as to Melendez's open letter?

Making Butch: An Historical Memoir of the 1970s

Sue-Ellen Case

Sue-Ellen Case is a professor of critical studies in the theatre department at the University of California, Los Angeles. The author of several books, Professor Case has been granted the Lifetime Achievement Award by both the American Society for Theatre Research and the Association for Theater in Higher Education. In this memoir of the San Francisco butch-femme scene, she offers a vivid picture of lesbian life at a time when individuals' gender identities were largely invisible to the mainstream culture. In particular, she locates the intersection of the butch-femme scene and the hippie counterculture that exploded in the Bay Area around 1970.

While watching the film *Last Call at Maud's*, I remembered my first night at Maud's: more, my many nights at Maud's.[1] For Maud's was my first bar, my coming-into-the-life bar, the bar I frequented several nights a week, the bar that centered my obsessive fantasies of a lesbian (under)world — the bar that loomed behind my article "Toward a Butch-Femme Aesthetic."[2] The film was about another Maud's. In part, it depicted a Maud's that did not exist, since the film was peopled by well-known feminist authors whom I had never seen there, but whose inclusion in the film seemingly added legitimacy to the bar's claim to centrality in the lesbian scene in San Francisco. In part, the film focused on the later Maud's, in which baseball provided some innocent center around which the drinking, drugs, and cruising could be relegated to more marginal roles. Perhaps all that cheery team-playing was partially a result of the feminist clean-up of the lesbian scene. At any rate, Maud's, the oldest women's bar in San Francisco, was my training ground, was the social center of the lesbian scene in the city, and now is no more.

My first night at Maud's was in the late 1960s. I pushed open its plain black door to discover two rather dimly lit rooms. The long bar occupied the first room. It was illuminated by various neon ads for beers, the warm, orange light from the juke box, and the garish surround of the pinball machine. The other room afforded a central view of the pool table, with its low-hanging lamp and a few tables along the walls. The old butch-femme scene hunkered down at the end of the bar itself, while a few hippie dykes straggled in to sit at the tables. The classical butches still played the pinball machine and occupied the central pool table. The hippie dykes played the juke box (demanding new tunes) and talked endlessly among themselves. Their conversation was not like the anecdotal monologues delivered by the classical butches, after a few beers, but were sometimes drug-inspired, enthusiastic descriptions of altered perception. The two groups regarded one another with suspicion.

It is this shared, but contested gaze that defines the intersection, the historical moment of this memoir. The time when hippie neo-butches encountered the classical ones. At Maud's: where lifestyle politics met ghettoized, closeted behavior; where middle-class drop-outs, students, and sometime professionals met working-class people who had slim, but tenacious hopes of doing better; where the "sexual revolution" broke the code of serial monogamy; where costume and hallucination affronted sober dress codes and drink. . . .

Like many others, I wore long, straight, hippie hair and bell-bottom hip-huggers, but felt I was "butch" (though I had never heard the term). They were men's pants, after all, with broad leather belts, and hippie men were sporting long hair as well. Nevertheless, I had to depend on the kindness of classical butches in order to learn the ropes of bar culture. They seemed quite obliging – I think it was my long hair. They drove me around in their big American cars, showing me the route of four bars which composed the itinerary of a weekend night. Maud's was both the starting place and the end-point along a route that included two bars in the Mission district and one over on the North Beach side of town. After the bars closed, the hearty might add an after-hours joint (for members only) in the Tenderloin district. Brunches at the boys' bars on Sunday provided an opportunity to see who had gone home with whom, and all that together composed a weekend in the life.

The butch-femme people included "Whitey" whom some may 5 remember from the film *The Word Is Out*—her parents had her confined to a mental institution for her sexual proclivity. I dated one of her girlfriends, a young innocent from Kansas City, who had met Whitey in the bars in her first two-week discovery of San Francisco and whom Whitey had rescued from the Midwest by arriving at her parents' door in Kansas City to whisk her off on the back of her motorcycle. That young girl later committed suicide. Other femmes I knew also went down: one who had worked in the publishing firm Little, Brown, until she ran off to join a lesbian commune° and became addicted to pills; a sex worker (called prostitutes at the time) who had her own "shop" in her apartment and sold stained glass windows on the side; the beautiful Eileen, the bar server, and Janice [sic] Joplin, who (it was said) sometimes frequented the place. Of course, lots of people were dying from drug use in the hippie culture and its environment. So there were mourning rituals in the hippie culture and in the bar culture.

---

commune: group of people living together and sharing possessions and responsibilities.

Strangely, among those I knew, it was the femmes who died. These were actually the neo-femmes, who somehow crossed the two cultures. The classic ones did better—they survived. One was called "the fox" because of her dyed red wig—she waited tables at a hamburger place called Zim's. She might still be there. She had already been there for several years. Some classic butches included "Red," who once won the pool championship with one hand, having broken her other in a bar fight, and "Ace," who drove a cab and had lived for years with a beautician, whose teased, dyed hair was truly monumental. I can remember one femme-femme couple, actually. They were both beauticians. No butch-butch couples, though—well, not until the androgynous look came into fashion. Then everyone looked like butches—"Girl Scout counselors," some of us called them, who wore plaid shirts and REI pants. They could be camping in a minute. They had their back packs close at hand.

The crowd was almost exclusive "white," a fact I did not notice at the time, even though, by day, I was involved in the student strike at San Francisco State which broke out over bringing ethnic studies onto campus. I could yell at a cop in riot gear about needing to break the "white" composition of the campus and then fail to notice its hold in the bars. My semi-closeted student status must have helped to isolate my political critique from my social one. In fact, as I remember, there was little discussion of the student strike in the bar. Of course, I didn't discuss the writings of Marcuse° in there either. Somehow, my own working-class upbringing had taught me to confine school words and concerns to the schoolyard. Still, I knew that the "black" women, as they were then called, hung out over in Oakland at their own bars and the Filipinas hung out in a place out by the Avenues. I don't remember any Latinas. Hippies were also a pretty white bunch, seemingly ignorant of the racist element in their "new world" of love and understanding. It doesn't seem to be much better today. . . .

Many elements and substances in the bars and bar life are addictive. I, myself, started going out four and five nights a week. I watched lots of people drop out, go on welfare, or gain some kind of disability pay, in order to live their whole lives there. Why not? It was painful to live under the dominating culture. And wearing a damned skirt in an office was confining. There was a dress code at San Francisco State, for example, stating that skirts and hose were required for all female instructors. I had a couple of knit suits that made riding a motor scooter to work rather treacherous. Inside, in the remove of the bar, it seemed like being a waitress, all decked out, and the center of dyke attention was a really glamorous job. . . .

Marcuse: Herbert Marcuse (1898–1979), German-American political theorist whose Marxist scholarship inspired radicals in the 1960s.

More to the point, however, is the feeling that the ghetto nature of our social life at that time encouraged us to collapse many of our aspirations and dreams into the mythic landscape of the bar, sometimes to the detriment of our futures.

Drinking accompanied the socializing and for some, that was 10 life-threatening. I have two friends from those days who are still struggling with alcoholism. Eroticizing commodity fetishism, as lifestyle politics will do, is also addictive. It's like Edie Sedgwick said in her book *Edie*, about life in the Warhol factory: after a while, with the drugs, they just spent all their time getting dressed up and ready to go out — eventually they never even made it out the door. The most fun was the dressing up, the make-up, the hair-styles. Saturdays were about getting ready, Saturday night partying and picking up, and Sundays about seeing who had done what with whom. The weekend was gone. So when the feminist movement came up with the idea called "substance abuse" it didn't seem as prudish and antique as it does now. In fact, it was an eye-opener. The organization called "sober dykes" was founded with great pride. Most drugs were put away, except for cocaine, which was touted then to be non-addictive. We later found out about that one, too. I'm not promoting an anti-alcohol, anti-drug attitude, nor even a 12-step approach to life. However, for some, the fact that the social life occurred only around alcohol was dangerous, even life-threatening. . . .

> "Maud's was my first bar, my coming-into-the-life bar, the bar I frequented several nights a week, the bar that centered my obsessive fantasies of a lesbian (under) world"

During the later 1970s, feminist coffee houses began opening in the city, along with a women's center, which included a lesbian space. So suddenly there were options for places to gather. If you couldn't afford to be around drinking, but still wanted to meet dykes, you had another possibility. People began exploring social relationships outside of the context of drinking and sexual practice. . . . But it is important to keep in mind that early on in those changing years, bars were still the only places to hang out and sex was the center of social relations. Addictions abounded and were explored with great gusto and we all kept returning to the magic circle that bounded those rites. In one way, it was a grand time. The imagination that would celebrate myth and ritual could find wonderful dreams in those bars. Yet constructing a ghetto out of choice, as some bars currently do, has a different valence from having no option but the ghetto. . . .

Maud's location, about three blocks from Haight Street, influenced the mix of people in the bar. The woman who wrote the book *Going Down on Janice* had opened a kind of sexy, hippie clothing store on Haight and could be seen in the bar on a Friday night. I felt comfortable going into her store to buy the men's clothes. She had the exciting reputation of peeking around the dressing-room curtain when you were undressing. Her butch lover, in full leathers, could be seen riding her Triumph chopper down Haight Street in the early evening. She was one of the few butch images to intrude into the het, hippie flower look. You see, hippies were into strong gender roles, with women baking bread and having babies, while men chopped wood and rolled joints. They didn't mix with the homosexual crowd, but many of the lesbians around that scene emulated some of its practices, such as living in communes. Theirs were as separatist communes, though. People at the bar often moved "out into the country" for a while, but many returned in a hurry. Some lesbian communes still persist in the south of Oregon. Others were founded in Grass Valley in California and in northern New Mexico. They were the subject of many conversations in the bars. We would pack up our cars and go out there for a week, just to look. The ones up in Sonoma County were close enough for the girls to come into town on the weekend and report on their successes with goat grazing and wood chopping. It was exotic. We were interested in flirting with these "milk maids," as we called them. I was having fantasies out of Restoration comedies. Fop that I would be.

So, anyway, I learned butch in the heat of this cauldron, which was brewing alternative subcultures in San Francisco. A new butch was born then, combining certain characteristics of the classical style with other influences. Because of feminism, cloning was already happening, toning down the masculine stance. Likewise, middle-class and student conventions altered the gestures, in terms of how you held your cigarette, for example, no longer between the thumb and first finger, which was definitely working-class, but more like Virginia Woolf, in that famous smoking photo of hers. Your seated posture was different as well. You might cross your legs and lean forward at the table, rather than hook your big shoes on the rungs of the bar stool and lean back. The volume of speech diminished, no more yelling "Hey, Red" when your friend entered the bar, while the volume of music rose, with the new electro sounds of the Jefferson Airplane, for instance. Dancing freed up, releasing one from the bondage of partnering — like sexual freedom, the flirtation was opened out into a wider, more flexible space on the dance floor. Finally, walking the walk definitely altered. Although we might have ridden motorcycles (I certainly did) we did not stomp about in our boots. Everyone was wearing boots, after all. If you had shoulders, you didn't need to mark the fact. Feminism made us interested in women and allowed us to be uninterested in men.

While we were butch, an identification with men would have seemed sordid. Many hippie men, with their long hair and soft ways, who were anti-Vietnam activists, running from the draft, were also trying to put aside the masculine. The idea of a politics around gays in the military would have been strange, indeed, to those against national military forces. Replicating what were perceived as the gestures of power and dominance had no attraction to those concerned with "equal rights," so to speak. We were "flower children" who were against all aggression. The Vietnam war made weaponry and hints of violence seem obscene. Hulking about, or strutting one's stuff would have been aggrandizing space and aping dominance. Thus, butch was about giving sexual pleasure, taking pride in lesbian identification, and being attracted to femmes. We were seeking to be "gentlemen," in the best sense of the word, if we understood butch to have any referent among men. A sense of gallantry could mark gestures as butch. You know, there was that Brit fashion of puffy sleeves—the courtier style. Listening to the Stones'° "my sweet lady Jane," encouraged fantasies as pages—exquisite ceremonies of butch bottoms.

However, the butch I learned was not acceptable to the classical 15 butches.

Sherman, who appears as a character in the novel *Sita*, laughed derisively at my long hair, my silly hippie pants, my flowered shirts, and my "execrable" taste in music. She had been elected the "King" of North Beach, in her men's long-sleeved shirts, her tough ways, and her abstract-expressionist painting style. She wore boxer shorts and men's pajamas and was probably "stone." We were not. We had been a part of the "sexual revolution," after all and wanted to experience it all. Sherman told me to just forget it and, by the way, to forget her beautiful girlfriend. I didn't. Some of those femmes liked the new-style butches. For one thing, we could "pass" when necessary, both in terms of sexual orientation and class manners. For another, we were struggling with some kind of feminist notion of equality and shared practices. . . .

Some called us "nelly butches" as a way to accommodate the new style. We took to wearing 1930s men's clothes from the thrift stores, with flowing, Dietrich-type pants and silk bow-ties. Why, we wondered, did butch necessarily mean dressing down, playing baseball or poker? To be honest, sometimes, when we watched those traditional butch-femme couples waltz around the floor, they resembled our parents, saying the

Stones: Rolling Stones, British rock band formed in 1962.

same things, like "cut your hair" and "don't listen to that loud, horrible music." We were alternatively amused and frustrated by the classic rhetoric of serial monogamy: repetitively "falling in love," "getting married," and then living with a "roommate" who, as they loved to insist, "used to be my lover but we don't sleep together anymore." This was the signal that they were moving on. It occasioned those bar fights and couple-identified postures. Hippie free love shared a devotion to sexual pleasure with the classic butches and femmes around the bars, but without the thrill of sneaking around. Bar fights just didn't fit with the idea of "make love not war." And then, those classic couples seemed so apolitical, at the time of street demonstrations. They didn't join them. Perhaps it was because they couldn't yet feel comfortable in the streets. . . .

While we're on contested critical terrain, let me return to the much-debated issue of the lesbian relationship to "camp" . . . Crowning the King and Queen of North Beach was an annual joint event. The boys' bars hosted some wonderful women entertainers whom the lesbians poured in to ogle. Tapes by the fabulous Ann Weldon° circulated in both bars. The drag° ball brought the leading queens around in their limos to visit the annual drag party at Maud's. And, as I mentioned before, the boys' bars hosted those Sunday brunches we all attended. Moreover, several of them served cheap dinners on certain nights of the week. We often met our gay friends there early in the evenings before making our way out into our gender-specific clubs. So, the practice of drag and the enjoyment of multiple sexual partners circulated between gay and lesbian bar cultures. Show people were on the fringes of the scene. Some girls who worked as "exotic dancers," as they preferred to be called, cynically performed flirtations with men on the stages of topless/bottomless clubs. Costumes were playing on the sidewalks of the Haight. Hallucination disjointed the "real." Some of us had seen not only Barbara Hammer's° films, but Andy Warhol's as well. Kenneth Anger° was around in the city. His movie, which begins with a big biker putting on his leathers and chains to "Blue Velvet,"° was the talk of the town. I talked with him once about trying to do some homosexual version of Oedipus. Shortly after that, he jumped, nude, onto the altar of Glide Memorial Church. Meanwhile, back at Maud's, the brutal, clipped discourse of bar butches still

---

Ann Weldon: American actress, singer, and activist.
drag: clothing more conventionally worn by the opposite sex, especially women's clothes worn by a man.
Barbara Hammer: American feminist film-maker (b. 1939).
Kenneth Anger: American experimental film-maker (b. 1927).
"Blue Velvet": popular song written in 1950 and covered by many artists.

circulated among the hippie descriptions of visions and hallucinations. Opening in there, between the clip and the float, in an environment of self-ironic flirtation within an urban homosexual scene, was a space for masquerading thoughts and inverting social codes. Clipped, ironic, playful travesties cast the mantle of camp across the scene. Not the whole scene, of course, but this particular graft of hippie and traditional.

At the same time as this permissive environment held great sway, violent homophobic practices still penetrated the removed spaces of the bars. Paying off the cops at the bar could be seen by anyone who wanted to look over there on party nights. It was still illegal to dance together in close contact and the local beat cops had to be encouraged not to come around. The raids around election time as "moral clean-ups" enforced a sense of the frailty of official liberality. One of the bars in Oakland allowed dancing in a back room, where a large red light blinked when the vice cops entered the front door. Everyone flew to their seats. A certain butch badge of daring could be sported by getting "86ed," or thrown out of the bar for a certain period of time. The owners had to be careful about the vice cops, so they would police untoward physical proximity, which we enjoyed in various dark corners. Frighteningly, there were still repeated episodes of male gangs hiding around the corner at the time of the bar's closing ready to gang rape the women who dared to walk down the pavement alone. This happened to two of my friends. We might swagger in the bars, sporting our butch outfits, but we put on a coat and hurriedly got on our bikes out in front, when we left the safety of the bar's confines.

In many ways, a certain sense of "butch" did not survive this moment. 20 The lesbian feminist movement turned away from role-playing into a privileging of androgyny, or non-gendered, or non-patriarchal, or "natural" styles, as they insisted. When butch re-emerged out the other side of that betrayal, it did so with a vengeance – so vengeful, in fact, that it associated its demeanor with gay men and the masculine, rather than with styles among women. Daddy-boy dykes and F2M associated with men in new, more fleshly ways. The swagger was back. Images of dominance were eroticized. Working-class styles were sported, even though, often, by middle-class butches. Leather harnesses, dildos, and piercings don't exactly suggest the gestures of gallantry, the way page haircuts and puffy sleeves once had done. In those days, I think the gyno-centric (as it was called then in feminist circles) was the magnetic pole of the imaginary, rather than the masculine. The masculine had been contaminated by its proximity to war.

Well, I am not calling for a vote on which is better. Instead, I want to make a different point, to conjecture that it was in the contrast between these two styles that the notion of style itself became visible in the subculture. Before hippies, butch and femme were not perceived as a style, but as "the way we are." At this point in history, one might argue, when hippies and butches actually regarded one another across the room, both became aware of a contest of styles. They were on their way to constructing a sense of lesbian "lifestyles." Their comparative practices redefined lesbian sexual practice as style and began to construct a sense of a self-conscious lesbian sociality, grounded first in the bars and later, in various kinds of locations. At the same time, because of the poets, the filmmakers, and the dress-shop owners, there arose a sense that there was a style of lesbian self-representation. Lesbians could begin to see themselves in the mirror in a way that only a few novels had provided them before. Now, they were represented in a certain way, partially influenced by the underground cinema practices in women's and gay films at the time, partially by the styles of the subculture itself. Now, by the time "lesbian style wars," as Arlene Stein called them in her article by the same title, were taking place in the late 1980s, the 1970s had become cast as a pre-style moment.[3] Although Stein makes some acute observations about the politics of "lifestyle," she grounds its emergence in the 1980s by reducing the 1970s to what she calls the "anti-fashion" movement within lesbian feminism. I think this has become a kind of commonplace assumption that I want to adjust here by introducing the hippie butch. At least in the urban center known as San Francisco, with its Haight-Ashbury hippie culture, its "Love-Ins,"° its Fillmore Auditorium, its local groups such as The Jefferson Airplane, its singers such as Joan Baez and Janis Joplin, its anti-war demonstrations, its student uprisings such as the one at San Francisco State and other events of the late 1960s and the 1970s, more than a strict hairy-legged, overall-wearing lesbian feminist was walking through the bar door. Sure, she was around and she was influential. But the encounter between the classic butch and the hippie butch was perhaps even more prescient in its focus on style, on issues of representing masculinity and sexual desire.

Hippies also presented the subculture with an interest in perception (via hallucination) and in the structuring of internal processes. If you look around now, these elements, although reconfigured, are still recognizably present. The student movement brought these kinds of studies onto the campus. Some people think we got them from importing French psychoanalytic studies. But I think they developed out of a subculture which smoked marijuana and indulged in long monologues about inner processes, or dropped acid and then dealt with the nature of perception, and out of a militant student movement that insisted that the streets, with all their priorities and social exigencies become part of the "student body."

Love-In: peaceful social gathering associated with the hippies of the 1960s.

Notes

1. *Last Call at Maud's/The Maud's Project*. New York: Water Bearer Films, 1993. The bar was Maud's on Cole Street in San Francisco, also known as The Study.

2. This article has been published in many places, to my embarrassment. I did not retain the copyright and it was released by the press. One accessible collection is Henry Abelove, Michéle Barale and David Halperin (eds), *The Lesbian and Gay Studies Reader* (New York and London: Routledge, 1993), pp. 294–306.

3. Arlene Stein, 'All dressed up but no place to go? Style wars and the new lesbianism,' *Outlook* (Winter 1989), 1(4), pp. 34–42.

Understanding the Text

1. Even in famously permissive San Francisco, lesbians in the 1960s and 1970s had an outlaw status. Give examples drawn from the text.

2. Case does not offer clear definitions of "butch" and "femme." Based on the reading, offer your own definitions.

3. What characteristics shared by the lesbian and hippie communities does Case identify?

Reflection and Response

4. Case presents butch-femme culture exclusively through the lens of personal memoir. What are the advantages of this rhetorical method? What are the weaknesses? Would a greater reliance on facts and figures give the reader a better understanding of lesbian culture in the early 1970s?

5. The bar scene provided a limited space in which the butch-femme subculture could flourish. In what other situations do such well-defined social spaces play an important role? Discuss in detail.

Making Connections

6. Research the status of gay men in places like San Francisco in the mid-twentieth century. How did their experiences differ from those of the butch-femmes? How did their experience mirror the butch-femme experience?

7. Case mentions the importance of dress codes, both formal (instructors at San Francisco State) and informal (the "nelly butch" look). Compose a short essay discussing how and why clothing plays a role in defining social boundaries and constructing subcultural identity.

Deafness as Culture

Edward Dolnick

Edward Dolnick grew up in a small town in Massachusetts. He had dreams of playing professional basketball, but instead became an award-winning journalist, writing for *The Atlantic*, the *New York Times Magazine*, the *Washington Post*, and, as the chief science writer, the *Boston Globe*. He is also the author of several books, including *The Rescue Artist: A True Story of Art, Thieves, and the Hunt for a Missing Masterpiece*, which won the 2006 Edgar Award in the Best Crime Fact category. In "Deafness as Culture," published in 1993, Dolnick focuses on a particularly contentious time in the Deaf community, as members debated issues of deaf identity, authenticity, and new auditory technology.

For millennia deafness was considered so catastrophic that very few ventured to ease its burdens. Isolation in a kind of permanent solitary confinement was deemed inevitable; a deaf person, even in the midst of urban hubbub, was considered as unreachable as a fairy-tale princess locked in a tower. The first attempts to educate deaf children came only in the sixteenth century. As late as 1749 the French Academy of Sciences appointed a commission to determine whether deaf people were "capable of reasoning." Today no one would presume to ignore the deaf or exclude them from full participation in society. But acknowledging their rights is one thing, coming to grips with their plight another. Deafness is still seen as a dreadful fate.

Lately, though, the deaf community has begun to speak for itself. To the surprise and bewilderment of outsiders, its message is utterly contrary to the wisdom of centuries: Deaf people, far from groaning under a heavy yoke, are not handicapped at all. Deafness is not a disability. Instead, many deaf people now proclaim, they are a subculture like any other. They are simply a linguistic minority (speaking American Sign Language) and are no more in need of a cure for their condition than are Haitians or Hispanics.

That view is vehemently held. "The term 'disabled' describes those who are blind or physically handicapped," the deaf linguists Carol Padden and Tom Humphries write, "not Deaf people." (The upper-case D is significant: it serves as a succinct proclamation that the deaf share a culture rather than merely a medical condition.) So strong is the feeling of cultural solidarity that many deaf parents cheer on discovering that their baby is deaf. Pondering such a scene, a hearing person can experience a kind of vertigo. The surprise is not simply the unfamiliarity of the views; it is that, as in a surrealist painting, jarring notions are presented as if they were commonplaces.

The embrace of what looks indisputably like hardship is what, in particular, strikes the hearing world as perverse, and deaf leaders have learned to brace themselves for the inevitable question. "No!" Roslyn Rosen says, by shaking her head vehemently, she *wouldn't* prefer to be able to hear. Rosen, the president of the National Association of the Deaf, is deaf, the daughter of deaf parents, and the mother of deaf children. "I'm happy with who I am," she says through an interpreter, "and I don't want to be 'fixed.' Would an Italian-American rather be a WASP?° In our society everyone agrees that whites have an easier time than blacks. But do you think a black person would undergo operations to become white?"

The view that deafness is akin to ethnicity is far from unanimously 5 held. "The world of deafness often seems Balkanized, with a warlord ruling every mountaintop," writes Henry Kisor, the book editor for the *Chicago Sun-Times* and deaf himself. But the "deaf culture" camp — Kisor calls it the "New Orthodoxy" — is in the ascendancy, and its proponents invoke watchwords that still carry echoes of earlier civil-rights struggles. "Pride," "heritage," "identity," and similar words are thick in the air.

Rhetoric aside, however, the current controversy is disorientingly unfamiliar, because the deaf are a group unlike any ethnic minority 90 percent of all deaf children are born to hearing parents. Many people never meet a deaf person unless one is born to them. Then parent and child belong to different cultures, as they would in an adoption across racial lines. And deaf children acquire a sense of cultural identity from their peers rather than their parents, as homosexuals do. But the crucial issue is that hearing parent and deaf child don't share a means of communication. Deaf children cannot grasp their parents' spoken language, and hearing parents are unlikely to know sign language. Communication is not a gift automatically bestowed in infancy but an acquisition gained only by laborious effort.

This gulf has many consequences. Hearing people tend to make the mistake of considering deafness to be an affliction that we are familiar with, as if being deaf were more or less like being bard of hearing. Even those of us with sharp hearing are, after all, occasionally unable to make out a mumbled remark at the dinner table, or a whispered question from a toddler, or a snatch of dialogue in a movie theater.

To get a hint of blindness, you can try making your way down an unfamiliar hall in the dark late at night. But clamping on a pair of earmuffs conveys nothing essential about deafness, because the earmuffs can't block out a lifetime's experience of having heard language. That experience makes hearing people ineradicably different. Because antibiotics

WASP: White, Anglo-Saxon Protestant.

have tamed many of the childhood diseases that once caused permanent loss of hearing, more than 90 percent of all deaf children in the United States today were born deaf or lost their hearing before they had learned English. The challenge that faces them—recognizing that other peoples' mysterious lip movements *are* language, and then learning to speak that language—is immeasurably greater than that facing an adult who must cope with a gradual hearing loss.

Learning to speak is so hard for people deaf from infancy because they are trying, without any direct feedback, to mimic sounds they have never heard. (Children who learn to speak and then go deaf fare better, because they retain some memory of sound.) One mother of a deaf child describes the challenge as comparable to learning to speak Japanese from within a soundproof glass booth. And even if a person does learn to speak, understanding someone else's speech remains maddeningly difficult. Countless words look alike on the lips, though they sound quite different, "Mama" is indistinguishable from "papa," "cat" from "hat," "no new taxes" from "go to Texas." Context and guesswork are crucial, and conversation becomes a kind of fast and ongoing crossword puzzle.

"Speechreading is EXHAUSTING. I hate having to depend on it," 10 writes Cheryl Heppner, a deaf woman who is the executive director of the Northern Virginia Resource Center for Deaf and Hard of Hearing Persons. Despite her complaint, Heppner is a speech-reading virtuoso. She made it through public school and Pennsylvania State University without the help of interpreters, and she says she has never met a person with better speech-reading skills. But "even with peak conditions," she explains, "good lighting, high energy level, and a person who articulates well, I'm still guessing at half of what I see on the lips." When we met in her office, our conversation ground to a halt every sentence or two, as if we were travelers without a common language who had been thrown together in a train compartment. I had great difficulty making out Heppner's soft, high-pitched speech, and more often than not my questions and comments met only with her mouthed "Sorry." In frustration we resorted to typing on her computer.

> "The world of the deaf is heterogeneous, and the fault lines that run through it are twisted and tricky."

For the average deaf person, lip-reading is even less rewarding. In tests using simple sentences, deaf people recognize perhaps three or four words in every ten. Ironically, the greatest aid to lip-reading is knowing how words sound. One British study found, for example, that the average deaf person with a decade of practice was no better at lip-reading than a hearing person picked off the street.

Unsurprisingly, the deaf score poorly on tests of English skills. The average deaf sixteen-year-old reads at the level of a hearing eight-year-old. When deaf students eventually leave school, three in four are unable to read a newspaper. Only two deaf children in a hundred (compared with forty in a hundred among the general population) go on to college. Many deaf students write English as if it were a foreign language. One former professor at Gallaudet, the elite Washington, D.C., university for the deaf, sometimes shows acquaintances a letter written by a student. The quality of the writing, he says, is typical. "As soon as you had lend me $15," the letter begins, "I felt. I must write you to let you know how relievable I am in your aid."

Small wonder that many of the deaf eagerly turn to American Sign Language, invariably described as "the natural language of the deaf." Deaf children of deaf parents learn ASL as easily as hearing children learn a spoken language. At the same age that hearing babies begin talking, deaf babies of parents who sign begin "babbling" nonsense signs with their fingers. Soon, and without having to be formally taught, they have command of a rich and varied language, as expressive as English but as different from it as Urdu or Hungarian.

At the heart of the idea that deafness is cultural, in fact, is the deaf community's proprietary pride in ASL. Even among the hearing the discovery of ASL's riches has sometimes had a profound impact. The most prominent ally of the deaf-culture movement, for example, is the Northeastern University linguist Harlan Lane, whose interest in the deaf came about through his study of ASL. When he first saw people signing to one another, Lane recalls, he was stunned to realize that "language could be expressed just as well by the hands and face as by the tongue and throat, even though the very definition of language we had learned as students was that it was something spoken and heard." For a linguist, Lane says, "this was astonishing, thrilling. I felt Like Balboa seeing the Pacific."

Until the 1960s critics had dismissed signing as a poor substitute for 15 language, a mere semaphoring of stripped-down messages ("I see the ball"). Then linguists demonstrated that ASL is in fact a full-fledged language, with grammar and puns and poems, and dignified it with a name. Anything that can be said can be said in ASL. In the view of the neurologist and essayist Oliver Sacks, it is "a language equally suitable for making love or speeches, for flirtation or mathematics."

ASL is the everyday language of perhaps half a million Americans. A shared language makes for a shared identity. With the deaf as with other groups, this identity is a prickly combination of pride in one's own ways and wariness of outsiders. "If I happened to strike up a relationship with a hearing person," says MJ Bienvenu, a deaf activist speaking through an interpreter, "I'd have considerable trepidation about my [deaf] parents' reaction. They'd ask, 'What's the matter? Aren't your own people good enough for you?' and they'd warn, 'They'll take advantage of you. You don't know what they're going to do behind your back.'"

Blind men and women often marry sighted people, but 90 percent of deaf people who marry take deaf spouses. When social scientists ask people who are blind or in wheelchairs if they wish they could see or walk, they say yes instantly. Only the deaf answer the equivalent question no. The essence of deafness, they explain, is not the lack of hearing but the community and culture based on ASL Deaf culture represents not a denial but an affirmation.

Spokespeople for deaf pride present their case as self-evident and commonsensical. Why should anyone expect deaf people to deny their roots when every other cultural group proudly celebrates its traditions and history? Why stigmatize the speakers of a particular language as disabled? "When Gorbachev° visited the U.S., he used an interpreter to talk to the President," says Bienvenu, who is one of the directors of an organization called The Bicultural Center. "Was Gorbachev disabled?"

Uneasy Allies

Despite the claims made in its name, though, the idea that deafness is akin to ethnicity is hardly straightforward. On the contrary, it is an idea with profound and surprising implications, though these are rarely explored. When the deaf were in the news in 1988, for instance, protesting the choice of a hearing person as president of Gallaudet, the press assumed that the story was about disabled people asserting their rights, and treated it the same as if students at a university for the blind had demanded a blind president.

The first surprise in the cultural view of deafness is that it rejects the   20 assumption that medical treatment means progress and is welcome. Since deafness is not a deprivation, the argument runs, talk of cures and breakthroughs and technological wizardry is both inappropriate and offensive—as if doctors and newspapers joyously announced advances in genetic engineering that might someday make it possible to turn black skin white.

Last fall, for example, *60 Minutes* produced a story on a bright, lively little girl named Caitlin Parton. "We don't remember ever meeting [anyone] who captivated us quite much as this seven-year-old charmer," it began.

Gorbachev: Mikhail Gorbachev (b. 1931), leader of the Soviet Union at the time of its collapse in 1991.

Caitlin is deaf, and *60 Minutes* showed how a new device called a cochlear implant had transformed her life. Before surgeons implanted a wire in Caitlin's inner ear and a tiny receiver under her skin, she couldn't hear voices or barking dogs or honking cars. With the implant she can hear ordinary conversation, she can speak almost perfectly, and she is thriving in school. *60 Minutes* presented the story as a welcome break from its usual round of scandal and exposé. Who could resist a delightful child and a happy ending?

Activists in the deaf community were outraged. Implants, they thundered in letters to *60 Minutes*, are "child abuse" and "pathological" and "genocide." The mildest criticism was that Caitlin's success was a fluke that would tempt parents into entertaining similar but doomed hopes for their own children. "There should have been parades all across America," Caitlin's father lamented months later. "This is a miracle of biblical proportions, making the deaf hear. But we keep hearing what a terrible thing this is, how it's like Zyklon B,° how it has to be stopped."

The anger should have been easy to anticipate. The magazine *Deaf Life*, for example, runs a question-and-answer column called "For Hearing People Only." In response to a reader's question well before *60 Minutes* came along, the editors wrote, "An implant is the ultimate invasion of the ear, the ultimate denial of deafness, the ultimate refusal to let deaf children be Deaf. . . . Parents who choose to have their children implanted, are in effect saying, 'I don't respect the Deaf community, and I certainly don't want my child to be part of it. I want him/her to be part of the hearing world, not the Deaf world."

The roots of such hostility run far deeper than the specific fear that cochlear implants in children are unproved and risky. More generally, the objection is that from the moment parents suspect their child is deaf, they turn for expert advice to doctors and audiologists and speech therapists rather than to the true experts, deaf people. Harlan Lane points to one survey that found that 86 percent of deaf adults said they would not want a cochlear implant even if it were free, "There are many prostheses from eyeglasses and artificial limbs to cochlear implants," Lane writes. "Can you name another that we insist on for children in flagrant disregard of the advice of adults with the same 'condition'?"

The division between the deaf community and the medical one seems 25 to separate two natural allies. Even more surprising is a second split, between deaf people and advocates for the disabled. In this case, though,

Zyklon B: cyanide-based pesticide used in the gas chambers of Nazi extermination camps.

the two sides remain uneasy partners, bound as if in a bad marriage. The deaf community knows that whatever its qualms, it cannot afford to cut itself off from the larger, savvier, wealthier disability lobby.

Historically, advocates for every disabled group have directed their fiercest fire at policies that exclude their group. No matter the good intentions, no matter the logistical hurdles, they have insisted, separate is not equal. Thus buildings, buses, classes, must be accessible to all; special accommodations for the disabled are not a satisfactory substitute. All this has become part of conventional wisdom. Today, under the general heading of "mainstreaming," it is enshrined in law and unchallenged as a premise of enlightened thought.

Except among the deaf. Their objection is that even well-meaning attempts to integrate deaf people into hearing society may actually imprison them in a zone of silence. Jostled by a crowd but unable to communicate, they are effectively alone. The problem is especially acute in schools, where mainstreaming has led to the decline of residential schools for disabled and the deaf and the integration of many such students into ordinary public schools. Since deafness is rare, deaf students are thinly scattered. As a result, half of all deaf children in public school have either no deaf classmates at all or very few. . . .

The world of the deaf is heterogeneous, and the fault lines that run through it are twisted and tricky. Now politics has worsened the strains. Frances Parsons, for example, is a much honored Gallaudet professor who, though deaf herself, has denounced "the extremists fanatically hawking ASL and Deafism." Such views have brought her hate mail and denunciatory posters and, once, a punch in the neck. Parsons sees her attackers as cultists and propagandists; they call her and her allies traitors and Uncle Toms.

Much of the dispute has to do with who is authentically deaf. Parsons is suspect because she speaks and has hearing parents. To be the deaf child of deaf parents has cachet, because this is as deaf as one can be. (The four student leaders of the Gallaudet protest were all "deaf of deaf.") To use ASL is "better" than to use a manual language that mimics English grammar and arranges ASL signs in English word order. "Those who are born deaf deride those who become deaf at six years or twelve years or later," the Gallaudet psychologist Larry Stewart observed in a bitter essay titled "Debunking the Bilingual-Bicultural Snow Job in the American Deaf Community." "ASL-users who do not use lip movements scorn those who sign with mouthed English, or, the other way around. Residential school graduates turn up their nose at mainstream graduates, or the reverse. And so it goes; a once cohesive community now splintered apart by ideology."

Understanding the Text

1. In what ways is American Sign Language (ASL) like any other language?
2. What are the many factors that make lip-reading difficult for a deaf person?
3. What does Dolnick mean when he says "The world of deafness often seems Balkanized" (par. 5)?

Reflection and Response

4. Despite the vehement objections of the Deaf community, most hearing individuals think of deafness as a disability. On what grounds do they think this? What is your position? Why?
5. Write a letter to the editor of *The Atlantic* in which you praise or criticize — or both — Dolnick's article. Bear in mind that letters to the editor are usually short and to the point.
6. Many Deaf activists draw parallels between Deaf identity and ethnic or racial identity. Are these analogies valid? Why or why not?

Making Connections

7. Research the current status of cochlear implants in the Deaf community. What is the state of the technology? How have attitudes toward cochlear implants changed since Dolnick's article was published in 1993?
8. ASL is a defining feature of Deaf culture. How do other subcultures discussed in this book use language as a means of maintaining group identity?

from *Hell's Angels*

Hunter S. Thompson

As a writer in the vanguard of the New Journalism of the 1960s, Hunter Thompson's personal engagement with the subjects he reported on helped shape the attitudes of a generation of writers. His book *Hell's Angels: The Strange and Terrible Saga of the Outlaw Motorcycle Gangs*, published in 1967, tells the story of the year he spent hanging out with the Oakland, California, chapter of the outlaw biker club and offers trenchant social commentary and inside glimpses into the Angels' lives. His association with the group ended abruptly in 1966 when he was beaten nearly to death by bikers who took offense at some of his comments. Thompson went on to author several more books on American politics and culture. He committed suicide in 2005.

My dealings with the Angels lasted about a year, and never really ended. I came to know some of them well and most of them well enough to relax with. But at first — due to numerous warnings — I was nervous about even drinking. I met a half dozen Frisco Angels one afternoon in the bar of a sleazy dive called the DePau Hotel, located in the south industrial section of the San Francisco waterfront and on the fringe of the Hunger's Point ghetto. My contact was Frenchy, one of the smallest and shrewdest of the outlaws, who was then part owner of a transmission-repair garage called the Box Shop, across Evans Avenue from the degraded premises of the DePau. Frenchy is twenty-nine, a skilled mechanic and an ex-submariner in the Navy. He is five foot five and weighs 135 pounds, but the Angels say he is absolutely fearless and will fight anybody. His wife is a willowy, quiet young blonde whose taste runs more to folk music than to brawls and wild parties. Frenchy plays the guitar, the banjo, and the tiple.

The Box Shop is always full of cars, but not all of them belong to paying customers. Frenchy and a rotating staff of three or four other Angels run the place, working anywhere from four to twelve hours a day most of the time, but occasionally taking off for a bike trip, an extended party or a run down the coast on a sailboat.

I talked to Frenchy on the phone and met him the next day at the DePau, where he was playing pool with Okie Ray, Crazy Rock, and a young Chinaman called Ping-Pong. Immediately upon entering the bar, I took off my Palm Beach sport coat, in deference to the starkly egalitarian atmosphere which the customers seemed to prefer.

Frenchy ignored me long enough to make things uncomfortable, then nodded a faint smile and rapped a shot toward one of the corner pockets.

I bought a glass of beer and watched. Not much was going on. Ping-Pong was doing most of the talking and I wasn't sure what to make of him. He wasn't wearing any colors, but he talked like a veteran. (Later I was told he had an obsession about getting in and spent most of his time hanging around the Box Shop and the DePau. He had no bike, but he tried to compensate by carrying a snub-nosed .357 Magnum revolver in his hip pocket.) The Angels were not impressed. They already had one Chinese member, a mechanic for Harley-Davidson, but he was a quiet, dependable type and nothing like Ping-Pong, who made the outlaws nervous. They knew he was determined to impress them, and was so anxious to show class, they said, that he was likely to get them all busted.

When the pool game ended, Frenchy sat down at the bar, and asked 5 what I wanted to know. We talked for more than an hour, but his style of conversation made me nervous. He would pause now and then, letting a question hang, and fix me with a sad little smile . . . an allusion to some private joke that he was sure I understood. The atmosphere was heavy with hostility, like smoke in an airless room, and for a while I assumed it was all focused on me—which most of it was when I made my initial appearance, but the focus dissolved very quickly. The sense of menace remained; it is part of the atmosphere the Hell's Angels breathe . . . Their world is so rife with hostility that they don't even recognize it. They are deliberately hard on most strangers, but they get bad reactions even when they try to be friendly. I have seen them try to amuse an outsider by telling stories which they consider very funny—but which generate fear and queasiness in a listener whose sense of humor has a different kind of filter.

Some of the outlaws understand this communications gap, but most are puzzled and insulted to hear that "normal people" consider them horrible. They get angry when they read about how filthy they are, but instead of shoplifting some deodorant, they strive to become even filthier. Only a few cultivate a noticeable body odor. Those with wives and steady girlfriends bathe as often as most half-employed people, and make up for it by fouling their clothes more often.[1] This kind of exaggeration is the backbone of their style. The powerful stench they are said to exude is not so much body odor as the smell of old grease in their crusty uniforms. Every Angel recruit comes to his initiation wearing a new pair of Levis and a matching jacket with the sleeves cut off and a spotless emblem on the back. The ceremony varies from one chapter to another but the main feature is always the defiling of the initiate's new uniform. A bucket of dung and urine will be collected during the meeting, then poured on the newcomer's head in a solemn baptismal. Or he will take off his clothes and stand naked while the bucket of slop is poured over them and the others stomp it in.

These are his "originals," to be worn every day until they rot. The Levis are dipped in oil, then hung out to dry in the sun—or left under the motorcycle at night to absorb the crankcase drippings. When they become too ragged to be functional, they are worn over other, newer Levis. Many of the jackets are so dirty that the colors are barely visible, but they aren't discarded until they literally fall apart. The condition of the originals is a sign of status. It takes a year or two before they get ripe enough to make a man feel he has really made the grade. . . .

Motorcycle outlaws are not much in demand on the labor market. With a few exceptions, even those with saleable skills prefer to draw unemployment insurance . . . which gives them the leisure to sleep late, spend plenty of time on their bikes, and freelance for extra cash whenever they feel the need. Some practice burglary, and others strip cars, steal motorcycles, or work erratically as pimps. Many are supported by working wives and girlfriends, who earn good salaries as secretaries, waitresses, and nightclub dancers. A few of the younger outlaws still live with their parents, but they don't like to talk about it and only go home when they have to—either to sleep off a drunk, clean out the refrigerator, or cadge° a few bucks from the family cookie jar. Those Angels who work usually do it part time or drift from one job to another, making good money one week and nothing at all the next.

They are longshoremen, warehousemen, truck drivers, mechanics, clerks, and casual laborers at any work that pays quick wages and requires no allegiance. Perhaps one in ten has a steady job or a decent income. Skip from Oakland is a final inspector on a General Motors assembly line, making around $200 a week; he owns his own home and even dabbles in the stock market. Tiny, the Oakland chapter's sergeant at arms and chief head-knocker, is a "credit supervisor" for a local TV appliance chain. He owns a Cadillac and makes $150 a week for hustling people who get behind on their payments.[2] "We get a lot of deadbeats in this business," he says. "Usually I call 'em up first. I come on real businesslike until I'm sure I have the right guy. Then I tell him, 'Listen, motherfucker, I'm givin' you twenty-four hours to get down here with that money.' This usually scares the shit out of 'em and they pay up quick. If they don't, then I drive out to the house and kick on the door until somebody answers. Once in a while I get a wise-ass trying to give me the run-around . . . then I pick up a couple of guys, lay a few bucks on 'em for the help, and we go out to see the punk. That always does it. I never had to stomp anybody yet."

---

cadge: to ask for or obtain something to which one is not entitled.

There are others with steady incomes, but most of the Angels work 10
sporadically at the kind of jobs that will soon be taken over by machines.
It is hard enough to get unskilled work while wearing shoulder-length
hair and a gold earring . . . it takes an employer who is either desperate
or unusually tolerant . . . but to apply for work as a member of a nation-
ally known "criminal motorcycle conspiracy" is a handicap that can only
be overcome by very special talents, which few Angels possess. Most
are unskilled and uneducated, with no social or economic credentials
beyond a colorful police record and a fine knowledge of motorcycles.[3]

So there is more to their stance than a wistful yearning for acceptance
in a world they never made. Their real motivation is an instinctive cer-
tainty as to what the score really is. They are out of the ballgame and
they know it. Unlike the campus rebels, who with a minimum amount of
effort will emerge from their struggle with a validated ticket to status, the
outlaw motorcyclist views the future with the baleful eye of a man with
no upward mobility at all. In a world increasingly geared to specialists,
technicians and fantastically complicated machinery, the Hell's Angels
are obvious losers and it bugs them. But instead of submitting quietly to
their collective fate, they have made it the basis of a full-time social ven-
detta. They don't expect to win anything, but on the other hand, they
have nothing to lose. . . .

The whole thing was born, they say, in the late 1940s, when most
ex-GIs wanted to get back to an orderly pattern: college, marriage, a job,
children—all the peaceful extras that come with a sense of security. But
not everybody felt that way. Like the drifters who rode west after Appo-
mattox, there were thousands of veterans in 1945 who flatly rejected the
idea of going back to their prewar pattern. They didn't want order, but
privacy—and time to figure things out. It was a nervous, downhill feeling, a mean kind of *Angst* that always comes out of wars . . . a compressed
sense of time on the outer limits of fatalism. They wanted more action,
and one of the ways to look for it was on a big motorcycle. By 1947 the
state was alive with bikes, nearly all of them American-made irons from
Harley-Davidson and Indian.[4] . . .

The Hell's Angels of the sixties are not keenly interested in their origins or spiritual ancestors. "Those guys aren't around anymore," [Hell's
Angels president Sonny] Barger told me. But some were—although in
1965 it wasn't easy to locate them. Some were dead, others were in prison
and those who'd gone straight were inclined to avoid publicity. . . .

Many of the Angels are graduates of other outlaw clubs . . . some of
which, like the Booze Fighters, were as numerous and fearsome in their
time as the Angels are today. It was the Booze Fighters, not the Hell's
Angels, who kicked off the Hollister riot which led to the filming of *The*

Wild One. That was in 1947, when the average Hell's Angel of the 1960s was less than ten years old.

Hollister at that time was a town of about four thousand, a farming 15 community an hour's fast drive south of Oakland, off in the foothills of the Diablo mountain range. Its only claim to fame in 1947 was as the producer of 74 percent of all the garlic consumed in the United States. Hollister was—and remains, to some extent—the kind of town that Hollywood showed the world in the film version of *East of Eden,* a place where the commander of the local American Legion post is by definition a civic leader.

And so it came to pass, on July Fourth of that year that the citizens of Hollister gathered together for the annual celebration. The traditional Independence Day rites—flags, bands, baton virgins, etc.—were scheduled to precede a more contemporary event, the annual motorcycle hill climb and speed tests, which the previous year had drawn contestants from miles around . . . valley boys, farmers, small-town mechanics, veterans, just a crowd of decent fellas who happened to ride motorcycles.

The 1947 Hollister hill climb and races also drew contestants from miles around . . . many miles, and many contestants. When the sun rose out of the Diablos on that Fourth of July morning, the seven-man local police force was nervously sipping coffee after a sleepless night attempting to control something like 3,000 motorcyclists. (The police say 4,000; veteran cyclists say 2,000—so 3,000 is probably about right.) It has been established beyond doubt, however, that Hollister filled up with so many bikes that 1,000 more or less didn't make much difference. The mob grew more and more unmanageable; by dusk the whole downtown area was littered with empty, broken beer bottles, and the cyclists were staging drag races up and down Main Street. Drunken fist fights developed into full-scale brawls. Legend has it that the cyclists literally took over the town, defied the police, manhandled local women, looted the taverns, and stomped anyone who got in their way. The madness of that weekend got enough headlines to interest an obscure producer named Stanley Kramer and a young actor named [Marlon] Brando. Shortly before her death, in 1966, Hollywood gossip columnist Hedda Hopper took note of the Hell's Angels menace and traced its origins back through the years to *The Wild One.* This led her to blame the whole outlaw phenomenon on Kramer, Brando and everyone else in any way connected with the movie. The truth is that *The Wild One*—despite an admittedly fictional treatment—was an inspired piece of film journalism. Instead of institutionalizing common knowledge, in the style of *Time,* it told a story that was only beginning to happen and which was inevitably influenced by the film. It gave the outlaws a lasting, romance-glazed image of themselves, a coherent reflection that only a very few had been able to find in a mirror . . . virile, inarticulate brutes whose good instincts got warped somewhere in the struggle for self-expression and who spent the rest of their violent lives seeking revenge on a world that done them wrong when they were young and defenseless.

Another of Hollywood's contributions to the Hell's Angels lore is the name. The Angels say they are named after a famous World War I bomber squadron that was stationed near Los Angeles and whose personnel raced around the area on motorcycles when they weren't airborne. There are others who say the Angels got their name from a 1930 Jean Harlow movie based on some scriptwriter's idea of an Army Air Corps that may or may not have existed at the time of the First World War. It was called *Hell's Angels* and no doubt was still being shown in 1950, when the restless veterans who founded the first Angel chapter at Fontana were still trying to decide what to do with themselves. While the name might have originated before any Hell's Angel was born, it was lost in the history of some obscure southern California military base until Hollywood made it famous and also created the image of wild men on motorcycles—an image that was later adopted and drastically modified by a new breed of outcasts that not even Hollywood could conceive of until they appeared, in the flesh, on California highways.

The concept of the "motorcycle outlaw" was as uniquely American as jazz. Nothing like them had ever existed. In some ways they appeared to be a kind of half-breed anachronism, a human hangover from the era of the Wild West. Yet in other ways they were as new as television. There was absolutely no precedent, in the years after World War II, for large gangs of hoodlums on motorcycles, reveling in violence, worshiping mobility, and thinking nothing of riding five hundred miles on a weekend . . . to whoop it up with other gangs of cyclists in some country hamlet entirely unprepared to handle even a dozen peaceful tourists. Many picturesque, outback villages got their first taste of tourism not from families driving Fords or Chevrolets, but from clusters of boozing "city boys" on motorcycles.

> "The main reasons the Angels are such good copy is that they are acting out the day-dreams of millions of losers who don't wear any defiant insignia and who don't know how to be outlaws."

In retrospect, eyewitness accounts of the Hollister riot seem timid compared to the film. A more accurate comment on the nature of the Hollister "riot" is the fact that a hastily assembled force of only twenty-nine cops

20

had the whole show under control by noon of July 5. By nightfall the main body of cyclists had roared out of town, in the best *Time* style, to seek new nadirs in sordid behavior. Those who stayed behind did so at the request of the police; their punishment ranged from $25 traffic fines to ninety days in jail for indecent exposure. Of the 6,000 to 8,000 people supposedly involved in the fracas, a total of 50 were treated for injuries at the local hospital. (For a better perspective on motorcycle riots it helps to keep in mind that more than 50,000 Americans die each year as the result of automobile accidents.)

Nobody has ever accused the Hell's Angels of wanton killing, at least not in court . . . but it boggles the nerves to consider what might happen if the outlaws were ever deemed legally responsible for even three or four human deaths, by accident or otherwise. Probably every motorcycle rider in California would be jerked off the streets and ground into hamburger.

For a lot of reasons that are often contradictory, the sight and sound of a man on a motorcycle has an unpleasant effect on the vast majority of Americans who drive cars. At one point in the wake of the Hell's Angels uproar a reporter for the *New York Herald Tribune*[5] did a long article on the motorcycle scene and decided in the course of his research that "there is something about the sight of a passing motorcyclist that tempts many automobile drivers to commit murder."

Nearly everyone who has ridden a bike for any length of time will agree. The highways are crowded with people who drive as if their sole purpose in getting behind the wheel is to avenge every wrong ever done them by man, beast or fate. The only thing that keeps them in line is their own fear of death, jail, and lawsuits . . . which are much less likely if they can find a motorcycle to challenge, instead of another two-thousand-pound car of a concrete abutment. A motorcyclist has to drive as if everybody else on the road is out to kill him. A few of them are, and many of those who aren't are just as dangerous—because the only thing that can alter their careless, ingrained driving habits is a threat of punishment, either legal or physical, and there is nothing about a motorcycle to threaten any man in a car.[6] A bike is totally vulnerable; its only defense is maneuverability, and every accident situation is potentially fatal—especially on a freeway, where there is no room to fall without being run over almost instantly. Despite these hazards, California—where freeways are a way of life—is by long odds the nation's biggest motorcycle market. . . .

Of all their habits and predilections that society finds alarming, the outlaws' disregard for the time-honored concept of an eye for an eye is the one that frightens people most. . . . Their claim that they don't start trouble is probably true more often than not, but their idea of provocation is dangerously broad, and one of their main difficulties is that almost nobody else seems to understand it. Yet they have a very simple rule of thumb; in any argument a fellow Angel is *always right*. To disagree with a Hell's Angel is to be *wrong*—and to persist in being wrong is an open challenge.

Despite everything psychiatrists and Freudian castrators have to say 25 about the Angels, they are tough, mean, and potentially dangerous as packs of wild boar. The moment a fight begins, any leather fetishes or inadequacy feelings are entirely beside the point, as anyone who has ever tangled with them will sadly testify. When you get in an argument with a group of outlaw motorcyclists, your chances of emerging unmaimed depend on the number of heavy-handed allies you can muster in the time it takes to smash a beer bottle. In this league, sportsmanship is for old liberals and young fools. . . .

One of the Frisco Angels explained it without any frills: "Our motto, man, is 'All on One and One on All.' You mess with an Angel and you've got twenty-five of them on your neck. I mean, they'll break you but good, baby."

The outlaws take the "all on one" concept so seriously that it is written into the club charter as Bylaw Number 10: "When an Angel punches a non-Angel, all other Angels will participate." . . .

The dividing line between outlaws and the square majority is subject to change at any moment, and many respectable clubs have queered their image overnight. All it takes is a noisy fracas, a police report, and a little publicity . . . and suddenly they're outlaws. In most cases this leads to the breakup of the club, with a majority of the members feeling hurt and scandalized that such a thing could have happened. But those few responsible for the trouble will no longer be welcome in respectable circles. Technically, they become "independents," but that term is a misnomer because any rider who applies it to himself is already an outlaw anyway. All he lacks is a club to join, and he will sooner or later find one. The motorcycle fraternity is very tight—on both sides of the law—and the most extreme viewpoints are represented by the American Motorcycle Association and the Hell's Angels. There is no status in the middle, and people who are serious enough about motorcycles to join an AMA club will not take rejection lightly. Like converts to Communism or Catholicism, Hell's Angels who were once AMA members take their outlaw role more seriously than the others.

The Angels are too personally disorganized to have any clear perspective on the world, but they admire intelligence, and some of their leaders are surprisingly articulate. Chapter presidents have no set term in office, and a strong one, like Barger, will remain unchallenged until he goes to jail, gets killed, or finds his own reasons for hanging up the colors. The outlaws are very respectful of power, even if they have to create their own image of it. Despite the anarchic possibilities of the machines they ride and worship, they insist that their main concern in life is "to be a righteous Angel," which requires a loud obedience to the party line. They are intensely aware of *belonging*, of being able to depend on each other. Because of this, they look down on independents, who usually feel so wretched—once they've adopted the outlaw frame of reference—that they will do almost anything to get in a club.

"I don't know why," said an ex-Angel, "but you almost have to join a 30 club. If you don't, you'll never be accepted anywhere. If you don't wear any colors, you're sort of in between—and you're nothing."

This desperate sense of unity is crucial to the outlaw mystique. If the Hell's Angels are outcasts from society, as they freely admit, then it is all the more necessary that they defend each other from attack by "the others"—mean squares, enemy gangs, or armed agents of the Main Cop.° When somebody punches a lone Angel every one of them feels threatened. They are so wrapped up in their own image that they can't conceive of anybody challenging the colors without being fully prepared to take on the whole army. . . .

For most of the year the Hell's Angels are pretty quiet. Around home, on their own turf, they cultivate a kind of forced coexistence with the local police. But on almost any summer weekend one of the half dozen chapters might decide to roam on its own, twenty or thirty strong, booming along the roads to some small town with a token police force, to descend like a gang of pirates on some hapless tavern owner whose only solace is a soaring beer profit that might be wiped out at any moment by the violent destruction of his premises. With luck, he'll get off with nothing more than a few fights, broken glasses or a loud and public sex rally involving anything from indecent exposure to a gang-bang in one of the booths.

These independent forays often make news, but it is on their two major runs—Labor Day and the Fourth—that the hell and headlines break loose. At least twice a year outlaws from all parts of the state gather somewhere in California for a king-size brain-bender.

A run is a lot of things to the Angels: a party, an exhibition and an exercise in solidarity. "You never know how many Angels there are until you go on a big run," says Zorro. "Some get snuffed, some drop out, some go to the slammer and there's always new guys who've joined. That's why the runs are important—you find out who's on your side." . . .

Main Cop: Thompson's term for centralized police authority.

Anybody who has ever seen the Angels on a run will agree that rural 35
Californians are likely to reject the spectacle as not right for their way of
living. It is a human zoo on wheels. An outlaw whose normal, day-to-
day appearance is enough to disrupt traffic will appear on a run with his
beard dyed green or bright red, his eyes hidden behind orange goggles,
and a brass ring in his nose. Others wear capes and Apache headbands,
or oversize sunglasses and peaked Prussian helmets. Earrings, *Wehrmacht°*
headgear and German Iron Crosses are virtually part of the uniform—like
the grease-caked Levis, the sleeveless vests and all those fine tattoos:
"Mother," "Dolly," "Hitler," "Jack the Ripper," swastikas, daggers, skulls,
"LSD," "Love," "Rape" and the inevitable Hell's Angels insignia. . . .

"When you walk into a place where people can see you, you want to
look as repulsive and repugnant as possible," said one. "We are complete
social outcasts—outsiders against society. And that's the way we want to
be. Anything good, we laugh at. We're bastards to the world and they're
bastards to us."

"I don't really care if people think we're bad," said another. "I think
this is what really keeps us going. We fight society and society fights us.
It doesn't bother me." . . .

The outlaw stance is patently antisocial, although most Angels, as
individuals, are naturally social creatures. The contradiction is deep-
rooted and has parallels on every level of American society. Sociologists
call it "alienation," or "anomie." It is a sense of being cut off, or left
out of whatever society one was presumably meant to be a part of. In
a strongly motivated society the victims of anomie are usually extreme
cases, isolated from each other by differing viewpoints or personal quirks
too private for any broad explanation.

But in a society with no central motivation, so far adrift and
puzzled with itself that its President[7] feels called upon to appoint a
Committee on National Goals, a sense of alienation is likely to be very
popular—especially among people young enough to shrug off the guilt
they're supposed to feel for deviating from a goal or purpose they never
understood in the first place. Let the old people wallow in the shame
of having failed. The laws they made to preserve a myth are no longer
pertinent; the so-called American Way begins to seem like a dike made
of cheap cement, with many more leaks than the law has fingers to plug.
America has been breeding mass anomie since the end of World War II.
It is not a political thing, but the sense of new realities, of urgency, anger
and sometimes desperation in a society where even the highest authorities seem to be grasping at straws.

Wehrmacht: unified armed forces of Nazi Germany from 1935 to 1946.

In the terms of our Great Society the Hell's Angels and their ilk are 40
losers—dropouts, failures and malcontents. They are rejects looking for a
way to get even with a world in which they are only a problem. The Hell's
Angels are not visionaries, but diehards, and if they are the forerunners or
the vanguard of anything it is not the "moral revolution" in vogue on college campuses, but a fast-growing legion of young unemployables whose
untapped energy will inevitably find the same kind of destructive outlet that "outlaws" like the Hell's Angels have been finding for years. The
difference between the student radicals and the Hell's Angels is that
the students are rebelling against the past, while the Angels are fighting the
future. Their only common ground is their disdain for the present, or
the status quo. . . .

The widespread appeal of the Angels is worth pondering. Unlike most
other rebels, the Angels have given up hope that the world is going to
change for them. They assume, on good evidence, that the people who
run the social machinery have little use for outlaw motorcyclists, and
they are reconciled to being losers. But instead of losing quietly, one
by one, they have banded together with a mindless kind of loyalty and
moved outside the framework, for good or ill. They may not have an
answer, but at least they are still on their feet. One night about halfway
through one of their weekly meetings I thought of Joe Hill on his way
to face a Utah firing squad and saying his final words: "Don't mourn.
Organize." It is safe to say that no Hell's Angel has ever heard of Joe Hill
or would know a Wobbly from a bushmaster, but there is something very
similar about the attitudes. The Industrial Workers of the World° had
serious blueprints for society, while the Hell's Angels mean only to defy
the social machinery. There is no talk among the Angels of "building a
better world," yet their reactions to the world they live in are rooted in
the same kind of anarchic, para-legal sense of conviction that brought the
armed wrath of the Establishment down on the Wobblies. There is
the same kind of suicidal loyalty, the same kind of in-group rituals and
nicknames, and above all the same feeling of constant warfare with an
unjust world. The Wobblies were losers, and so are the Angels . . . and if
every loser in this country today rode a motorcycle the whole highway
system would have to be modified.

There is an important difference between the words "loser" and "outlaw." One is passive and the other is active, and the main reasons the
Angels are such good copy is that they are acting out the day-dreams of
millions of losers who don't wear any defiant insignia and who don't
know how to be outlaws.

Industrial Workers of the World: commonly termed "Wobblies," the IWW was an
international labor union founded in Chicago in 1905.

Notes

1. The Angels' old ladies are generally opposed to B.O. "My old man went for two months once without taking a shower," a girl from Richmond recalls. "He wanted to see what it would be like to live up to the reputation people gave us . . . I've got sinus and I can't smell that good anyhow, but it finally got so bad I sez, 'Go pull out the other mattress — I ain't gonna asleep with you till you shower'."

2. Numerous court appearances crippled Tiny's income toward the end of 1965, and in June of 1966 he was forced to take an indefinite leave of absence to attend his own trial on a charge of forcible rape.

3. By the middle of 1966 the war in Vietnam had put several of the Angels back in the money. The volume of military shipping through the Oakland Army Terminal caused such a demand for handlers and loaders that Hell's Angels were hired almost in spite of themselves.

4. Now defunct.

5. Now defunct.

6. Preetam Bobo tells a story about a man in a "big new car" who forced him off the road on Highway 40 one Sunday afternoon in the 1950s. "The dirty little bastard kept running up on my taillight," said Preetam, "until finally I just pulled over and stopped. The other guys had seen it, so we decided to teach the bastard a lesson. Man, we swarmed all over him . . . We whipped on his hood with chains, tore off his aerial and smashed every window we could reach . . . all this at about seventy miles an hour, man. He didn't even slow down. He was terrified."

7. Eisenhower.

Understanding the Text

1. What is a Hell's Angels "run"? Why is it central to their identity as a group?

2. Describe the typical member of the Hell's Angels in the 1960s, including ethnicity, economic status, educational background, personal beliefs, and geographic history.

3. Why is Hollister, California, central to the story of the Hell's Angels?

Reflection and Response

4. How does the Hell's Angels initiation ceremony, in which their jeans are permanently fouled, serve as a symbol for what they see as their status in the world? What other aspects of outlaw-motorcycle culture symbolically support this view of themselves?

5. Although Thompson insists that the Hell's Angels see themselves as "losers," as social outcasts who have no chance of integrating into mainstream society, they nonetheless reproduce many of the values of the American mainstream. Discuss the ways in which the Angels are actually traditional, even conservative, in their outlook and way of life.

6. As with much of Thompson's book-length study of the Hell's Angels, this selection begins with a personal anecdote about the time he spent riding with them. Does this kind of insider journalism give him more credibility as a writer or undermine his factual claims about the subculture? Does a journalist, who traditionally aims for objectivity, cross a line when he becomes part of his own story? Is the distinction between objective journalism and personal experience even relevant?

Making Connections

7. At one point, Thompson parallels the Hell's Angels and the Wobblies (Industrial Workers of the World), a radical community prominent in the early twentieth century. Research the Wobblies and write a short essay discussing the ways in which this group challenged the prevailing values of their time.

8. Thompson explicitly links the early motorcycle outlaws to the demobilized soldiers who moved west after the Civil War in 1865 and became, in many cases, the prototypical American cowboys and gunslingers. How do the motorcycle outlaws continue the long tradition of American rebellion, individualism, and autonomy? How do their values reflect the values of the men who roamed the Old West?

9. Watch *The Wild One*, the 1953 film that introduced the American public to the outlaw-biker subculture. In what ways does this film provide a template for the Hell's Angels development as a community? How did members pattern their behavior and appearance on the Hollywood representation of their community? What other subcultures have been influenced by media representations of themselves?

Military BRATS = Bright. Resilient. Active. Talented. Successful.

BJ Gallagher

The author of more than twenty books, BJ Gallagher holds a degree in sociology. For many years she served as the manager of training and development for the *Los Angeles Times*, and has conducted seminars for a host of multinational corporations. Gallagher's work has been featured on the *CBS Evening News*, the *Today Show*, *Fox News*, PBS, CNN, and many other programs. Her book *Peacock in a Land of Penguins* was an international best-seller, translated into twenty-one languages. Having grown up in an active-duty military family, Gallagher speaks out on behalf of military children.

What's in a name? Plenty! Names are very personal, very powerful, in conveying identity, family lineage, historical tradition, group affiliation, and much more.

When I was a girl, my name was Barbara. It was a lovely name that my parents gave me when I was born. "Barbara" conveys intelligence, strength, and just the right amount of femininity, without being too frilly. I liked my given name—but apparently other people didn't, because they were always shortening it to "Barbie," "Babs," "Bobbie," or just plain "Barb" (which I hated). As a child, I couldn't find my voice to correct people: "Excuse me, my name is Barbara. Please call me Barbara." Instead I would just grit my teeth in silent resentment while others changed my name willy-nilly without my consent.

When I turned 18 and graduated from high school in Illinois and headed west to attend college in Southern California, it seemed the perfect time to reconfigure my name so that people would stop shortening it. I decided to go with my initials, "BJ"—short for Barbara Jo. *"That'll fix 'em,"* I thought to myself. *"They can't shorten that!"* My mother had always referred to me as "BJ" on her calendar, with reminder notes to herself: "BJ to the orthodontist" or "BJ to piano lesson" or "BJ's parent/ teacher meeting." It felt good to reclaim my name in a way that would stop other people from messing with it.

Today, military brats are having a similar struggle with their own name. I care about the issue because I am one of those brats. I am the daughter of an Air Force pilot who served his country for 30-plus years, fighting in three wars, moving his family dozens of times across three continents. I am my father's daughter. I'm a military brat—always have been, always will be.

But recently I learned that someone is messing with our name. Two women, Debbie and Jennifer Fink, have taken it upon themselves to change the name that generations of military kids have worn as a badge of honor. The Finks have decided that we should be called CHAMPS instead of BRATS. These civilian women have not served in uniform—nor were they raised in military families—yet they have decided that they know what's best for the children of today's armed forces!

For the sake of discussion, let's give the Fink ladies the benefit of the doubt and assume that their intentions are good. Still, good intentions do not give you the right to change a child's name without her consent—nor do good intentions give you the right to change the name of an entire group of millions of children (and adult children) without their consent.

What's next? Are you going to try to ban the term "rug rat" in favor of "carpet cutie"? Are you going to replace "ankle biter" with "foot kisser"? Do you plan to insist that *The Little Rascals* be re-named "The Little Angels" instead? When will the language police stop your misguided attempts to whitewash other people's reality?

Seriously, the whole political correctness thing has gotten way out of control. The Finks' campaign to change "BRATS" to "CHAMPS" is both ridiculous and insulting. The term "military brat" is a timeless, traditional badge of honor. Who are the Finks to change our name without our permission?

> *"BRAT is not just an American term of endearment — it is an internationally recognized term that unites military children around the world."*

Perhaps the Finks just didn't do their homework. Since they have no military background, they don't understand military culture, in which BRAT is a term of affection and respect, connoting a certain element of spunkiness and adventurousness.

In civilian culture, the term "brat" means "spoiled child" so it's understandable that the Finks might be confused about the very different meaning of the term "military brat." But in military culture, kids are anything *but* spoiled—we are disciplined, responsible, and we have enormous respect for authority. The Finks' intentions may be good, but their campaign is way off target.

If one were of a cynical mindset, one might suspect that the Fink's re-branding campaign is simply a money-making boondoggle—a creative way to sell books and get grants from organizations that support military families. But ask any of today's service members and their families, and they will tell you that such funds would be far better spent on suicide-prevention programs for service members, financial counseling for military families, training more service dogs for veterans with PTSD, and other services and support. A campaign to change the name of military brats is money wasted on something none of us asked for and none of us want.

BRAT is not just an American term of endearment—it is an internationally recognized term that unites military children around the world. While the precise origin of the term "military brat" is unknown, there is some evidence that it dates back hundreds of years into the British Empire, and originally stood for "British Regiment Attached Traveler." Military cultures in Australia, India (also called Fauji Brats), Canada (also called Base Brats), Pakistan, the Philippines, New Zealand, the United Kingdom (also called Pad Brats or Patch Brats). Also known as "camp followers," there have been such military dependent subcultures in many parts of the world for thousands of years.

I didn't like people changing my name when I was a girl and I don't like people doing it now. My name is BJ Gallagher and I am a military brat. I am the child of a warrior. I am spunky and spirited. My father trained me to be fearless. He set high standards and pushed me to be an achiever. He trained me to lead. He taught me the value of honesty and integrity. He showed me how to respect the chain of command, while not abdicating my personal accountability.

I may not have been able to speak up when I was a child and people tried to change my name, but I'm not a little girl anymore. I can speak up now. I am not anybody's "little CHAMP." I am a military BRAT . . . and proud of it.

Understanding the Text

1. What occasion prompts Gallagher to write her essay?
2. What is the difference between the definition of the word "brat" in everyday usage and in military-family usage?

Reflection and Response

3. Unlike the members of other subcultures, military brats seem anything but rebellious. How do they nonetheless challenge the dominant culture?
4. Gallagher begins her essay by pointing out the power of names in conveying identity, group affiliation, and historical traditions. In fact, she responds with indignation to attempts to change timeworn appellations. Discuss at least three examples of the power of particular group names.
5. How does Gallagher establish a specific tone? How does her use of language reflect her personality?

Making Connections

6. Not only do the children of military families constitute a distinct community but members of the military themselves might be considered a subculture. Investigate military life and reflect on how the values and practices of soldiers and support personnel form a distinct system within the larger American culture.

7. Visit Debbie and Jennifer Fink's Operation C.H.A.M.P.S. website (http://www. operationchamps.org). Do you think that changing the name of the children of military personnel from *brats* to *champs* is warranted? What might be an argument in favor of the name change?

The Unwanted

William Finnegan

William Finnegan is a long-time staff writer at the *New Yorker*. The author of several books, Finnegan has twice won the John Bartlow Martin Award for Public Interest Magazine Journalism. A longer form of "The Unwanted" won the Sidney Hillman Award for Magazine Reporting in 1998 and was republished as part of his book *Cold New World*, which portrays the dismal conditions of various marginalized American communities at the turn of this century. In this piece, Finnegan recounts the months he spent with the adolescent skinheads — violent, working-class white supremacists — of Lancaster, California.

"**S**harp" stands for Skinheads Against Racial Prejudice. It is not, as I first thought, a local Antelope Valley sect. Skinheads claim Sharp throughout the United States, in Europe, even, reportedly, in Japan. There is no formal organization — just an antiracist ideology, a street-fighting tradition, and a few widely recognized logos, usually worn on jacket patches. Sharp's *raison d'etre* is its evil twin, the better-known white-supremacist and neo-Nazi skinhead movement. . . . Many, if not most, skinheads in this country are actually nonpolitical (and nonracist) and simply resent the disastrous public image that the boneheads give them. Sharps do more than resent it.

"It's all about working-class" — this was the surprising reply I kept getting from the Antelope Valley Sharps when I first asked why they were skinheads. All of them, I found, were amateur social historians, determined to rescue the skinhead movement — or simply skinhead, as they call it — from the international disrepute into which it had fallen. In their version, which seems broadly accurate, the original skinheads emerged in England in the mid-sixties out of other youth cultures, notably the "hard mods"° and the Rude Boys, stylish Jamaicans who wore porkpie hats° and listened to reggae and ska.° Skinheads were clean-cut, working class, nonracist ("two-tone"), and tough. They loathed hippies for reasons of both class and hygiene, loved soccer and beer, fighting and ska, scooters and Fred Perry tennis shirts. . . . They wore extra-shiny boots, extra-wide Levi's, and narrow braces. The meticulous, distinctive look they developed has been described as a "caricature of the model worker."

hard mods: 1960s working-class British subculture known for drug use and dapper clothing.
porkpie hat: man's hat with a flat crown and a brim turned up all around.
ska: uptempo Jamaican musical genre originating in the 1950s.

134

For a detailed history of skinhead, the Antelope Valley Sharps all urged on me a book, published in Scotland, called *Spirit of '69: A Skinhead Bible.*

By the seventies, the movement had been hijacked, according to the Sharps, by the anti-immigrant National Front in England. Skinheads had already become notorious for "Paki-bashing," but that was at first less racial, the Sharps insisted, than territorial. In any case, it was the second wave of British skinhead that crossed over to the United States, in the late seventies, as part of the great punk-rock cultural exchange, and by then neo-Nazism and white supremacism were definitely in the mix. Traditional American racist and neo-Nazi groups began to see the political potential in skinhead in the mid-eighties, and a host of unholy alliances were formed between racist skinheads and old-line extremist organizations such as the Aryan Nations, White Aryan Resistance, the Church of the Creator, and the Ku Klux Klan. The Anti-Defamation League, which monitors neo-Nazi skinheads in more than thirty countries, estimated in 1995 that there were only thirty-five hundred active neo-Nazi skinheads in the United States—a figure apparently derived from a narrow definition of its subjects, since there were, from everything I could tell, more white-supremacist gang members than that in California alone. But after a decade of hate crimes and racist violence, white-power skinheads were becoming increasingly familiar figures in the American social landscape, particularly among teenagers, who tended to know much more about them and their rabid views than adults did.

"The boneheads are looking *forward* to a race war."

"They like Bic their heads, and grow out a little goatee so they look 5 like the devil, just to scare other kids."

"They're all on some harsh drug."

"*Somebody's* got to stand up to these guys," Darius Houston said.

Six or seven Sharps were sitting around Jacob Kroeger's mother's house in Lancaster. They were a picturesque lot in their boots and braces, their extra-short ("flooded") jeans, their Andy Capp-type "snap caps."° . . . Some sported "suedeheads,"° others had skulls that gleamed. Most were white kids and, though girls came and went, it was clear that all the main players were boys. They were voluble with me, and easy with each other, even though the mood that evening was rather grim and besieged. This was late 1995, and Darius Houston's girlfriend, Christina Fava, had just been involved in a nasty incident with the Nazi Low Riders. It seemed that a girl from the NLRs had called her a "nigger lover" in a hallway

---

snap caps: flat, billed caps worn by the type of working-class British man portrayed in the Andy Capp cartoon series.
suedehead: close-cropped hair used to distinguish members of an offshoot of skinhead subculture.

at Antelope Valley High School, where Christina was a junior. A black student named Todd Jordan, who knew and cared nothing about skinheads, had become involved on Christina's side, and the next day half a dozen NLRs had jumped Todd on a deserted athletic field, stabbing him five times with a screwdriver. Todd was now in the hospital. The doctors were saying that he would not play basketball—he was on the school team—again. Christina, for her part, was transferring to a new school.

And this wasn't the only violent attack of the preceding weeks. Less than a month before, some two dozen NLRs and their allies had stormed Jacob's house during a party, knocking down the front door, chasing everyone out, breaking windows, smashing holes in the walls. The house was still being repaired, as I could see, and there was some question about whether or not it had been insured against Bonehead Attack.

Somehow, I said, being a Sharp seemed to mean, more than anything 10 else, a lot of fighting with white-power skinheads.

I was wrong, I was assured.

"It's the music, the fashions, the friendships, the whole lifestyle."

"Everybody's got everybody else's back."

"It's all about working class."

This curious, almost un-American class consciousness among the 15 Antelope Valley Sharps turned out, upon examination, to be a very American miscellany. The kids themselves came from a wide range of backgrounds, everything from two-parent middle-class families to drug-addled welfare mothers who dumped them on the streets as adolescents. For some, "working-class" meant, I learned, simply having a job, any job, as opposed to being a "bum." For others, it was synonymous with "blue-collar," and it distinguished them from richer kids who might decide to be skinheads and buy all the gear but who weren't really streetwise and so might just have to be relieved of their new twelve-hole Doc Martens.

Sharp membership was itself in constant flux. Earlier that year, there had been scores of kids in the valley claiming Sharp, but the antics of some of the "fresh cuts" had started causing problems for the inner circle, who were tougher and more deeply committed to skinhead and had to tell the new guys to cool it. There were still dozens of kids "backing it up" when I started visiting—young antiracists who said they were punk rockers or traditional skinheads or unity skins—but only a handful actually claiming Sharp. Hanging out with the Sharps and their allies, I came to see that there was, in fact, much more to their little brotherhood than rumbling with the boneheads. They were a haven, a structure, a style, a sensibility, set against the bleakness, uncertainty, and suffocating racial tension of teenage life in the valley.

For Darius, in particular, Sharp was a godsend. An orphan since his mother died when he was thirteen, he had been a skater and a punk rocker before discovering skinhead. As a half-black kid in a largely white town, being raised by various white relatives—it was his white mother's family that had settled in the Antelope Valley—he had always been something of an outsider. Skinhead, as he understood it, was a complete, ready-made aesthetic and way of life. It was exotic yet comfortable; it fit. He identified with its "blue-collar pride," underground energy, and its music, and he was soon playing bass in a multiracial ska band called the Leisures. Darius was a stickler for the dress code. Indeed, one of his main complaints about the boneheads seemed to be that they were always doing "cheesy" things like writing slogans in felt pen on the jeans and T-shirts and bomber jackets, instead of getting proper patches. He was planning, he told me, to get a huge tattoo on his back of a crucified skinhead with the caption THE LAST RESORT, which was, among other things, the name of a legendary skinhead music shop in London. Unfortunately, the mere idea of a black skinhead drove neo-Nazi skinheads into a fury, so Darius had been fighting on a regular basis for years. He was a skilled fighter—he once showed me a kick-boxing trophy he had won—but the backup that the other Sharps provided was still, for Darius, a lifesaver. Going to school had become too dangerous, so he was on independent study. After graduating, he said, he planned to join the Navy and become a medical technician. He was eighteen, beefy, soft-spoken, watchful, with skin the color of light mahogany. When we met, he was homeless and had been sleeping on a couch in Jacob's mother's house.

> "Sharp's *raison d'etre* is its evil twin, the better-known white-supremacist and neo-Nazi skinhead movement."

Billy Anderson, another Sharp, was sleeping on the other couch. He was seventeen, pink-skinned, big-boned, round-faced. He came from a chaotic family, plagued by alcoholism and drug abuse. According to both Billy and his older sister, a punk rocker who lived down below, their mother, who had been on public assistance most of her life, was a methamphetamine addict, given to tearing up carpets and tearing out phone wires in search of secret microphones; her current husband was an alcoholic; her previous husband was a tweaker; their favorite aunt died of a heroin overdose; and their father, who lived in a trailer park in Compton, was a pothead. "It's so wack to see your parents all tweaked on drugs," Billy said. "That's why I've never tried any drugs." Drinking and fighting were all right, though, he thought, particularly if you were fighting boneheads, whose crudity and racism gave the name of his beloved skinhead a white-trash taint. Like Darius, Billy was on independent study when we met and was planning to join the Navy. He had been into skinhead since he was fifteen, and he always seemed to be "dressed down"—in immaculate, classic skinhead gear—which was a feat, since he was usually homeless and broke.

Jacob Kroeger still had his hair when we first met, though he was getting ready to become a full-fledged Sharp. Eighteen, sardonic, fair-haired, he was a rare, second-generation Lancaster native. Jacob struck me as a street-fighting liberal (an even rarer breed), so affronted by the boneheads' racism that he was ready to defend his town's good name with his fists. After a clash with the NLRs that left one of them with a gash in his scalp, Jacob told me, "I just hope it knocks some *sense* into his head." His mother was often away with a boyfriend, leaving her house—a modest ranch-style bungalow in a seedy older tract—to become, at least for a while, the Sharps' main hangout. . . .

The Malones' house was NLRs' hangout. . . . Though I stopped by 20 many times, day and night, I never saw Mrs. Malone there. She worked in a plastics factory in Pasadena, more than an hour's drive away, and, according to Tim, she left the house at dawn and got home only late in the evening. When I first met Tim, who was seventeen, he had just spent two months in jail; he had been locked up as a suspect in the Todd Jordan stabbing, but had been released for lack of evidence. He was wiry and well built, with close-cropped dark hair and, tattooed on the back of his neck, an Iron Cross. He described himself as "more of the Gestapo Storm Trooper type than a political Nazi—the type that's ready to go to war over things. There's gonna be a race war around the year 2000."

I asked Tim how he had become a Nazi. He said that his father had been a Hell's Angel, "so it was kind of inherited." His dad drank, did speed, and abused his mother—that was why his parents broke up. The family had lived in a black neighborhood in Montclair, east of Los Angeles, where Tim, at the age of ten, joined a local Crips set for self-protection. He was the middle brother of three, and his joining a black gang did not please his brothers. "Both my brothers was punk rockers, into speed metal, and they used to beat me up, trying to teach me a lesson," he said. "I thank them for it now. I was on the wrong road. You gotta stick with your own race. Now ain't nothing I hate more than a wigger." (This charming term means "white nigger.") The news that Tim was an ex-Crip° helped explain why he often sounded like a white thug doing a flawless imitation of a black thug. He even had a set of elaborate

---

Crip: member of an extensive, mainly African-American gang centered in Los Angeles.

hand and arm gestures that I had never before seen a white kid use—the same moves gangsta rappers use in performance. . . .

The ranks of the boneheads were swelling, Tim said. Everywhere he went in the Antelope Valley, guys were throwing Nazi salutes at him. "Some of them I don't even know," he said. "We get hooked up that way." Standing in the Malones' front yard, talking with Tim and his friends, I did notice a startling number of passing cars honking in greeting, with white arms often jutting out the windows. The NLRs would respond with quick, stiff-armed salutes and the occasional deep shout, "White power!" Then they would grin. This, I thought, was why the local Sharps called their hometown Klancaster.

"When we first come up here, there was hardly any blacks," Tim told me. "So there wasn't much trouble. But then they started hearing about this place, wanting to come up here, starting stuff, thinking they're hard. So we're just trying to push 'em back."

The NLRs' main enemies, however, were the Sharps. "Most all Sharps are straight pussies," Tim said vehemently. "They're just a bunch of preppy white boys who want to run with the blacks because they're afraid to fight them."

The one Sharp who most infuriated Tim and his friends was, of course, 25 Darius Houston. "There's no such thing as a black skinhead," Tim fumed. "Skinheads are *white*. Everybody knows that. Darius is bullshit."

I asked Tim if he knew where skinhead originated.

"Germany," he said. He wasn't sure when.

I asked if he had ever read anything about skinheads.

"There really ain't no book about skinheads," he said. (There are many.) He had heard about a magazine, though, a neo-Nazi "skinzine" called *Blood and Honor*, published in Long Beach, California. He asked if I could help him find some copies. "They'll hold some concerts out here for us, we heard."

On the whole, the neo-Nazi skinheads I met in the Antelope Valley 30 seemed to have only vague, subpolitical connections to the white-supremacist world beyond their turf—through the methamphetamine trade, through prison gangs and outlaw motorcycle gangs, through racist music . . . They knew and admired groups like the Ku Klux Klan and White Aryan Resistance but, as far as I could tell, had little or no contact with such organizations.

● ● ●

Sharps often struck me as a fragile, if not endangered species. It was partly their hated identification with their enemies, the racists, by the public. One Christmas Eve a group of Sharps, including Darius, Johnny

Suttle, Billy Anderson, and Jacob Kroeger, tried to attend a midnight mass in Lancaster. They slipped into a rear pew, perfectly silent and respectful. Then they noticed that the other worshippers were looking over their shoulders in alarm. This was a largely black and Latino congregation, and when they saw skinheads, they saw possible racist attack. The Sharps were asked to leave, and weeks later they were still bummed out about it. "We're pariahs," Jacob said.

As pariahs, the Sharps dearly loved to "clique up," as they called it, or even just to run into one another unexpectedly. Once, while I was on the highway with a bunch of Sharps, a fresh cut named Fred recalled the time he looked over and saw, in the car next to him, a bunch of Sharps. "It was so cool! Just right there on the freeway!" I asked Fred how he knew the other car wasn't boneheads. "Because it was a nice car," he said matter-of-factly. "And I've never heard of a rich bonehead, have you?"

We were traveling at the time in a two-car convoy and, when the other car broke down, we had to cram nine passengers into my rented sedan. Some of the Sharps were beside themselves with excitement. Justin Molnar kept shouting, "We are rolling *so deep!*" He made it sound like we were the Corner Pocket Crips on patrol in the 'hood. In fact, we were going to a ska show at the Whiskey A Go Go, the venerable club on Sunset Boulevard.

That was a curious evening. Only the headliners, a band called Hepcat met with the complete approval of the Antelope Valley Sharps. The other acts had all "sold out," it seemed, in various ways—they played their ska too fast, or mixed in some Satanism, or some punk. . . . Johnny Suttle was also disgusted by action down in the mosh pit. "You're not *supposed* to pit to this music," he told me angrily. "All these hippies and punks think they can just shave their heads and throw themselves around at a ska show like they own the place, like they're real skins. They're not. They can't."

After the show, in the parking lot behind the club, Johnny stunned 35 me by suddenly throwing open the door of my car and scrabbling frantically under the front seat, shouting, "Where's my blade?" Before I could ask what he thought he was doing, he came up with an evil-looking throwing knife and was gone. It seemed that someone had spotted a group of boneheads, and dozens of skins from the ska show crowd were now off in hot pursuit. As things turned out, they didn't catch them, but Johnny and the others returned grimly exhilarated from the chase. I was unhappy about the knife, and said so. Nobody seemed overly impressed. I was also appalled that the Sharps were so quick to decide that perfect strangers were mortal enemies. How did they know their prey were

boneheads? Boneheads, after all, hate ska and rarely come to Hollywood. They just knew, they said. You could tell.

You really could tell, I found, at another show I attended with the Sharps. It was an oi show in San Bernardino. Oi music, which gets its name from a Cockney greeting, is a hard form of punk rock, and it appeals to the whole range of skinheads. The headliners at the San Bernardino show were a cult band from Britain called the Business, who had been around so long that they even appeared in *The Skinhead Bible*. The Antelope Valley Sharps were deeply thrilled to be seeing them, and before the show I took snapshots with Johnny's camera of each of them standing next to bored-looking members of the band. Darius, Jacob, Juan, Johnny, and four or five others had made the long trip over the mountains in a heavy rain. San Bernadino is an old, hard-used city east of Los Angeles. On a recent listing of 207 American cities ranked as places for bringing up children, San Bernadino came in number 207. The oi show was held in an old wrestling arena near the railroad tracks.

There were several hundred skinheads inside, most of them white but many of them Latino or Asian. Cliques milled around, exchanging elaborate tribal greetings with other cliques and taking snapshots together. All was mellow, all was unity, I was assured. No boneheads had come. A couple of punk bands played, and there was some moderate thrashing in the pit, which was a big, brightly lit, cement-floored space in front of the stage. I retreated to one of the wooden bleachers that rose on three sides of the arena. And that's where I was, looking down on the crowd, when the Orange County Skins arrived. They were in uniform and information. Their uniform consisted of black combat boots, white trousers, and the white tank tops known as "wife beaters." Their formation was a sort of flying wedge, which knocked people aside with swift, efficient violence as they swept toward the middle of the pit. There were no more than thirty of them, but they were all big, muscular white guys and their paramilitary coordination overwhelmed each bit of startled resistance. They easily seized the center of the arena, under the lights, turned to the stunned crowd, and raised their arms in Nazi salutes, bellowing, "White power! White power!"

There was a lengthy pause, during which everyone seemed to consider the boots of the invaders. Whoever approached them first was certain to get his teeth kicked in.

Then the crowd rushed the boneheads, and a bloody mélée began. It seemed to be all boots and fists. Security at the door had been very tight—a guard had even taken away my pens, tartly demonstrating how someone could jab out my eyes with one of them—so the possibilities for injury presumably had some limits. I caught glimpses of Sharps I

knew, flailing away—particularly Darius, who is tall and, as a black skin, seemed to be the focus of a great deal of Nazi fury. But Darius stayed on his feet, blessedly, and seemed to have plenty of help as he spun and kicked and punched. There were a couple of distinct rounds of fighting, as the arena's security force struggled to push the combatants apart. The Nazis were badly outnumbered but preternaturally fierce, and each time they seemed to be contained and moving toward the exit they regrouped and attacked in another direction.

Understanding the Text

1. What is the difference between a "Sharp" and a "bonehead"?

2. Why do the Sharps call their hometown "Klancaster"?

3. One of the skinheads that Finnegan portrays declares, "We're pariahs" (par. 31). What does he mean?

Reflection and Response

4. What methods does Finnegan use in his quest to understand the skinhead subculture? How do his methods influence his style of writing?

5. Several of the skinheads that Finnegan writes about come from homes plagued by violence, alcoholism, drug abuse, and broken marriages. How might such conditions affect the values and practices of the skinhead subculture?

6. Discuss in depth the role of music in the skinhead scene. What kind of music do the skinheads prefer? Why? How does it function as a way of unifying the group?

Making Connections

7. Finnegan mentions that the father of one of the Nazi Low Riders was a member of the Hell's Angels motorcycle gang. Although they originated in different times and places, what characteristics do these two subcultures share? Explain possible reasons for these commonalities, with specific reference to Hunter S. Thompson's "Hell's Angels" (p. 117).

8. Research the original skinhead movement in England, and then discuss the differences between the British and American versions of the subculture. In your informed opinion, what accounts for these differences?

Carsten Koall/Getty Images

3 | How Do Subcultures Challenge Authority?

Although subcultures arise for a variety of reasons, most are defined to some degree by resistance to authority. The communities represented in this chapter are all intentionally oppositional, characterized largely by radical resistance. Clinical psychologist Bruce Levine opens the discussion by challenging his profession's eagerness to label those with "deficits in rule-governed behavior" as mentally ill. For Levine, these individuals are not dangerous nonconformists but a source of innovation and cultural energy. In fact, many of the communities featured in this book have a significant impact on the dominant American culture precisely because they enact a powerful, attractive nonconformity.

Several of these openly defiant groups are associated with particular musical genres. In "Muhammad Rocked the Casbah," Lydia Crafts describes a new version of an old subculture — punk — as incarnated by American Muslims. Sociologist Ross Haenfler investigates how the highly visible hip hop subculture negotiates problems of race and gender. In "A Little Too Ironic," Kristen Schilt analyzes a 1990s music subculture, Riot Grrrl, as a community of empowerment for young women. In each of these cases, music serves many purposes: to unite people through common experience, to express shared values, to exclude the uninitiated, and to challenge the mainstream.

In their open opposition to the dominant culture, most of these subcultures have a public presence. Alex Forman, writing in 1967, extols the virtues of the San Francisco–area hippies who sought to establish a new economic model of human interaction. The feminist bicyclists that Ariel Climer describes in "Riding to Resist" also believe in taking their politics to the streets in order to address problems in their communities, while the raw-food renegades in Dana Goodyear's "Raw Deal" must go underground to protect themselves from law enforcement.

In perhaps the ultimate act of resistance, the subculturists featured in George Gurley's "Pleasures of the Fur" reject humanness itself in favor of

photo: Carsten Koall/Getty Images

animal identities. In every case, these communities embrace their outsider status, creating freedoms not offered to them by mainstream American life. As you read, consider your own place on the spectrum of rebellion. What values do you embrace? What values do you reject? How do these values shape your view of the world? What role do you play in your circle of acquaintances and friends? What role do you play — or would you like to play — in the larger social world?

Why Anti-Authoritarians Are Diagnosed as Mentally Ill

Bruce Levine

Bruce E. Levine received his Ph.D. in clinical psychology from the University of Cincinnati and practices in Ohio. He is a regular contributor to *CounterPunch*, *AlterNet*, *Truthout*, *Z Magazine*, and the *Huffington Post*, and has been published in numerous other magazines. An activist advocating for reform in the treatment of mental health problems, Levine is a member of Psychologists for Social Responsibility, the International Society for Ethical Psychology & Psychiatry, and MindFreedom. In reading "Why Anti-Authoritarians Are Diagnosed as Mentally Ill," consider how Levine's examination of "disruptive disorders" applies to the subcultures featured in this chapter.

In my career as a psychologist, I have talked with hundreds of people previously diagnosed by other professionals with oppositional defiant disorder, attention deficit hyperactive disorder, anxiety disorder and other psychiatric illnesses, and I am struck by (1) how many of those diagnosed are essentially *anti-authoritarians*, and (2) how those professionals who have diagnosed them are not.

Anti-authoritarians question whether an authority is a legitimate one before taking that authority seriously. Evaluating the legitimacy of authorities includes assessing whether or not authorities actually know what they are talking about, are honest, and care about those people who are respecting their authority. And when anti-authoritarians assess an authority to be illegitimate, they challenge and resist that authority — sometimes aggressively and sometimes passive-aggressively, sometimes wisely and sometimes not. . . .

Mental Illness Diagnoses for Anti-Authoritarians

A 2009 *Psychiatric Times* article titled "ADHD & ODD: Confronting the Challenges of Disruptive Behavior" reports that "disruptive disorders," which include attention deficit hyperactivity disorder (ADHD) and opposition defiant disorder (ODD), are the most common mental health problem of children and teenagers. ADHD is defined by poor attention and distractibility, poor self-control and impulsivity, and hyperactivity. ODD is defined as a "a pattern of negativistic, hostile, and defiant behavior without the more serious violations of the basic rights of others that are seen in conduct disorder"; and ODD symptoms include "often actively defies or refuses to comply with adult requests or rules" and "often argues with adults."

Psychologist Russell Barkley, one of mainstream mental health's leading authorities on ADHD, says that those afflicted with ADHD have deficits in what he calls "rule-governed behavior," as they are less responsive to rules of established authorities and less sensitive to positive or negative consequences. ODD young people, according to mainstream mental health authorities, also have these so-called deficits in rule-governed behavior, and so it is extremely common for young people to have a "dual diagnosis" of AHDH and ODD.

> "Do we really want to diagnose and medicate everyone with 'deficits in rule-governed behavior'?"

Do we really want to diagnose and medicate everyone with "deficits in   5 rule-governed behavior"?

Albert Einstein, as a youth, would have likely received an ADHD diagnosis, and maybe an ODD one as well. Albert didn't pay attention to his teachers, failed his college entrance examinations twice, and had difficulty holding jobs. However, Einstein biographer Ronald Clark (*Einstein: The Life and Times*) asserts that Albert's problems did not stem from attention deficits but rather from his hatred of authoritarian, Prussian discipline in his schools. Einstein said, "The teachers in the elementary school appeared to me like sergeants and in the Gymnasium the teachers were like lieutenants." At age 13, Einstein read Kant's° difficult *Critique of Pure Reason* — because Albert was interested in it. Clark also tells us Einstein refused to prepare himself for his college admissions as a rebellion against his father's "unbearable" path of a "practical profession." After he did enter college, one professor told Einstein, "You have one fault; one can't tell you anything." The very characteristics of Einstein that upset authorities so much were exactly the ones that allowed him to excel.

By today's standards, Saul Alinsky, the legendary organizer and author of *Reveille for Radicals* and *Rules for Radicals*, would have certainly been diagnosed with one or more disruptive disorders. Recalling his childhood, Alinsky said, "I never thought of walking on the grass until I saw a sign saying 'Keep off the grass.' Then I would stomp all over it." Alinsky

---

Kant: Immanuel Kant (1927–1804), German philosopher who argued that human reason creates the structure of experience.

also recalls a time when he was ten or eleven and his rabbi was tutoring him in Hebrew:

One particular day I read three pages in a row without any errors in pronuncia-tion, and suddenly a penny fell onto the Bible . . . Then the next day the rabbi turned up and he told me to start reading. And I wouldn't; I just sat there in silence, refusing to read. He asked me why I was so quiet, and I said, "This time it's a nickel or nothing." He threw back his arm and slammed me across the room.

Many people with severe anxiety and/or depression are also anti-authoritarians. Often a major pain of their lives that fuels their anxiety and/or depression is fear that their contempt for illegitimate authorities will cause them to be financially and socially marginalized; but they fear that compliance with such illegitimate authorities will cause them exis-tential death.

I have also spent a great deal of time with people who had at one time in their lives had thoughts and behavior that were so bizarre that they were extremely frightening for their families and even themselves; they were diagnosed with schizophrenia and other psychoses, but have fully recovered and have been, for many years, leading productive lives. Among this population, I have not met one person whom I would not consider a major anti-authoritarian. Once recovered, they have learned to channel their anti-authoritarianism into more constructive political ends, including reforming mental health treatment.

Many anti-authoritarians who earlier in their lives were diagnosed   10 with mental illness tell me that once they were labeled with a psychiatric diagnosis, they got caught in a dilemma. Authoritarians, by definition, demand unquestioning obedience, and so any resistance to their diag-nosis and treatment created enormous anxiety for authoritarian mental health professionals; and professionals, feeling out of control, labeled them "noncompliant with treatment," increased the severity of their diagnosis, and jacked up their medications. This was enraging for these anti-authoritarians, sometimes so much so that they reacted in ways that made them appear even more frightening to their families.

There are anti-authoritarians who use psychiatric drugs to help them function, but they often reject psychiatric authorities' explanations for why they have difficulty functioning. So, for example, they may take Adderall (an amphetamine prescribed for ADHD), but they know that their attentional problem is not a result of a biochemical brain imbalance but rather caused by a boring job. And similarly, many anti-authoritarians in highly stressful environments will occasionally take prescribed benzodiazepines° such as Xanax even though they believe it would be safer to occasionally use marijuana but can't because of drug testing on their job.

It has been my experience that many anti-authoritarians labeled with psychiatric diagnoses usually don't reject *all* authorities, simply those they've assessed to be illegitimate ones, which just happens to be a great deal of society's authorities.

Maintaining the Status Quo

Americans have been increasingly socialized to equate inattention, anger, anxiety, and immobilizing despair with a medical condition, and to seek medical treatment rather than political remedies. What better way to maintain the status quo than to view inattention, anger, anxiety, and depression as biochemical problems of those who are mentally ill rather than normal reactions to an increasingly authoritarian society.

The reality is that depression is highly associated with societal and financial pains. One is much more likely to be depressed if one is unemployed, underemployed, on public assistance, or in debt. And ADHD-labeled kids do pay attention when they are getting paid, or when an activity is novel, interests them, or is chosen by them.

In an earlier dark age, authoritarian monarchies partnered with 15 authoritarian religious institutions. When the world exited from this dark age and entered the Enlightenment, there was a burst of energy. Much of this revitalization had to do with risking skepticism about authoritarian and corrupt institutions and regaining confidence in one's own mind. We are now in another dark age, only the institutions have changed. Americans desperately need anti-authoritarians to question, challenge, and resist new illegitimate authorities and regain confidence in their own common sense.

In every generation there will be authoritarians and anti-authoritarians. While it is unusual in American history for anti-authoritarians to take the kind of effective action that inspires others to successfully revolt, every once in a while a Tom Paine,° Crazy Horse,° or Malcolm X° come along. So authoritarians financially marginalize those who buck

---

benzodiazepines: class of tranquilizing drugs.
Tom Paine: English-American political agitator and author (1737–1809).
Crazy Horse: war chief of the Oglala Sioux responsible for Custer's defeat at the Little Big Horn in 1876.
Malcolm X: born Malcolm Little (1925–1965), achieved fame as a confrontational civil-rights activist and Nation of Islam leader.

the system, criminalize anti-authoritarianism, psychopathologize anti-authoritarians, and market drugs for their "cure."

Understanding the Text

1. Why are people diagnosed with ADHD often given a "dual diagnosis" of ODD?
2. Levine suggests that many individuals' anxiety and depression do not require medical treatment. What issues do we as a society need to address instead?
3. What does Levine mean when he says that anti-authoritarians "fear that compliance with such illegitimate authorities will cause them existential death" (par. 8)?

Reflection and Response

4. Nearly everyone has experienced the tension between abiding by the rules and challenging the rules. Referring to examples from your own life, where do you place yourself on the authoritarian/anti-authoritarian spectrum?
5. Levine says that we live in "an increasingly authoritarian society" (par. 13). Do you agree? What counterarguments can be made in response to this claim?
6. What valuable role do anti-authoritarians play in society? Give several specific examples.

Making Connections

7. Using outside research, write a brief essay showing how anti-authoritarianism is historically important to American national identity.
8. Does authoritarianism only find expression in mainstream culture, or are there authoritarian subcultures as well? Discuss.

San Francisco Style: The Diggers and the Love Revolution

Alex Forman

Writing for the July 1967 issue of *Anarchy* magazine, Alex Forman offers a first-hand account of the arrival of the Summer of Love, the great hippie gathering in San Francisco. In 1966, Forman left his conventional middle-class life to join the new counterculture centered in the Haight-Ashbury district. He says, "It was like paradise there. Everybody was in love with life and in love with their fellow human beings to the point where they were just sharing in incredible ways with everybody." The Digger community that sprang up in the 1960s borrowed their name from a seventeenth-century group of British Protestant anarchists who put their beliefs about radical equality and ecological stewardship into practice by farming on public lands.

Growing out of give-and-take between the New Left[0] and the old Beat[6] generation, a hippy culture blossomed in San Francisco in late 1965. Two new factors which made the hippy culture a very distinct phenomenon were, first, a feeling of community (emphasized by individuals frustrated in the New Left), and second, the use of LSD. Cutting across the economic and social differences of many alienated Americans, almost all quite young, a new tribal love culture took root in the Haight-Ashbury district of the city. The new force unleashed by LSD constituted the primary unifying factor in a grouping which ranged from the sometimes violent Hell's Angels motorcycle club to meditating Zen Buddhists. This new culture was at first amorphous but it soon took on the shape of a bohemian community complete with its own merchant class: the hip merchants.

> "Growing out of give-and-take between the New Left and the old Beat generation, a hippy culture blossomed in San Francisco in late 1965."

Haight-Ashbury's new love community acquired members primarily from the swollen ranks of alienated young people who were also discovering the "love trip." Conversations on streets in the Haight-Ashbury became filled with talk of love, and then, suddenly appearing in the autumn of

---

New Left: broad political movement of the 1960s and 1970s consisting mainly of educators and public intellectuals, often associated with the Free Speech Movement and hippie activity.
Beat: the Beat Generation, comprised of authors whose work explored the dark side of American culture and politics in the 1940s and 1950s.

1966, was a group calling itself the Diggers. It began to distribute free food in the local park—food donated by individuals and collected from the surpluses of local markets. The new group also attempted to provide housing for the growing number of young people who had become convinced that they should create a new, loving society. . . .

At first the coming of the new Diggers was lauded by the entire hippy community. The "Digger thing" of giving things away spread into the community—and beyond into the high schools and colleges of the city. There was a powerful new force in the air as one walked down Haight Street and saw people giving away flowers, fruits and candies. The Diggers in a sense became a new morality, the opposite of industrial capitalism's grab-bag marketplace morality. The moral position of the Diggers can be seen in the fact that after they had been pushed out of various offices by the police and health departments, they were given an office and kitchen privileges by a neighborhood church. They were looked upon soon as the most beautiful part of the community and then began to be labelled by some as a "community service." It was at this point that an inevitable split occurred, for the Diggers did not want to be a community service—they wanted the community itself to be based on the new morality. A conflict began between the Diggers and the hip merchants.

It was fairly obvious that the merchants were getting rich without helping the hippies on the streets, many of whom were dependent on the Diggers. At a meeting one of the more vocal Diggers asked why, if they were a community service, did they find it so hard to get aid from the community. They wished to see money used to buy space for people—living space, growing space, space to create the new world. Such aims conflicted with those of the business-minded merchants. A full-scale break was developing.

Meanwhile, the Diggers' magic acquired them two farms which are   5 now being established as future food suppliers as well as colonies of freedom from the city hassle. In April of 1967 the movement jumped across an ethnic barrier with the beginning of a Black Man's Free Store in the heart of the Negro ghetto. It was at this time—with the establishment of free-stores in the black community and the Haight-Ashbury, with the beginning of farms and the break with the merchants—that the Diggers [began to stress] concrete political realities. They spoke now of need for some kind of revolution—and especially in the Black Man's Free Store the work is viewed as the beginning of a revolution. . . .

This is not to imply that the Diggers are giving up on love. If anything, there's now more love than before. But they're becoming more aware of the system that prevents love, more aware of the strength of competitive industrial capitalism, since it's threatening their own community.

This awareness was demonstrated when four individuals associated with the Diggers, each from a different section of San Francisco, sent a letter to the city government [demanding] a system of free storehouses to be replenished when empty. The letter argued that our industrial system is capable of feeding everyone if organized for that purpose, and stated that it's a moral and psychological necessity that this be done. Reading this leaflet in the Black Man's Free Store, gazing out the window at prostitutes selling their bodies — beautiful black bodies on a sunny afternoon — I realized that such changes were indeed a necessity. But the Diggers alone can't implement them. It will take a massive alliance of the alienated young people and the political left. Yet the Diggers continue working toward their goal — working through the medium of love, as illustrated by the following exchange heard in the Black Man's Free Store as it opened in April:

Rembrandt (a sign-painter passing by): I see that you guys are opening a store. Do you want a sign painted?

Roy (a former freedom-fighter in Mississippi, now organizer of the store): Well, this is a free-store so we can't pay you anything, but if you want to paint a sign . . . you see, we give things away.

Rembrandt: I never give anything away and nobody has ever given me anything.

Roy: Nobody's ever given you anything? . . . See that box of spray paints — if you can use them they're yours. Do you have any money? Here's thirty cents for bus fare.

Rembrandt: I don't understand. What are you guys doing here?

Roy: See that big appliance and furniture store across the street, with the sign about cashing welfare checks? Well, that's where all the people on welfare go . . . I've taken them there myself. The woman who runs the place came in here awhile ago and asked what we were doing. When I told her we were setting up a free-store she told me that I was in the wrong neighborhood — that we didn't need a free-store here. She said I should go to the Haight-Ashbury. Then she became really excited and said that we just couldn't do this here and she would stop it. Well, the point is that we're here to give things away so that the people on welfare can have enough money to live better than now. It's the beginning of a revolutionary movement for change.

Rembrandt: I see. Well, why don't I paint a nice big sign on the window saying "Watch For Our Grand Opening Day" and write "Free Food, Clothes and Appliances" — that'll really scare her.

Rembrandt (after painting): Listen, I have a truck I can borrow so I'll
come back and give you guys some glitter and help move
some stuff. (He leaves.)

Roy: He really did his thing, didn't he? Did you dig it? We turned
that cat on to doing his thing and he did it, man, he really
did it.

Understanding the Text

1. Forman assumes that his audience knows who the "hip merchants" (par. 1)
   are. What do you think he means by the term?

2. When he first encounters the Black Man's Free Store, why is Rembrandt, the
   sign-painter, confused?

Reflection and Response

3. Although the hippies of the San Francisco Bay Area ultimately failed to
   establish a new society based on love, freedom, and unity, many of the
   hippie ideals became a part of mainstream society. What are some of these
   ideals? Do you believe that these ideals continue to have a function today? If
   so, where do we find such principles enacted in contemporary society?

4. Why do you think that the owner of the appliance business objected so
   strongly to the Black Man's Free Store across the street from her store?
   What do you think the woman found objectionable about giving away free
   goods? Is such a model feasible on even a small scale today?

5. That Forman was writing this article in 1967 puts him in a unique position to
   comment on the rise of hippie subculture. How would his article be different
   if he were writing today about the events of 1967?

Making Connections

6. The Diggers took their name from the group of radicals who followed Gerrard
   Winstanley at the time of the English Civil War in 1649. Research these
   proto-anarchists and explain how their beliefs and practices resonated with
   the San Francisco hippies who called themselves Diggers.

7. Forman, writing at the time of the rise of the hippie subculture, claims that
   LSD is the "primary unifying factor" (par. 1) in the subculture. How have
   drugs, either legal or illegal, played a role in defining other subcultures? Why
   are some drugs more suited to one subculture than to another?

8. Research the Summer of Love, when more than a hundred-thousand hippies
   descended on San Francisco to participate in the new lifestyle. What was
   the Diggers' response to this invasion? What challenges tested hippie
   subculture during this time? What happened at the end of the summer?

9. Several other subcultures in this book, including the Hell's Angels and the
   femme-butch community portrayed by Sue-Ellen Case, formed in the San
   Francisco Bay Area. Why do you suppose this location has been such fertile
   ground for alternative communities and ways of life?

Muhammad Rocked the Casbah

Lydia Crafts

Michael Muhammad Knight's loosely autobiographical novel *The Taqwacores* has the rare distinction of spawning a real-world subculture: Punk Islam. Muslim kids around the United States discovered the book and banded together into a rebellious punk subculture containing elements of Islamic faith, hardcore music, and punk-style anarchy. Here, freelance journalist Lydia Crafts tells the story of a disaffected Muslim teenager in San Antonio, Texas, who, after reading Knight's novel, brought the values and practices of the characters into his own life. This article originally appeared in *Texas Monthly*.

Kourosh Poursalehi was a 16-year-old Sufi° from San Antonio in 2004 when he created a song that made a fictional punk-rock movement come alive. Hypothesizing that no one in the world was like him, Poursalehi went looking for other Muslim punks and discovered *The Taqwacores*, a novel written by Muslim-convert Michael Muhammad Knight about a fictional underground Muslim punk-rock scene in upstate New York. In the book, the punks called themselves taqwacore—a combination of the Arabic word *taqwa*, meaning consciousness of God, and hardcore.

Poursalehi thought the taqwacores were real and set out to meet them. He found a poem written by Knight at the beginning of the book called "Muhammad was a Punk Rocker" that portrays the Prophet rebelling against the oppressors of his time, smashing idols and sporting a spiky hairdo. Poursalehi put the poem to music—spawning the first-ever taqwacore song.

The poem embodies Knight's vision of Muslim punk. Born in the 1970s, punk rockers purposefully sing off-color lyrics, wear politically incorrect labels, and stamp their bodies with tattoos in the name of individual freedom and opposition to the status quo. The Prophet Muhammad was punk, according to Knight, because he was a nonconformist who fought for what he believed. A growing number of young Muslims who resist their parents' orthodox views, but also struggle with the values of their non-Muslim friends, are embracing punk. Muslim punk provides a place to forge a new identity for young Muslims confused about religion and their role in American society, particularly as they are bombarded by negative stereotypes of Muslims in a post-9/11 America. At the same time,

---

Sufi: member of an esoteric, mystical sect of Islam.

Muslim punk offers a palpable way to express anger toward the orthodoxies of fundamentalist Islam.

Once Poursalehi completed his song, he sent a recording to Knight, who lives in upstate New York. Knight had written "Muhammad was a punk rocker" after returning from Pakistan, where he studied Islam for six hours a day and almost joined the Chechen mujahedeen before growing disillusioned with his faith. As a Muslim, Knight felt trapped. Whenever he questioned his faith, other Muslims accused him of having "no *adab*," which translates in Arabic to "no manners." He discovered punk in college and fell in love with its philosophy of never apologizing for having a different point of view. Still, he yearned for a spiritual life. He wrote "Muhammad was a punk rocker" and then the novel, fantasizing about a place where Muslims would accept him. When Knight heard Poursalehi's song for the first time, he was ecstatic.

"I had it play on repeat over and over, and I couldn't believe what was 5 happening," Knight said. "I had just put something out there into the world, not knowing if it'd have meaning for anyone else, and then here I was listening to this kid sharing it, making it his own."

A few days after hearing Poursalehi's song, Knight took a road trip to Boston to meet Shahjehan Khan and Basim Usmani. Both would gain worldwide recognition as the lead guitarist and singer, respectively, for a Muslim punk band called The Kominas.

Khan and Usmani had also recently read *The Taqwacores* and had contacted Knight to share their admiration for the book.

Basim Usmani, lead vocalist and guitarist for The Kominas, performs at Silver Factory Studios in Los Angeles. Gary Friedman/Getty Images

A self-described Muslim delinquent, Khan met Usmani playing hooky from Sunday school at their mosque in Wayland, Massachusetts. Khan had a fairly sheltered childhood in a suburban town outside Boston. It wasn't until he enrolled in the University of Massachusetts at Amherst, soon after September 11th, that he experienced prejudice.

Khan said "weird barriers" arose between him and other students—he found the cafeteria ethnically divided, and his floormate went so far as to tell Khan that Muslims cause all the problems in the world. Following a two-month drug binge, Khan dropped out. He moved home and enrolled in the University of Massachusetts at Lowell, where he and Usmani rekindled their friendship. Usmani had just read *The Taqwacores*, and he gave Khan his copy. The book reawakened Khan's interest in Islam—for the first time he felt he could identify with Muhammad as someone who had also struggled against society to make his own way.

"I started thinking maybe I was Muslim all along," Khan said. "Part of   10 being Muslim is questioning authority and making mistakes and blazing your own trail."

Khan remembers that Knight pulled up to Usmani's house in Lexington, Massachusetts, blaring "Muhammad was a punk rocker" with the windows on his green Buick Skylark rolled down. He lived in the car at the time and had a makeshift bed in the backseat. Usmani and Khan climbed inside the car and spent the afternoon driving around listening to Poursalehi's song. Usmani had recently introduced Khan to punk and burned him a CD called "Punk 101." They had taken a stab at writing music together, but had yet to finish a song. "Muhammad was a punk rocker" demonstrated that there were like-minded Muslims out there.

"It was nuts," Khan said. "I couldn't believe there was this kid down in Texas writing this music. I don't remember what my exact feeling was at the time, but I remember I was excited and thinking that this was the beginning."

San Antonio, with its small Muslim population, may seem an unlikely birthplace for Muslim punk. Given San Antonio's dominant culture, however, it's understandable why Poursalehi would embrace taqwacore. Poursalehi grew up thinking no one was like him. Traveling to his house in northern San Antonio, it's easy to see why. On a 10-mile stretch of Stone Oak Parkway, there are at least 10 churches, several Christian schools, and billboards proclaiming, "Jesus is Lord." The Cornerstone Church, a 17,000-member Christian-Zionist megachurch, sits at Poursalehi's exit, and several more churches lie along the main road to his house. Out of San Antonio's 1.2 million people, the Catholic Diocese of San Antonio alone claims 680,000 members, and the San Antonio Baptist Association has 265 church affiliates. By contrast, 30,000 Muslims live in San Antonio, including recent converts.

Poursalehi went through his teenage years during a time that this small Muslim community felt under siege. Sarwat Husain, who chairs the Council for American-Islamic Relations in San Antonio and collects data on hate crimes in the area, said discrimination against Muslims reached its peak immediately following September 11. Four Muslim-owned gas stations were torched, women donning *burqa*° were physically attacked on the streets, and children were beaten up at school. While hate crimes against Muslims still occur, Husain said the community now has more support from city leaders.

As a Sufi, Poursalehi faced double discrimination. Narjis Pierre, a Sufi 15 and author living in San Antonio, said that Muslim immigrants sometimes bring misconceptions about Sufis from their homelands. Often described as a mystical tradition within Islam, Sufism began in resistance to corrupt Islamic rulers. Sufis have continued to resist oppressive regimes in the modern era (for example, the predominantly Sufi Kurds in Northern Iraq fought Saddam Hussein). As a response to their resistance, Pierre said, rulers have marginalized Sufis, deeming their faith heretical. "In many countries, Sufis have been seen as innovators and heretics, and this 'ignorance' may be carried over to Europe-America and given on to their [Muslim immigrant] children," she said.

Poursalehi never shared his Sufi upbringing with his peers. He continues to be reluctant to discuss his Sufi background. He says the religion bothers him because it's too closely tied to money. In spite of his resistance to Sufism, Poursalehi admits it influenced him. He even credits religion with piquing his musical interest through the Sufi practice of *dhikr*,° which involves remembering God through chanting divine names. Often Sufis achieve an ecstatic state with dhikr. Poursalehi describes music as a similarly mystical experience.

"Music is like another world for me," he said. "It's like when you're a little kid and you think of a fairytale land. That's how strong music is for me."

Poursalehi found punk music at age 14. He started listening to The Fearless Iranians from Hell, a San Antonio punk group that has striking similarities to many taqwacore bands. The Fearless Iranians would perform with ski masks to make fun of stereotypes about Muslims being terrorists. Around the time Poursalehi discovered punk, San Antonio had a lively punk-rock scene. Poursalehi supported local bands and regularly

---

burqa: enveloping garment worn by some Islamic women to cover their bodies when in public.
dhikr: form of devotion in which the worshiper is absorbed in the rhythmic repetition of the name of God.

attended concerts at venues such as Sin 13 and Sanctuary. He said he found a connection between punk shows and religion.

"In both areas, there's a strong sense of energy going around and unity almost," he said. "It's about people coming together for the same cause and the same concerns. It was crazy hearing a live show. It put chills through your body, and I decided I wanted to do that."

It's been three years since Poursalehi made the first taqwacore song. 20 Since then, he has created a punk band called Vote Hezbollah (the name's a joke), the Kominas have established a cultlike following, and numerous other taqwacore bands have sprung up across the country. The Muslim punks have established relationships online. Last summer they all met on the first-ever Muslim punk-rock tour. Knight bought a bus for $2,000 on eBay, painted it green with small red camels, and wrote "taqwa" on the front. Five bands, including the Kominas and Vote Hezbollah, toured for 10 days from Boston to Chicago.

During the trip, the Muslim punks encountered the same issues they have struggled with separately. The Islamic Society of North America invited them to perform at its conference in Chicago. For the first 10 minutes, the concert was a success—young Muslims packed the conference, cheering the taqwacore bands from their respective male and female sections. But when a female group, Secret Trial Five, took the stage, conference leaders called the police and had the taqwacore bands kicked out—Muslim women are forbidden to sing in public. The taqwacore groups also had to deal with discrimination. On the road, other drivers flipped them off. One driver held a "Fuck Allah" sign up to his window.

This time, however, rather than bottling up their anger, the Muslim punks responded with humor, mostly dark. The Kominas performed songs with provocative lyrics such as "suicide bomb the gap," and "Rumi was a homo" (a stab at an anti-gay imam in Brooklyn). The musicians started a joke band named Box Cutter Surprise, after the knives used to hijack planes on September 11th. Marwan Kamel, from a band on tour called Al-Thawra, Arabic for "revolution," said members created the group to shock audiences.

"The sole purpose was to light a fire under people's asses," Kamel said. "We were totally exploiting Americans' fear of terrorism, but maybe that's what everyone needs right now."

On tour, the taqwacore bands allowed each other to embrace their contradictions as young Muslim Americans confused about their religion, identity, and place in the world. They prayed together, philosophized about Allah, visited mosques in Harlem and Ohio, shouted their grievances about President Bush and generally thought for themselves.

> "I think all the prophets and imams were punk rockers... They were all labeled as weird; they all fought against the evils that had become common in their societies."

"I began to feel a balance between 25 my identity as a Muslim and an American," Khan said. "It was literally the most amazing experience of my life."

This fall the Muslim punks returned to their homes across the country. Some of the bands, like the Kominas and Vote Hezbollah, are working on albums, and they're all planning a European tour.

Other Muslims have picked up their guitars and turned up their amps, and more bands promise to join the taqwacores on their trip. Jeremy (who doesn't use a last name and also goes by Bilal) is a Muslim-convert from Fort Worth who recently started writing punk music. He converted to Islam after attending Baptist Middle School, where his teachers rarely gave him satisfactory answers to his questions about the Bible (such as, why can Christians eat pork?). He went on a spiritual quest and came across *The Taqwacores*. Then he began talking to Knight and other Muslim punks online. Jeremy dreams of writing music that will spread a peaceful image of Islam. The first taqwacore song to inspire him? "Muhammad was a punk rocker."

"I think all the prophets and imams were punk rockers," Jeremy said. "They were all labeled as weird; they all fought against the evils that had become common in their societies. They were all persecuted . . . Abraham broke idols of wood and stone, and Jesus broke conceptual idols, and Muhammad broke both."

Understanding the Text

1. What does "tacqwacore" mean? How did the term originate?
2. What is Sufism? What connection between Sufism and music does Poursalehi identify?

Reflection and Response

3. "[T]he prophets and the imams were punk rockers," claims one tacqwacore adherent (par. 28). Do you agree or disagree that figures such as Abraham, Jesus, and Muhammad represent the kind of resistance and rebellion typified by punk culture? Discuss in detail.
4. The tacqwacore subculture is unusual in that it began as a work of fiction. How have other subcultural identities been shaped by media depictions, whether in novels, movies, television, or social media?

5. In his novel *The Tacqwacores* Michael Muhammad Knight writes that the words "punk" and "Islam" are like "flags": they symbolize abstract ideas to which people attach whatever meanings they want. How do you personally interpret the words "punk" and "Islam"? Given your interpretation, do you think these two "flags" can fly together?

Making Connections

6. Investigate one of the many other punk subcultures — rude boys, riot grrrls, crust, oi, straight edge, etc. What are the distinct characteristics of the particular group? How do their values, beliefs, and practices differ from other punk subcultures?

7. Find a copy of Michael Muhammad Knight's novel *The Tacqwacores*. Why might readers believe that the Muslim punk subculture depicted in this book already existed? What elements contribute to the verisimilitude (the sense of reality) of the novel?

The Appropriation and Packaging of Riot Grrrl Politics

Kristen Schilt

Perhaps the most significant social change of the last half-century has been the economic and political rise of women in American society. Although we often define resistance and rebellion in terms of masculine aggression — e.g., motorcycle gangs, punks, skinheads, skaters, taggers — female subcultural movements have also aggressively challenged the dominant culture. Kristen Schilt, a sociologist at the University of Chicago, examines one of the most anti-authoritarian female subcultures of the late-twentieth century, Riot Grrrl, in order to understand the promises and problems of female aggression. Elsewhere, Schilt has done fascinating research into inequalities in the workplace, beliefs about the biological origins of gender and racial differences, and the place of science in the popular imagination.

The Emergence of the Riot Grrrls

Riot Grrrl began in 1991, when a group of women from Washington, D.C., and Olympia, Washington, held a meeting to discuss how to address sexism in the punk scene. Inspired by recent antiracist riots in D.C., the women decided they wanted to start a "girl riot" against a society they felt offered no validation of women's experiences. The name "Riot Grrrl" emerged. The use of the word "girl" came from a desire to focus on childhood, a time when girls have the strongest self-esteem and belief in themselves (White 397). The rewriting of the word as "grrrl" represented the anger behind the movement; it sounded like a growl (Carlip 9). Because the founding women had ties to punk, a genre known for using performance and shock value as tools of protest, Riot Grrrl had a more radical orientation than other feminist organizations such as the National Organization for Women. As Emily White commented in *Rock She Wrote: Women Write About Rock, Pop and Rap*, "Riot Grrrl co-opted the values and rhetoric of punk, fifteen years after the fact, in the name of feminism—or as they call it 'revolution-girl style now'" (397).

At its inception, Riot Grrrl issued a manifesto stating its philosophy and intent. The manifesto was published in various Riot Grrrl "zines," such as *Riot Grrrl* and *Bikini Kill*. Zines (short for "fanzines") are home-made publications with limited distribution. Zines became an important part of the punk scene in the late 1970s because punks liked "producing a paper unhampered by corporate structure, cash and censorship" (Burchill and Parsons 37). Zine-making was a predominantly male domain, however. Mark Perry, one of the early punk zine makers, wrote in one issue of *Sniffin' Glue*: "Punks are not girls, and if it comes to the crunch we'll have no options but to fight back" (Reynolds and Press 323).

In the hands of the Riot Grrrls, however, zines became a medium for discussing taboo subjects, such as rape, incest, and eating disorders. Zine-making offered girls a way of forming connections with other girls who shared their experiences. The formation of these connections allowed girls to see their own personal experiences with rape and assault as part of a larger political problem. As Hillary Carlip wrote in *Girlpower*, "In zines, [Riot Grrrls] are finally free to express themselves fully, to be heard, and also to realize they are not alone" (34). Zine-making offered many girls a forum in which to discuss the marginalization they felt in the predominantly male punk scene and to discuss sexism and harassment with other girls and women who shared similar experiences.

Bikini Kill was one of the earliest Riot Grrrl-associated zines. The first issue, which came out in 1991, was primarily written by Kathleen Hanna and Tobi Vail, members of the band Bikini Kill. Issue 2 contained a version of the Riot Grrrl manifesto, which listed many reasons why Riot Grrrl was necessary:

Riot Grrrl is: BECAUSE we know that life is much more than physical   5
survival and are patently aware that the punk rock 'you can do anything'
idea is crucial to the coming angry grrrl rock revolution which seeks to save
the psychic and cultural lives of girls and women everywhere, according to
their own terms, not ours. ("Riot Grrrl is" 44)

The zine also included an article on fat oppression and a list of the top ten sexist responses to feminist beliefs and suggestions on how to rebut them. Tobi Vail also produced a zine entitled *Jigsaw*. The jigsaw puzzle was a metaphor frequently used by Bikini Kill to describe the confusion of girls who were trying to see where they fit into a male-dominated world. In the liner notes of the Bikini Kill self-titled 1994 CD, Kathleen Hanna writes, "Don't freak out cuz [sic] the jigsaw is laying on the floor and it's not all the way done and has been there for 4 whole hours now, resist the freak out. You will get it . . . it's all part of the process."

In addition to circulating information about feminism, zines were used as

> "... the punk rock 'you can do anything' idea is crucial to the coming angry grrrl rock revolution which seeks to save the psychic and cultural lives of girls and women everywhere, according to their own terms, not ours."

a forum to confront racism in the punk scene. Allison Wolfe, the singer for Bratmobile, edited a zine called *Girl Germs*. Wolfe criticized the white privilege in the punk (and Riot Grrrl) scene and tried to get others to recognize and confront it in themselves. Other zines, such as *Gunk*, offered more in-depth critiques of the predominantly white scene and what could be done about it. *Gunk*'s editor, Dasha, writes, "I used to laugh at this whole white bread punk scene, but now I'm not laughing as much as I'm getting annoyed" ("I'm Laughing" 3). She also discusses the implications of punks who claim the status of "white niggers" and what the term means to an African-American punk like herself.

Reading other girl-zines enabled girls to see their experiences of racism, abuse, and harassment as political issues rather than isolated personal incidents. As the word spread about these homemade magazines that told unbowlderized° versions of adolescent girls' lives, more and more girls attempted to reach out to other girls through the girl-zine network. When *Sassy*, a popular teen magazine from the early nineties, published the addresses of several Riot Grrrl zines, many of them were forced to stop production because they couldn't handle the flood of mail they received. Many of the Riot Grrrl zine makers felt that this was a testament to how zines validated girls' experiences and made them feel that they were not alone.

Forming Connections through Music

Similar to girl-zines, the bands associated with Riot Grrrl used their music to express feminist and antiracist viewpoints. Bikini Kill, Bratmobile, and Heavens to Betsy (all Riot Grrrl-associated bands) created songs with extremely personal lyrics that dealt with topics such as rape, incest, and eating disorders. Again, girls who heard these songs had the experience of realizing how their own personal problems fit into larger political structures. Members of Riot Grrrl-associated bands also received scores of letters from girls who wanted to relate how these lyrics had affected their lives.

When I interviewed Kathleen Hanna in 1998, she said,   10

I still have been getting as many letters as I did in the first two months of Riot Grrrl. I still get as many letters about feminism, about all kinds of things—girls with eating disorders, girls who are being sexually assaulted in their homes—see I get the same kind of mail. The same amazing mail.

bowdlerize: edit wording and remove passages that are considered improper or offensive.

That the volume of mail had not decreased in eight years underscores the ability of bands like Bikini Kill to address issues that speak to many girls' lives.

In the Bikini Kill song "Feels Blind," Kathleen Hanna addresses how society teaches women to hate themselves. The words, "As a woman I was taught to always be hungry/yeah women are well acquainted with thirst/we could eat just about anything/we could even eat your hate up like love," show how self-hatred can emerge in the form of an eating disorder, or in the tolerance of an abusive relationship. Another song, "Don't Need You," proclaims that "don't need you to say we're cute/don't need you to say we're alright/don't need your protection/don't need your kiss goodnight," rejecting stereotypical heterosexual relationship dynamics. In her pre-Bikini Kill bands, Hanna is equally uncompromising in her lyrical subjects. On "Kalvinator," from her 1990 band, Viva Knieval, Hanna sings, "If I were a boy I might be small time powerful like you/ and I might even fuck a girl who's like me," ridiculing the sexist attitudes of male musicians in the punk scene. She follows the same theme in the Wondertwins song, "If I Were a Real Woman," describing a "real woman" as a "sunburnt baby waiting for you." These lyrics offer a critique of the social construction of the "perfect" woman.

Bratmobile, another Riot Grrrl-associated band, also explores socially constructed stereotypes of women. In the song "Teenager," Allison Wolfe sings, "I'm not jaded to the bone/I'm not little Miss Knowledge/I'm not hooked up to the phone/I'm not just a piece of college/I'm a teenager," illustrating how girls don't fit into perfect, rigid classifications. . . .

The Press vs. Riot Grrrl

Proponents of Riot Grrrl wanted to reach out to as many girls as possible, but were reluctant to use mainstream media for that purpose. The performance style of many of the bands shocked some journalists, leading to negative and condescending articles about Riot Grrrl. Kim France writes of Riot Grrrl in 1993, "They do things like scrawl SLUT and RAPE across their torsos before gigs, produce fanzines with names like *Girl Germs* and hate the media's guts. They're called Riot Grrrls, and they've come for your daughters" ("Grrrls" 23). In interviews I have conducted with founders of Riot Grrrl, they maintain that writing "SLUT" and "RAPE" on arms and stomachs was intended to draw attention to constraints placed on women's sexuality and to publicize issues such as sexual abuse and rape that were largely ignored by the media. Riot Grrrl emphasized the importance of placing taboo subjects, such as sexual abuse, out in the open. At Bikini Kill shows, microphones were often passed around so that the audience could share stories of sexual abuse. But while most reports about Riot Grrrl mentioned the body writing, no reporters delved into why Bikini Kill employed these tactics or connected it to the serious issues of incest in middle-class white America.

Stories about Riot Grrrl often were misinformed, antagonistic, or banal. In the liner notes to Bikini Kill's self-titled 1994 CD, Tobi Vail outlines why the group refused to do interviews: too often the band had been misrepresented and taken out of context, making them appear immature and ridiculous. In *Angry Women in Rock*, Andrea Juno quotes Kathleen Hanna as saying that *Newsweek* purchased a picture of her and friends at the beach in bikinis to print with the article about Riot Grrrl (85). The photo was purchased in an effort to discredit her feminism; she was in a band called Bikini Kill, yet she wore bikinis. Hanna tells Juno that *The Washington Post* ran a story on Bikini Kill (without interviewing the band) and incorrectly reported that Hanna claimed her father had raped her. Hanna had many relatives in D.C. and the article caused her a lot of embarrassment and hurt her family. Other reports were simply condescending. A reporter from *The Evening Standard* wrote of Riot Grrrl, "Their ideas may be babyish. But at least they have some" (Leonard 243). *Melody Maker*, the leading music journal in England, writes, "The best thing that any Riot Grrrl could do is to go away and do some reading, and I don't mean a grubby little fanzine" (Leonard 243). The authors of these articles gave Riot Grrrl a cursory glance and dismissed the movement as juvenile and unimportant.

Zine editors tried to rise to the challenge of defending Riot Grrrl. Bethany, writing in *Gunk*, says, "Bikini Kill is now an alternative image of women. The media only gets one image; it can be distorted. They don't know Kathy, Tobi, Billy or Kathleen" ("Beth's Letter" 11). Sasha, the editor of *Cupsize* writes, "Most people took their *SPIN* soundbite accounts of Riot Grrrl and ran with them, feeling free to apply the label to any feminist or female rocker" ("Riot Grrrl" 28). In a reaction to the negative press, women who identified as Riot Grrrls initiated a media blackout. However, this anti-media stance only increased the number of negative, uninformed stories about Riot Grrrl. Gottlieb and Wald conclude their article on Riot Grrrl, saying that if Riot Grrrl truly wanted to offer its form of feminism to the masses, they needed to abandon their belief in the power of the subculture and start working with the media (271). This statement, however, misses the point of Riot Grrrl. As Marion Leonard° notes, "The goal of many of those involved [in Riot Grrrl] was not to

15

Marion Leonard: Senior Lecturer in the Department of Music at the University of Liverpool.

gain mass attention but to encourage girls and women to communicate with each other" (247). Some members of Riot Grrrl remained steadfast in their rejection of the media and others remained open to the media. Whatever the stance of individual Riot Grrrls, however, the media soon lost interest and stories about the death of Riot Grrrl began to appear in 1995 and 1996. . . .

The appropriation of subcultures by the mainstream is a continuous and not inherently negative process. If one girl feels empowered by the Spice Girls' "girl power" slogan or Alanis Morissette's angry tirade, then something positive can occur. However, I believe that the problems with the commodification of the radical feminist message of Riot Grrrl run very deep. Riot Grrrl's success with girls lay in its ability to "foster an affirmative mode of public female self-expression" that didn't "exclude, repress, or delegitimize girls' experiences" (Gottlieb and Wald 267). It was about making connections with other girls and women and start-ing to build a feminist and political consciousness. Riot Grrrl gave girls ideas on how to make their own music. It was a realistic assumption that girls inspired by Bikini Kill could and would start their own bands. But how realistic was it for girls to aspire to be the next Alanis Morissette or Baby Spice? If you can't sing or dance, where does that leave you? Riot Grrrl-associated bands may not have been musically perfect but they encouraged self-expression. While Morissette and [Fiona] Apple deal with some of the political issues promoted by Riot Grrrl, they sing without the desire to inspire girls to try their own forms of expression. Simon Firth noted in 1981, "girl culture, indeed, starts and finishes in the bedroom" (228). Riot Grrrl revolutionized this idea, making the bedroom a place to produce zines, hold all-girl meetings, or play guitar. Girls who were inspired by the message of Riot Grrrl were not encouraged to be passive listeners; they were inspired to find an active way to practice new ideas about feminism.

The new genre of women in rock took many lessons from Riot Grrrl and the largely ignored women of the punk years: the anger towards patriarchy is present, the discussion of sexual abuse, and even the acknowledgment of female desire. But the message is diluted. The Period Pains, a teenage all-girl band from England, offer a critique of the Spice Girls' empty "girl power" slogans in their song "Spice Girls: Who Do You Think You Are?" The lines "you can't even sing / wear bikinis on stage" and "you're not girls you're women / you're boring and you're lame" show that some teenagers notice the discrepancies between words and actions. There is no shared experience or advice in how to move towards healing, as there is in Riot Grrrl material. There is no encourage-ment for girls to use music as a form of expressing anger towards a world that marginalizes them. There is nothing but the empty promise of "the future is female" (Douglas 21). That future may seem bleak if you don't look good in spangled bustiers and hot pants.

References

"Beth's Letter." *Gunk* (n.d.): 11.

Burchill, Julie, and Tony Parsons. *The Boy Looked at Johnny: The Obituary of Rock and Roll*. London: Pluto Press Limited, 1978.

Carlip, Hillary. *Girlpower: Young Women Speak Out!* New York: Warner Books, 1995.

Frith, Simon. *Sound Effects: Youth, Leisure and the Politics of Rock'n'Roll*. New York: Pantheon Books, 1981.

Gottlieb, Joanne, and Gayle Wald. "Smells Like Teen Spirit: Revolution and Women in Independent Rock." *Microphone Fiends: Youth Music and Youth Culture*. Ed. Andrew Ross and Tricia Rose. New York: Routledge, 1994: 250–74.

Hanna, Kathleen. "Jigsaw Youth." Liner Notes, *Bikini Kill*. Compact disc by Bikini Kill. Kill Rock Stars, 1994.

"I'm Laughing so Hard It Doesn't Look Like I'm Laughing Anymore." *Gunk* (n.d.): 3–4.

Juno, Andrea. "Kathleen Hanna." *Angry Women in Rock*. New York: Juno Books, 1996: 82–103.

Leonard, Marion. "'Rebel Girl You are the Queen of my World': Feminism, Subculture, and Grrrl Power." *Sexing the Groove: Popular Music and Gender*. Ed. Sheila Whiteley. New York: Routledge, 1997: 230–56.

Reynolds, Simon and Joy Press. *The Sex Revolts: Gender, Rebellion and Rock'n'Roll*. Cambridge, MA: Harvard University Press, 1995.

"Riot Grrrl." *Cupsize 3* (n.d.): 8, 28–29.

"Riot Grrrl is . . . ." *Bikini Kill 2* (circa 1991): 44.

Spice World. Dir. Bob Spiers. Columbia Pictures, 1996.

Vail, Tobi. "Bikini Kill is Made Up of Four Individuals." Liner Notes, *Bikini Kill*. Compact disc by Bikini Kill. Kill Rock Stars, 1994.

White, Emily. "Revolution Girl Style Now." *Rock She Wrote: Women Write About Rock, Pop and Rap*. Ed. Evelyn McDonnell and Ann Powers. New York: Dell Publishers, 1995: 396–408.

Understanding the Text

1. To what extent can the rise of Riot Grrrl be attributed to a reaction against sexism? Provide evidence from the reading to support your answer.

2. Explain the role of "zines" in the Riot Grrrl subculture. How did they fulfill the main aims of Riot Grrrl?

3. What historical time period gave rise to Riot Grrrl?

Reflection and Response

4. How does Schilt's academic perspective on Riot Grrrl shape our understanding of the subculture? How might another perspective — an article from the *Bikini Kill* zine, for example — alter our understanding?

5. Corin Tucker of the bands Heavens to Betsy and Sleater-Kinney has accused the music press of misinterpreting Riot Grrrl: "I think it was deliberate that we were made to look like we were just ridiculous girls parading around in our underwear. They refused to do serious interviews with us, they misprinted what we had to say, they would take our articles, and our fanzines, and our essays and take them out of context." Why do you think that the mainstream music press was so dismissive of Riot Grrrl?

6. How does Schilt use authoritative quotations to establish the conversation about the topic of Riot Grrrl?

Making Connections

7. Trace the history of one of the Riot Grrrl bands — Bikini Kill, Bratmobile, Heavens to Betsy, Excuse 17, Huggy Bear, Cake Like, Skinned Teen, Emily's Sassy Lime, Sleater-Kinney, etc. Where are the women now? How have they kept the subculture alive? How have they influenced mainstream culture?

8. Schilt points out that Riot Grrrl was more radical than the late-twentieth-century feminism represented by the National Organization for Women (NOW). Research NOW, then respond to Schilt's claim. Is it valid? In what ways does Riot Grrrl continue to shape feminist discourse?

9. Research the spread of American Riot Grrrl to other parts of the world, focusing on a specific country and band. How has this international Riot Grrrl band resisted political oppression and gender restrictions?

Riding to Resist: L.A. Bicyclists Brave Death to Empower Communities

Ariel Climer

Ariel Climer is a freelance video editor and a community activist involved in Ridazz bicycle culture in Los Angeles. This article originally appeared on the website Occupy.com, a nonprofit media channel dedicated to "amplifying the voices of the global 99 percent." In her writing, Climer shows how activist subcultures can expand their circle of concern beyond their immediate needs to encompass the larger community. As you read, consider the reasons that this subculture, which melds a number of personal and political concerns, has emerged at this particular historical moment.

Riding bikes in Los Angeles is like riding with family: we celebrate and commune even when the only blood between us is road rash from near-death falls. Our family rides against traffic and the dominant culture. We have evolved from our origins as young punks and brought all ages of bicycle activists out of their homes and into the streets to form innovative and radical groups whose two-wheeled tools address specific and far-reaching community needs.

We reach far across the city like the roots of the ficus trees that disrupt L.A. sidewalks. Our parents, the Midnight Ridazz, modeled the counterculture for us. Three women began the Midnight Ridazz as a simple, small ride with a few friends. They organized around "fun and inclusive love, not divisive anger," recalled Don "Roadblock" Ward, one of the first riders, speaking in a retrospective interview with KCET.

The rides grew from six participants to almost 2,000 and sparked a cycling movement across the city. The alternative culture of the Ridazz drew in diverse cyclists, but it especially welcomed those outside the mainstream: the underdressed, the radicals, the jokers. These rides exemplify the simple joy of riding, while emphasizing the political act — in America at least — of using a bicycle as a primary mode of transportation.

Today, the Ridazz have grown like old oaks and now inspire other projects that uphold the rights of cyclists. Rides and riders have multiplied as the Internet facilitates posting and hosting rides. In 2013, invitations to over 500 unique rides showed up on the Midnight Ridazz website — events hosting anywhere from five to 500 riders, each action with its own subculture and highlighting a different area of the city. Rides that have grown "classic," like L.A.'s Critical Mass and C.R.A.N.K. Mob, still frequent the scene alongside newer ones.

With all of these bicycles in the streets, accidents still abound in 5
Southern California. But we continue to fight for our rights. The Eastside Riders and Los Ryderz on the south side of Los Angeles honor fallen
friends monthly in the Bike Ride for Safety and Justice, named in honor
of Benjamin Torres who was killed in a hit-and-run in Gardena.

Torres's untimely death is a reminder of the dangers of riding in a
city dominated by the car. By honoring fallen riders, advocates continue
to bring awareness to both bikers and drivers — and, in many cases, to
demand justice. The blog Biking in LA keeps a saddening record of the
cycling death statistics, reporting 89 deaths in Southern California in
2013 — and an increase in L.A. County bicycling deaths by 54 percent
this year alone.

Policy advocates in Los Angeles like the Los Angeles County Bicycle
Coalition alongside statewide bicycle advocacy groups, have worked to
pass California's 3-foot law that will go into effect in September 2014,
requiring drivers to pass bicycles with a 3-foot buffer.

Bike advocates have also helped bring about the city's Anti-Harass-
ment ordinance, which the *L.A. Times* explains "makes it a crime for drivers to threaten cyclists verbally or physically," as well as allows cyclists to
take drivers to civil court — the first ordinance of its kind in the country.
Though the risks remain, the Los Angeles cycling community continues
to fight to expand its rights and develop new laws that protect it.

We also cook for each other and we eat together. Groups like Food Not
Bombs/Comida No Bombas in Los Angeles use bicycles to further the fair
distribution of food and resources. These groups prepare hot food such as
soups, beans, rice, burritos and other dishes to serve free to low-income
people, which they deliver using bicycles with homemade trailers.

Two Los Angeles City Council members want to ban feeding the 10
homeless in public and make the food service provided by these bicycle groups illegal. In response, bike members joined a large protest in
December that generated attention on the corner of Hollywood and
Vine, a location where many homeless people spend time.

Even *Forbes* magazine recently called the motion one of the five "most
ridiculous government bans of 2013." The cyclists of Los Angeles will
continue to serve, even if unjust laws become prohibitive.

We also take care of each other. Using the bicycle as a healing tool,
the Ovarian Psycos, an all-womyn-of-color cycling collective, has developed a unique culture through all-womyn/queer/femme-identified rides
every full moon. Through various events — like discussions led by a
women's center worker, or an ancestor ceremony to honor those before
them — the Ovarian Psycos strive to heal their communities spiritually,
emotionally and physically using bicycles as the outlet. They also help get

"We harness bicycles as a means of promoting our own autonomy, healing our communities, and bringing about a future free of oppression."

female-identified people on bicycles in a city where ridership increased by 32 percent from 2009–2011 alone, according to the Los Angeles Bicycle Coalition—but where female participation still accounts for less than 20 percent. The Ovarian Psycos have garnered widespread attention, encouraging the proliferation of their annual Clitoral Mass ride to six cities across the nation in its second year.

We are a united community. Some of the most supportive bicycle groups ride the streets of the south side of Los Angeles. Los Ryderz and the Eastside Riders Bicycle Club join to form the United Riders, providing youth access to health workshops, community issue-themed rides, rallies, clean-up days and community fairs. The National Institute on Out-of-School Time recommends that children and youth have "access to and sustained participation in quality programming with strong partnerships with schools, families and the community." The United Riders are part of this equation, responding to social needs using bicycles as a tool.

In Los Angeles, we work together to carry out radical change in unique ways. We harness bicycles as a means of promoting our own autonomy, healing our communities, and bringing about a future free of oppression. The culture we counter is not just the culture of cars, but a debilitating economic system and isolating individualism. Through bicycles we create chosen families. In family, we begin to heal, and in healing, we find the strength to resist.

Understanding the Text

1. In paragraph 2 Climer says, "We reach far across the city like the roots of the ficus trees that disrupt L.A. sidewalks." What does this analogy mean?
2. Who are the Ovarian Psycos, and why does Climer consider them an important part of rider subculture?
3. What injustices do the rider groups aim to address?

Reflection and Response

4. For the radical bike riders, what negative values does "car culture" represent? Do you agree with this position?
5. Climer repeatedly mentions using bicycles as "tools." What does she mean by this? What do radical bicyclists want to fix? How do their concerns reach beyond their immediate needs?

Making Connections

6. Climer's article originally appeared on the website Occupy.com. Research the Occupy social-rights movement. Can the Occupy movement be considered a subculture? Why or why not? What are the main objectives of the Occupy groups and what effect have they had in the world?

7. Investigate the rise of the original Midnight Ridazz in Los Angeles. Who were they? Where did they come from? What motivated them?

8. Discuss how other subcultures use a particular object or tool to achieve specific aims.

Hip Hop—"Doing" Gender and Race in Subcultures

Ross Haenfler

Sociologist Ross Haenfler is one of the nation's foremost experts on youth subcultures. The author of several scholarly books on the subject, he focuses on subcultures in everyday life, with a special interest in how individuals' changing values and beliefs lead to larger social change. Punk, hardcore, and straight-edge subcultures particularly influenced Haenfler as a young person, so it's not surprising that much of his research and writing addresses masculinity in various music scenes, including the one portrayed here: hip hop. He currently teaches courses on sociological theory, deviant subcultures, and masculinity at Grinnell College in Iowa.

Hip Hop Culture—Status and Roles in the Scene

Hip hop is a *culture*, not simply a musical form, and an underground subculture has grown steadily alongside hip hop's mainstream popularity. One might claim to listen to hip hop music without really being part of the subculture, which encompasses much more than a musical style and street fashion. Hip hop culture, as outlined by Afrika Bombatta and the Zulu Nation,° consists of four basic elements, or art forms: DJ-ing, MC-ing, breakdancing, and graffiti. DJ-ing, as you might expect, involves playing records for a crowd. However, the hip hop DJ does much more than simply play one song after another. Rather, she or he uses two turntables simultaneously, jumping back and forth between records, mixing in samples, scratching over the music, and pumping up the crowd with chants, cheers, and call and response. As part of a hip hop group, the DJ lays down beats that the MC(s) raps over. An MC (Master of Ceremonies or Microphone Controller), popularly called a rapper, writes and performs rhymes over a beat. Rap's most basic definition is a vocal laid down over music (Ridenhour and Jah 1997). Technically, one could rap over country, classical, jazz, or any other type of music. Rap groups, such as the legendary Run DMC, include one or more MCs and a DJ like Jam Master Jay, although solo artists are much more popular today. Their songs include samples, or small pieces of other artists' songs; hence, part of a James Brown song might end up in more contemporary rap music.

Having emerged alongside DJ-ing and MC-ing, b-boying (also called break-dancing) is the dance form most associated with hip hop culture.

Afrika Bombatta and the Zulu Nation: South Bronx disc jockey (b. 1957) who helped create and define early hip hop music and dance, primarily through a group of socially aware rappers.

B-boying requires exceptional balance, strength, and skill, as dancers regularly assume difficult poses ("freezes") such as holding their entire bodies up on one hand or "power moves" such as spinning on their heads. Breaking is an exhibition or showcase style, where one dancer at a time takes center stage, showing off her or his moves as others watch and wait to take their turn. Some breakers form teams, or "crews," and face off in b-boy competitions.

The final element of hip hop culture is graffiti art, sometimes called graf or bombing. Though typically viewed as deviant vandalism or associated with gangs, the hip hop world considers graffiti a true art form. Writers gain fame and respect for their art and symbolically lay claim to urban space (Macdonald 2001). Each "street artist" coins her or his own "tag," their personal logo or signature that other writers identify, and more experienced artists create "pieces" (short for "masterpiece"), which are larger, more elaborate murals depicting their tag (ibid.). In an interesting (and practical) twist that reflects some mainstream recognition of graffiti art, some cities have erected "safe walls" where graffiti is not only legal but encouraged. Although graffiti culture has often been connected with hip hop, many artists have little or no connection with the scene, considering themselves their own, unique subculture (Pray 2005).

DJs, MCs, b-boys, and graf artists are all examples of statuses in the hip hop scene. . . . Different people hold the same status; for example, there are many individuals with the status of MC or b-boy. Each person simultaneously holds many different statuses. You, for example, might be some combination of a student, an employee, a sister or brother, a mother or father, an athlete, and a member of a church, mosque, or synagogue. Each status comes with a set of expected behaviors and/or obligations, called roles. A role is the set of behaviors associated with a status. In hip hop, the status of graf artist entails performing the artist role by designing and painting tags and murals.

Holding the status of MC requires performing the roles of lyricist and 5 live performer. Members of every subculture hold at least one status and perform multiple roles. Someone who is completely involved in hip hop culture is known as a "head" (Ridenhour and Jah 1997). Authentic "headz" know hip hop history and take an active role in shaping its future. Like "hardcore" punks, they are more committed to the scene than the average hip hopper. Each of the four hip hop statuses demand, in their own ways, respect (see Macdonald 2001). While arguably every member of any subculture might be searching for or demanding some kind of respect, hip hoppers more regularly and explicitly articulate this demand themselves. The importance of respect comes from African Americans and other marginalized groups who have faced struggle, discrimination, and a *lack* of respect.

Hip Hop, Urban Life, and Racism

In 2005, shortly after Hurricane Katrina wreaked havoc upon the U.S. gulf coast, rapper Kanye West claimed during a telethon that "George Bush doesn't care about black people." His comments, reflecting the widespread frustration with mismanaged federal relief efforts, raised unaskable questions: Did race play a factor in the delay, given that most of the stranded New Orleans residents were black? Would aid have arrived faster had the victims been white? These were uncomfortable questions for a society that prides itself on fairness and equality for all.

> "Hip hop is one response to inner city urban life and an ongoing dialogue regarding racism and race relations in the United States."

Hip hop is one response to inner city urban life and an ongoing dialogue regarding racism and race relations in the United States. Rap music and hip hop culture originally flourished in marginalized communities that experienced poverty and racism. Subcultures, according to Brake (1985), point out the inconsistencies in the larger culture, the gaps between a society's values and its reality. People in the United States value the "American Dream" that claims that those who work hard will be rewarded with upward mobility and secure, stable lives for their families. The reality is that many people work hard yet remain in poverty with inadequate access to health care, affordable housing, and good education. Hip hop regularly points out these inconsistencies. Even in Japan, often believed to be a racially homogenous nation, hip hoppers shine a spotlight on ethnic discrimination against "outcaste" groups such as *burakumin*,° who face bias finding jobs and marriage partners (Condry 2006).

Race in the United States

The United States has had a troubled history of race relations, to say the least, from slavery and Jim Crow laws to school segregation and debates over affirmative action and reparations for slavery. Many of today's youth, especially white youth, believe that racism was by and large an unfortunate problem of the past, resolved for the most part during the civil rights era. The occasional racist incident aside, many Americans believe that equal opportunity exists for all, regardless of the color of one's skin. Undeniably we have as a nation made some progress toward racial equity, and relationships between whites and nonwhites have significantly improved. We are a diverse country in which many different

---

burakumin: outcast group at the bottom of the Japanese social order.

ethnicities work, live, and socialize together. Yet problems persist, including racist violence. The terrorist attacks of September 11, 2001, renewed stereotypes of people of Middle Eastern descent and raised concerns about racial profiling. African and Native Americans make up a disproportionate number of the poor and the prison population. The country still struggles over immigration policies, with politicians and pundits taking opposing stands on illegal immigration. These struggles reflect a racial ideology—the widely held system of beliefs about race—that on the surface champions equal opportunity while covering significant inequality, tension, and racism. Far from being a harmonious, "color blind" society, race significantly impacts our lives and profoundly affects how we experience the world.

Like many people, you might believe that individuals of different colors are somehow fundamentally different from one another, that race somehow determines characteristics like intelligence, work ethic, morality, and propensity for criminal behavior. Sociologists, however, recognize that there are no fixed or permanent characteristics of race. Race encompasses biological traits such as skin color, facial structure, and hair texture that society considers meaningful. However, the actual meanings of race are socially constructed; what people think about race depends on their social surroundings, varies from place to place, and changes over time. There is no fixed biological meaning associated with race; in fact, race doesn't necessarily depend upon the color of one's skin, as was evident in nineteenth- and early twentieth-century immigration to the United States when waves of Italian, Irish, Polish, and other immigrants were not considered "white" (Margolis 2005). Racism is a belief system asserting that one race is inherently inferior to another (Healey 2005). Again, racism is not entirely based upon skin color—racism existed between the Hutus and Tutsis of Rwanda despite the fact that both groups are black, virtually indistinguishable in terms of skin tone. People's perceptions of skin color and race vary from culture to culture. In France, for example, racism is based more upon immigrant status than skin color (Lamont 2003). Racism always, however, involves a more powerful group judging a less powerful group as somehow morally inferior.

Although race is socially constructed, it still has vital consequences for   10 what we believe and the opportunities we have. The cultural meanings connected with race influence our perceptions of people. Young black men, in particular, are often presumed to be "troublemakers or criminals" (Anderson 1991, 167). Chicano youth are viewed as gang members or illegal workers. Even people who think of themselves as "color blind" or opposed to racism often subscribe to negative stereotypes. Racial scapegoating, or blaming social problems on a racial or ethnic category, fuels anti-immigrant movements today that blame unemployment and the health care crisis on Mexicans and other Latinos. Likewise, our racial category often influences our perceptions of others. Consider that after the devastating 2005 Hurricane Katrina 12.5 percent of whites believed race played a factor in rescue attempts, whereas 60 percent of African Americans felt that if the victims had been white they would have been evacuated faster. Regardless of the reality, a racial divide in perceptions still exists.

Hip hop as a culture has consistently challenged the notion that racism has disappeared by drawing attention to the lives and problems of inner city youth. Remember that subcultures often uncover the hidden contradictions in society (Brake 1985). Hip hop, in a sense, asks how a country that prides itself on its freedoms and opportunities still harbors poverty and racism. It emerged in the midst of "white flight," or the migration of whites (and often industry) from urban to suburban areas — the urban middle class stagnated or shrank, leaving in its wake deteriorating schools and a scarcity of jobs. The hip hop response initially followed two veins, "sixties-inspired hip hop nationalism" and "Afro-centric hip hop nationalism" (Decker 1994, 99–100). Black nationalism draws upon black power movements of the 1960s and 1970s, condemning the disenfranchisement of contemporary poor, urban blacks. Afrocentric nationalism glorifies pre-colonial African empires, promoting a spiritual connection to African heritage and freedom from Western/colonial thought and oppression: Beyond these historic inspirations, today's underground hip hop (for example, dead prez and Immortal Technique) focuses on additional issues such as corporate control of the media, war, and welfare. As an initially urban phenomenon, hip hop culture constitutes a symbolic "taking back" of urban areas (Rose 1994b). Graf artists tag their names and paint murals on trains, buildings, and public spaces, staking out territory and remaking their surroundings. Early DJs tapped into streetlight electricity to throw block parties, and b-boys often performed on street corners. . . .

Sexual Politics of Hip Hop — Gangsta Rap and Women Rappers

While conscious hip hop often articulates a socially progressive message, other strands are profoundly misogynistic. One aspect of male privilege, or the unearned advantages associated with being male, is the dominance of popular culture by men that often results in music/movies/

TV produced by men, for men, from men's point of view. Like heavy metal, some rap lyrics, rap videos, and rap record covers degrade women, treating them as voiceless sexual playthings. Gangsta rappers in particular regularly depict women as devious and domineering, relegating them to little more than potential sexual conquests. White rap artist Eminem drew substantial criticism (despite support from openly gay pop star Elton John) for songs depicting violence against women and homosexuals. NWA criticized the police and debased women in the same songs. Just as punks and skinheads have contradictory elements, rap often simultaneously critiques racism while reinforcing sexism.

No subgenre of rap gains more negative attention than gangsta rap. While artists claim they are simply singing about their experiences of ghetto life, critics charge rappers like Snoop Dog and 50 Cent with glorifying violence and sexual domination. The now-defunct Parent Music Resource Center waged a campaign against rap (and metal), targeting 2 Live Crew in particular for its raunchy lyrics. Bragging about one's physical and sexual power is part of the hypermasculine image gangsta rappers cultivate. Influenced by Al Pacino's portrayal of Sicilian mafia boss Michael Corleone in *The Godfather* and his role as a Cuban gangster in *Scarface*, self-described "gangstas" prove and perform their masculinity through two primary roles: the "tough guy" and the "player of women" (see Oliver 1989). Prior to his murder in 1996, rapper Tupac Shakur, with "Thug Life" tattooed across his muscular torso, exemplified the "cool pose" prevalent among young men and ubiquitous in gangsta rap, and 50 Cent carries on the tradition today.

The "cool pose" generally entails baggy clothing, a cocky swagger, physical intimidation, and sexual prowess (Majors and Billson 1992). It is a performance, meant to convey specific meanings to whomever happens to be the "audience." Interactionist° theories of gender focus in part on how we *do*, or create, the meanings of gender through our everyday actions. Candace West and Don Zimmerman (1987, 140) claim that "a person's gender is not simply an aspect of what one is, but, more fundamentally, it is something that one does, and does recurrently, in interaction with others." Rather than a fixed characteristic, gender is an "interactional accomplishment." We produce, reinforce, and sometimes challenge what "masculine" and "feminine" mean in our interactions with others. You've probably seen guys "proving" their masculinity by showing off or women producing "femininity" by carefully managing

---

interactionist: describing the study of how individuals shape, and are shaped by, society.

their makeup and hair. In hip hop, particularly in gangsta rap, young men perform the cool pose and so reinforce a fairly narrow masculine script.

• • •

Lacking viable legitimate opportunities to attain culturally valued 15 statuses and rewards, some people will turn to illegitimate means to succeed (Merton 1957). In particular, young men who are unable to fulfill the roles that society says "real" men should fulfill (such as having a high-paying, high-status job and providing for a family) may seek to compensate in the only ways available to them: athleticism, violence, and bragging about their sexual conquests (Rose 1994b). This dynamic is hardly restricted to young black men, as our discussions of skinheads and heavy metal fans demonstrate. Indeed, the sexism and racism in youth subcultures may merely reflect, sometimes dramatically, the patriarchal, white supremacist values of the larger society (hooks 1994). Black rappers' misogynist attitudes may conceal the anger, pain, and depression that go along with the struggles many of them face (Morgan 1999).

Women Rappers

Women in hip hop have not sat idly by while men degrade or exclude them. While in many ways mainstream hip hop culture glorifies patriarchal masculinity, some female artists use rap music and culture to encourage and empower women. . . .

Cheryl L. Keyes (2002, 189) identifies four categories of female rappers: "Queen Mother," "Fly Girl," "Sista with Attitude," and "The Lesbian." The Queen Mother, exemplified by Queen Latifa early in her career, portrays herself as African royalty, dispensing knowledge and guidance to her people, demanding respect for black women, and often dressing in stylized African clothing. Fly Girls, such as the members of Salt-N-Pepa and TLC, wear the latest fashionable clothing while delivering an image of strong, independent, empowered women in charge of their sexuality. Like the Fly Girl, the Sista with Attitude (such as Lil' Kim) is an independent woman, only with a more aggressive, in-your-face, "bad girl" posture, sometimes even reclaiming the word "bitch" as a positive label. The Lesbian, of which Queen Pen is the exemplar, addresses lesbian identity from a black woman's perspective, a daring challenge in the often homophobic rap world. Although these categories are merely loose archetypes, they give an idea of the diversity of women's performances of gender in the hip hop world.

Although from a certain point of view female rappers are engaging in feminist resistance, according to Rose (1994a) and Morgan (1999), feminism has not resonated with many black women, who associate it with white women and an anti-male attitude. They are wary of a feminist movement that emphasizes gender inequality at the expense of racial inequality and are sometimes reluctant to criticize sexist black men for fear of further marginalizing that group. In addition to balancing calls for sexual and racial equality, women in hip hop are caught between challenging men's sexual exploitation of women and confidently asserting their sexuality (Pough 1999). Traditionally, white feminism has focused more on stopping sexist exploitation (by challenging pornography, for example) than on celebrating women's sexuality and sexual power. Yet women in hip hop sometimes wear skimpy outfits and dance "suggestively." Is dancing with little clothes on an example of shameless exploitation or a statement of sexual power? Can feminists demand an end to the objectification of women without denying their sexuality? Hip hop feminist Joan Morgan (1999, 74–78) claims that the responsibility lies on both men and women to challenge the sexism in hip hop, writing, "Any man who doesn't truly love himself is incapable of loving us in the healthy way we need to be loved" and "sistas have to confront the ways we're complicit in our own oppression." She insists that the hip hop community can be "a redemptive, healing space for brothers and sistas" (ibid., 80). Still, the financial rewards of sexist mainstream hip hop will likely confine much of conscious hip hop to the underground.

Hip Hop and White Suburban Youth — The "Performance of Race"

Although hip hop sprang from African American communities, it has since spread throughout the world. MCs from Japan to Brazil adapt the medium to their own circumstances, and in the United States Latino, Asian, and Native American youth have all joined the hip hop revolution. However, the largest consumers of hip hop music in the United States are white youth; the subculture has spread from the inner city to suburban America (Kitwana 2005), and various white performers have found mainstream success — Beastie Boys, Vanilla Ice, Marky Mark (now actor Mark Wahlberg), and most recently Eminem. In the early 1990s, Cornell West (2001) foresaw the "Afro-Americanization of white youth" as young black athletes and entertainers gained significant attention and were subsequently admired and emulated by young, white, and (mostly) male fans. Perhaps nothing more clearly illustrates this trend than the mass appeal of hip hop.

The rise of hip hop's appeal to white youth has sparked a politically 20 incorrect moral panic — in short, some white adults, whose conceptions of blackness are mostly negative, worry that their children are trying to "be black" (Kitwana 2005). Exactly what attracts white youth to rap music is difficult to say, especially since rap often contains explicit critiques of dominant (white) society. But perhaps this critique holds the attraction; what could be more subversive to an adolescent than to glorify the very artists who condemn your own (and therefore your parents') group? In the early 1990s, white kids who wore Public Enemy shirts likely unnerved their elders, stoking the "Fear of a Black Planet" the group represented. Interestingly, adolescent white males identify with the violence and sexism of gangsta rap rather than the anti-racist themes of political hip hop. The performance of a narrow, powerful, sexual version of black masculinity may lie at the heart of rap music's attraction. It could be that white kids are also alienated from mainstream American life and its uncertain job opportunities, stagnant wages, and growing inequality (ibid.). Yet apart from popular rap music, hip hop as an underground culture is likely attractive because it offers a community that, ideally, nurtures artistic and political expression and becomes a voice for struggling kids of all races (ibid.).

The phenomenon of white hip hoppers offers a clear example of how we construct race. White kids who adopt (in their minds) "black" manners of speech, dress, and demeanor earn the label "wigger"—that is, "white nigger" (Roediger 1998; Kitwana 2005). So-called wiggers evoke a variety of responses from their peers. Some, white and black, reject whites who "act black" or who "wish they were black" as inauthentic poseurs. For racist whites in particular, the word is a slur directed at other whites who violate their racial norms. Sometimes, however, the label is a term of endearment used by blacks to designate whites "seriously embracing African American cultural forms and values, in contrast to 'wanna-be' dabblers in the externalities of rap" (Roediger 1998, 360). The confusion or strangeness that white hip hoppers evoke demonstrates that we act out our race as well as our gender and that a flawed (or unconventional) performance is deviant. Several movies and TV shows illustrate conventional performances of race. In the movie *Can't Hardly Wait* (1998) a white kid "acts black" and *White Chicks* (2004) depicts two black men posing as white women. Both situations are funny to the audience precisely because they break the expectations of how we perform racial identity. Likewise, black kids who act "white," such as the Carlton character on the old TV show *Fresh Prince of Bel Air,* face derision from their peers for failing to follow the unwritten rules of racial performance. Pointing out racial performances is not meant to essentialize or stereotype any racial group—in other words, there is not one way to "act" white, Asian, Latino, black, or any other grouping, because there is no essential whiteness, Asian-ness, or Latino-ness. Nevertheless, we have unspoken norms and expectations regarding how people of different races and ethnicities act, and when people bend or break these rules we notice.

• • •

We all hold a variety of statuses. Sometimes those statuses contradict one another in important ways. Status inconsistency occurs when a subculturist holds two or more seemingly contradictory statuses. Imagine a gutter punk who comes from a loving middle class family or a gangsta rapper from the suburbs. Thus, when he raps about street life, 50 Cent is not simply relating his experience; he is reminding his audience of his authentic roots. White rappers must reconcile their whiteness with a cultural form still associated primarily with African Americans. They may face even greater pressure to show their rap credentials, hence Eminem's continual reminders that he struggled to rise above a humble background and his surrounding himself with a largely African American entourage. I am not questioning these artists' credibility, but clearly rappers construct and manage their authenticity as much as any other group, and authenticity depends, in part, on demonstrating one's racial and social class credentials.

You may be wondering if white hip hop fans develop a sort of racial consciousness, an ability to examine their own privilege, question racist beliefs, and grapple with social problems affecting people of color. Does hip hop have these positive outcomes? There is some evidence that hip hop has fostered a multicultural perspective and raised consciousness about race (Kitwana 2005). However, it may be that most whites are simply consuming a "black" art form without having to really engage with black people. One can purchase hip hop music, watch music videos, and so on without ever actually encountering a black person. Some people fear that white kids have appropriated hip hop, as they appropriated rock and roll, and have removed it from its racial and political context (ibid.). Furthermore, it could be that white kids feel that identifying with a "black" cultural form is in itself revolutionary—in a sense, they might feel they are "doing their part" without really changing anything. After all, white youth have rejected their "white-ness" as an act of rebellion since at least the early 1900s.

Conclusions

Hip hop culture has the potential to draw attention to racism and provide disadvantaged youth with a forum in which to build solidarity and fight oppression. While many youth are drawn to hip hop for the image, the bling, and simply the music, some build the multicultural communities politicians talk about but rarely realize. However, much of commercial rap music glorifies violence and remains misogynistic. Similar to punk, there is a significant gap between the underground hip hop culture and the mainstream, commercialized music. Hip hop also demonstrates how members of sub-cultures "do" gender in many different ways. The meanings of gender, like race, are socially constructed and are therefore flexible and changeable. Well-meaning people of all races hope for a "color blind" society, meaning a society that, in the words of Martin Luther King, Jr., judges individuals "on the content of their character, not by the color of their skin." For most of us, this seems like a worthy goal. Conscious hip hop reminds us, however, that we have not yet achieved that ideal and, moreover, to be colorblind blinds us to the continuing real impacts of racism in our society.

References

Brake, Mike. 1985. *Comparative Youth Culture: The Sociology of Youth Culture and Youth Subcultures in America, Britain, and Canada*. London: Routledge and Kegan Paul.

Condry, Ian. 2006. *Hip-Hop Japan: Rap and the Paths of Cultural Globalization*. Durham, NC: Duke University Press.

Decker, J.L. 1994. "The State of Rap: Time and Place in Hip Hop Nationalism." In *Microphone Friends: Youth Music and Youth Culture*, ed. Andrew Ross and Tricia Rose, 99–121. New York: Routledge.

hooks, bell. 1994. *Outlaw Culture: Resisting Representations*. New York: Routledge.

Keyes, Cheryl L. 2002. *Rap Music and Street Consciousness*. Urbana and Chicago: University of Illinois Press.

Kitwana, Bakari. 2005. *Why White Kids Love Hip Hop: Wangstas, Wiggers, Wannabes, and the New Reality of Race in America*. New York: BasicCivitas Books.

Lamont, Michele. 2003. "Who Counts as 'Them'? Racism and Virtue in the United States and France." *Contexts* 2 (4): 36–41.

Macdonald, Nancy. 2001. *The Graffiti Subculture: Youth, Masculinity, and Identity in London and New York*. New York: Palgrave Macmillan.

Majors, Richard, and Janet Mancini Billson. 1992. *Cool Pose: The Dilemmas of Black Manhood in America*. New York: Lexington Press.

Margolis, Eric. 2005. "White Ethnics." Photo essay in *Race, Ethnicity, Gender and Class: The Sociology of Group Conflict and Change*. 4th ed., Joseph F. Healey. Thousand Oaks, CA: Pine Forge Press.

Merton, Robert K. 1957. *Social Theory and Social Structure*. Glencoe, IL: Free Press.

Morgan, Joan. 1999. *When Chickenheads Come Home to Roost: My Life as a Hip Feminist*. New York: Simon and Schuster.

Oliver, William. 1989. "Sexual Conquest and Patterns of Black-on-Black Violence: A Structural-Cultural Perspective." *Violence and Victims* 4: 379–390.

Pough, Gwendolyn. 1999. *Check It While I Wreck It: Black Womanhood, Hip-Hop Culture, and the Public Sphere.* Lebanon, NH: Northeastern University Press.

Pray, Doug (director). 2005. *Infamy.* Chatsworth, CA: Image Entertainment. Documentary film.

Roediger, David. 1998. "What to Make of Wiggers: A Work in Progress." In *Generations of Youth: Youth Cultures and History In Twentieth-Century America,* ed. Joe Austin and Michael Nevin Willard, 358–366. New York: New York University Press.

Rose, Tricia. 1994b. "A Style Nobody Can Deal With: Politics, Style, and the Postindustrial City in Hip Hop." In *Microphone Friends: Youth Music and Youth Culture,* ed. Andrew Ross and Tricia Rose, 71–88. New York: Routledge.

Ridenhour, Carlton, and Yusuf Jah. 1997. *Fight the Power: Rap, Race, and Reality.* New York: Delta.

Understanding the Text

1. What does Haenfler mean by "status" in the context of hip hop subculture? What are some of the statuses described in the reading?

2. According to Haenfler and others cited in the reading, what social and economic factors gave rise to hip hop subculture?

3. Explain what sociologists mean when they say that race is "socially constructed"?

Reflection and Response

4. Keeping in mind Haenfler's examples, develop your own examples of how race and ethnicity is constructed and performed.

5. The author points out that stereotypes are not always supported by empirical evidence, but that nonetheless perception matters. How does this observation translate into your own real-world experience, in either a positive or negative way?

6. What is your own relationship to hip hop, both as a musical genre and as a subculture? Are you a fan? Indifferent? Baffled? Inspired? Explain.

Making Connections

7. Choose a contemporary hip hop act and analyze both the music and the practitioners in terms of the themes Haenfler develops in his article.

8. Research the graffiti/tagger subculture mentioned here and in Mark Stryker's article in chapter five (p. 285). What role does respect play in the subculture? Why is it such a central value? What other subcultures place respect in such a central position?

Raw Deal

Dana Goodyear

Dana Goodyear has been a staff writer for the *New Yorker* since 1998, and is the author of two collections of poetry. As a poet, she imbues her journalistic writing with a singular clarity and lyricism. The following article is drawn from one chapter in her 2013 book *Anything That Moves: Renegade Chefs, Fearless Eaters, and the Making of a New American Food Culture*, which, as the title indicates, investigates the fascinating world of outlaw food preparation and consumption. Goodyear lives in Venice, California, and is a faculty member at the University of Southern California.

Even before James Stewart, the leader of the milk-trafficking gang known as the Rawesome Three, hired an attorney from one of the top marijuana-defense firms in Los Angeles, the analogy was plain: raw milk is the new pot, only harder to get. For more than a year, Rawesome, a members-only food club that Stewart ran from a lot in Venice, California, was the subject of a nine-agency investigation, in which undercover agents infiltrated the network of dairy dealers supplying the club. . . . The operatives, including the feared California Department of Food and Agriculture investigator Scarlett Treviso (code-named La Rue), mingled with customers and, using what Stewart's lawyer said were "purse cams and pole cams," photographed Rawesome's cooler, dry-goods trailer, and open-air produce market. They also took pictures from the street: members passing through a large corrugated metal gate with a sign that read "Rawesome Foods—Raw and Organic—Out of the Ordinary and Downright Extraordinary."

Rawesome, an expensive, all-cash specialty store devoted to radically unprocessed food, attracted a clientele of health-seekers, yoginis, celebrities, and the seriously ill. At Rawesome they could buy provisions that were otherwise inaccessible: unheated honey from the Bolivian highlands (outside the fallout range of the A-bomb° tests), sun-dried cashews from Bali, raw cow colostrum, goat whey, and camel milk from a dairy selling it for "craft use." In the meat cooler, there were raw bison kidneys, spleen, hearts, and testicles, which customers often sliced open and ate on the spot. "We had some real vampires going through there," a former Rawesome worker, who lived for a time in a shipping container on the lot, said. "Everyone wanted to suck the cow's udder." Liv Tyler and Mandy Moore shopped there occasionally. Mariel Hemingway was a regular, as were Peta Wilson and Vincent Gallo. Fred Segal, the boutique

A-bomb: atomic bomb.

owner, ordered a box of food every week, and John Cusack's personal chef, Rawesome workers said, was forbidden to shop anywhere else.

Early on the morning of August 3rd, as one of the coconut juicers — known around Rawesome for their stoned demeanor and their unsocialized way of wearing mud masks in public—started extracting the day's supply, there was a knock at the gate. Outside, more than a dozen agents from the F.D.A., the county health department, and the Franchise Tax Board had assembled, in raid jackets and tactical vests; armed L.A.P.D. officers provided security. Stewart, a robust sixty-four-year-old with a beachcomber's mustache and a wardrobe of Hawaiian shirts, was arrested and put in handcuffs. He had nine thousand dollars in his pocket, because he'd been planning to go downtown to pick up merchandise. His fruit money was entered into evidence. Over the next several hours, a crowd of about a hundred Rawesome members gathered to watch as agents loaded produce onto a flatbed truck. When the agents dumped some eight hundred gallons of raw dairy down the kitchen drain, members wept.

The same day, the police rounded up the rest of the Rawesome Three. In Santa Paula, sixty miles away, they hit Healthy Family Farms, a small operation that supplied the club with poultry, eggs, and, for a time, raw goat products from a forty-head herd that Rawesome boarded there. The farmer, Sharon Palmer, a single parent who manages the farm with her three teenagers, was arrested. A fifty-nine-year-old graphic designer named Eugenie Victoria Bloch, a Rawesome member who helped sell Palmer's products at farmers' markets, was also arrested, outside her home in Los Angeles. Stewart, Palmer, and Bloch were charged with felony counts of conspiracy; Stewart and Palmer were charged with an additional two felonies, for running an unlicensed milk plant and processing milk products without pasteurization,° and with various misdemeanors, including counts of poor sanitation and improper labeling. (All three pleaded not guilty to all the charges.) Stewart's bail was set at a hundred and twenty-three thousand dollars, with the stipulation, common in drug cases, that he be held until the court could ascertain that the bail was not "feloniously obtained"—high stakes for a grocer.

At a hearing in October, thirty supporters wearing white T-shirts that read "RAW MILK HEALS" gathered outside the courtroom. Many were baffled by what had befallen their neighborhood market. "Rawesome was an intelligent local food ecosystem. It was alive, and it was regulating itself on a level so far beyond what the U.S.D.A. or the F.D.A. means when it says 'food safety,'" Camilla Griggers, who teaches English at a nearby

pasteurization: heating process that kills microbes in food and drink.

college, said. "That we would be dragged through the court system on a food-safety issue is so laughable. Rawesome was a gourmet club par excellence of the best food you could get anywhere in the world."

Raw milk stirs the hedonism° of food lovers in a special way. Because it is not heated or homogenized and often comes from animals raised on pasture, it tends to be richer and sweeter, and, sometimes, to retain a whiff of the farm—the slightly discomfiting flavor known to connoisseurs as "cow butt." "Pasteurization strips away layers of complexity, layers of aromatics," Daniel Patterson, a chef who has used raw milk to make custard and eggless ice cream at Coi, his two-Michelin-star restaurant in San Francisco, said. "Right now, at the beginning of spring, the milk is at its sweetest. The cows are getting a lot of herbs that are really verdant and green, and the milk has a higher fat content." Another respected California chef, who uses raw cream to make butter, ice cream, and a *cajeta°* he describes as "haunting," told me, "Dairy is the single most delicate and sensitive indicator of terroir I have encountered. When you take milk or cream and pasteurize it and homogenize it, you've killed the originality." He helped a nearby farmer buy three cows (from a breed carefully picked for the character of its milk) and is part of a small herd share, an agreement of uncertain legality whereby consumers own a percentage of a herd and are entitled to a certain amount of the milk. The chef said that his farmer insisted on cash payments, no paper trail. "Only recently have they allowed receipts to go through my bookkeeper, but even now we don't say what it's for," he told me. "We say 'cow services.'"

> "The new wave of refined American cuisine has a regressive side, wrapped up in nostalgia for an imagined past."

The new wave of refined American cuisine has a regressive side, wrapped up in nostalgia for an imagined past. Never mind the immersion circulators and the hydrocolloids; progressive cooking is an act of recovery. Patterson, who is both a kitchen technologist and a forager, told me, "We make a huge effort at Coi to look like we're making no effort at all." To chefs like him, unprocessed milk does not just taste better; it is sentimental and, more important, it is pure. "Raw milk is a primary touchstone of that sort of agrarian, old-fashioned way of life," Patterson said.

Suspicion of technology has long been associated with the raw-milk movement. In the nineteen-thirties, a Cleveland dentist named Weston A. Price travelled around the world studying isolated populations

---

hedonism: pursuit of pleasure.
cajeta: Mexican dish made of sweetened, carmelized goat's milk.

experiencing their first exposure to "the displacing foods of modern commerce." In *Nutrition and Physical Degeneration*, which has become a central text for the movement, he wrote that people who ate unprocessed, indigenous foods had strong teeth, regular bone structure, and overall good health, whereas those who had adopted an American diet—refined sugar, white flour, pasteurized and skim milk, and hydrogenated° oils—had cavities, facial deformities, and other problems, which they passed along to their children.

Advocates of raw milk hold that pasteurization kills enzymes that make food digestible and bacteria that contribute to a healthy immune system. Drinking raw milk, they say, confers numerous health benefits—vitality, digestive vigor, strong teeth, clear skin—and even has the power to treat serious ailments, such as diabetes, cancer, and autism. Sally Fallon Morell, the founder of an advocacy group informed by Price's work, recommends feeding raw milk to infants. Carola Caldwell, a registered nurse who drove several hours from Lake Arrowhead to shop at Rawesome, overrode years of medical training to feed her son raw milk and meat. She told me that the diet had cured him of extreme allergies, chemical sensitivity, and moodiness. "Within three weeks of starting raw food, he became a different child," she said.

There has been little science to support these claims. The closest thing 10 to an objective body of data appeared last August, with the publication of a large-sample study linking children's consumption of unheated "farm milk" to reduced rates of asthma and allergies. The researchers, based in Europe, where raw milk is more widely accepted, determined that whey protein was the protective element, but they stopped short of advising people to consume raw milk, because of the risk of pathogens. The next step, they wrote, would be to develop "ways of processing and preserving a safe and preventive milk."

Milk—rich in protein, low in acid—is one of the best growth mediums on the planet. Bacteria love it. Unpasteurized milk can carry salmonella, campylobacter, and E. coli O157:H7, the strain that came to public attention in the nineties, when four children died after eating contaminated meat at Jack in the Box. Listeria has been traced to queso-fresco-style raw-milk cheeses, sometimes known as "bathtub cheese," a reference to unsanitary home-production methods. A study published by the C.D.C. in February found that pathogens in raw milk can be especially harmful to children and others with weakened immune systems; in the sixty raw-dairy outbreaks between 1993 and

---

hydrogenated: referring to the treatment of oils with hydrogen to increase the shelf life of food.

Raw milk stored in glass jars and kept at 36–38° F. lasts for seven to ten days. Improper storage allows microbial contaminants to multiply. Robert F. Bukaty/AP Images

2006 in which the victims' ages were known, two-thirds were younger than twenty. Only a small fraction of the population—between one and three per cent—drinks raw milk, and fewer than two hundred cases of foodborne illness are attributed to it each year. Still, its popularity is rising, which is a great concern to regulators. The C.D.C. study reported that raw dairy was a hundred and fifty times more likely than pasteurized products to cause an outbreak.

• • •

Raw milk has always been legal in California, but the preponderance of regulation has made it hard to come by. In the late nineties, not long after James Stewart started selling raw milk, the state's largest provider shut down its raw operation, leaving, by Stewart's count, eight licensed raw-milk cows in California. As he searched for new supplies, he heard from Mark McAfee, a former paramedic who had inherited his grandparents' farm, in Fresno. "I called up James and said, 'I've got two hundred and fifty cows here, all certified organic or on grass,'" McAfee told me. "He says, 'I'll be there in three hours.'" According to McAfee, Stewart single-handedly rebuilt the market for raw milk in Southern California, and introduced him to the nutritionist Aajonus Vonderplanitz,° a former *General Hospital* actor who claims to have cured himself of multiple cancers by eating a diet of raw meat, eggs, and milk, and sharply restricting his water intake. (Vonderplanitz, who calls his approach the Primal Diet, says that for a treat he bleeds meat into raw milk: "Tastes like ice cream!") Vonderplanitz became an investor in the farm, and his followers became McAfee's customers. Organic Pastures is now, by McAfee's estimation, the largest raw dairy in the world, with four hundred and thirty cows. It produces twenty-four hundred gallons of milk a day, which retails for sixteen dollars a gallon. . . .

But embracing bacteria is part of the raw-milk ethos. In order to shop at Rawesome, you had to sign an agreement saying that you preferred your food to "contain microbes, including but not limited to salmonella, E. coli, campylobacter, listeria, gangrene and parasites" and liked your eggs "completely unrefrigerated and unwashed from the chicken and covered with bacteria and poultry feces." Members not only rejected government food-safety standards as inapplicable to their nutritional requirements; they found them to be dangerous, because they allow for food to be treated with radiation and antibacterial chemicals. In an earlier raid on Rawesome, in 2010, the California Department of Food and Agriculture took samples of cheese made by a dairy in Missouri and found that they tested positive for trace amounts of listeria. "We told them we threw it out, but I don't think we did," a former U.S.D.A. employee who worked at Rawesome for two years told me. "Listeria really didn't matter."

Milk, be it human or cow, is the first food to which most humans are exposed; it is unlike other products both for consumers, who associate it with basic nourishment, and for regulators, who see its oversight as a grave responsibility. Michele Jay-Russell, of the Western Institute for Food Safety and Security at U.C. Davis, said, "From a public-health perspective, milk has fallen into the category of water. Providing a clean milk and water supply is fundamental to what the government sees as its job. If the government were stopping people from selling impure water, it's hard to imagine there would be a great public outcry." But Jay-Russell acknowledges the frustration of consumers who can't get a product that they feel they need. "The crux of the conundrum is: why shouldn't it be their choice?"

One winter morning, with a heavy fog lying over Los Angeles, the 15 Dairy Fairy, a Rawesome member who quietly assumed Stewart's procurement responsibilities after the bust, got in her car and headed for the drop. Every week, she takes orders from the Rawesome diaspora for raw

Aajonus Vonderplanitz: American nutritionist and activist (1947–2013).

dairy, sauerkraut, and meat, most of it transported from out of state in truck space rented from a large produce operation. To compensate her for her time, she is given a box of groceries, which is meaningful, since she works freelance, and she and her boyfriend spend about five hundred dollars a week on food. (Their dog eats raw, too.)

Since August, the drop had gone down in public parks across the city, but the Dairy Fairy had decided that was too risky. One day, at a convenience store, she noticed a man selling cars off the lot. "I was like, That's kind of shady," she said. "So I went and talked to the owner. He said, 'I'm from Egypt—I love raw milk!' I trade him milk for us to park our truck here." The beauty of the location, she said, is that trucks come and go all day long; no one notices the milk truck, unmarked and inconspicuous, parked in a corner of the lot.

The truck was waiting when she arrived. A young couple popped out; the woman had a pixie cut and was wearing knee-high yellow-and-black athletic socks from a CrossFit gym. The man helped the Dairy Fairy unload from her trunk two cases of black-market raw butter, made with cream from a nonfat-yogurt operation in New England, which sold for sixteen dollars a pound. "This stuff is sacred!" the Dairy Fairy said. The butter-maker, she said, demanded that they rendezvous in strange spots to make the handoff: cash up front for butter. The last time, it had been at LAX. This time, she had had to meet him by the side of the road in Pasadena.

As the sun burned through the fog, the former members of Rawesome started to arrive: skinny women on bicycles, old ladies with tote bags, a C.P.A.° in a shiny black BMW S.U.V. Vincent Gallo—pink sunglasses, lumberjack shirt, moccasins—came for his box, which included goat yogurt made by someone who used to work at Rawesome. "I go up in the mountains and get the raw goat milk," the yogurt-maker said. "I actually have to sign a waiver saying I won't bring anyone up there or say who they are. They are top secret."

A few weeks later, the Dairy Fairy called me. She'd had an uncomfortable conversation with the butter-maker, who has a successful gourmet business and sees no advantage in exposing his dealings in contraband dairy. "He said, 'You were the drug dealer! The drug dealer does not talk to the media!'"

To many in the national food-freedom movement, raw milk is the test 20 case. Two years ago, a nonprofit legal organization that helps raw-milk farmers sued the F.D.A. to lift the ban on interstate sales. (The suit was dismissed. . . .) In responding, the F.D.A. asserted, "There is no absolute

---

°C.P.A.: certified public accountant.

right to consume or feed children any particular food." Statements like this stoke anxiety about the government's intentions. "Raw milk is just symbolic of this attitude of government regulators that they are the ones that make the decisions about what foods we can have," David Gumpert, a journalist who advocates for raw milk on his blog, *The Complete Patient,* says. "You have this trend now toward irradiation. It's not required, but it's been sanctioned by the F.D.A. The next step may be for the F.D.A. to require that all spinach has to be irradiated."

The story of Stewart and his club was taken up by bloggers outraged at what they saw as federal overreach and disproportionate enforcement. In recent years, the F.D.A. has raided Amish and Mennonite farms that supply unpasteurized dairy products to out-of-state food clubs; earlier this year, a farmer in Pennsylvania was driven out of business. The raid at Rawesome appeared to be an escalation of a strategy that raw milkers think aims to kill the business entirely. Mike Adams, the editor of the Web site Natural News, compared undercover regulating agents to the East German Stasi,° and warned of. "I believe we are very close to entering the age of a shooting war between farmers and the F.D.A.," he wrote. "I would encourage the F.D.A. agents who are no doubt reading this to strongly consider: Is your war against raw milk worth risking your life?"

Lately, raw milk has found political support in a somewhat unexpected quarter: among Tea Partiers and libertarians. At a December town-hall meeting in New Hampshire, Ron Paul, who introduced legislation to overturn the federal ban on interstate sales, received a round of applause when he said, "I would like to restore your right to drink raw milk anytime you want." At the end of January, James Stewart and a group of supporters converged at a hotel in Las Vegas, to attend the Constitutional Sheriffs Convention, an event put on by Richard Mack, a former sheriff from Arizona who successfully challenged a provision of the Brady Bill before the Supreme Court and is now running for Congress as a Republican from Texas. Mack, who told me that he'd spoken at "more Tea Party events than Sarah Palin," had drawn a hundred sheriffs, from across the country, who feel that the federal government is infringing on individual rights.

Among the booths—Gun Owners of America, the John Birch Society,° Freeze-Dry Guy ("Freeze-dried foods for uncertainties")—was a table piled with raw cheeses and fresh produce. The vegetables had come from a sustainable Nevada farm that had recently become a food-freedom darling when a health inspector showed up at a "farm to table" dinner and made

Stasi: secret police of formerly communist East Germany.
John Birch Society: ultra-conservative advocacy group founded in 1958.

the farmer pour bleach on the vegetables, maintaining that, because she could not determine how long ago they had been cut, they were unfit even for pigs. That night, Stewart and the sheriffs would attend an "ice-cream speakeasy" hosted by several Raw Milk Freedom Riders—mothers who practice civil disobedience by crossing state lines with raw milk—featuring product that had been criminally transported from California.

Stewart was in a buoyant mood. The Rawesome trial was proceeding slowly, but he was meeting people he thought might be able to help him—like-minded California sheriffs and Oath Keepers, a group of soldiers, cops, and concerned civilians whose purpose is to remind officials that they have sworn to uphold the Constitution. Several of them, wearing black T-shirts with the silhouette of a Lexington minuteman holding a musket, stood near the entrance, checking credentials. "I know why the crackdown is happening," Stewart said. "Because we're winning. They're in freak-out mode. They're seeing all these fires going all over the place, and the only way they believe they can crack down is to do it on a nationwide basis, so they create fear and hysteria."

A buffet was set up in the middle of the room, with cold cuts, pasta 25 salad, and bags of chips. Mack, an imposing figure in cowboy boots, a turquoise shirt, and a loosened teal-colored tie, loaded up a plate. "I grew up absolutely hating milk," he told me. "I would gag on it! Now when I drink their milk, maybe it tastes better to me because it's freedom milk. It just has a little rebellious flavor in it. To me, it's the new civil rights. It's Rosa Parks."

Mack wandered over to the farm booth and asked one of the women there if she had eaten. "We brought our food, 'cause this is genetically modified," she said, pointing at the bag of popcorn in his hand. Someone poured Mack a glass of milk, and he turned to face the roomful of sheriffs—old fellows, mostly, with holstered handguns at their hips. The raw milkers cheered as Mack took a big, showy sip and called out, "Freedom milk! Freedom milk!"

The romance of the small farmer is a powerful thing in the American food marketplace. Sharon Palmer, who had taken up farming after a career in business, sought to connect Healthy Family Farms to this story, describing it as a "sustainable, pasture-based farm," where all the animals—chickens, ducks, Cornish game hens, lambs, cows, milk-fed pigs—are raised "from birth" and harvested by hand. When she was arrested in August, she again positioned herself as part of a larger narrative, telling the *Ventura County Star*, "It's not just about me. It's happening all over the country. I am very, very hopeful that this will become apparent that this is government abuse."

But just because a farm is small does not mean that the farmer always makes good decisions about how he raises the food you eat. A community that resists labelling and inspection as government intrusion puts itself at the mercy of its suppliers. And although Rawesome is held up by those who mourn it as a paradigm of intimate, enlightened consumership, its members may have known less about the origins of their food than they thought. A few years ago, a splinter group, led by Aajonus Vonderplanitz, began to question the integrity of Healthy Family Farms, claiming that the chicken and the eggs were outsourced and contained high levels of mercury and sodium. (Palmer and Stewart admitted to briefly selling eggs from another farm, but dispute the lab tests.) The former U.S.D.A. employee who worked at Rawesome said that she was furious to discover that the chickens she believed to be exclusively pasture-fed were in fact finished on corn. "There's no such thing as non-G.M.O. corn feed!" she said.

After the Rawesome Three were arrested, Palmer's practices came under greater scrutiny. The bail-motion papers, signed by the deputy D.A. who brought charges, said that seized records revealed that she was "buying thousands of dollars' worth of meat, poultry, and eggs from other venders and reselling it at farmers' markets and at Rawesome." (Palmer maintains that this merchandise was part of a side business supplying restaurants.) Her pre-agrarian past also came uncomfortably into view. Several years before starting the farm, while working at a mortgage company owned by her then-husband, she was implicated in a reverse-mortgage scam that led to felony charges, including one claiming that she had defrauded an elderly woman of her Malibu home. After spending nine months in county jail, she took a plea bargain and was released. "When I came home, all I wanted was to do something good for my kids and my community—that's why I chose farming," Palmer told me. "Look where I ended up: in the middle of the milk mess."

Throughout the winter, Stewart remained optimistic—he had the 30 Oath Keepers on his side, and was eager to reopen Rawesome soon. His case had been assigned to a new D.A., whom he hoped might be more lenient. But additional charges could be pending; although Stewart wasn't charged with violating the federal ban on interstate commerce, agents had collected evidence about his relationship with an Amish farmer in Pennsylvania. When I talked to the farmer—an enterprising man whose operation reportedly makes nearly two million dollars a year—he said, "I'm living by the faith of God that he will provide our needs, that if the F.D.A. comes after us it will have been God's plan."

Understanding the Text

1. What does Goodyear mean when she writes that "raw milk is the new pot, only harder to get" (par. 1)?

2. According to enthusiasts, what are some of the benefits of raw milk?

3. Those who endorse eating raw food range across a wide political and social spectrum. What beliefs unite them? Use textual evidence from the essay to support your answer.

Reflection and Response

4. Proponents of the raw-food movement often cast their arguments as objections to government intrusion into the most basic aspects of their lives. In your estimation, where should the lines be drawn when it comes to government regulation of private choices? Does the government have the right — or even the responsibility — to tell citizens what they may and may not eat? Are there other instances of government regulation that can serve as guidelines for raw-food policies?

5. One raw-milk supporter tells Goodyear that "it tastes better to me because it's freedom milk. It just has a little rebellious flavor to it. To me, it's the new civil rights. It's Rosa Parks" (par. 25). Is this claim justified?

6. Goodyear points out that the "romance of the small farmer" is part of what drives the raw-food movement. Why do you suppose the family farm remains a touchstone of American experience, despite the fact that only two percent of the population actually farms? Discuss in detail.

Making Connections

7. Does food, symbolically and literally, play a role in other subcultures? If so, how? Why do you think that food is such a contested topic when it comes to identity and belonging?

8. What characteristics does the raw-food community share with at least one other subculture featured in this book? Consider lifestyles, beliefs, rhetoric, values, and goals.

Pleasures of the Fur

George Gurley

George Gurley is a popular columnist for the *New York Observer* and a contributor to several national magazines, including *Playboy*, *Marie Claire*, and the *New York Times*. The *Huffington Post* has referred to him as one of New York's "indispensable" people, whose late-night exploits generally leave his "dignity in disarray" but offer a window onto the pageantry of New York society. In many respects, he is a journalistic heir to writers such as Hunter S. Thompson, featured in chapter two. In the following dispatch from Chicago, originally published in *Vanity Fair*, Gurley engages with members of an extreme subculture: men who identify as animals.

A moose is loitering outside a hotel in the Chicago suburb of Arlington Heights. The moose — actually a man in a full-body moose costume — is here for a convention . . . and so is the porcupine a few feet away, as well as the many foxes and wolves.

Even the people in regular clothes have a little something (ferret hand puppet, rabbit ears) to set them apart from the ordinary hotel guests. One man in jeans and a button-down shirt gets up from a couch in the lobby and walks over to the elevator, revealing a fluffy tail dragging behind him. The elevator doors open. Inside, a fellow is kissing a man with antlers on his head.

The other hotel guests look stunned.

"We're a group of people who like things having to do with animals and cartoons," a man in a tiger suit tells a woman. "We're furries."

"So cute," the woman says.

Welcome to the Midwest FurFest.

Here, a number of "furries" — people whose interest in animal characters goes further than an appreciation of *The Lion King* — are gathering together.

At 7:30 p.m., near the front desk, three men known as Pack Rat, Rob Fox, and Zen Wolph are scratching one another's backs — grooming one another, like macaques in a zoo. "Skritching," they call it. I am tempted to turn around and run. Instead I find myself talking with Keith Dickinson, a self-described "computer geek." Not long ago, this man, a 37-year-old from Kansas City, Kansas, was so depressed he could barely bring himself to go to the grocery store. And then it hit him. He started to believe that, somewhere deep down, he was actually . . . a polar bear.

"In normal society," Dickinson says, "two people who hardly know each other do not walk up and scratch each other's backs. But when you're one of the furs, it's one big extended family."

Next to him is his skinny, longhaired, fedora-wearing sidekick, a 10
23-year-old art student named Ian Johnson (nametag: r. c. rabbitsfoot).
Last year, Johnson, who has brought the ashes of his dead cat to the
FurFest, persuaded Dickinson to attend another furry convention in
Memphis, and that's what did it.

"It's a new way of looking at the world," Dickinson says. "It's like
looking at it with baby eyes, or cub eyes."

"You regress into a child when you come to a convention," Johnson
says, "because it's that kind of camaraderie, or childishness."

Riding with Ostrich

It's night. Ostrich has to run an errand. We get into his Chevrolet Metro
and speed away from the Sheraton, toward the nearest mall. The headlights illuminate the road ahead.

Ostrich, whose real name is Marshall Woods, is a compact guy in a
denim jacket and blue jeans. He's 39 years old and works as a network
administrator at a rubber company in Akron.

"When I was very, very young, I knew I wanted to be some type of ani- 15
mal," he says. "I didn't necessarily want to be the animal, but I wanted
to have the animal shape, as far back as I can remember. It's that way for
a lot of people."

He did normal things, like playing in the high-school marching band . . .
but he couldn't stop thinking about cartoon animals. Throughout his
teenage and college years, he hid his furriness, thinking it was a "babyish
thing."

"What the hell," he says. "Now I'm old and I'm warped, everybody
knows it, so I don't bother hiding anything anymore!"

It wasn't until 1994 that he came upon others who shared his interest. He was a chemist at the time, collecting dinosaur stuff on the side.
One day he went to a comic-book shop and discovered *Genus*, a furry
comic-book series with sexy characters. "And I looked at it and I was like,
Whoa! This looks pretty much exactly what I'd like to read—I gotta have
one of these," he recalls.

Now he writes a newsletter for Ohio Furs, an organization of furries
with 87 members.

He got his name after taking some ballet classes and not being very 20
good at it. "I was sincere but not impressive," he says. "I guess I was technically competent, but not very much fun to watch. And I was compared
to the ostrich ballerinas in *Fantasia*. They are trying very hard, but they
are not quite there."

In 1998, Ostrich put up a Web site where you can see his animal drawings, his animal-themed poems and short stories (one of which was published in *Pawprints*, a magazine for furries), his instructions on how to build a fursuit, and pictures of himself engaged in animal-centered activities. Like the time he made a solo trip to Sea World. "There's something just inherently cheerful about ducks," reads the text next to one picture on his Web site. "They seem almost ridiculously optimistic about the world and their place in it." Next to a photo of sea lions, the caption reads: "Do they have any idea how cute they look when they beg? Who could refuse them?"

For a while, he concedes, he was a "plushie," which is the word for a person who has strong—usually erotic—attachment to stuffed animals. He even wrote a plushie newsletter for a while, but gave it up. "It doesn't really interest me now," he says. "I just like to have the stuffed animals around. I would still say I'm a plushophile—I'm just not that interested in it that much sexually. In a casual way, but not really seriously." . . .

Some Furry Theory

There are many kinds of furries, but they all seem to have a few things in common. Something happened to them after a youthful encounter with Bugs Bunny or Scooby Doo or the mascot at the pep rally. They took

Furries gather at a 2016 convention. These events take place all over the world and include such activities as dancing, arts and crafts, and fashion shows. Carsten Koall/Getty Images

"After being bombarded by tigers telling them what cereal to eat, camels smoking cigarettes, cars named after animals, airplanes with eyes and smiles, shirts with alligators, they decided their fellow human beings were not nearly so interesting as those animal characters."

refuge in cartoons or science fiction. After being bombarded by tigers telling them what cereal to eat, camels smoking cigarettes, cars named after animals, airplanes with eyes and smiles, shirts with alligators, they decided their fellow human beings were not nearly so interesting as those animal characters.

But it wasn't so liberating, having these intense feelings, when you thought you were the only person on earth who had them. The second big revelation for most furries came when they got on the Internet. Not only were there others like them, they learned, but they were organized! They started having conventions in the early 90s. Now, such gatherings as the Further Confusion convention in San Jose, California, and Anthrocon in Philadelphia, attract more than 1,000 furry hobbyists apiece. (The Midwest FurFest is a smaller "con," with about 400 attending.) There are other conventions, too—even summer camps.

The furry group has its own customs and language. "Yiff" means sex, "yiffy" means horny or sexual, and "yiffing" means mating. "Fur pile" denotes a bunch of furries lying on top of one another, affectionately, while skritching. "Spooge" is semen—a possible outcome of a fur pile. A "furvert" is anyone who is sexually attracted to mascots and such.

Many furries have jobs related to science and computers. They role-play on a Web site called "FurryMUCK," a chat-room kingdom where users pretend they're red-tailed hawks, foxes, and polar bears.

A high number of furries are bearded and wear glasses. Many resemble the animal they identify with (especially wolves and foxes, the most popular "totems"). Some have googly, glazed, innocent eyes. A few are crazy-eyed. . . .

Calling Dr. Pervert

Sex researcher Katharine Gates has written about Fox Wolfie Galen, among others, in her book *Deviant Desires: Incredibly Strange Sex* (Juno Books, 2000). Now she was sitting down in the living room of her Brooklyn Heights apartment, where she lives with her husband. In the book, Fox Wolfie Galen called sex with stuffed animals a "sacramental act."

"How can you not laugh?" Gates said. "I mean, because it's absurd. Even ordinary sex is pretty damn absurd when you think about it. It's pretty silly, it's pretty awkward, and so I don't think it would be fair to point the finger entirely at these people—but, no, it's funny. And the people who do it for the most part have a great sense of humor about it. Galen is a good example."

Gates, who is 36 years old, said some plushophiles may not be 30 "relationship-suitable": "In some cases—and this might be cruel to say—but we may be wired for the zeta male, the lowest male, to turn to other pursuits besides the pursuit of another human being. These people need a way of having intimacy and pleasure, too." . . .

A Badger Speaks

Back at the convention, it's rehearsal time in the Sheraton's Chicago Room. Onstage, a chicken puppet is "bock-bock-bock"-ing along to "Born to Be Wild." An engineer from Long Island named Lincoln (nametag: j. badger) sits down at a table. "You have to understand something," he says. "I was a very shy person. And a couple years ago, something broke, and I'm not shy anymore. Then I became a manager at work and so it improved my whole life!"

I ask J. Badger if there was wild sex going on at the con. "I don't want to know about it. And I think it's up to the con committee to keep that out of public view. The public should not even be aware." He has heard about "things" that went on at furry conventions in California, with its large population of wild San Francisco-based furries and its nexus of furrydom near Disneyland. J. Badger prefers a family-oriented furry experience. "If you don't make it for the kids, you will not have a next generation," he says.

A few rows ahead of J. Badger, a guy is skritching a pal's neck with his bear claw. "You have to understand, that is just human affection; that has nothing to do with furry," J. Badger says.

Besides gardening and volunteer work, these days J. Badger attends about 10 furry and science-fiction conventions a year. "I also do other conventions that I will not talk about," he says. "There are other conventions that are for adults only and I go to those."

Onstage now, three bears are playing air fiddle and plastic fish for 35 guitars while a hillbilly song plays. It has a catchy chorus:

> *Wearing my mask, yay!*
> *Looking like a bear, yay!*
> *Wearing my mask and looking like a bear*
> *I'm a rac-cooooon!*

Now it's showtime. The Chicago Room is full of furries. "Y'all ready for a good three, four hours of entertainment?" says Tyger Cowboy, the master of ceremonies.

Babs Bunny is the first act. Basically, it is someone in a bunny outfit hopping around while singing Cyndi Lauper's "Girls Just Want to Have Fun" in a high-pitched voice.

A group of furries in cat regalia do a few songs from *Grease*. A little boy in the front—a son of the convention chairman, Robert King—has his fingers in his ears.

The Squirrelles sing "You Can't Hurry Love." An Elmo muppet does "Tiptoe Through the Tulips." Ten seconds into the number, a wolf creeps up and rips Elmo apart. The place goes nuts. . . .

A Skritch Session

The Eagles are playing loud inside Trophies, the hotel sports bar. Football 40
is on the big screens. The crack of pool balls can be heard over "Hotel California." Tyger Cowboy is holding court at a table and working on a Reuben and an iced tea. His real name is Christopher Roth, and he's a 36-year-old travel agent who has booked flights for many of the furries present. "I am a tiger in a human body, yes. I am very feline. I am very neurotic about having my paws sticky. They have to be washed. Yecch!"

Roth lives in St. Louis, with his mate, Jack Below (Spiked Punch), the wolf trapped in a human body. They're both well-known furries, and they run arf, a support group of furries, who do things together such as visit hospitals and volunteer at the zoo. Tyger Cowboy, who has been in the fandom for three years, also runs the UniFURsal mailing list in St. Louis. He was picked on growing up. He lived near a nature preserve and was very "animal-oriented." Later, he says, he played semi-pro hockey and rode broncos in the Texas Gay Rodeo. But now he lives for furrydom.

The guy next to him is wearing a dog collar and a black T-shirt that reads, BAD DOG, NO BISCUIT. His name is Robert Norton. He is 23 years old and works at Wal-Mart while attending technical school in Wisconsin, but he's really a . . . "I'm a Rottweiler," he says. "A lot of my friends used to say I acted like a canine, especially Rottweilers. I've had Rottweiler breeders tell me I remind them of one of their dogs. Certain expressions I do. I chew on furniture. Little mannerisms. If somebody says the wrong thing and it upsets me, I've been known to spontaneously start growling at them without realizing it. I kind of got myself in trouble at work doing that. I growled at a customer."

It's time for the charity auction, and Tyger Cowboy has to get into his seven-foot tiger-kitten costume; he is offering a five-minute skritch to benefit Tiger Haven in Tennessee, an animal sanctuary damaged by a fire in which four tiger cubs died.

Up in Room 822 ("Furry Central," they were calling it), Tyger Cowboy strips down to his tight white briefs. Norton, morphing into his Rottweiler persona, gets on the floor and begins gnawling on a chair. Behind him is another man who fancies himself a Rottweiler; he gives Norton a vigorous back rub. Rottweiler number one starts exhaling loudly. "He's drooling again," Tyger Cowboy says. "Felines rule, dogs drool."

He puts on his tiger head and then, with his right paw, beckons me 45 closer to him.

He put his claws on my head . . . and gives me my first skritch. "You have a cat?" he says.

"Yes."

"Just think. You've been petted by a cat!"

The Coffee Mug of Dreams

The bespectacled auctioneer is Dr. Samuel Conway (furry name: Uncle 50 Kage). He's a biomedical researcher and a furry celebrity of sorts. He is auctioning off the mallet belonging to Tyger Cowboy's mate, Spiked Punch.

"Spiked will give you a nice big hug if you buy his mallet," Uncle Kage says theatrically. It sells for a hundred dollars.

Soon, Uncle Kage is showcasing a coffee mug with Native American art depicting the transformation of a young brave into a wolf. "Don't we all wish—isn't this all of our dreams? I have $30 for the mug that depicts our dream, the transformation of a man into a wolf—let's hope he stays that way, because it's unthinkable to go back . . . Sold for $30!"

The Cat and the Fox

In the vendors' room, furries are buying comic books, cartooning kits, swords, axes, and tomahawks. A sign on the table reads, NO CHILDREN. Behind it is a wild-haired, busty woman named Bushy Cat. She is an artist whose drawings show erotic furry fantasies, with fantastic anatomies drawn in glorious detail.

Back in 1997, Bushy Cat was going nowhere. Her animal art wasn't selling at craft fairs. "I was ready to work at McDonald's," she says. "I wasn't clearing any money at all, and no recognition."

Then she went to Anthrocon in Philadelphia, where she found out 55 what sells. With binders full of X-rated drawings, she went to conventions in Tennessee, California, Washington—all over—and put 30,000 miles on Greyhound.

Jurann Foxtail, a 24-year-old dot-com worker, stops by. He is a "huge collector" of "yiffy" art. He says his life changed after he saw Disney's *The Fox and the Hound* at age four. "For weeks I begged my parents to be the fox," he says. "I wanted to be the fox. 'I want to be the fox, Mommy, I want to be the fox!' 'You can't be the fox, you're a person!' 'Oh, that's no fun.'" . . .

The Griffin in the Bar

Matt Davis, a slender 30-year-old dude with black close-cropped hair, is in the hotel bar. His T-shirt reads, MY SEXUAL PREFERENCE IS NOT YOU. Davis drove up to the Midwest FurFest with a few other furs from Arkansas. He's a security guard and furry artist who fantasizes about being a griffin, which would make him half eagle, half lion.

"I'd be a security-guard griffin," he says. "I could fly and patrol the area." He would have a griffin mate who would look like him but "a little bit thinner-boned" and "adorable."

"I've had fantasies that I've spent a long hunt through the forest catching my prey and bringing home to my nest moose and deer, something like that. Something large. Carrying it home to my nest, where my mate is waiting for me, and after eating, we engage in ferocious sex and fall asleep cuddling together in the nest."

With him is a rotund fellow with long blond hair. He says he is the 60 March Hare (real name: O. Holcomb). "Being human, first of all, we're not all that cute," he says. "In fact, we're butt-ass ugly. Second of all, intelligence, while it is a wonderful thing, is not that wonderful. Having what we think is understanding and then realizing it's not is more painful than being hunted down and killed by your predator." Being furry, on the other hand, is a solution to life. "It gives me thunder," says the March Hare. "I can walk into any situation and go, 'I am the dude!' It's like having a switch, a psychological switch you can tap into and turn something on." It helps even when he's flipping burgers. "You have 30 orders up there," he says. "If I wasn't the hare, I wouldn't be fast enough to get those 30 orders out—and in under three minutes—and be the dude."

The Furry-Haters

Later on in the bar, at two a.m., a dozen 30-ish patrons, part of a wedding party, are making noise. I hear the word "faggots."

"They're freaks," says a blonde who gives her name as Sylvia.

"No," says Johnny. "*Star Trek* people that have lost *Star Trek*. Now they run around with mouse costumes on. Very disturbing."

"A bunch of freaks running around!" Sylvia insists. "What is the purpose of the fur costume?"

"Pretty much guys that can't deal with society," Johnny says. "There's 65
more to it than the costumes—they're blatant homosexuals."

"Bestiality!" Sylvia says.

"It's a shame, because there's a lot of people here who are getting the
wrong impression of Chicago," says Johnny. "Like, a bunch of queers running around in a mouse costume. It, uh, it just makes me sick." . . .

Toward a Furry Future

A month after the Midwest FurFest, I call Ostrich at his apartment in
Ohio. He has been sitting around drawing a picture of a fox and playing with his cat. The FurFest was a success, he says. "I've heard nothing
but good about it," Ostrich says. "I've heard two complaints about it,
and they're both from known malcontents." He confirms there was a fair
amount of wild sex at the convention: "Oh, yeah, I know there was for a
fact. I probably would have been involved in it if I hadn't been so busy."

Was he still hopeful about the possibility of genetic engineering?

"Oh, yeah. That's pretty much the future of the world—there's no 70
way around it. If I can live another 30 or 40 years, I might live several
hundred more. Obviously, I'd like to rework my body to make my physical body conform more to my body image. I'd want a tail, I'd want some
fur, and, basically, some cute cartoon eyes and stuff. The technology for
that's coming. I don't think it's as far off as most people think."

Understanding the Text

1. Although there are many kinds of furries, what do they all have in common?
2. How was the rise of the Internet partly responsible for the formation of the
   furry subculture?
3. Sex researcher Katherine Gates suggests that some people may be "wired
   for the zeta male, the lowest male, to turn to other pursuits besides the pursuit of another human being" (par. 30). What does she mean by "zeta male"
   in this context?

Reflection and Response

4. Most people now believe that one is "born that way" in terms of gender
   identity. Many furries go even further, asserting that they were born with an
   animal identity. Do you believe that this is the case? Explain.
5. The "furry-haters" in the hotel bar denounce the furries as "guys that can't
   deal with society" and "blatant homosexuals." How would a member of the
   furry community defend himself against this characterization?

Making Connections

6. In describing how he approaches writing one of his articles, George Gurley says that "total immersion" is his method, and that "the ideal thing would be to go into it knowing as little as possible" about the subject. What is the benefit of this method of journalism? In what other situations could this open-minded exploration be a useful working method?

7. Gurley says that most furries have jobs related to science and computers. Why do you think this is the case? What other subcultures feature science and computer professionals? What characteristics do these subcultures have in common?

Carsten Koall/Getty Images

4 | What Values Do Subcultures Share with Main-stream America?

James and Laura Dowd introduce this chapter by arguing that American subcultures are not so much separate from the mainstream as part of a spectrum of social groupings that make up our common culture. From this perspective, a marginalized community's values and practices often overlap with those of other marginalized groups. In addition, subcultures share much with mainstream culture. We all experience the same geography, national history, and broad social realities, despite our frequent inability to understand the lives of our fellow citizens.

Travis Culley, in his essay on bike messengers, and Leslie Heywood, in her study of bodybuilders, both identify the core American values of hard work and autonomy as the animating factors of their respective subcultures. For these authors, personal commitment to the physical body parallels America's projection of aggression and dominance in the world.

Bob Frost, in his brief history of Chicano lowriders, also deals with the projection of values into larger social spheres, as young Mexican Americans claim access to shared public space through the most American of all symbols: the automobile. Frost's article demonstrates how the theme of individual autonomy, a constant in mainstream American life, animates lowrider culture.

The ethos of individualism is central to the survivalist subculture that Kim Murphy reports on in "The American Redoubt." It is no accident that the survivalist movement sprang up in the American West. In the national imagination the West has always been the last frontier, the place to live free of the dominant culture. As a Western institution, the rodeo has long represented this free-spirited Americanness, as Glenden Brown argues in "Femininity and Toughness: What Rodeo Queens Tell Us about America." The West is also the setting for the flourishing Mormon polygamous community profiled by Scott Anderson, whose reporting for *National Geographic* suggests that mainstream American values such as hard work and strong, intact families are alive and well in unconventional places.

Douglas Haddow's "Hipsters: The Dead End of Western Civilization" concludes the section. Haddow revisits this subculture of educated twentysomethings to claim that hipsters, by incorporating crass American values of consumerism and ahistorical nostalgia, have doomed themselves to irrelevance. As you read, pay particular attention not only to what these subcultures openly borrow from the dominant culture but also to how they represent themes that inform our national identity.

The Center Holds: From Subcultures to Social Worlds

James J. Dowd and Laura A. Dowd

In this scholarly article, originally published in *Teaching Sociology*, James J. Dowd and Laura A. Dowd challenge the concept of subcultures as "either deviant, marginalized groups or heroic resisters against the hegemonic culture." They present a more nuanced conception of subcultures as existing along a continuum of social groups. The Dowds are sociologists at the University of Georgia and, during their long careers, have published dozens of academic articles and books focusing on social theory and life-span human development. The Dowds wrote "The Center Holds" specifically to introduce the concept of subcultures in undergraduate sociology courses.

Subcultures and the Continuum of Assimilation

[D]oes the United States have a common culture or is it better understood as a loose network of many overlapping subcultures? . . . [I]t is our contention that subcultures exist along a continuum of social assimilation that may be defined both objectively and subjectively. By social assimilation we mean, objectively, the frequency with which one interacts with members of groups other than one's own and, subjectively, the perceived sense of integration with the wider society that results from continual interaction with those outside one's immediate social groups. If one is socially assimilated in a socially and ethnically diverse society like the United States, one has regular and frequent interaction with individuals not of one's own ethnicity, religion, or regional identity. Subjectively, one is socially assimilated into the surrounding (dominant) culture if one feels competent to conduct routine social interaction with others who are members of the larger culture and different from oneself. The assimilated individual possesses a subjective taken-for-granted sense of understanding and familiarity with the tacit rules governing social intercourse within the larger, dominant culture.

"[D]oes the United States have a common culture or is it better understood as a loose network of many overlapping subcultures?"

With this preface in mind, we can define the ideal subculture as a group whose members (1) interact frequently with one another; (2) share a common world view, or *Weltanschauung*, that has at its center that attribute that defines the group most thoroughly; and (3) remain unwilling or unable to assimilate into the larger, dominant culture; that is, to have one's identification with the subculture become "normalized" and unproblematic. Subcultures may also be distinguishable from members of the dominant cultural group on the basis of their physical appearance, style of clothing and adornment, and other cultural signifiers such as language or dialect.

Based on this definition, we can identify at least three major types of subcultures which may be identified in terms of the probability of their eventual assimilation. The first of these groups, the one most likely to assimilate, includes the youth subcultures that have been studied extensively. . . .

Youth subcultures are the most widely cited (but not the only) instance of what we might call a temporary subculture. Any group that is physically isolated from the wider society for periods of time is likely to take on the characteristics of temporary subcultures. Examples would include inmates doing time inside a prison or perhaps a military unit stationed on a base away from its homeland, such as a United Nations peacekeeping force garrisoned in a temporary camp far from home.[1]

The second of the subcultural groups we encounter as we move away   5 from the cultural center and toward the less-likely-to-assimilate pole on the assimilation continuum are ethnic minority groups, particularly those who have recently immigrated to a society, who are culturally distinct and not fully assimilated.[2] These groups may develop some facility in the language of the dominant culture but will also attempt, in almost all cases, to maintain the group's boundaries through norms favoring marital endogamy and through cultural rituals and practices that uphold group values, customs, and traditions (Gonzales 2001; Takaki 1998; Tuan 1999). Such ethnic subcultures constitute the most often studied case and ideal instance of the sociological concept of subculture.

A third type of subculture — and the one least likely to assimilate — includes all groups defined not on the basis of an ascribed status characteristic like ethnicity, but rather on an achieved, or volitional, characteristic such as a common world view, political or religious beliefs, or lifestyle preference (Talbot 2000). This third type of subculture is much more difficult to identify because its existence is signaled by neither language nor marriage patterns. In addition, such subcultures are similar to yet distinct from voluntary associations, social networks, or other such loosely aggregated groups whose members share a particular pastime, avocation, interest, hobby, or other such commonality of focus or behavior. A religious cult such as the ill-fated Heaven's Gate, whose members live apart from the larger world and maintain a distinctive set of beliefs around which their existence as a group is defined, is an example of such a volitional belief subculture. Radical political groups, particularly those like the Weather Underground or the Earth Liberation Front, whose activities bring them into direct confrontation with law enforcement agencies, also represent instances of a belief subculture. Such belief subcultures would also constitute excellent examples of what we could describe as countercultures.

With this criterion of separateness at the center of our understanding of subcultures, it is difficult to agree with those who consider groups of artists, such as rock musicians or visual artists, to constitute distinctive subcultures (Muggleton 2000) even though they, as well as groups such as those who actively participate in paramilitary exercises or body-building regimes, may be distinguished by their appearances or practices. If regular interaction occurs between such groups and non-group members from the wider society and if these groups participate more or less in the common culture of that wider society, their subcultural status would seem more symbolic than real. . . .

A Common Culture?

Having defined subcultures as groups with three identifiable, measurable characteristics, we now turn to the question of the prevalence of subcultures in contemporary society. Are subcultures common to the extent that modern societies like the United States may be understood as consisting of overlapping networks of subcultures?

The answer depends on two considerations: (1) where the boundaries are drawn; that is, where on the continuum of subcultural characteristics the sociologist would place the edge or boundary of the subculture; and (2) the nature of the common culture; that is, those factors or variables considered to be essential, defining elements of the common culture. Concerning boundaries: if we place the marker at three or more standard deviations from the mean, then the United States clearly is not an overlapping network of subcultures. If, however, we move the marker closer to the mean, which would effectively define many more groups as subcultures, then the claim that the United States comprises a complex network of overlapping subcultural groups becomes true by definition. Using a marker very close to the mean would place almost all groups . . . outside the center. Using this approach, some sociologists have offered as examples of subcultures older people living in housing facilities for the aged, rodeo cowboys, universities (Newman 1997) and a wide variety of occupational groups, including truck drivers, transit police, test pilots, cab drivers, artists, construction workers, philosophers, athletes, and even sociologists. With this boundary marker, it is inevitable that one would almost certainly reach Henslin's conclusion (2001:49) that "U.S. society contains tens of thousands of subcultures."

The second issue one must consider in order to answer the ques- 10 tion of whether subcultures are common or rare is the specific meaning attributed to the concept of common culture. . . . [C]ontemporary American society is fairly pluralistic, accommodative and relatively autonomous (in the sense of not being directly controlled by ruling political or religious elites). Yet although the "thinking, doing, and having" of American society are not shared equally or similarly valorized by all of its members, a common culture exists nonetheless. . . .

The dominant culture in the United States is held together by forces emanating from five different, but related, sources. The first is the economy; that is, the system of multinational capitalism in which we all are implicated and from which we derive our livelihood. Fundamental to the common culture of contemporary American society is participation as rational actors in this system in order to acquire the capital necessary to purchase needed or desired food, shelter, and other material and cultural products. For this reason alone, we share common frustrations, anxieties, and satisfactions generated by the experience of being workers in a capitalistic economy. The second force is education. To prepare for work and life, we each undergo a similar (but certainly not equal) educational experience in which we encounter a varied but structurally similar set of courses that attempt to impart basic language, vocational, and citizenship skills, as well as familiarity with the laws and customs of American society. This training includes an exposure of the student to both the manifest and "hidden" curricula of the schools (Apple 1990; Bourdieau 1977; Bowles 1971). Another force is technology. We encounter a similar mechanical and electronic world through our use of automobiles, washing machines, coffee pots, television sets, telephones, high-tech electronics, and other similar devices. Technology is an aspect of the material culture of a society, and American culture in particular is saturated with technological devices, the mastery of which is increasingly necessary for participation in social life. For example, over 95 percent of American homes have a television set, television being the medium through which common understandings of our culture are disseminated through the plots and contrivances of situation comedies, athletic competitions, soap operas, and talk shows.

The fourth aspect of the common culture in American society is consumption.

Russell Jacoby (1994:37) argues against the idea that every group has a distinct culture, which is the implication of the "culture as a toolkit" view. Instead of a society of subcultures in which one would speak of "the culture of the poor, of drug addicts, of dog fanciers, etc., we are joined together in a culture of work, consumption, and acquisition." In other words, we are all shoppers. The fifth source of American common culture is memory—a shared knowledge of the loss and sacrifice associated with war, including the Civil War, World War II, and the Vietnam War; disaster; and heroic accomplishments. It includes a familiarity with the exploits or feats of common cultural heroes such as George Washington, Babe Ruth, Eleanor Roosevelt, John Glenn, Joe Louis, Amelia Earhart, Jonas Salk, John F. Kennedy, Oprah Winfrey, and Bill Gates as well as that of those, such as Al Capone, Marilyn Monroe, Jacqueline Kennedy Onassis, James Dean and others remembered for their celebrity or notoriety.

In sum, subcultures certainly exist but, like hunters and gatherers in the face of an increasingly industrialized world, their distinctive ways of life are vulnerable to the relentless encroachment of global capitalism and the standardizing pressures of its associated culture industries.

Subcultures, Social Words, and the Idiocultures of Social Groups

. . . As we have already discussed, the notion of subculture is usually asso-   15
ciated either with an ethnic group that is generally isolated and/or on the periphery of society or with a group holding a distinctive world view that results in minimal social interaction with the wider society. In either case, the concept of subculture defines a continuum on which subcultures range in exclusivity, world view, and assimilation. Subcultures are dynamic entities and over time tend increasingly to adopt the cultural practices of the wider society or the common culture. At the extreme margin are those groups whose political and cultural beliefs remove them almost entirely from participation in the surrounding culture (for example, a cloistered and secluded religious order).

Far more common are those groups described first by Strauss (1978, 1982) as social worlds sharing a distinctive way of life yet participating to a greater or lesser extent in the common culture. In the interactionist tradition, a social world essentially represents a universe of discourse.[3] Strauss insisted, however, that the concept should not be limited to the linguistic realm. The social world is much more concrete, denoting not just shared symbols but also "palpable matters like activities, member- ships, sites, technologies, and organizations . . ." (Strauss 1978:121). Social worlds exist within the wider culture with relatively little tension between their practices and beliefs and those of other social worlds. Some distinctive cultural elements, including a particular linguistic jar- gon, are almost certain to develop within social worlds. In short, a social world may be thought of as a certain way of life that develops around a particular activity. This activity will be the central focus of not just one particular social group but of a loose network of social groups, including occupations, professions, organizations, and institutions. Examples abound and would include any group that devotes considerable time to a specific pursuit, whether it be military training, bird-watching, college teaching, art collecting, ultramarathoning, race track gambling, or beer tasting. We can speak, for example, of the distinctive social worlds of country music musicians, of nudists, of pedigree dog breeders, of academia, of college sorority sisters, and so on.

As an example, the social world of academics is not restricted simply to the occupation of college professors but includes the colleges and universities that employ them; the professional associations to which they belong and which accredit them; the publishers with whom they negotiate book contracts; the students they teach, evaluate, and advise; and the common experiences of library research, writing research grants, writing essays, enjoying sabbaticals, reading journals of opinion, listening to NPR, and so on. The social world of country music, in contrast, involves musicians, song writers, studio technicians, radio stations, recording companies, festival organizers, road crews, business managers, merchandise manufacturers and distributors, television interviews, long weeks on the road, and the experience of dealing with agents and promoters.

From the perspective of those who are not part of a particular social world, the individuals belonging to it and its networks might be considered a bit different but certainly not extreme. . . .

Conclusions

. . . The approach we have taken in this paper begins with the assumption that subcultures exist at some distance from the cultural center of society and are characterized primarily by a limited degree of social interaction with those outside their group, which in turn fosters the perpetuation of a distinctive world view. Over time, however, the cultural power of the wider society is such as to reel groups at varying locations on the cultural periphery in toward the center—that is, to assimilate them. The dominant culture exerts a powerful centripetal force, drawing subcultures in towards the center and reducing much of their subcultural distinctiveness. In most cases, especially that of ethnic subcultures, the residue of older cultural patterns exists as a form of memory or what Gans (1979) has termed "symbolic" ethnicity. For a group to retain its subcultural distinctiveness for any significant length of time requires considerable effort and vigilance. Time is corrosive, and the common culture exerts a very powerful homogenizing force on all societal members.

• • •

The increasing complexity of American society has generated countless 20 social worlds even as it has witnessed the continuing absorption of former subcultures into the social center. . . .

The problem with subcultures is their tendency towards intolerance and ethnocentrism. Although assimilation of subcultures within the wider cultural milieu brings with it a loss of tradition and a certain sense of disconnection, much can be gained as well. The child of immigrant parents may feel a nagging sense of ambivalence, role distance, and even disloyalty as a result of having to straddle two different ways of life. However, she is also likely to be fluent both in her family's dialect and that practiced among friends and associates in the wider culture and to move effectively between these worlds. Knowing both worlds gives her a degree of autonomy that her parents almost certainly lacked. Our participation in one or several social worlds today may not carry the same sense of cultural power and depth that resounded in the rituals and practices of less complex and differentiated societies. Yet despite the incapacity of our social worlds to provide the same sense of foundational, primordial attachments that subcultures once provided (and in some cases still do provide), the comfortable sense of familiarity we have with the ideas, practices, and technologies of our local social groups and the larger social worlds in which we live, work, and recreate provides a cultural framework that, although imperfect, satisfies the human search for meaning.

References

Apple, Michael. 1990. *Ideology and Curriculum.* New York: Routledge.

Bourdieau, Pierre. 1977. "Cultural Reproduction and Social Reproduction." Pp. 487–511 in *Power and Ideology in Education.* Edited by A. H. Halsey and J. Karabel. New York: Oxford.

Bowles, Samuel. 1971. "Unequal Education and the Reproduction of the Social Division of Labor." *Review of Radical Political Economics* 3:1–30.

Gans, Herbert J. 1979. "Symbolic Ethnicity: The Future of Ethnic Groups and Cultures in America." *Ethnic and Racial Studies* 2:1–19.

Gonzales, Juan. 2001. *Harvest of Empire: A History of Latinos in America.* New York: Penguin USA.

Henslin, 2001. *Sociology: A Down-to-Earth Approach.* 5th ed. Boston, MA: Allyn & Bacon.

Jacoby, Russell. 1994. *Dogmatic Wisdom: How the Culture Wars Divert Education and Distract America*. New York: Doubleday.

Muggleton, David. 2000. *Inside Subculture: The Postmodern Meaning of Style*. New York: Berg/NYU.

Newman, David M. 1997. *Sociology: Exploring the Architecture of Everyday Life*. 2d ed. Thousand Oaks, CA: Pine Forge Press.

Strauss, Anselm. 1978. "A Social World Perspective." *Studies in Symbolic Interaction* 1:119–28.

———. 1982. "Social Worlds and Legitimation Processes." *Studies in Symbolic Interaction* 4:171–90.

Takaki, Ronald. 1998. *Strangers From a Different Shore: A History of Asian Americans*. Rev. ed. San Francisco, CA: Back Bay Books.

Talbot, Margaret. 2000. "A Mighty Fortress: Inward Christian Soldiers." *The New York Times Magazine*, February 27, pp. 34–41.

Tuan, Mia. 1999. *Forever Foreigners or Honorary Whites?: The Asian Ethnic Experience Today*. New Brunswick, NJ: Rutgers University Press.

Notes

1. Of these two examples, the prison constitutes the better case of a subculture. Because the prison itself is a permanent structure and a total institution, there is an equally permanent and total subculture that exists within it; for individual inmates, however, exposure to that subculture continues only for the length of their term. The soldiers garrisoned overseas presents a weaker example, given the prior internalization of the common culture and the likelihood that the base will provide them with at least some of the amenities and reminders of home. In both the case of youth subcultures and temporary subculture, there exists a very high probability of their members' eventual assimilation into the wide society. For this reason, we focus almost all of our attention in this paper on those subcultures that are more enduring and which exist within the larger society rather than inside total institutions.

2. Earlier in the history of the United States, it was also possible to speak of regional subcultures that, because of their relative isolation from other regions, developed distinctive beliefs, practices, and dialects. This was true most especially in the American south. This predominately rural part of the country maintained a distinctive view of the world that was largely influenced by the defeat of the Confederate forces during the Civil War (the War for Southern Independence). Today, due to several factors that include the increased migration into the south from other parts of the country and the rapid economic development of this region, its exclusivity, distinctiveness, and inability to assimilate have all decreased significantly.

3. Fine and Kleinmann's (1979) interactionist analysis of subcultures, written at the same time as the Strauss work on social worlds but apparently without knowledge of the Strauss paper, takes a similar approach, arguing that subcultures are not social groups but universes of discourse.

Understanding the Text

1. What three main types of subcultures do the authors identify? Give one example of each type.

2. According to the Dowds, what five forces hold together the dominant culture of the United States?

Reflection and Response

3. The authors suggest that a failure to master technological devices renders a person incapable of participating in social life. Do you agree? Why or why not? What significant social problems arise from a lack of technological knowledge?

4. The Dowds provide a list of cultural heroes to illustrate one of the five sources of American common culture. Whom would you add to their list? Why? Discuss at least three people.

5. The sociologist Herbert Gans calls the older cultural patterns of immigrant subcultures "symbolic ethnicity." In other words, the group retains cultural forms but not cultural meaning. Think of an assimilated ethnic group in contemporary America and write a short essay about the ways in which the group retains the symbolism of its ethnic origins.

Making Connections

6. The Dowds point out that it is common to find groups that have distinct social worlds yet participate "to a greater or lesser extent in the common culture" (par. 16). Choose one of the subcultures from this book and discuss the extent to which the group participates in mainstream culture. Consider the factors that pressure subcultures to assimilate and conform.

7. Research one of the radical religious or political groups mentioned in the article — Heaven's Gate, the Weather Underground, the Earth Liberation Front — and compose an essay in which you discuss the historical context of the subculture's formation, as well as the lasting effects, if any, on mainstream culture.

from Building Otherwise: Bodybuilding as Immersive Practice

Leslie Heywood

Feminist scholar and bodybuilder Leslie Heywood has contributed widely to the literature on the bodybuilding community. A professor at SUNY-Binghamton, Heywood has authored nine books, ranging from poetry to academic studies of sports and the women's movement. Here she calls upon her own experience in the gym to guide her through an academic analysis of late-twentieth-century bodybuilding as a projection of American ideologies of world dominance and industrial power.

In this narrative I wish to make three central claims: 1) that competitive, steroid-based body-building and its long-term detrimental health effects can be read as a synecdoche for globalization and its "grow or die" imperatives that ignore externalities such as long-term environmental damages; 2) that bodybuilding was more fully part of the mainstream in the late 1980s/early 1990s than it is now for specific economic and cultural reasons, and that, as a strangely literal embodiment of the economic global fetish with capital growth, bodybuilders now seem like a historical anachronism, out of step with more austere times; 3) the "New Austerity" emphasis allows us to explore the potentiality of bodybuilding in a different modality: that of immersive practice.

But Before the "Goodbye to All That": Postmodern Fantasy, American Exceptionalism, and the Transcendence of the Flesh

Postmodernism° was the word that aspired to describe the era of surfaces, the elision of content, the "image is everything" rush of consumerism that characterized the deregulated 1980s, a deregulation that ushered in the era of "globalization," and that preached an equality of image if nothing else. Every day was a form of theater, people playing with signifiers to make their look present the message of the day, image of the day, "self" of the day. A carnival of surfaces, a "be-all-that-you-can-be" free for

---

postmodernism: late twentieth-century philosophy of art and culture which rejects grand theories and certainties.

all. Postmodern theory pronounced the death of the self, the author, and that everything was text—that is, an endlessly rearrangeable collection of signs that had no fixed, pre-determinate pattern or shape, and this was the true nature of reality according to this mode of conception. The perfect world for the emergence of the bodybuilder as a dominant cultural image, and bodybuilding as a mainstream practice.

"That's when it hit me," Fussell writes, describing his reactions to his fellow bodybuilders as he ate and lifted and dieted down with the best of them.

Bad theater. Every word they uttered, every move they made seemed rehearsed—as rehearsed, in fact, as any performance I'd seen on stage. That explained the pregnant pauses before delivering the lines I knew from the magazines. Line like 'You gotta stay hungry,' or 'you work hard, good things will happen.' Much of being a bodybuilder, I gathered, meant playing at being a bodybuilder. (Fussell 1991:48)

A very literal form of "play" in which your own body is the construction site, the bodybuilder's dream is the dream of endlessly re-arrangeable flesh, the manipulation of the material without limits, the ultimate victory over "nature": "while my legs spasmed through the night," writes Fussell, "I'd dream of Tom Platz, the so-called 'Golden Eagle.'" Precisely describing the way a postmodern sensibility informs bodybuilding, he writes that:

more than any other bodybuilder, [Platz had] given up everything to reverse the course of nature. He had been born with a miserable structure, his hips wider than a yardstick, his shoulders narrower than a ruler. But through sheer industry, through set after set of 315-pound squats for 50 straight reps, through training sessions interspersed with vomit and blood, Tom hurdled these obstacles and became Mr. Universe. (Ibid.: 77)

You don't like the body you were born with? You don't like the shape to which your genetics have contributed? That's ok, that's just fine, because you can physically remake yourself however you'd like. Here Fussell gets at the way the concept of postmodern plasticity combines with earlier ideologies of self-determination—ideologies intrinsic to the larger cultural dream of American exceptionalism—to create a cultural context in which bodybuilding could flourish for a time.

In a brilliant analysis of the ideology of American exceptionalism, literary cultural critic Donald Pease defines that "exceptionalism" as "a

Bodybuilders pose in a Mixed Pairs competition. Michael Bradley/Getty Images

fantasy through which U.S. citizens bring contradictory political and cultural descriptions into correlation with one another through the desires that make them meaningful" (Pease 2009:8). Those desires are connected to the desire for autonomy, the celebration of the individual (and America as a nation of unique individuals), and the desire to start fresh, unencumbered by the past or one's origins. Those correlations have a long history related to the United States' foundation as a colony that rebelled against its sovereign to create alternative political, social, and cultural structures:

American exceptionalism has been taken to mean that America is "distinct" (meaning merely different) or "unique" (meaning anomalous), or "exemplary" (meaning a model for other nations to follow), or that it is "exempt" from the laws of historical progress (meaning that it is an "exception" to the laws and rules governing the development of other nations). (Ibid.:8)

Perhaps most influential to the American psyche is "the belief that 10 the U.S. was unencumbered by Europe's historical traditions" (ibid.: 11). While the desire for a sense of personal sovereignty and power seen in bodybuilders may have universal inflections, there may be a particular

"Americanness" for bodybuilding in that the ideology/fantasy of American exceptionalism has parallels with a bodybuilder's preoccupation with difference from "the masses." Like the bodybuilder who seeks to escape his genetic somatotype and remake himself to a better purpose and image, the ideology of American exceptionalism sought to excise the political, social, and individual body from its European, and particularly British, antecedents° and start again a new foundation, the earlier foundation razed clean. The preoccupation with breaking free from the past, forgetting and ignoring the past, and starting to build anew is one that has been directly imported into bodybuilding psychology and subculture.

> "[T]here may be a particular 'Americanness' for bodybuilding in that the ideology/fantasy of American exceptionalism has parallels with a bodybuilder's preoccupation with difference from the masses."

Anomalous,° exemplary, and unencumbered—these three adjectives are key descriptors of bodybuilding lore, absolutely central to beliefs about the fundamental project bodybuilding becomes. As Fussell describes the attitude he and his fellow builders share: "I want to look like something you've never seen before." . . . It's saying, or rather screaming, "More than anything else in the world, whatever it takes, I don't want to be like you. I don't want to look like you, I don't want to talk like you, I don't want to *be* you" (Fussell 1991:137). This uniqueness is something that is worked hard for, achieved, an undeniable difference encoded in the flesh. A difference worth, apparently, compromising one's long-term health, and even dying for: "I told myself that taking steroids was a Faustian bargain. I was selling my soul to the devil in exchange for transcending what was permitted to ordinary mortals. I was my own alchemist, I said, transmuting the base metal of myself, the dross, into gold" (ibid.: 122). Transmuting° the dross° into gold, building a physique that is valued for its difference, exempt from the physical laws that limit the development of others, providing a physical ideal to which others could or should aspire, Fussell enacts the fundamental exceptionalist drama of the body-builder, neatly combining its different strands into a living, breathing work of transformed flesh.

---

antecedent: thing or event that logically precedes another.
anomalous: deviating from what is normal or expected.
transmuting: changing in form or substance.
dross: waste material, rubbish.

Historically speaking, bodybuilding began at the turn of the twentieth century, was mainstreamed in the 1980s when Arnold Schwarzenegger as The Terminator became the masculine ideal, and began to fall out of favor at the end of the 1990s, when on a mass scale gyms converted themselves to "fitness centers" and "no grunting" became a fitness center rule. At my own gym, my training partners and I were reprimanded by the gym owner for letting the local newspaper take a picture of us training for a fitness article—we were "too big," he said. He was running a fitness center, not a gym, and he didn't want to intimidate anyone. We talked about it indignantly for days, but we knew our days were numbered. Now, chains such as Planet Fitness market a "no judgment zone" where supposedly everyone can train without being evaluated for the quality of their physique, and grunting from the strain of lifting heavy weights is explicitly forbidden in gym rules. The brief moment of bodybuilding hegemony was dead.

"Grow or Die": Economic and Bodily Imperatives in the Late Twentieth Century

This trajectory wasn't random, rather neatly following the expansion of the global economy and deregulation and the relentless emphasis on economic growth despite externalities. Like a global economy gone wild in an excess of production and consumption, not considering any of the environmental costs, the clear-cut forests, destruction of marshland, the dammed-up streams, many bodybuilders—especially competitive but also non-competitive—ingested various kinds of steroids and all kinds of pharmaceuticals in the effort to pump themselves up. And pump they did—bodybuilders in the 1990s and through to today became almost impossibly big, starting with Doria Yates and running through to Ronnie Coleman, who is more than 300 lbs in contest shape. Even bodybuilders themselves are questioning this direction:

Notice how ESPN showed a lot of bodybuilding shows back in the 80's and early 90's. Turn the TV on right now and you will see water polo, chess, hot dog eating contests, and poker. But not bodybuilding. Our sport has always been a sub-culture, but with the mass monsters of today we took out every chance we had to succeed and make bodybuilding mainstream. I look at this as neutral, because bodybuilding is not a normal activity, and that's a part of why I love it and it's special to me. It's not for everyone. Personally I like the mass monsters because it sets out new goals in which me or you could go after [sic]. It shows that it's possible to achieve. I believe that for bodybuilding fans the turn around to size is somewhat good, but when it comes to the general public we are taking ten steps back. (Bigcalves, "In The World of Bodybuilding, How Big is Too Big?" http:// www.bodybuilding.com/fun/topicoftheweek130.htm, accessed June 10, 2010)

"The general public," which may have embraced extreme muscularity 15 as an ideal more in the mid-1980s through mid-1990s than it does today, seems to have reverted to its characterization of bodybuilders as excessive narcissists. Aware of and sympathetic to the kind of stigmatization bodybuilders face, Lee Monaghan's study of the knowledge specific to bodybuilding subculture attempts to put bodybuilding drug use into perspective:

the reported global "abuse" of steroids among gym members — anomalous with the supposed healthism of exercise and widely considered dangerous and polluting—renders "bodybuilder" synonymous with the pejorative label "risk taker" in many people's minds. Within Western scientific and popular discourse such deviancy is claimed to manifest in the materiality of the body. A possible long-term hazard of drug-assisted bodybuilding, not immediately apparent but instead dependent upon the probing of biomedical science, is damage to internal bodily organs such as the liver, kidneys, and cardiovascular system. Moreover, the marking of deviancy on "excessively" muscular female bodies is in a more recognizable fashion—the inscription and project of powerful cultural meaning—represents another possible risk for those bodybuilders who transgress the normative ideal of the "fit-looking" body. (Monaghan 2000: 1–2)

As Monaghan so convincingly shows, bodybuilders are well aware of public perceptions and exist in perpetual dialogue with them even as they pride in their difference from dominant standards. Monaghan's study "explores the sustainability of the 'risky' practice of bodybuilding as participants endeavor to construct and maintain 'appropriate' bodies and identities" (Monaghan 2000: 2). . . .

As Monaghan points out, "bodybuilders" are far from a monolithic category, with variability informing the overall conceptions of the "ideal" body in terms of location, individuals within a specific location, and variability of that conception over a bodybuilder's lifespan. My analysis, while allowing that there are a wide range of reasons why people bodybuild, and very different understandings and formulations of its meaning, focuses largely on the underlying premise—that growth (in this case physical growth of the already-mature body, facilitated by the [over] consumption of food, supplements, and in some cases, steroids) is good. Whatever meaning an individual bodybuilder may assign to his/her growth, I'm interested in exploring the symbolic connections between over-consumption as an individual practice related to bodybuilding, and over-consumption as an externality produced by the global economic fetish with growth. Just as the growth mandate in the global economy produces externalized environmental damage that results in phenomena such as climate change, the extinction of species, over-utilization of resources and destruction of habitat, the growth mandate in a bodybuilder's individual life is often similarly externalized. Moreover, the ideological shift from a blind emphasis on growth to a more moderate emphasis is paralleled by a similar shift in the mainstream fitness industry from the hypermuscularity of bodybuilders as an ideal to the more general category of "fitness" as an ideal. While no one has the right to prescribe for any individual what is "too big," it can be observed that the "greening" of marketing and its emphasis on avoiding wastefulness has had the effect of further stigmatizing bodybuilders and their growth projects. My further point is that, as in all sports, bodybuilding in its competitive modality tends to incur externalities in a way that training in an immersive modality does not.

Of any sport, bodybuilding marks the ultimate postmodern dream, the transcendence of genetics, of the non-conforming flesh, and for American builders, at least, that dream is shot through with the residues of ideologies of American exceptionalism — America is different, and it is its "duty" to grow and dominate and show everyone else the way, just as bodybuilders see themselves as exceptional and greater forms of humanity than others. Mr. Universe and all that sign implies, the bodybuilder's dream of surfaces is the drama of size, and the drama of size has its shadow side, its barely concealed externalities of excess and waste:

EAT BIG, SLEEP BIG, TRAIN BIG was the iron edict obeyed by all of us. In our 20 *muscle stable, we averaged 5,000 calories a day. The stove was constantly burning, the oven baking, the refrigerator cooling, the cupboards storing . . . Nimrod injected himself on a daily basis with Vitamin B12 in order to maintain his extraordinary appetite. Vinnie could be heard throwing up every afternoon from an excess of food even his body couldn't take . . . to us, food represented fuel for the future. Every chicken breast and beef flank we ate was consumed in the hope that it would help make us into the giants we dreamed of being. (Fussell 1991:132, Emphasis in Text)*

Eating to the point of excess, consuming more than the body can process, bodybuilding's primary drama is first one of scale — of continual, unlimited growth—and it shares this aspect with the global economy, whose "grow or die" imperatives have "taken place without reference to environmental consequences such as global warming, ozone layer depletion, and the loss of irreplaceable scare resources" (Brown 2005: 565). . . .

Notes

Brown, Chris (2005) "Westfailure?" in David Held and Antony McGrew (eds.) *The Global Transformations Reader* (New York: Polity Press).

Fussell, Samuel Wilson (1991) *Muscle: Confessions of an Unlikely Bodybuilder* (New York: Avon Books).

Kaye, Kristin (2005) *Iron Maidens: The Celebration of the Most Awesome Female Muscle in the World* (New York: Thunder's Mouth Press).

Monaghan, Lee (2000) *Bodybuilding, Drugs, and Risk* (London and New York: Routledge).

Pease, Donald F. (2009) *The New American Exceptionalism* (Minneapolis: University of Minnesota Press).

Understanding the Text

1. In what way does Heywood see bodybuilding as immersive? Does she consider this immersion good or bad?

2. What is "American exceptionalism"? More specifically, what does the term mean in the context of bodybuilding?

Reflection and Response

3. How does Heywood use the research and writing of other authorities as a way of getting to her own argumentative points? Why is this strategy more effective than using outside sources only as support for her argument?

4. Paraphrase Heywood's argument that bodybuilding subculture represents core American values, as well as reflects political and social anxieties. Does she make a valid argument? Explain.

5. What makes bodybuilding more than just an activity shared by random individuals? In other words, if you were a sociologist, what grounds would you have for claiming that bodybuilders in the late-twentieth century comprised an actual subculture?

Making Connections

6. Although Heywood argues that bodybuilders now seem to belong to the last century, bodybuilding has clearly not died out. To what extent has bodybuilding, broadly defined, been reconfigured in contemporary mainstream culture?

7. Heywood specifically equates bodybuilding with "the economic global fetish with capital growth" (par. 1) — in other words, as the embodiment of the values of modern capitalism itself. In what other, non-economic ways can we interpret bodybuilding?

8. "You don't like the body you were born with? You don't like the shape to which your genetics have contributed? That's okay, that's just fine, because you can physically remake yourself however you'd like" (par. 7). The bodybuilder's desire to reconfigure his or her body to match an ideal image echoes the claims that George Gurley makes about furries (p. 197). What parallels can we draw between the two subcultures?

from *The Immortal Class: Bike Messengers and the Cult of Human Power*

Travis Culley

This selection is drawn from *Immortal Class: Bike Messengers and the Cult of Human Power* (2002), Travis Culley's book-length account of his time as a bike messenger in Chicago. Culley's original aim was to collect an anthology of writing from the community of bike messengers, but after failing to find a publisher, he wrote this poetic account of his own experiences instead. It was published to great fanfare. He holds an MFA in writing from the School of the Art Institute of Chicago, and in 2003 was named the alumnus of the year by his alma matter, New World School of the Arts.

6:48 a.m.

As I bolt headlong down from the Michigan Avenue Bridge to Madison Street, each dark Bauhaus° shape blurs into the cold stone facade of its Gothic neighbor. I keep on, coasting in the pedals, taking a wide right turn westbound on a vacant three-lane street through the center of downtown. This first delivery of the day shakes off my morning lag, pumping warmth through my veins, bringing the first bit of sweat to my brow. The air is clean; my head is clear. I look for a left turn onto Wells.

This morning, before the computers are booted up, the banks unlocked, and the stock market scrolls clicked on, I am running delivery routes under the city's yellow streetlights. The elevator banks are empty and the traffic lights, at what will soon be congested intersections, hold and change for no one. Most deliveries I make at this hour are to locked offices, where packages are slid beneath dim glass doors. I move as quickly and efficiently as I can, preserving my energy. A day of messengering is like a hard drug: you never know how rough it will be until you've slept it off.

Out here, while I'm coasting unobstructed through the shadows of morning, the world seems at perfect peace. The whole city is still and relaxed. Even buildings get their beauty sleep. Coming out of the spinning doors of the Morton Salt Building, I keep a swift rhythm skipping down the cold steps, heading to the Grinch, my yellow Cannondale road bike, locked to the bridge railing overlooking the riverbank. While the sky changes with dawn, a steady stream of people crowd the revolving

---

Bauhaus: German art school that combined crafts and the fine arts (1919–1933).

doors over my left shoulder. Their eyes are half open, their manner calm; they smile softly like babies still tucked into bed.

I enjoy this quiet time when the city's rhythm is slow. I can empathize with the early-morning modesty, and I share the reflective awe that I see in the pious postures of people walking. This respect will fall away when the colors in the sky turn blue and the city awakes. These same quiet faces will struggle for a spare minute, a phone number, a positive response from a supervisor or a client. Sincere people doing honest work will be driven into shouting matches, compelled to insult each other, tempted to quit right on the spot.

I'm with them every step of the way. I have seen the red faces and   5 the feelings of distrust as shoulders brush in crowded yet silent elevators. I have seen the masklike smiles they wear through stressful meetings about bottom lines. And yet I know none of these wandering souls. I talk to very few of them; they are somehow another species. Their machinery and their mythology move in one direction only. They stand packed into tight spaces, they look up to the brass trim of elevators, and they rise like they are spirits ascending to a gilded afterlife. Is it a floor number they are after? A title that will follow their name? A certain number of digits in their salary? Perhaps they just want a little safety? I don't know. But they are on a path and they will kill to stay on that path.

Every day I see them, good people yelling at each other, running past each other, and stepping over each other. I see them at their worst: in the public space, on the street, where no one is looking and no one cares.

I don't have time to be caught up in the sorrow of this. As my eyes have grown tired of fanning over as many as a million people in a single day, my heart has grown weary of caring for them. My relationship to these people of the city is reduced to suffering the silence of elevators with them, or walking through the ritual pickup and dropping off of packages with them, or muscling through traffic where "please" and "thank you" are lost to the aggravating assault of car horns and uncalled-for profanities. I have found that these good people, so engrossed by their own private struggles, are often incapable of conversation or a courteous word. They are concentrating, holding up the weight of their self-made worlds, trying to find higher ground.

While these masses groan over the decisions they have made and the responsibilities they have undertaken, I float above. I am free of their ideas of good and bad, rich and poor, right and wrong. As an uncommon laborer I may not amount to much in their eyes, but I am free of their judgment. I am sometimes seen as a social misfit, a freeloader, a junkie, but I am also envied for the color, the vigor, the picture of America I can find while they push their way through the weekday treadmill routine. . . .

Transcending age, sex, color, and all of that divisive sociopolitical bull-shit, the courier industry is supported by very like-minded people. Many of us are artists and musicians, usually in our twenties. Most of us have been broke long enough to be masters of survival and have dreamt big enough to avoid the constraints of a salaried existence. I came to this city to succeed in the theater. I survive as a courier. Cadence for cash and Money for miles—these are the mantras of many a struggling genius. We work for materials and we herald our poverty for the liberties it grants us. Every week or so on the street I meet another ambitious biker who has a bag full of handbills for their next big show or their next exhibition or their next club gig.

Beyond these surface similarities, there is a deep and unspoken bond 10 between couriers. When one is down, others carry the weight. When one is hurt, others are there to help. Some days the work can be so intense that bikers dehydrate, panic, end up confused or lost, or get messages scrambled on the radio. We have to look out for one another. Bikers get hurt, and when we do, we are often our only family. . . .

8:43 a.m.

The bike messenger is a lone ranger; he comes in to the industry from god knows where and offers himself up to sometimes incomprehensi-bly extreme situations. Every day he overcomes an avalanche of obstruc-tions, he makes miracles happen to win what is essentially a little game he plays with time. Companies will support a biker who can fight down any obstacle. . . .

If the company ever tries to discipline a messenger, two things can happen. An inexperienced biker will try to improve. This means going faster or trying to cover up mistakes—often losing his own inner calm, his *style* on the street. Eventually he will screw up and get hurt. If the biker is above being disciplined, if he is confident in his technique, he will just go to another company to work his magic.

Simply put, the relationship between the biker and the company is one of mutual gain. There is no ass to kiss and no contract to sign. It all comes down to the brutally simple premise that no matter the distance, the climate, the time of day, or the cir-cumstance, if the package is on time the agreement between the courier and the company remains solid. But accom-plishing this can be deadly. When it

"When it all comes down, the biker stands alone where there are no shadows, no one to help him, and nothing to hide behind."

all comes down, the biker stands alone where there are no shadows, no one to help him, and nothing to hide behind. The messenger must take personal responsibility right down to the asphalt with him. This is lesson one.

10:02 a.m.

I sit watching streams of cars and buses scuffling along. The sky ripples upward in a stream of rising fumes. I can feel the seconds pass as my thoughts keep time. Whenever there is a moment of rest I meditate on the world, the street, the day, the psychological wear and tear of modernism, of urbanity. I make sure that my pen is lodged in the right place and that I have a spare. I stretch my legs to keep my knees from tightening up. I think about the other bikers I can hear on the radio and what I should expect of the next ten seconds or so. I think about how I can do my job faster, with less effort. I forecast.

In another twenty minutes the streets will clear out. Cabbies will cir- 10 cle, looking for work, or sit in long lines at hotels, cracking open doors to lean out and spit. In offices, the phones will light up with personal calls and lunch plans will be discussed in private. I will get a group of daily shuttles that will occupy me for an hour or so.

The city that once seemed so chaotic and wild to me now seems like a perfectly choreographed ballroom dance. I have learned to see in the city a distinct sense of order, a special geometry, a realm of necessity behind each unplanned lunge and skid. The Loop has its own laws of nature that the biker must come to terms with. There are many such axioms, like *Cops north of the river are too corrupt to enforce laws* and *Bikes are invisible in traffic—always pass on the left.* These lessons come with experience and some common sense, but not all of these laws are so easy to learn or to integrate into a routine.

One of the most difficult lessons I've had to learn is that the city responds to the emotional, the philosophical—the *subjective predisposition* of the messenger. Like in a dream or hallucination, the city comes to reflect the messenger, determining how long he will be able to sustain the job by how well he can live with himself.

Pat, Number Thirty-four, is an example. If you come into the job angry, the most unexpected obstacles will drive your temper into the ground. The aggressive drivers and slow-walking pedestrians will become your nemeses. Pat quit eventually, after getting into a fight with another cabdriver. As we all know, cabs are a great excuse for getting upset, but Pat rubbed the cliché to soreness. . . .

11:21 a.m.

Many jobs can offer beautiful, challenging experiences, but none are quite like this.

Beyond all of the stress, the fatigue, and the often bizarre expressions of humanity that I find on a daily basis, I can appreciate this work for what it has shown me, how it has challenged me, and who it has allowed me to become. But this very deep satisfaction did not come quickly. It came only when I first realized that, as a bike messenger, I could *succeed*. 20

Success for a biker depends essentially upon two things: how well you can keep a rhythm and how well you can keep a temper. The first challenge is finding the rhythm of the city. This takes time, sensitivity, and a little bit of soul. The next challenge—keeping the temper—requires inner strength. But once you are *there* and you can hear the city's rhythm and look her in the eye, finding order in the chaos, then, at that instant, all of the obstacles that can confound an amateur will dissipate. The timing of when to hydrate, when to stretch, when to go headlong down Michigan Avenue—all becomes clear. . . . Congested streets seem empty. Intersections and red lights are pierced effortlessly. The routine of locking up the bike is choreographed to perfection and can be accomplished in three seconds or less. . . .

11:55 a.m.

I find it difficult to paint a picture of messengering as a blissful day job, a worklike recreation for sunny days in a big city. Yes, there are many moments that feel like celebrations of human power and personal freedom. When the sun is high and the breeze is cool, amid streams of joggers and tourists crowding parks for music festivals, with blue skies all around, I am the first to stop and be grateful for this side of my work. I savor the scenes I can stumble across on my way through the Gold Coast with a hot package going to a high-rise condo in the park. There are days that end with the light radio banter of friends on a gorgeous afternoon, saying things with intended coolness like:

"Thirty-nine to base. I am clean here in heaven, holding a cold Sam Adams and hoping to stay that way."

"10-4. You've had a hard day, Number Thirty-nine. Why don't you kick your heels up and watch the girls. Will I be seeing you in the A.M.?"

"That's a big 10-4, boss. Heels are up. Thirty-nine is out." 25

I have a right to enjoy these rare times because, more often than not, I am trying to keep my knuckles from going numb, my safety glasses from fogging up in the cold, and my packages dry. As a messenger, I spend much of my time in steel freight elevators that whistle at high speeds through tall shafts of stale air. Scratched into their industrial gray sidings are the senseless and profane scribbles of mailroom clerks. I deliver thick checks to old men in spacious condos who get twenty-four-hour care from live-in nurses. I spend some part of my day with young women who answer phones behind big desks. They scramble for pens because they know I am in a rush, and sign for each package as if it's urgent. I suppose it *is* urgent, but they can take all the time in the world and I won't rush them because they are, for me, probably the one part of my day I can always enjoy. The rest of my day is spent sprinting through traffic or waiting in a courier center with six other smelly bikers who are in line for packages from the Sears Tower.

Some of my day is spent back at base matching the day's delivery receipts with the dispatcher's floaters (the office's crudely cut paper forms that each order is written on). Throughout a workday, these floaters are collected in a stack and pinned together by magnets against the board, a metal sheet that is leaned up above the dispatcher's desk. After an order has been dispatched to a biker, Zero scribbles down the biker's number on the floater and sticks it on this board, under that biker's magnet, for him or her to go through later. We turn this matching time into bitch sessions that have us laughing to tears, making party plans or racing plans for the weekend. When our paperwork is done, we usually leave behind us a table littered with torn receipts and half-empty beer bottles, some of which end up atop the old refrigerator.

Messengering is not an easy job. It can be filled with anguish and humiliation, it can offer hardship so much deeper than the minor frustrations of traffic and rude doormen. In my time on the street, I have been hunted by cars, and hit by them. I have been chased and have returned chase to many unruly antagonists. I've been doored, thrown, clobbered, threatened, and pinned between cars. I have been in fistfights with motorists. I have cracked mirrors and scratched paint jobs. I have stood in the middle of traffic with my arms spread wide, demanding to be run down by a vehicle. This kind of conflict is just part of the job; such trials are so common now that I only talk about them if there are injuries or court dates. Somehow, through the unique difficulties that the journey of every single day brings, the job gets done and the board gets cleared, bringing with it a feeling of victory that never tires because each day seems only to get worse.

The longer you work out here, the sooner you begin to see yourself as somehow different, somehow exempt from the so-called universal laws of life and death. You become part of a class that, in order to continue, must believe itself unstoppable. This heightened feeling gives the messenger a confidence, a speed, and an agility of almost metaphysical proportions.

We cling to the dream of being untouchable, part of an immortal class 30 of winged angels, hailed for speed and strength. It moves us forward when danger comes too close, when "Man down" is heard on the radio and we can't be distracted, and when we feel too exhausted to go another mile yet we will continue. We will find our destinations, catch the elevator to the right floors, deliver the packages, and be ready for more. We messengers fight through extreme fatigue, overstimulation, frostbite, and dehydration.

With resilience and determination we are able to survive stunts and endure stresses that seem impossible to the casual observer. The pride taken in this feat makes us part of a unique world of young, colorful soldiers who look death in the face and make a living evading her.

Understanding the Text

1. Why does Culley claim that conflict is an important part of the bike messenger's life?

2. What are the two elements of success for a bike messenger?

3. Who is the typical member of the bike-messenger subculture?

Reflection and Response

4. When Travis Culley published his book about his experiences as a bike messenger in Chicago, many of his fellow messengers criticized him for failing to portray the boredom, the pain, and the varied experiences of the workers. Do you feel that his description of the bike messenger's life is sufficient? Why or why not?

5. In several passages, Culley offers a portrait of normal working life as a kind of imprisonment. Why does he do this? Are there any counterarguments to Culley's claims about the humdrum existence of ordinary Chicagoans?

6. What do you think of Culley's title? How does he elaborate on the theme suggested by the title?

Making Connections

7. There are several other bike subcultures in the United States, including one mentioned in this book ("Riding to Resist," p. 170). Investigate one of these other communities and develop a short essay discussing how the members construct a sense of exclusivity based on their often dangerous activities.

8. Culley suggests that the bike messenger is the contemporary equivalent of the cowboy. To what extent is this a valid analogy? Discuss the myth of the American cowboy in detail, then connect it to the life and work of the bike messenger.

The Polygamists

Scott Anderson

The son of a U.S. government worker, Scott Anderson grew up in Taiwan and Korea. Since 1994, he has reported extensively from war-torn regions, publishing articles in *Harper's*, *Vanity Fair*, *Esquire*, the *New York Times Magazine*, and other periodicals. In addition, he has authored several novels and nonfiction works, many of which deal with armed conflicts around the world. In this reading, originally published in *National Geographic* magazine, Anderson turns his attention to the more peaceful landscape of the American Southwest, where outlaw polygamous Mormon communities continue to thrive.

The first church members arrive at the Leroy S. Johnson Meeting House in Colorado City, Arizona, at about 6 p.m. Within a half hour the line extends out the front doors, down the side of the building, and out into the parking lot. By seven, it stretches hundreds of yards and has grown to several thousand people—the men and boys dressed in suits, the women and girls in Easter egg–hued prairie dresses.

The mourners have come for a viewing of 68-year-old Foneta Jessop, who died of a heart attack a few days ago. In the cavernous hall Foneta's sons form a receiving line at the foot of her open casket, while her husband, Merril, stands directly alongside. To the other side stand Merril's numerous other wives, all wearing matching white dresses.

Foneta was the first wife.

Colorado City is a town with special significance for those of Foneta's faith. Together with its sister community of Hildale, Utah, it is the birthplace of the Fundamentalist Church of Jesus Christ of Latter-Day Saints (FLDS), a polygamous offshoot of the Mormon Church, or LDS. Here in the 1920s and '30s, a handful of polygamous families settled astride the Utah-Arizona border after the leadership of the Mormon Church became increasingly determined to shed its polygamous past and be accepted by the American mainstream. In 1935 the church gave settlement residents an ultimatum: renounce plural marriage or be excommunicated. Practically everyone refused and was cast out of the LDS.

At the memorial service for Foneta, her husband and three sons give 5 testimonials praising her commitment to the covenant of plural marriage, but there is an undertone of family disharmony, with vague references by Merril Jessop to his troubled relationship with Foneta. No one need mention that one of Merril's wives is missing. Carolyn Jessop, his fourth wife, left the household in 2003 with her eight children and went on to write a best-selling book on her life as an FLDS member. She

235

describes a cloistered environment and tells of a deeply unhappy Foneta, an overweight recluse who fell out of favor with her husband and slept her days away, coming out of her room only at night to eat, do laundry, and watch old Shirley Temple movies on television.

At the conclusion of the service, most of the congregation walk over to the Isaac Carling cemetery for a graveside observance. I assume the enormous turnout—mourners have come in from FLDS communities in Texas, Colorado, and British Columbia—stems from the prominent position Foneta's husband holds: Merril Jessop is an FLDS leader and the bishop of the large chapter in West Texas. But Sam Steed, a soft-spoken, 37-year-old accountant acting as my guide, explains that elaborate funerals are a regular occurrence. "Probably between 15 and 20 times a year," he says. "This one is maybe a little bigger than most, but even when a young child dies, you can expect three or four thousand people to attend. It's part of what keeps us together. It reminds us we're members of this larger community. We draw strength from each other."

Few Americans had heard of the FLDS before April 2008, when law enforcement officials conducted a raid on a remote compound in West Texas known as the Yearning for Zion Ranch. For days after, television viewers witnessed the bizarre spectacle of hundreds of children and women—all dressed in old-fashioned prairie dresses, with elaborately coiffed hair—being herded onto school buses by social workers and police officers.

That raid had been spurred by phone calls to a domestic violence shelter, purportedly from a 16-year-old girl who claimed she was being sexually and physically abused on the ranch by her middle-aged husband. What lent credibility to the calls was that the residents of YFZ Ranch were disciples of the FLDS and its "prophet," Warren Jeffs, who had been convicted in a Utah court in 2007 for officiating at the marriage of a 14-year-old girl to a church member.

The raid made for gripping television, but it soon became clear that the phone calls were a hoax. And although authorities had evidently anticipated a violent confrontation like the 1993 shoot-out at the Branch Davidian compound in Waco—SWAT teams were brought in, along with an armored personnel carrier—the arsenal at the YFZ Ranch consisted of only 33 legal firearms. A Texas appeals court later found that authorities had not met the burden of proof for the removal of the more than 400 children, and most were returned to their families within two months. . . .

From the bluff behind his Hildale home, Joe Jessop has a command- 10 ing view of the Arizona Strip, an undulating expanse of sagebrush and piñon-juniper woodland that stretches south of the Utah border all the way to the northern rim of the Grand Canyon, some 50 miles away.

Below are the farm fields and walled compounds of Hildale and Colorado City, which Joe refers to collectively by their old name, Short Creek. "When I first came to Short Creek as a boy, there were just seven homes down there," says Joe, 88. "It was like the frontier."

Today, Short Creek is home to an estimated 6,000 FLDS members—the largest FLDS community. Joe Jessop, a brother of Merril, has contributed to that explosive growth in two very different ways. With the weathered features and spindly gait of a man who has spent his life outdoors and worked his body hard, he is the community's undisputed "water guy," a self-taught engineer who helped with the piping of water out of Maxwell Canyon back in the 1940s. He's had a hand in building the intricate network of waterlines, canals, and reservoirs that has irrigated the arid plateau in the decades since.

A highly respected member of the FLDS, Joe is also the patriarch of a family of 46 children and—at last count—239 grandchildren. "My family came to Short Creek for the same reason as everyone else," he says, "to obey the law of plural marriage, to build up the Kingdom of God. Despite everything that's been thrown our way, I'd say we've done a pretty good job."

Members of the faith describe the life that the Jessops and other founding families have built as idyllic, one in which old-fashioned devotion and neighborly cooperation are emphasized and children are raised in a wholesome environment free of television and junk food and social pressures. Critics, on the other hand, see the FLDS as an isolated cult whose members, worn down by rigid social control, display a disturbing fealty to one man, the prophet Warren Jeffs—who has claimed to be God's mouthpiece on Earth.

To spend time in Hildale and Colorado City is to come away with a more nuanced view. That view is revealed gradually, however, due to the insular nature of the community. Many of the oversize homes are tucked behind high walls, both to give children a safe place to play and to shield families from gawking Gentiles, as non-Mormons are known. Most residents avoid contact with strangers. *National Geographic* was given access to the community only on the approval of the church leadership, in consultation with the imprisoned Warren Jeffs.

In keeping with original Mormon teachings, much of the property 15 in Hildale and Colorado City is held in trust for the church. Striving to be as self-sufficient as possible, the community grows a wide variety of fruits and vegetables, and everyone, including children, is expected to help bring in the yield. Church members also own and operate a number of large businesses, from hotels to tool and machine manufacturers. Each Saturday, men gather at the meetinghouse to go over a roster of building and maintenance projects around town in need of volunteers. In one display of solidarity, the men built a four-bedroom home, from foundation to roof shingles, in a single day.

> "Although living arrangements vary — wives may occupy different wings of a house or have their own granny cottages — the women tend to carve out spheres of influence according to preference or aptitude."

This communal spirit continues inside the polygamous home. Although living arrangements vary — wives may occupy different wings of a house or have their own granny cottages — the women tend to carve out spheres of influence according to preference or aptitude. Although each has primary responsibility for her own children, one wife might manage the kitchen, a second act as schoolteacher (virtually all FLDS children in Hildale and Colorado City are homeschooled), and a third see to the sewing. Along with instilling a sense of sorority, this division of labor appears to mitigate jealousy.

"I know it must seem strange to outsiders," says Joyce Broadbent, a friendly woman of 44, "but from my experience, sister wives usually get along very well. Oh sure, you might be closer to one than another, or someone might get on your nerves occasionally, but that's true in any family. I've never felt any rivalry or jealousy at all."

Joyce is a rather remarkable example of this harmony. She not only accepted another wife, Marcia, into the family, but was thrilled by the addition. Marcia, who left an unhappy marriage in the 1980s, is also Joyce's biological sister. "I knew my husband was a good man," Joyce explains with a smile as she sits with Marcia and their husband, Heber. "I wanted my sister to have a chance at the same kind of happiness I had."

Not all FLDS women are quite so sanguine about plural marriage. Dorothy Emma Jessop is a spry, effervescent octogenarian who operates a naturopathic dispensary° in Hildale. Sitting in her tiny shop surrounded by jars of herbal tinctures she ground and mixed herself, Dorothy admits she struggled when her husband began taking on other wives. "To be honest," she says, "I think a lot of women have a hard time with it, because it's not an easy thing to share the man you love. But I came to realize this is another test that God places before you — the sin of jealousy, of pride — and that to be a godly woman, I needed to overcome it."

What seems to help overcome it is an awareness that a woman's primary role in the FLDS is to bear and raise as many children as possible, 20

---

naturopathic dispensary: store for alternative-medical herbs.

to build up the "celestial family" that will remain together for eternity. It is not uncommon to meet FLDS women who have given birth to 10, 12, 16 children. (Joyce Broadbent is the mother of 11, and Dorothy Emma Jessop of 13.) As a result, it's easy to see why this corner of the American West is experiencing a population explosion. The 100 or so babies delivered in the Hildale health clinic every year have resulted in a median age of just under 14, in contrast with 36.6 for the entire U.S. With so many in the community tracing their lineage to a handful of the pioneering families, the same few names crop up over and over in Hildale and Colorado City, suggesting a murkier side to this fecundity: Doctors in Arizona say a severe form of a debilitating disease called fumarase deficiency, caused by a recessive gene, has become more prevalent in the community due to intermarriage.

The collision of tradition and modernity in the community can be disorienting. Despite their old-fashioned dress, most FLDS adults have cell phones and favor late-model SUVs. Although televisions are now banished, church members tend to be highly computer literate and sell a range of products, from soaps to dresses, via the Internet. When I noticed how few congregants wore glasses, I wondered aloud if perhaps a genetic predisposition for good eyesight was at work. Sam Steed laughed lightly. "No. People here are just really into laser surgery."

The principle of plural marriage was revealed to the Mormons amid much secrecy. Dark clouds hovered over the church in the early 1840s, after rumors spread that its founder, Joseph Smith, had taken up the practice of polygamy. While denying the charge in public, by 1843 Smith had shared a revelation with his closest disciples. In this "new and everlasting covenant" with God, plural wives were to be taken so that the faithful might "multiply and replenish the earth."

After Smith was assassinated by an anti-Mormon mob in Illinois, Brigham Young led believers on an epic 1,300-mile journey west to the Salt Lake Basin of present-day Utah. There the covenant was at last publicly revealed and with it, the notion that a man's righteousness before God would be measured by the size of his family; Brigham Young himself took 55 wives, who bore him 57 children.

But in 1890, faced with the seizure of church property under a federal antipolygamy law, the LDS leadership issued a manifesto announcing an end to plural marriage. That certainly didn't end the practice, and the LDS's tortured handling of the issue—some church leaders remained in plural marriages or even took on new wives after the manifesto's release—contributed to the schism between the LDS and the fundamentalists.

"The LDS issued that manifesto for political purposes, then later 25 claimed it was a revelation," says Willie Jessop, the FLDS spokesman. "We in the fundamentalist community believe covenants are made with God and are not to be manipulated for political reasons, so that presents an enormous obstacle between us and those in the LDS mainstream."

Upholding the covenant has come at a high price. The 2008 raid on the YFZ Ranch was only the latest in a long list of official actions against polygamists—persecutions for simply adhering to their religious principles, in the eyes of church members—that are integral to the FLDS story. At various times both Utah and Arizona authorities attempted to crack down on the Short Creek community: in 1935, in 1944, and most famously, in 1953. In that raid some 200 women and children were hauled to detention centers, while 26 men were brought up on polygamy charges. In 1956 Utah authorities seized seven children of Vera Black, a Hildale plural wife, on grounds that her polygamous beliefs made her an unfit mother. Black was reunited with her children only after agreeing to renounce polygamy.

Melinda Fischer Jeffs is an articulate, outgoing woman of 37, and she gives an incredulous laugh when describing what she's read about the FLDS. "Honestly, I can't even recognize it!" the mother of three exclaims. "Most all of what appears in the media, it makes us sound like we're somehow being kept against our will."

Melinda is in a unique position to understand the conflicting views of this community. She is a plural wife to Jim Jeffs, one of the prophet's nephews and an elder in the FLDS. But she is also the daughter of Dan Fischer, a former FLDS member who has emerged as one of the church leadership's most vociferous critics. In 2008 Fischer testified before a U.S. Senate committee about alleged improprieties within the FLDS, and he now heads an organization that works with people who have been kicked out of the church or who have "escaped." When Fischer broke with the church in the 1990s, his family split apart too; today 13 of his children have left the FLDS, while Melinda and two of her half siblings have renounced their father.

"And that is not an easy thing," Melinda says softly, "obviously, because I still love my father. I pray all the time that he will see his errors—or at least, stop his attacks on us."

If there is one point on which FLDS defenders and detractors might 30 agree, it is that most of the current troubles can be traced to when its leadership passed to the Jeffs family, in 1986. Until then, the FLDS had been a fairly loosely run group led by an avuncular man named Leroy Johnson, who relied on a group of high priests to guide the church. That ended when Rulon Jeffs took over following Johnson's death. After being declared the prophet by the community, Rulon solidified the policy of one-man rule.

Charges that a theocratic dictatorship was taking root in the Arizona Strip grew louder when, after Rulon's death in 2002, the FLDS was taken over by his 46-year-old son, Warren. Assuming the role of the prophet, Warren first married several of his father's wives—and then proceeded to wed many more women, including, according to Carolyn Jessop, eight of Merril Jessop's daughters. Although many FLDS men have multiple wives, the number of wives of those closest to the prophet can reach into the double digits. A church document called the Bishop's Record, seized during the Texas raid, shows that one of Jeffs's lieutenants, Wendell Nielsen, claims 21 wives. And although the FLDS would not disclose how many plural wives Warren Jeffs has taken (some estimate more than 80), at least one was an underage girl, according to a Texas indictment.

Although the issue of underage marriage within the church has garnered the greatest negative media attention, Dan Fischer has championed another cause, the so-called Lost Boys, who have left or been forced from the community and wound up fending for themselves on the streets of Las Vegas, Salt Lake City, and St. George, Utah. Fischer's foundation has worked with 300 such young men, a few as young as 13, over the past seven years. Fischer concedes that most of these boys were simply "discouraged out," but he cites cases where they were officially expelled, a practice he says increased under Jeffs.

Fischer attributes the exodus partly to a cold-blooded calculation by church leaders to limit male competition for the pool of marriageable young women. "If you have men marrying 20, 30, up to 80 or more women," he says, "then it comes down to biology and simple math that there will be a lot of other men who aren't going to get wives. The church says it's kicking these boys out for being disruptive influences, but if you'll notice, they rarely kick out girls."

Equally contentious has been the FLDS restoration of an early Mormon policy of transferring the wives and children of a church member to another man. Traditionally, this was done upon the death of a patriarch so that his widows might be cared for, or to rescue a woman from an abusive relationship. But critics argue that under Jeffs this "reassignment" became one more weapon to hold over the heads of those who dared step out of line.

Determining who is unworthy has been the exclusive province of the prophet. When in January 2004 Jeffs publicly ordered the expulsion of 21 men and the reassignment of their families, the community acquiesced. Jeffs's diary, also seized during the Texas raid, reveals a man who micromanaged the community's every decision, from chore assignments and housing arrangements to who married whom and which men were ousted—all directed by revelations Jeffs received as he slept. He claimed that God guided his every action, no matter how small. One diary entry reads: "The Lord directed that I go to the sun tanning salon and get sun tanned more evenly on their suntanning beds."

In 2005 a Utah court transferred control of the trust that oversees much of the land in Hildale and Colorado City from the FLDS leadership to a state-appointed fiduciary;° the church is currently waging a campaign to recover control of the trust. As for Jeffs, after spending over a year on the lam avoiding legal issues in Utah — and earning a spot on the FBI's Ten Most Wanted list — he was caught and is currently serving a ten-year-to-life sentence as an accomplice to rape. He awaits trial on multiple indictments in Arizona and Texas. The 11 other church members awaiting trial in Texas include Merril Jessop, who was indicted for performing the marriage of Jeffs to an underage girl.

Yet Jeffs's smiling portrait continues to adorn the living room of almost every FLDS home. In his absence, his lieutenants have launched a fierce defense of his leadership. While conceding that underage marriages did occur in the past, Donald Richter, contributor to one of the official FLDS websites, says the practice has now been stopped. As for the Lost Boys, he argues that both the numbers involved and the reasons for the expulsions have been greatly exaggerated by the church's enemies. "This is only done in the most extreme cases," Richter says, "and never for the trivial causes they're claiming. And anyway, all religious groups have the right to expel people who won't accept their rules."

Certainly Melinda Fischer Jeffs hasn't been swayed by the ongoing controversy. "Warren is just the kindest, most loving man," she says. "The image that has been built up about him by the media and his enemies is just unrecognizable to who he really is." Like other church members, Melinda has ready answers for most of the accusations leveled against Jeffs and is especially spirited in defending the policy of reassignment. According to her, it is almost always initiated at the request of a wife who has been abandoned or abused. This is debatable. In his diary Jeffs recounts reassigning the wives of three men, including his brother David, because God had shown him that they "couldn't exalt their ladies, had lost the confidence of God." One of his brother's wives had difficulty accepting the news and could barely bring herself to kiss her new husband. "She showed a great spirit of resistance, yet she went through with it," Jeffs records. "She needs to learn to submit to Priesthood."

Yet Melinda's defense of Jeffs underscores one of the most curious aspects of the polygamous faith: the central role of women in defending it. This is not new. In Brigham Young's day a charity rushed to Utah to establish a

fiduciary: involving trust, particularly in matters of financial management.

safe house for polygamous women seeking to escape this "white slavery"; that house sat virtually empty. Today FLDS women in the Hildale–Colorado City area have ample opportunity to "escape"—they have cell phones, they drive cars, there are no armed guards keeping them in—yet they don't.

Undoubtedly one reason is that, having been raised in this culture, 40 they know little else. Walking away means leaving behind everything: the community, one's sense of security, even one's own family. Carolyn Jessop, the plural wife of Merril Jessop who did leave the FLDS, likens entering the outside world to "stepping out onto another planet. I was completely unprepared, because I had absolutely no life skills. Most women in the FLDS don't even know how to balance a checkbook, let alone apply for a job, so contemplating how you're going to navigate in the outside world is extremely daunting."

It would seem there's another lure for women to stay: power. The FLDS women I spoke with tended to be far more articulate and confident than the men, most of whom seemed paralyzed by bashfulness. It makes sense when one begins to grasp that women are coveted to "multiply and replenish the earth," while men are in extraordinary competition to be deemed worthy of marriage by the prophet. One way to be deemed worthy, of course, is to not rock the boat, to keep a low profile. As a result, what has all the trappings of a patriarchal culture, actually has many elements of a matriarchal one.

There are limits to that power, of course, for it is subject to the dictates of the prophet. After hearing Melinda's stout defense of Jeffs, I ask what she would do if she were reassigned.

"I'm confident that wouldn't happen," she replies uneasily.

"But what if it did?" I ask. "Would you obey?"

For the only time during our interview, Melinda grows wary. Sitting 45 back in her chair, she gives her head a quarter turn to stare at me out of the corner of one eye.

On a sunny afternoon in March 2009, Bob Barlow, a friendly, middle-aged member of the FLDS, gives me a tour of the YFZ Ranch in West Texas. The compound consists of about 25 two-story log-cabin-style homes, and a number of workshops and factories are scattered over 1,700 acres. At the center sits a gleaming white stone temple. It is remarkable what the residents have created from the hardscrabble plain. With heavy machinery, they literally made earth out of the rocky terrain, crushing stone and mixing it with the thin topsoil. They planted orchards and gardens and lawns and were on their way to creating a self-sufficient community amid the barren landscape. All that ground to a halt after the 2008 raid.

"The families are slowly coming back now," Barlow says. "We'll come out the other side of this better and stronger than before."

I suspect he's right. So many times in the history of Mormon polygamy the outside world thought it had the movement on the ropes only to see it flourish anew. I'm reminded of this one afternoon in Colorado City when I speak with Vera Black. Now 92 and in failing health, Vera is the woman whose children were taken from her by Utah authorities in 1956 and returned only after she agreed to renounce polygamy. Within days of making that promise, she was back in Short Creek with her children and had renewed her commitment to the everlasting covenant.

Now living with her daughter Lillian, Vera lies in a daybed as her children gather around. Those children are now in their 50s and 60s, and as they recount the story of their long-ago separation — both from their mother and their faith — several weep, as if the pain were fresh.

"I had to make that promise," Vera says, with a smile, "but I crossed 50 my fingers while I did it."

Understanding the Text

1. What does the term "sister-wife" mean?
2. Anderson describes contemporary polygamy as a "collision of tradition and modernity" (par. 21). What does he mean by this?
3. Who are the Lost Boys? What reason is there to suspect that many of them have been expelled from the community for reasons other than disruptive behavior?

Reflection and Response

4. Critics maintain that polygamy as practiced in contemporary times privileges male power and desires. Do you agree?
5. In what ways do polygamous households replicate traditional middle-class values? To what extent do religious convictions undermine these bourgeois values?
6. What is the effect of Anderson's starting his article with a long narrative?
7. When does the constitutional guarantee of the free exercise of religion exceed social limits? Besides polygamy, what are some examples of religious practices that conflict with legal standards?

Making Connections

8. How does the lifestyle of the polygamous Mormons in the American Southwest parallel that of the Amish in Pennsylvania? In what ways can they be compared to the Hasidim in Brooklyn?
9. Research the history of polygamy in the United States, discussing both the practical and ideological reasons for the practice among both Mormons and non-Mormons.

The American Redoubt, Where Survivalists Plan to Survive

Kim Murphy

Kim Murphy is a longtime foreign and national correspondent who became an editor of the *Los Angeles Times* in June 2013. She won a Pulitzer Prize in 2005 for her coverage of Russia's struggles with terrorism. Murphy has reported from around the globe on events ranging from the Deep Water Horizon oil spill in the Gulf of Mexico to the Aurora, Colorado, theater massacre. The *Times* former bureau chief in Moscow and London, she now makes her home in the Pacific Northwest. In "The American Redoubt," she reports on the survivalists who have chosen this geographic area as their final retreat from what they see as an apocalyptic future for American society.

The American Redoubt: It lies in the rural high country of Montana, Idaho, Wyoming, eastern Washington and Oregon.

For a growing number of people, it's the designated point of retreat when the American economy hits the fan. When banks fail, the government declares martial law,° the power grid goes down. When warming oceans flood the coasts and a resurgent Russia takes out targets on the Eastern Seaboard.

Though white separatists for years have called for a racial homeland in the inland Pacific Northwest, an even bigger movement of survivalists, Christian fundamentalists, and political doomsayers is fueling the idea of a defensible retreat in the high country west of the Rockies.

Armed with stocks of brown rice, weapons, battery-operated radios and razor wire, many are preparing isolated homesteads that can quickly be turned into armed fortifications when groceries disappear from stores and hordes of desperate city-dwellers flee a flu pandemic or run out of oil.

> "Though white separatists for years have called for a racial homeland in the inland Pacific Northwest, an even bigger movement of survivalists, Christian fundamentalists, and political doomsayers is fueling the idea of a defensible retreat in the high country west of the Rockies."

---

martial law: suspension of ordinary law by the military during times of crisis.

The guru of the movement is James Wesley Rawles, a former Army ⁵
intelligence officer and author of the bestselling novel *Survivors: A Novel
of the Coming Collapse*. The book tells of military veterans who lead bands
of tough-minded Americans through a period of marauding rioters and
the collapse of the supply chain and technology, and of a provisional
government "determined to take over America and destroy the freedoms
upon which it was built."

Rawles, who got his start as an editor at *Defense Electronics* magazine
and a technical writer at Oracle Corp., in 2005 started what has become
one of the country's most widely read survival blogs, which claims to
attract up to 300,000 unique visitors a week. He published one of the
bibles of modern survivalist tactics, *How to Survive the End of the World as
We Know It*, in 2009.

Places like northern Idaho and western Montana have always been
ripe territory; the low mountains around Bonners Ferry, Idaho, and
Montana's Flathead Valley have long had more than their share of cabins
populated by wary loners. But now Rawles has given a name to this idealized retreat—the American Redoubt—and framed the geography.

It's impossible to say how many have heeded the call—analysts say
it's probably not all that many so far—but adherents say that's because
the need is only now becoming apparent. Boise was home to a survivalist
trade show last year featuring electric generators, dehydrated food, and
water-purification devices.

With the rising federal debt and prospects for another credit crisis,
Rawles said in a telephone interview, "It could turn into a full-scale economic rout in short order. And under circumstances like that, I have
encouraged my readers for many years to relocate themselves in lightly
populated agricultural regions that are well removed from major population centers, where there'll be large-scale rioting and possibly looting in
the event of an economic crisis."

Rawles has already beaten his retreat, but don't ask him to where.   ¹⁰

The most he'll say is he lives on a ranch—presumably in Redoubt
territory—west of the Rocky Mountains. He has livestock, he has three
years' worth of food stockpiled, he has a functioning garden, and he's got
the weapons he needs to hold back the hordes if they find him.

"Because of the nature of my blog, I'm in an almost unique situation,
in that I might be considered the go-to guy for 160,000 survival blog
readers," Rawles, 51, said of the secrecy surrounding his location.

"I don't want to be that guy. I don't want anyone knowing where I
live, because some morning I may wake up and find my barnyard full of
tents and yurts and RVs."

A "Crossover Following"

On his blog, one of a large and growing number of survivalist websites, Rawles emphasizes that he is a "non-racist"—that Christians, Messianic Jews and Orthodox Jews are welcome to join the retreat, no matter what their race. Buddhists and "New Age crystal channelers," on the other hand, would be better advised to retreat elsewhere. He pays homage to "Galt's Gulch," novelist Ayn Rand's concept of a hidden retreat for disaffected capitalists.

"The preparedness movement has grown at the fastest rate I have seen 15 in my entire lifetime—faster than in the late '70s, when the Iran hostage crisis had people very concerned, much faster than in the late '90s, when people were concerned about Y2K," Rawles said. The interview was conducted on a phone with the area code he had when he lived in Livermore, California.

"I think a substantial amount of society, in the aftermath of Hurricane Katrina and the Japanese earthquake and tsunami and nuclear meltdowns, people have definitely recognized the fragility of society and they're taking rational steps to mitigate the risks," he said.

While the majority of his readers are conservative Christian Republicans, he said that "there's a tremendously large and growing segment of my readership that are left of center, Birkenstock-wearing greenies. There's as much crossover with the folks that are interested in local sustainable agriculture and green building techniques as there is with the tea party movement."

In Idaho and northwestern Montana, hotbeds of American Redoubt sentiment, websites offer help finding jobs in the new homeland until the time for full retreat is at hand, as well as lists of sympathetic churches ("reformed" congregations dominate the A-list). Some feature real estate agents capable of finding that 20-acre hilltop parcel, invisible from the road, with its own solar power. (Try Revolutionary Realty in northern Idaho or IdahoJoe Realty, run by Joe Rohner of Boise, who bills himself as a "redoubt realtor.")

"Interest is growing. A lot of people have come here, and a lot that none of us know about, because a lot of them do it on their own," Rohner said. "It's a growing movement that's not very centralized, and probably never will be, because these people tend to be kind of secretive anyway."

Chuck Baldwin, a prominent conservative preacher and radio 20 host—and 2008 presidential candidate for the Constitution Party—has bought in.

"Over a period of about three years, my family and I . . . just really put our heads together and tried to look at some of the things we saw coming. And we came to the conclusion that where we had lived for over 30 years probably was not where we wanted to stay, in light of what we saw on the horizon," Baldwin said in an interview. He decamped from Florida with his grown children, their families, and his in-laws to Kalispell, Montana, in 2010.

"I hope and pray that things don't get drastic. But at the same time, only a very foolish and naive person could think that America can continue to spiral into this deficit-spending . . . money system that we have established over the last few decades," said Baldwin, who is now a candidate for lieutenant governor in Montana.

Looking Toward the Future

In a message to his supporters, Baldwin credited Rawles' vision of the American Redoubt for helping shape his own vision for his family's future. "It is our studied opinion that America is headed for an almost certain cataclysm," Baldwin wrote. "As Christians, we suspect that this cataclysm could include the judgment of God. As students of history, we believe that this cataclysm will most certainly include a fight between Big-Government globalists and freedom-loving, independent-minded patriots. I would even argue that this fight has already started."

Concerning allegations that some of Montana's white separatists have attended his church services, Baldwin is dismissive.

"To try to associate our move here with some kind of a racist bent is 25 lunacy," he said. "When you talk about depriving people of their normal accessibility to food and medicine and clothing and shelter and things that are part and parcel of what we would consider normal life, I don't think that's racial at all."

Baldwin has appropriated some of Rawles' checklist items on his own website for those he is now encouraging to populate the Redoubt.

Develop a home-based business, he says; bring your guns; home-school your kids.

"Make a clean break by selling your house and any rental properties," he advises. "You aren't coming back."

Understanding the Text

1. What does the term "redoubt" mean?
2. According to the article, who is the typical American survivalist? Consider profession, religion, family, race, political persuasion, and other relevant characteristics.
3. Why is calling John Wesley Rawles the "guru" of the movement ironic?

Reflection and Response

4. As Murphy writes, the American Northwest has long been "ripe territory" for survivalists. What are some of the factors that make this geographical area attractive for those who believe in the imminent collapse of society?

5. Obviously, the United States faces — and has always faced — a multitude of problems, from a troubled economy to racial antipathy to environmental damage. Is a retreat from society an appropriate response? Are there justifications for the survivalists' fear of a coming cataclysm?

6. How do the values and practices of modern survivalists have roots in the life of nineteenth-century frontier America?

Making Connections

7. On the Internet, find one of the many survivalist blogs or websites and perform a rhetorical analysis of the text. What kind of language is used? Why? How is the language tailored to the audience? What kinds of arguments and supporting evidence are evident? What is missing from the discussion?

8. The back-to-the-land hippies of the late 1960s also isolated themselves in rural areas far from mainstream society. Research these communal groups in order to identify similarities and differences between them and the primarily right-wing survivalists. How were their motivations similar? What values do they share? How are these values profoundly American?

Low and Slow: The History of Lowriders

Bob Frost

Born in St. Paul, Minnesota, and educated at Brown University, Bob Frost spent many years as the Sunday magazine editor for the *San Jose Mercury News*. In addition, he has been a contributor to the *History Channel Magazine*, *West*, and many other publications. More recently, Frost founded HistoryAccess.com and currently serves as the site's editor-in-chief. The lowrider community he discusses here has a long history in Frost's adopted state, California. The term "lowrider" refers both to a style of customized vehicle fitted with hydraulic systems that allow the chassis — or base frame — to be raised or lowered and to the group of people who drive them.

In Southern California in the 1950s and early '60s, young Chicanos created a car style called "lowrider" that expressed the pride and playfulness of Mexican American culture.

The peak of lowrider culture came in the 1970s on Whittier Boulevard in Los Angeles, a wide commercial street that cut through the *barrio* of the city. Gliding along Whittier on Saturday nights in the '70s were brightly-painted cars modified by young Mexican American men to ride low to the ground, fitted with special hydraulics to make them bounce up and down. These drivers had little interest in the rubber-burning speed of their hot-rodding peers. The guiding principle here was *bajito y suavecito*: low and slow.

The Whittier "cruise" was a social event of large importance, an exciting arena where *la raza* (the people) could come together to have fun, where young men and women could check each other out, and where a proud political and historical consciousness could be articulated.

Lowriders, wrote journalist Ted West in 1976, "express the refusal of a young Chicano American to be Anglicized. There has never been a clearer case of the automobile being used as an ethnic statement." Lowriding continues today—under the radar compared to the '70s, but thriving.

Opinions vary on what constitutes today's lowriders, but many hobby- 5
ists would agree with anthropologist Ben Chappell that the style includes a lowered chassis, hydraulic suspension, custom wheels ("rims") often with spinners, narrow tires, engravings on the windows, multi-layer lacquer jobs, lush custom interiors with accessories such as chain-wheel steering and crushed velvet, and a streamlined exterior with multiple colors, designs, and/or murals.

barrio: ghetto neighborhoods

The history of lowriders is complex. One aspect of the story begins in the 1920s when auto ownership skyrocketed in Southern California. You needed a car to get anywhere in spread-out Los Angeles and environs; Henry Ford sold a lot of Model T's there starting in 1908; by the middle '20s, the region had a rate of auto ownership of one car for every 2.25 people, compared with a nationwide average of one for every seven.

Used cars were available in L.A. in seemingly unlimited quantities for very little money. In the 1920s, young men from various ethnic groups bought used Model T's, along with Model A's and other vehicles, stripped off the fenders and other extraneous parts to lighten the weight, and modified the engines to get more speed. These were the world's first hot rods, called "hop ups" and "gow jobs" in those days. The guys would drive east to the Mojave Desert and race across dried-up lake beds.

> "In Southern California in the 1950s and early '60s, young Chicanos created a car style called 'lowrider' that expressed the pride and playfulness of Mexican American culture."

Hot-rodding was a robust presence in L.A. for years. By the 1940s some hot-rodders were becoming less interested in speed and more interested in streamlined style and comfort. They began building what became known as custom cars. They would take, say, a 1936 Ford, and lower the rear of its chassis with cutting torches, getting it as close to the pavement as the law allowed. They would bend and modify the frame. They'd cover

A lowrider performs a "three wheel motion," a maneuver in which the driver makes a turn or circle, shifting the weight of the vehicle to the rear and causing the front wheel to lift off the ground. Shutterstock/Suzanne Tucker

the rear wheels with fender skirts. They'd round the corners and remove the name badges. The '36 Ford, formerly boxy and boring, evolved into something low, long, wide, sleek, mysterious, and exciting.

The custom car scene of the '40s was multicultural. So, for example, two Mexican-American brothers, Gil and Al Ayala, operated a well-known custom body shop on Olympic Boulevard in East Los Angeles, swapping ideas with customers of all races.

The custom car hobby began to change in the late 1950s and early   10
'60s. Many riders, mainly whites, turned away from the low, sleek look, and moved toward flamboyance, bubble tops, a funky futuristic look, and speed. This trend was pushed to its extreme by Ed "Big Daddy" Roth and the Kustom Kulture movement. But in East Los Angeles, Chicanos didn't follow the new trend, sticking to the time-honored technique of lowering and streamlining older cars. And they added a remarkable innovation: hydraulics, a distinguishing feature of the modern lowrider.

Lowrider hydraulics were originally aircraft hydraulic systems (pumps, dumps, cylinders). Young Chicanos attached this gear to the undercarriage of cars to create an adjustable suspension. Riders could flip a switch to raise a car's body a few inches to glide safely over an obstacle and to pass a police inspection, and then flip the switch back, returning the car to its low, cool, pavement-scraping stance. This evolved into dramatic up-and-down bouncing, known as hopping.

One car buff, quoted by author Paige R. Penland in *Lowrider: History, Pride, Culture,* recalled his introduction to the technology: "These guys were telling me about cars with hydraulics that made them go up and down. I said, 'What in the world would anybody want their car to go up and down for? That's the most ridiculous thing I ever heard of.' Then one day there was a Chevy going by. He hit the switch and the front end of the car went down. Boy, from then on, I was hooked. You just had to see it."

So, by the early 1960s, lowriders with hydraulics were a Chicano art form, distinctly separate from Ed Roth and the rest of the custom car scene. Lowriders with hydraulics were not only cool, they were playful—a good example of *rasqua-chismo,* described by scholar Tomas Ybarra-Frausto as a "bawdy, spunky" Chicano sensibility—"witty, irreverent, and impertinent"—that seeks to "subvert and turn ruling paradigms upside down," re-creating American icons, such as cars, with "oppositional meaning and function." Scholar Brenda Jo Bright puts it another way: hydraulics in lowriding represent "the politics of laughter."

Another chapter in the history of low-riders involves California demographics. Starting in 1900, the state's Mexican population grew rapidly due to a massive influx of immigrants seeking jobs in agriculture and manufacturing. By the end of World War II Los Angeles had one of the world's largest urban Mexican populations.

Mexicans in L.A., writes historian James D. Hart, got low wages, were 15
crowded into *barrios*, and were generally scorned by whites. Young people were stigmatized as *pachucos* (juvenile hoodlums). The "*pachuco* generation" was a term used by historian Carey McWilliams to describe these
American-born kids who reached maturity in the early 1940s.

The parents of the pachuco generation, McWilliams writes, generally
stayed close to home, seldom venturing from East L.A. into the downtown sector. By contrast, the new generation was "by no means so docile
and tractable as their parents" and was lured to the "downtown shopping
districts, to the beaches, and, above all, to the glamour of Hollywood."
They made their journeys by car, and they liked to drive in style. Police
harassed them but cruising continued — a bold assertion of freedom
in the land of the free. They were "laying a claim," writes scholar Ben
Chappell — "this is my city, my street, as much as anyone else's."

Understanding the Text

1. How did the geography of Los Angeles encourage the development of lowrider culture?
2. Define the term "pachuco."
3. Where did "hydraulics" come from and how do they work?

Reflection and Response

4. How does the lowrider subculture challenge the question of who has the
   right to occupy shared public spaces?
5. Frost claims that by the early 1960s lowriders were an art form that reflected
   specific Chicano sensibilities. What exactly are the subcultural values we can
   identify by analyzing the typical lowrider? You might want to locate some
   pictures online.
6. Explain the distinction between hot-rodders and lowriders. What are the
   historical roots of this split in Southern California car culture? How is this
   distinction based in ethnic differences? Does this distinction persist today?

Making Connections

7. In reference to lowriders, Ted West writes, "There has never been a clearer
   case of the automobile being used as an ethnic statement" (par. 4). In a brief
   essay, discuss other objects that are used by particular subcultures to make
   statements about ethnicity, politics, or gender.
8. Connect the way in which the lowriding pachucos laid claim to city streets
   to other subcultures (taggers, skaters, bikers, street kids), focusing on the
   similarities that gave rise to these communities, as well as the similarities in
   their responses to marginalization from the mainstream.

Femininity and Toughness: What Rodeo Queens Tell Us about America

Glenden Brown

Glenden Brown was born and raised in Utah, and educated at Grinnell College and the College of William and Mary. Although his family came to Utah in the 1840s with Brigham Young, the second President of The Church of Jesus Christ of Latter-day Saints, Brown has parted from his Mormon heritage and is now, in his own words, "a general pain in the butt to the conservative leadership of our state." In this article from *The Daily Kos*, Brown writes about attending one of the signature events of the American West: the rodeo. He sees in the rodeo the performance of roles long valued in the West, particularly the cowgirl's carefully maintained melding of femininity and toughness.

I got to spend the better part of my weekend at the Miss Rodeo Utah contest.

The day offered fascinating insights into the performance of gender, gender roles, patriotism, and American identity. Claiming direct descent from the Old West, rodeo asserts that it is a genuine, unbroken tradition from the Old West. Cowboys and cowgirls play specific gender roles within the subculture, roles built around a shared set of values — passion for horses, the myth of the open prairie and wide open spaces, hard work, and a particular form of patriotism.

Rodeo is a constructed subculture, self-aware that it is a creation while asserting its identity as the carrier of an American tradition, proclaiming that it embodies and represents a form of American-ness that is unique to rodeo, uniquely American, and essential to our national history. Rodeo's stylized dress and language is intended to evoke the past. Every aspect of rodeo is a deliberate creation of the people involved. Like the suburb in John Dorst's *The Written Suburb,* it is the creation of people who are self-aware and self-consciously creating their subculture. Rodeo — starting with acceptable clothing all the way through its choice of words to describe itself — is an intentional creation of the people involved. Rodeo is reminiscent of Disney in that aspect — it is not authentic in the sense that it doesn't occur naturally and yet it is authentic in the sense that it is the expression of the ideals and values of the people involved. A psychologist might see it as a form of projection in which participants project their personal, idealized values and morals onto the canvas of rodeo.

Throughout the contest — which is similar to any other beauty pageant — we were told about the girls' hard work — rising early to buck bales of hay, shovel out stalls, lug water, train and groom horses, then turning to their day job — for most contestants that is school. Tough work as a theme recurs repeatedly in rodeo's public awareness, as does the notion of toughness itself.

The queens embody a stylized femininity — long, lustrous, perfect hair, 5 perfect smiles that never slip, elaborate, brightly-colored leather dresses covered with glittering rhinestones, boots equally brightly colored, and perfectly-shaped hats — that portrays female beauty in a very specific way but which is discussed as only one aspect of their identity. Rodeo queens are tough; these are big strapping American girls who get thrown off horses, who buck bales of hay and rope cows, who are physically tough. In some events, the queen contestants are expected to actually feed and care for their horses to demonstrate they can do it.

In contrast, rodeo cowboys' masculinity is equally stylized but rigorously spare, even spartan in its simplicity. Standard attire is a long-sleeved shirt, jeans, wide leather belt with prominent belt buckle (a standard prize for winning events), boots, and hat. The long-sleeved shirt is regarded as a prac-

> "Rodeo is a constructed subculture, self-aware that it is a creation while asserting its identity as the carrier of an American tradition."

tical piece of clothing for back country riding — the long sleeves protect against thorns, brambles, and other environmental hazards. This standard attire is worn by both males and females. For the boys and men, it emphasizes the broad shoulders and narrow hips of the idealized masculine body shape — very different than the padded, helmeted body created for football (I see parallels between rodeo and rugby in many ways). Girls and women in rodeo — aside from the queens — seem to downplay or minimize displays of femininity, preferring to present themselves as highly capable horsewomen. . . . The queens, though equally capable on horseback, stand out in the crowd — their sequins and rhinestones on boots, jeans, and hats gleam in the arena in contrast to the simpler attire of other competitors. Yet, there are constant reminders of the differences between the genders.

The world of rodeo keeps strict and separate gender roles — men don't do women's events and women aren't welcomed in men's events. Rodeo is rigidly heterosexual. These two aspects are mutually reinforcing. Yet, I saw more than a few gay cowboys. Like most Americans, rodeo people are casually accepting of gay men (one of the key people involved in Miss Rodeo Utah is an openly gay man with a partner and adopted child), but that acceptance doesn't fully extend to the contest or event. Cowboys are straight (gay rodeo is unmentioned). Heterosexuality is enacted in many places—starting with little boys in oversized cowboy hats escorting the queen contestants. . . . Toughness is generally a masculine quality—and certainly the men's events require it—bronc and bull riding are physically hard. At multi-day events, it's not uncommon to see the contestants walking gingerly the day after their rides.

I grew up around horses. I've been bucked off, stepped on, kicked—I've trained a horse that wanted to buck and rear to read my body language and do what I wanted. I've also put a bridle on my horse and taken off for an afternoon of riding bareback in the hills, returning covered in sweat and dirt. Hard work in the world of rodeo is literal physical work—caring for and training a horse is physically demanding. The hard work that rodeo announcers cite for audiences is sweaty and dirty. Rodeo queens are expected to be able to do that work; they may be gorgeous, beautiful women but their beauty isn't all they are. These aren't the pampered hissy-fit-throwing beauty queens of the pageant circuit. . . .

The rodeo queen contestants are a tiny minority of the number of people who participate in rodeo. They are not exempt from the standards of rodeo—the matter-of-fact we're-here-to-do-a-job attitude that celebrates shit on your boots, dirt on your face and sweat on your brow. More than a few people at yesterday's events were former queens and contestants. . . .

The cowboy is tough—he gets bucked off a horse or a bull, lands in the   10 dirt in the arena, jumps up, brushes himself off, and heads for the exit. Or, if he's even tougher, he stays on the bronc or the bull, tougher still if he wins the event. The animals are dangerous simply because they're so big. They land even one hoof on you while you're on the ground, and you'll have shattered ribs and a crescent-shaped bruise that lasts days.

Break something, dislocate it, you wait till it heals and you head back to the arena. The toughness required for rodeo is real, but it is also a projection, a deliberate creation and invocation of the myth of the lone, tough cowboy out in the back country herding the cattle, roping the runaways and so on.

Tough men need tough women. Rodeo queens must be tough. They are judged on horse riding—they have to demonstrate they can control a horse and make it do what they want. Horses are beautiful creatures but not the smartest of domesticated animals. Despite their size, they scare easily, and a frightened horse can move with lightning speed away from whatever is scaring it. It's not uncommon around horses to watch as a horse suddenly heads right while their rider seems cartoonishly to linger in the air where just a moment ago, the horse was standing. Training a horse takes patience and determination and no small skill. A rodeo queen showing that her horse will do what she wants it to is demonstrating far more than what you see—if your horse runs the pattern correctly, it means you've ridden it enough, that you've been bucked off, stepped on, kicked.

As an example of American womanhood, rodeo women are not Marilyn Monroe with her soft face and voice and voluptuous curves, nor are they Britney Spears with her naughty school-girl vulnerability and emotional imbalances. Rodeo queens are more like Rosie the Riveter or Pink—determined, smart, capable, their femininity married to a physical and emotional toughness that shrugs off pain and defeat. During the fashion show portion of the event, the rodeo queens showed themselves as beautiful young women—but they weren't erotically beautiful. Everything in the fashion show demonstrated physicality—these are women who can walk, stride, keep their balance. It may sound absurd, but what was on display was their athleticism not their fashion sense.

Very few people are actual cowboys any more. Most herding is done with four-wheel ATVs or pickup trucks, and semis and trains carry live stock across the country. You don't need a squad of cowboys to drive the herd to the stockyards in Kansas City. The world of the cowboy lasted a few short decades and has long since vanished into history. Much of country music celebrates what it means to be a cowboy in a set of memes

Miss Thunder Mountain Pro Rodeo Queen, Ashlyn Opgrande, rides in a parade during the Portland Rose Festival 2015. shutterstock.com

and metaphors that are readily familiar to most Americans — trucks, horses, suffering, dogs, women doing men wrong or being done wrong by bad men. One of the songs blaring from the speakers yesterday proclaimed that cowboys love smoky bar rooms and the open range and beautiful women. Cowgirls, we were told repeatedly, are living a fairy-tale dream come true of being a rodeo queen and a cowgirl riding her horse in the clean country air. But rodeo cowboy or cowgirl is a persona that the contestants put on and take off. It's a mask — perhaps masque is a better term. Elaborately theatrical, rodeo creates and invents an image of the Old West, of the working cowboy/girl, rather than being a realization of the working cowboy/girl world.

Country singer Chris Ledoux wrote and recorded extensively about 15 the rodeo lifestyle based on his own experiences as a professional on the rodeo circuit. His career followed an odd trajectory — he was essentially the subculture artist of rodeo, nearly disappeared from the scene entirely, had his career revived in the late '90s, and had a series of hits. Ledoux's songs capture the experience of being a rodeo cowboy — of working the circuit, of the physical abuse rodeo visits upon contestants, the loneliness and isolation, the long hours of travel. Rodeo has recreated the experience of the Old West. Physical hardship, loneliness, travel. These are all hallmarks of the cattle drive.

There are no cattle drives anymore. Rodeo is performance; it is a form of professional theatre. Frequent proclamations by rodeo announcers of "working cowboy" and cowboy/girl toughness are ritualistic invocations of value rather than statements of fact. Those invocations betray the awareness among rodeo contestants and organizers that this is a constructed subculture, that for all their straight-faced seriousness, they aren't real working cowboys and cowgirls. A few might actually live on working ranches or farms, but most do not. Rodeo rhetoric romanticizes the Old West while ritually re-enacting its tropes. Like many other American subcultures, it looks backwards, yearning for an earlier time while its members live comfortably in the diverse, urban world that most Americans inhabit.

Rodeo is inseparable from a very particular form of patriotism. The flag, the pledge are part of rodeo life. It is perhaps unfair, but rodeo's patriotic displays and proclamations strike me as comforting myths, as attempts to create something not naturally experienced. If we must constantly tell ourselves how patriotic we are, perhaps we aren't so very patriotic after all.

Invoking the myth of the Old West, rodeo self-consciously holds itself out as a reminder to the rest of us — that we should recapture lost values and behaviors of the Old West. Myths of self-reliance, individualism, manliness, a matter-of-fact, get-to-it-get-it-done attitude. Most of all, it invokes a myth of America — as a frontier nation testing itself against nature. The rodeo queen in her stylized glory, invoking her toughness, is a reminder that the frontier has vanished and that the rancher long ago lost out to the farmer. It's complex and complicated, a reflection of deep anxiety about the loss of something that is uniquely American. The rodeo queen . . . serves no literal purpose, but she serves a profound psychological purpose, symbolizing the transformations of our culture and offering a role model for tough femininity.

Understanding the Text

1. Brown compares rodeo queens to Rosie the Riveter. Who was this figure, and why is she an appropriate parallel to the rodeo queen?

2. The author writes that the "rodeo cowboy or cowgirl is a persona that the contestants put on and take off. It's a mask — perhaps masque is a better term" (par. 14). Explain what he means by "persona" and "masque."

Reflection and Response

3. What does the author mean when he says that "rodeo is a constructed subculture, self-aware that it is a creation" (par. 3)? In what ways do the rodeo queens perform their roles?

4. In the end, Brown claims that the rodeo queen "serves no literal purpose, but she serves a profound psychological purpose, symbolizing the transformations of our culture" (par. 18). Do you agree that the rodeo queen embodies values and practices that are undergoing stress in mainstream culture? Why or why not?

5. On the assumption that no text is complete, what practical advice can you give the author to improve the article? Consider organization, evidence and examples, diction, and other stylistic points, bearing in mind that the author likely has good reasons for making the choices that he has made.

Making Connections

6. What other subcultures featured in this book draw heavily on the mythology of the American West, particularly the symbol of the cowboy/cowgirl? What values do these subcultures have in common? Why is the West such an enduring presence for members of these communities?

7. Listen to a couple of songs by country singer Chris Ledoux, who "wrote and recorded extensively about the rodeo lifestyle based on his own experiences as a professional on the rodeo circuit" (par. 15). How does Ledoux both capture the life of the rodeo subculture and "perform" the role of the rodeo cowboy?

Hipster: The Dead End of Western Civilization

Douglas Haddow

If there is a subculture that defined America at the turn of the twenty-first century, it was that of the hipster. A great deal of ink has been spilled and a great number of opinions aired — often by those who ostensibly belong to the hipster community — criticizing the values and practices of these twentysomething urbanites. Douglas Haddow contributes to this critique in an essay that originally appeared in *AdBusters*, an anti-consumerist, culture-jamming magazine. Haddow is a Vancouver-based freelance journalist who has written for numerous publications, including the *Guardian*, *Colors*, *Vice*, and *Slate*. He is also the communications coordinator for the Canadian drug policy coalition.

I'm sipping a scummy pint of cloudy beer in the back of a trendy dive bar turned nightclub in the heart of the city's heroin district. In front of me stand a gang of hippiesh grunge-punk types, who crowd around each other and collectively scoff at the smoking laws by sneaking puffs of "fuck-you," reveling in their perceived rebellion as the haggard, staggering staff look on without the slightest concern.

The "DJ" is keystroking a selection of MP3s off his MacBook, making a mix that sounds like he took a hatchet to a collection of yesteryear billboard hits, from DMX to Dolly Parton, but mashed up with a jittery techno backbeat.

"So . . . this is a hipster party?" I ask the girl sitting next to me. She's wearing big dangling earrings, an American Apparel V-neck tee, non-prescription eyeglasses and an inappropriately warm wool coat.

"Yeah, just look around you, 99 percent of the people here are total hipsters!"

"Are you a hipster?"   5

"Fuck no," she says, laughing back the last of her glass before she hops off to the dance floor.

Ever since the Allies bombed the Axis into submission, Western civilization has had a succession of counter-culture movements that have energetically challenged the status quo. Each successive decade of the post-war era has seen it smash social standards, riot and fight to revolutionize every aspect of music, art, government and civil society.

But after punk was plasticized and hip hop lost its impetus for social change, all of the formerly dominant streams of "counter-culture" have merged together. Now, one mutating, trans-Atlantic melting pot of styles, tastes and behavior has come to define the generally indefinable idea of the "Hipster."

An artificial appropriation of different styles from different eras, the hipster represents the end of Western civilization—a culture lost in the superficiality of its past and unable to create any new meaning. Not only is it unsustainable, it is suicidal. While previous youth movements have challenged the dysfunction and decadence of their elders, today we have the "hipster"—a youth subculture that mirrors the doomed shallowness of mainstream society.

> "An artificial appropriation of different styles from different eras, the hipster represents the end of Western civilization — a culture lost in the superficiality of its past and unable to create any new meaning."

Take a stroll down the street in any major North American or European city and you'll be sure to see a speckle of fashion-conscious twentysome-things hanging about and sporting a number of predictable stylistic trademarks: skinny jeans, cotton spandex leggings, fixed-gear bikes, vintage flannel, fake eyeglasses and a *keffiyeh*°—initially sported by Jewish students and Western protesters to express solidarity with Palestinians, the keffiyeh has become a completely meaningless hipster cliché fashion accessory. 10

The American Apparel V-neck shirt, Pabst Blue Ribbon beer and Parliament cigarettes are symbols and icons of working or revolutionary classes that have been appropriated by hipsterdom and drained of meaning. Ten years ago, a man wearing a plain V-neck tee and drinking a Pabst would never be accused of being a trend-follower. But in 2008, such things have become shameless clichés of a class of individuals that seek to escape their own wealth and privilege by immersing themselves in the aesthetic of the working class.

This obsession with "street-cred" reaches its apex of absurdity as hipsters have recently and wholeheartedly adopted the fixed-gear bike as the only acceptable form of transportation—only to have brakes installed on a piece of machinery that is defined by its lack thereof.

Lovers of apathy and irony, hipsters are connected through a global network of blogs and shops that push forth a global vision of fashion-informed aesthetics. Loosely associated with some form of creative output, they attend art parties, take lo-fi pictures with analog cameras, ride their bikes to night clubs and sweat it up at nouveau disco-coke

---

keffiyeh: Bedouin Arab scarf worn as a headdress.

parties. The hipster tends to religiously blog about their daily exploits, usually while leafing through generation-defining magazines like *Vice*, *Another Magazine* and *Wallpaper*. This cursory and stylized lifestyle has made the hipster almost universally loathed.

"These hipster zombies . . . are the idols of the style pages, the darlings of viral marketers and the marks of predatory real-estate agents," wrote Christian Lorentzen in a *Time Out New York* article entitled "Why the Hipster Must Die." "And they must be buried for cool to be reborn."

With nothing to defend, uphold or even embrace, the idea of "hipster- 15 dom" is left wide open for attack. And yet, it is this ironic lack of authenticity that has allowed hipsterdom to grow into a global phenomenon that is set to consume the very core of Western counterculture. Most critics make a point of attacking the hipster's lack of individuality, but it is this stubborn obfuscation that distinguishes them from their predecessors, while allowing hipsterdom to easily blend in and mutate other social movements, sub-cultures and lifestyles.

Standing outside an art-party next to a neat row of locked-up fixed-gear bikes, I come across a couple girls who exemplify hipster homogeneity. I ask one of the girls if her being at an art party and wearing fake eyeglasses, leggings and a flannel shirt makes her a hipster.

"I'm not comfortable with that term," she replies.

Her friend adds, with just a flicker of menace in her eyes, "Yeah, I don't know, you shouldn't use that word, it's just. . . ."

"Offensive?"

"No . . . it's just, well . . . if you don't know why then you just shouldn't 20 even use it."

"Ok, so what are you girls doing tonight after this party?" "Ummm . . . We're going to the after-party."

Gavin McInnes, one of the founders of *Vice*, who recently left the magazine, is considered to be one of hipsterdom's primary architects. But, in contrast to the majority of concerned media-types, McInnes, whose "Dos and Don'ts" commentary defined the rules of hipster fashion for over a decade, is more critical of those doing the criticizing.

"I've always found that word ["hipster"] is used with such disdain, like it's always used by chubby bloggers who aren't getting laid anymore and are bored, and they're just so mad at these young kids for going out and getting wasted and having fun and being fashionable," he says. "I'm dubious of these hypotheses because they always smell of an agenda."

Punks wear their tattered threads and studded leather jackets with honor, priding themselves on their innovative and cheap methods of self-expression and rebellion. B-boys and b-girls announce themselves to anyone within earshot with baggy gear and boomboxes. But it is rare, if not impossible, to find an individual who will proclaim himself a proud hipster. It's an odd dance of self-identity—adamantly denying your existence while wearing clearly defined symbols that proclaim it.

"He's 17 and he lives for the scene!" a girl whispers in my ear as I sneak 25 a photo of a young kid dancing up against a wall in a dimly lit corner of the after-party. He's got a flipped-out, do-it-yourself haircut, skin-tight jeans, leather jacket, a vintage punk tee and some popping high tops.

"Shoot me," he demands, walking up, cigarette in mouth, striking a pose and exhaling. He hits a few different angles with a firmly unimpressed expression and then gets a bit giddy when I show him the results.

"Rad, thanks," he says, re-focusing on the music and submerging himself back into the sweaty funk of the crowd where he resumes a jittery head bobble with a little bit of a twitch.

The dance floor at a hipster party looks like it should be surrounded by quotation marks. While punk, disco and hip hop all had immersive, intimate and energetic dance styles that liberated the dancer from his/her mental states—be it the head-spinning b-boy or violent thrashings of a live punk show—the hipster has more of a joke dance. A faux shrug shuffle that mocks the very idea of dancing or, at its best, illustrates a non-committal fear of expression typified in a weird twitch/ironic twist. The dancers are too self-aware to let themselves feel any form of liberation; they shuffle along, shrugging themselves into oblivion.

Perhaps the true motivation behind this deliberate nonchalance is an attempt to attract the attention of the ever-present party photographers, who swim through the crowd like neon sharks, flashing little blasts of phosphorescent ecstasy whenever they spot someone worth momentarily immortalizing.

Noticing a few flickers of light splash out from the club bathroom, I 30 peep in only to find one such photographer taking part in an impromptu soft-core porno shoot. Two girls and a guy are taking off their clothes and striking poses for a set of grimy glamour shots. It's all grins and smirks until another girl pokes her head inside and screeches, "You're not some club kid in New York in the nineties. This shit is so hipster!"—which sparks a bit of a catfight, causing me to beat a hasty retreat.

In many ways, the lifestyle promoted by hipsterdom is highly ritualized. Many of the party-goers who are subject to the photoblogger's snapshots no doubt crawl out of bed the next afternoon and immediately re-experience the previous night's debauchery. Red-eyed and bleary, they sit hunched over their laptops, wading through a sea of similarity to find their own (momentarily) thrilling instant of perfected hipster-ness.

What they may or may not know is that "cool-hunters" will also be skulking the same sites, taking note of how they dress and what they consume. These marketers and party promoters get paid to co-opt youth culture and then re-sell it back at a profit. In the end, hipsters are sold what they think they invent and are spoon-fed their pre-packaged cultural livelihood.

Hipsterdom is the first "counterculture" to be born under the advertising industry's microscope, leaving it open to constant manipulation but also forcing its participants to continually shift their interests and affiliations. Less a subculture, the hipster is a consumer group—using their capital to purchase empty authenticity and rebellion. But the moment a trend, band, sound, style or feeling gains too much exposure, it is suddenly looked upon with disdain. Hipsters cannot afford to maintain any cultural loyalties or affiliations for fear they will lose relevance.

An amalgamation of its own history, the youth of the West are left with consuming cool rather that creating it. The cultural zeitgeists of the past have always been sparked by furious indignation and are reactionary movements. But the hipster's self-involved and isolated maintenance does nothing to feed cultural evolution. Western civilization's well has run dry. The only way to avoid hitting the colossus of societal failure that looms over the horizon is for the kids to abandon this vain existence and start over.

"If you don't give a damn, we don't give a fuck!" chants an emcee   35 before his incitements are abruptly cut short when the power plug is pulled and the lights snapped on.

Dawn breaks and the last of the after-after-parties begin to spill into the streets. The hipsters are falling out, rubbing their eyes and scanning the surrounding landscape for the way back from which they came. Some hop on their fixed-gear bikes, some call for cabs, while a few of us hop a fence and cut through the industrial wasteland of a nearby condo development.

The half-built condos tower above us like foreboding monoliths of our yuppie futures. I take a look at one of the girls wearing a bright pink keffiyeh and carrying a Polaroid camera and think, "If only we carried rocks instead of cameras, we'd look like revolutionaries." But instead we ignore the weapons that lie at our feet—oblivious to our own impending demise.

We are a lost generation, desperately clinging to anything that feels real, but too afraid to become it ourselves. We are a defeated generation, resigned to the hypocrisy of those before us, who once sang songs of rebellion and now sell them back to us. We are the last generation, a culmination of all previous things, destroyed by the vapidity that surrounds us. The hipster represents the end of Western civilization — a culture so detached and disconnected that it has stopped giving birth to anything new.

Understanding the Text

1. What does Haddow's tone reveal about his attitude toward the hipster subculture? How does it affect the reader's perception of the subculture? What, specifically, does he object to about hipsters?

2. How do hipsters build "street cred" by appropriating cultural objects from working-class America? What do you think accounts for the hipsters' preoccupation with these cultural objects?

3. What does Haddow mean when he claims that hipsters are less a subculture than a consumer group?

Reflection and Response

4. Despite Haddow's objections, what positive values and practices do you see in the hipster subculture?

5. Do you agree with the author's claim that today's youth "are a defeated generation, resigned to the hypocrisy of those before us. . . . a culture so detached and disconnected that it has stopped giving birth to anything new" (par. 38)

Making Connections

6. Compare Haddow's essay to Anatole Broyard's "A Portrait of the Hipster" (p. 86). How has the subculture changed since the late 1940s? What values and practices of the subculture have remained the same?

7. How does the concept of "authenticity," central to the definition of the hipster, play a role in defining other subcultures represented in this anthology?

8. In response to Haddow's essay, journalist Jake Mohan has written:

   As much as the cantankerous square in me wants to see hedonistic young-sters taken down a peg, I think this essay might be giving hipsters a bit too much credit, overestimating both their cultural impact and longevity while longing nostalgically for a chimerical sense of past "cool" whose own authenticity is itself suspect. "An amalgamation of its own history, the youth of the West are left with consuming cool rather than creating it," Haddow claims. But is this sort of inversion really so unprecedented? Are hipsters the first generation to practice it? And isn't it more accurate to say that all youth everywhere, not just hipsters, end up doing both the creating and the consuming of culture, with the advertising and entertainment industries serving as mediators?

   How do you, in turn, respond to Mohan's questions?

Carsten Koall/Getty Images

5

What Happens When Subcultures Go Mainstream?

T his last chapter is meant to provoke questions about the legitimacy of subcultures when the mainstream so enthusiastically embraces them that they lose their outsider status and the "freedom of the margins." When this happens, subcultures inevitably adapt or die. They either positively motivate new movements within the larger culture and, in turn, are energized by wider cultural acceptance, or they vanish from the radar, victims of their own success. Cody Delistraty opens the discussion with "Commercializing the Counterculture," both a lament for the way that music festivals have become massive commercial enterprises and a call for festivals to recover their original resistance to the imperatives of mainstream commerce.

Brittany Julious deepens the discussion about the tendency of popular subcultures — in this case, ones based on cutting-edge African American music — to be absorbed into the dominant culture, robbing the scene of its valuable outsider status. Dylan Clark picks up this theme at the end of the chapter in his autopsy of punk subculture, which had to suffer the fate of being killed by the demands of consumer culture in order to live again in post-millennial form.

Once the values and practices of marginalized communities have been "naturalized," we no longer recognize their subcultural origins and meanings. Comedian Patton Oswalt argues, humorously, that the geek community of his youth has been so fully absorbed by the internet that it has been robbed of all significance. Similarly, Brett Scott maintains that the outlaw status of hackers has morphed into the ethos that drives the commercial interests of Silicon Valley tech companies.

Mark Stryker, in his journalistic piece on Detroit street art, examines the tensions that arise when criminal street-art is reconfigured as commercially viable gallery art, pointing out that the taggers' original political and social commentary is thereby effectively silenced. Something similar happened to the rave scene, according to Michaelangelo Matos, when the collective identity of ravers as underground rebels was reformulated by the massive exposure of the internet. As each of these authors argues, if a subculture offers its members meaningful status and ways of engaging with the world, there is a very good chance that, like it or not, they will be embraced by mainstream culture.

Commercializing the Counterculture: How the Summer Music Festival Went Mainstream

Cody C. Delistraty

Cody Delistraty is the associate producer of the *Charlie Rose Show* and has worked at the Council on Foreign Relations, UNESCO, and NBC Universal in both New York and Paris. A writer and historian, Delistraty's work has appeared in the *New York Times*, the *Paris Review*, *The Atlantic*, and the *New Yorker*, among other periodicals. In this piece from *Pacific Standard* magazine, Delistraty questions whether the enormous popularity of music festivals — once a hallmark of the counterculture — threatens the very values that make them so appealing.

At the bottom of a dirt path marked by a yellow question mark painted crudely onto a circular piece of wood, a soothing voice can be heard: "The power is in the exhale. Release yourself. Lose yourself."

"Now," the voice says, "Feel your heart move into your neighbor's heart. Now bring it back to yourself once more." It is 1 p.m. at the What the Festival in Dufur, Oregon, and an afternoon session of "Good Times Yoga" is being held in the Illuminated Forest. Trek deeper into the Illuminated Forest and you'll find a Japanese tea lounge; a makeshift Buddhist temple; and various art installations, like a wooden unicorn, a life-size stag made only of mirrors, and a massive dream catcher. Emerge from the trees to discover a hookah° lounge furnished with vintage couches and coffee tables. Continue further into the middle of the festival—passing the organic coffee vendors and the fire twirlers until you get to the pool party helmed by a chilled out DJ—and you'll be reminded that female toplessness is technically legal, that not everyone makes wise tattoo decisions, and that questions like, "Who here is on acid?" are sometimes answered with resounding cheers and a sea of raised hands.

It's difficult to tell if the What the Festival, abbreviated as WTF, which includes stage names such as the "Effin' Stage," the "OMG Lounge," and the "Late-Option Lounge" (or "LOL Stage"), is making an ironic stab at mainstream culture or a clumsy attempt at cultural relevance, but it is clear that the nascent festival in rural Oregon sees itself as an alternative to better-known and more popular summer music and arts festivals (Coachella, Sasquatch, Lollapalooza, Bonnaroo, and the Electric Daisy Carnival).

hookah: water-pipe for smoking tobacco.

The summer music and arts festival has long been a hub for fringe culture and a jumping-off point for political and social protests. Woodstock, the quintessential counterculture festival in upstate New York, was a definitive moment for racial and sexual equality. It marked the rise of hippie culture in the Baby Boomer generation and sparked a countercultural trend throughout the world. England also took part, establishing its own hippie culture at the Isle of Wright Festival in 1970, a year after Woodstock, where bands like Led Zeppelin and Ten Years After attracted an estimated 600,000 attendees, breaking the record for largest musical event of its time. Three years later, Australia hosted the 10-day Aquarius Festival in Canberra, where rock musicians and experimental theater actors performed side by side in what's been called "the launching pad for Australia's hippie movement."

Today, some modern festivalgoers are looking to return to these coun- 5
tercultural roots. "I feel like there are a lot of manufactured events that have gone mainstream and are really materialistic," says Craig Erickson, a writer from Portland, Oregon, who attended the What the Festival for the first time this year. "I wanted to come out here because I heard it was a lot more low-key. I feel like you can get weird here. It's a different mindset." But, despite Erickson's enthusiasm, the age of the countercultural festival seems to have long since passed.

In *Music, Power, and Politics*, Annie Janeiro Randall, an Oxford-educated musicologist, argues that the first hippies—"proto-hippies"—emerged in Germany at the beginning of the 20th century, and used the works of Nietzsche, Goethe, and Hesse to support their rejection of urbanization and desire to return to nature and spiritual life. The movement, known as *Wandervogel*, or "migratory bird," was introduced to the United States in the 1950s when many of these proto-hippies left Germany after World War II, moving especially to areas with warm climates like southern California. The beatniks, led by Jack Kerouac and Allen Ginsberg, helped propel hippie culture popularity in the U.S. in the 1960s, and, after 1967, when the three-day Monterey Pop Festival marked the beginning of the "Summer of Love," hippie culture became a well-known subculture in American society.

It became so popular, in fact, that a July 1967 issue of *Time* magazine ran a cover story entitled "Youth: The Hippies," which summed up the hippie ethos this way:

Do your own thing, wherever you have to do it and whenever you want. Drop out. Leave society as you have known it. Leave it utterly. Blow the mind of every straight person you can reach. Turn them on, if not to drugs, then to beauty, love, honesty, fun.

However, in 1969, when Charles Manson, who was viewed by many as a hippie (a dropout musician living in California), orchestrated the murders of actress Sharon Tate and Leno and Rosemary LaBianca,° the world quickly grew disenchanted with hippie culture. The televised trial of the Chicago Seven (a group of seven people who conspired to cross state lines to incite a riot in protest of President Lyndon Johnson's Vietnam War policies) also demonstrated the radical side of hippies to a mass American audience and led to their further social exclusion. By the mid-70s, hippie culture had all but fizzled out.

Those who still identified with the term hippie became nomads, and for those who were still a part of hippie culture or simply wanted to live by hippie values, festivals became the predominant way to meet, meditate, create art, experiment with drugs and sexuality, and listen to music. Until very recently, this subculture has continued to thrive, albeit in smaller numbers than 50 years ago, meeting at a variety of countercultural events held throughout the country.

Burning Man, a week-long event where participants build a city in   10 Nevada's Black Rock Desert, is perhaps the best example of the modern counterculture festival. Although Burners may not refer to themselves as hippies, most fancy themselves counterculturalists. The event, which is home to all-night dance parties and massive art installations including the eponymous effigy that's burned at the end of the week, started as essentially a temporary commune where goods and services were traded in a "gift economy": favors unconditional, monetary exchanges irrelevant. It was a direct rebuttal to the hegemony of capitalism and to corporate sponsorship, the festival version of Occupy Wall Street,° a push-back against the type of world presaged by David Foster Wallace's *Infinite Jest*, in which everything is mediated by advertising and branding.

Recent issues with ticket sales (where single buyers bought up dozens of tickets and immediately sold them off at rates too expensive for most Burning Man regulars) and the fact that Silicon Valley CEOs have begun shelling out for guided VIP Burning Man "experiences" (creating socio-economic tiers at the festival), however, have led to the degradation of the festival's original countercultural values.

Likewise, the five-day Glastonbury Festival near Pilton, Somerset, England, which began as a "free festival" where everything was free of charge in exchange for volunteering, now costs £215 and is sponsored

---

Sharon Tate, Leno Bianca, Rosemary Bianca: random victims of the Manson Family's 1969 murder spree in Los Angeles.
Occupy Wall Street: protest movement that began in 2011 in New York's financial district to draw attention to global economic inequality.

by the mobile phone company Orange. So too Lightning in a Bottle, a "transformational" festival meant to inspire "social cohesion" in California's Angeles National Forest lost much of its countercultural cachet when a sophisticated police sting that bordered on entrapment led to the arrests of 58 attendees for drug deals, mainly for the sale of small amounts of marijuana.

Long gone are the painted Volkswagen buses, talk of "free love," and shoulder-length hair for men, but it's only recently that the festivals associated with those things have also begun to disappear, replaced by a new breed of festival that's tailored to a different group entirely: hipsters.

Hipsters, who intentionally and ironically pervert supposed mainstream values, oftentimes share the external appearance of hippies: the long beards, the psychedelic drugs, and the rejection of "popular culture" from Katy Perry to luxury cars. Yet a hipster is not the same as a hippie for he is not a bohemian, but rather, as *New York Times* columnist David Brooks writes in *Bobos in Paradise: The New Upper Class and How They Got There,* a bourgeois-bohemian, or "bobo." The hipster is able to play the role of the bohemian while simultaneously wielding the resources of the bourgeois.

Festival-goers attend Bonnaroo Arts and Music Festival in Manchester, Tennessee. The festival is famous for the sweltering heat and number of attendees — during the festival it becomes Tennessee's sixth largest city. FilmMagic/Getty Images

What has caused the modern destruction of the countercultural 15
festival—and, by extension, the systematic degradation of the modern
counterculture movement—is not so much dubious police raids or over-
priced tickets, but the fact that modern festivalgoers genuinely believe
they are taking part in something countercultural while they are in fact
participating in the mainstream. Hipsters are not hippies, and to think
that camping for a few days without showers, smoking weed and popping Molly (the popular methylone-based drug—essentially a distilled
form of ecstasy), and living without responsibilities save for which musician to see next makes one a cultural revolutionary is an inherently
flawed stream of logic.

Although the hipster believes he is embracing counterculture and
anti-establishment through his rejection of the mainstream, he is in fact
less intent on social change and more keen on getting ahead of and setting cultural trends—even as these trends are often mediated through
capitalism. Implicit, yet nonetheless important "rules" of hipsterdom
include drinking the "right" brand of beer, such as Pabst Blue Ribbon (as
it was once associated with the blue-collar worker) and the importance
of wearing the "right" brand of sunglasses ($200 Ray-Bans? Sure! Equally
pricey Persols? So gauche).

Such care for manufactured trends and material goods is antithetical to
the counterculture ethos. The reason the hipster is so adamantly pursued
by corporations, brands, and commercial interests is that as an upper-
middle-class, 18-to-35-year-old, he is not only a part of the most desired
demographic but also a willing consumer, something the hippie never was.

At this year's South by Southwest festival in Austin, Texas, or SXSW,
which combines concerts with a film competition and art installations,
the comedian Jimmy Kimmel sent his crew to ask festivalgoers if they
had heard of made-up musical acts such as "Contact Dermatitis," "Neil
Patrick Harassment," and "DJ Heavy Flow." Too ready to be perceived as
up on the latest musical trends, the interviewees responded empathically
in the affirmative: "[I've] heard a couple songs" from DJ Heavy Flow's
album, *The Toxic Shock Experience,* says one girl; "I heard it, but I'm not
really into it," says another guy on the rap-country music of the fictional
Willie Nelson Mandela. It is entertaining and funny to watch these people caring so much about trends, about what other people think, and
about being perceived as cool, but it is also an obvious line in the sand
between hipsters and counterculturalists.

But like many dying subcultures (even those who read physical books
still have a few surviving bookstores to shop in) there may be a few last
bastions of hope for the counterculturalist.

Two years ago I wondered if the inaugural What the Festival could 20 become this generation's counterculture festival. This year's event attracted another steady crowd from the West Coast; Vancouver, Seattle, Portland, and San Francisco were all represented. The attendees weren't quite hipsters but they weren't quite hippies either: There didn't appear to be any driving social conscience behind the festival (save for perhaps eco-friendliness—e.g. composting bins, hemp milk), desire to "drop out" of society, or overt motivation to turn people on to "drugs . . . beauty, love, honesty, [or] fun," as the *Time* article wrote of hippies. But based on nearly two-dozen interviews and two years of attendance, it is clear that these festival-goers aren't the upper-middle-class twentysomethings looking for a place to prove their coolness bona fides or to try new synthetic drugs, as it tended to be with the attendees I spoke to at Coachella, Bonnaroo, and Sasquatch.

The volunteer-created Counter Culture Festival in Utrecht, Netherlands, and the pagan, new-age Yaga Gathering in Varena, Lithuania, also exist in this nebulous space. Hippie culture may be dying, but a new subculture—a sort of purgatory between hipster and hippie—may be arising.

Even as Burning Man, Glastonbury, and Lightning in a Bottle have begun to succumb to commercialization, and Coachella, Lollapallooza, Sasquatch, Bonnaroo, Firefly, and the Electric Daisy Carnival are wellsprings for hipsterdom and corporate interests, there are some festival-goers who are unwilling to accept overt advertising and branding or the know-it-all coolness that exists in hipsterdom.

The question is whether these contemporary counterculturalists can maintain their identity in the face of more popular festivals where attendance skyrockets into the hundreds of thousands. For the What the Festival, the Counter Culture Festival, and the Yaga Gathering, having a few thousand attendees is viewed as a success. Yet all new subcultures must start small. And their attendees hold strong convictions about future growth.

"We're a part of this thing called the neo-geo Renaissance," says Kyle O'Neil, an independent publisher from Oregon's Lincoln City Coast. "This is what's going on all around us: a Renaissance. There's been many of them, and every single one of them has led with art."

> "The question is whether these contemporary counterculturalists can maintain their identity in the face of more popular festivals where attendance skyrockets into the hundreds of thousands."

Dressed in a rainbow tank top, O'Neil paused to finish practicing his   25
fire staff twirling routine. "We're finding that path."

Understanding the Text

1. According to Delistraty, what is the main reason for the commercialization of the hippie/festival counterculture?
2. What does Delistraty mean by "manufactured trends and material goods" (par. 17)?

Reflection and Response

3. Do any of Delistraty's claims deserve greater development or support from authoritative sources? Which ones? Explain.
4. Is there a valuable role for the music festival beyond the expression of countercultural values? Make your case, citing specific evidence.
5. If you have attended a major music festival, write an in-depth account of your experience.

Making Connections

6. Delistraty attributes the demise of hippie culture to such events as the Manson Family murders and the trial of the Chicago Seven in 1969. Research the large social and economic changes that occurred in the late 1960s and 1970s to develop a more nuanced and detailed argument about the reasons for the fading of hippie culture.
7. How would the Diggers portrayed in Alex Forman's "San Francisco Style" (p. 151) (1967) respond to a contemporary festival such as Burning Man?

The Hacker Hacked

Brett Scott

Brett Scott is a London-based journalist who writes about financial activism and social and environmental finance. He is the author of *The Heretic's Guide to Global Finance: Hacking the Future of Money* (2013), in which he uses the figure of the hacker as a model for readers wishing to challenge the global financial system. He has written for such publications as the *Guardian*, *Wired*, and *Aeon Mag*, and has appeared on BBC *World Update*, BBC *Newsday*, the *Keiser Report*, and Arte TV. In the essay below, Scott contends that hacking, once the provenance of outsider computer geeks, has been gentrified by the relentless pressures of Silicon Valley, turning hacking from a challenge to authority into an activity at the center of entrepreneurial capitalism.

Any large and alienating infrastructure controlled by a technocratic elite is bound to provoke. In particular, it will nettle those who want to know how it works, those who like the thrill of transgressing, and those who value the principle of open access. Take the U.S. telephone network of the 1960s: a vast array of physical infrastructure dominated by a monopolistic telecoms corporation called AT&T. A young Air Force serviceman named John Draper—aka Captain Crunch—discovered that he could manipulate the rules of tone-dialing systems by using children's whistles found in Cap'n Crunch cereal boxes. By whistling the correct tone into a telephone handset, he could place free long-distance calls through a chink in the AT&T armor.

Draper was one of the first *phone phreakers*, a motley crew of jokers bent on exploring and exploiting loopholes in the system to gain free access. Through the eyes of conventional society, such phreakers were just juvenile pranksters and cheapskates. Yet their actions have since been incorporated into the folklore of modern hacker culture. Draper said in a 1995 interview: "I was mostly interested in the curiosity of how the phone company worked. I had no real desire to go rip them off and steal phone service."

But in his book *Hackers: Heroes of the Computer Revolution* (1984), the journalist Steven Levy went so far as to put up Draper as an avatar of the "true hacker" spirit. Levy was trying to hone in on principles that he believed constituted a "hacker ethic." One such principle was the "hands-on imperative":

Hackers believe that essential lessons can be learned about the systems—about the world—from taking things apart, seeing how they work, and using this knowledge to create new and even more interesting things.

277

For all his protestations of innocence, it's clear that Draper's curiosity was essentially subversive. It represented a threat to the ordered lines of power within the system. The phreakers were trying to open up information infrastructure, and in doing so they showed a calculated disregard for the authorities that dominated it.

This spirit has carried through into the modern context of the inter-   5
net, which, after all, consists of computers connected to one another via physical telecommunications infrastructure. The internet promises open access to information and online assembly for individual computer owners. At the same time, it serves as a tool for corporate monopolists and government surveillance. The most widely recognized examples of modern "hackers" are therefore groups such as Anonymous and WikiLeaks. These "cypherpunks" and crypto-anarchists are internet natives. They fight — at least in principle — to protect the privacy of the individual while making power itself as transparent as possible.

This dynamic is not unique to the internet. It plays out in many other spheres of life. Consider the pranksters who mess with rail operators by jamming ticket-barrier gates to keep them open for others. They might not describe themselves as hackers, but they carry an ethic of disdain towards systems that normally allow little agency on the part of ordinary individuals. Such hacker-like subcultures do not necessarily see themselves in political terms. Nevertheless, they share a common tendency towards a rebellious creativity aimed at increasing the agency of underdogs. . . .

Despite the hive-mind connotations of faceless groups such as Anonymous, the archetype of "the hacker" is essentially that of an *individual* attempting to live an empowered and unalienated life. It is *outsider* in spirit, seeking empowerment outside the terms set by the mainstream establishment.

Perhaps it's unwise to essentialize this figure. A range of quite different people can think of themselves in those terms, from the lonely nerd tinkering away on DIY radio in the garage to the investigative journalist immersed in politicized muckraking.° It seems safe to say, though, that it's not very hacker-like to aspire to *conventional* empowerment, to get a job at a blue-chip company while reading *The Seven Habits of Highly Effective People.* The hacker impulse is *critical*. It defies, for example, corporate ambitions.

• • •

The hacker is ambiguous, specializing in deviance from established boundaries, including ideological battle lines. It's a trickster spirit, subversive and hard to pin down. And, arguably, rather than aiming towards

muckraking: early twentieth-century reform-minded journalism dedicated to exposing corporate corruption and social ills.

some specific reformist end, the hacker spirit is a "way of being," an attitude towards the world.

Take, for example, the urban explorer subculture, chronicled by Bradley Garrett in *Explore Everything: Placehacking the City* (2013). The search for unusual detours—through a sewer system, for example—is exhilarating because you see things that you're not *supposed* to be interested in. Your curiosity takes you to places where you *don't belong*. It thus becomes an assertion of individual defiance of social norms. The byproduct of such exploration is pragmatic knowledge, the disruption of standard patterns of thought, and also dealienation—you see what's behind the interfaces that surround us, coming closer to the reality of our social world. 10

This is a useful sensibility to cultivate in the face of systems that create psychological, political and economic barriers to access. In the context of a complex system—computer, financial or underground transit—the political divide is always between well-organized, active insiders versus diffuse, passive outsiders. Hackers challenge the binary by seeking *access*, either by literally "cracking" boundaries breaking in or by redefining the lines between those with permission and those without. We might call this *appropriation*.

A figure of economic power such as a factory owner builds a machine to extend control. The activist Luddite° might break it in rebellion. But the hacker explores and then modifies the machine to make it self-destruct, or programs it to frustrate the purpose of its owners, or opens its usage to those who do not own it. The hacker ethic is therefore a composite. It is not *merely* exploratory curiosity or rebellious deviance or creative innovation within incumbent systems. It emerges from the intersection of all three.

The word "hacker" came into its own in the age of information technology (IT) and the personal computer. The subtitle of Levy's seminal book—*Heroes of the Computer Revolution*—immediately situated hackers as the crusaders of computer geek culture. While some hacker principles he described were broad—such as "mistrust authority" and "promote decentralization"—others were distinctly IT-centric. "You can create art and beauty on a computer," read one. "All information should be free," declared another.

Ever since, most popular representations of the hacker way have followed Levy's lead. Neal Stephenson's cyberpunk novel *Snow Crash* (1992) featured the code-wielding Hiro as the "last of the freelance hackers."

Luddite: early nineteenth-century bands of English workers who destroyed machines that threatened their jobs.

The film *Hackers* (1995) boasted a youthful crew of jargon-rapping, keyboard-hammering computer ninjas. The media stereotype that began to be constructed was of a precocious computer genius using his technological mastery to control events or battle others. It remains popular to this day. In the James Bond film *Skyfall* (2012), the gadget-master Q is reinvented by the actor Ben Whishaw as a young hacker with a laptop, controlling lines of code with almost superhuman efficiency, as if his brain was wired directly into the computer.

In a sense, then, computers were the making of the hacker, at least as   15 a popular cultural image. But they were also its undoing. If the popular imagination hadn't chained the hacker figure so forcefully to IT, it's hard to believe it ever would have been demonized in the way it has been, or that it could have been so effectively defanged.

Computers, and especially the internet, are a primary means of subsistence for many. This understandably increases public anxiety at the bogeyman figure of the criminal "hacker," the dastardly villain who breaches computer security to steal and cause havoc. Never mind that in "true" hacker culture—as found in hackerspaces, maker-labs and open-source communities around the world—the mechanical act of breaking into a computer is just one manifestation of the drive to explore beyond established boundaries. In the hands of a sensationalist media, the ethos of hacking is conflated with the act of cracking computer security. Anyone who does that, regardless of the underlying ethos, is a "hacker." Thus a single manifestation of a single element of the original spirit gets passed off as the whole.

Through the lens of moral panic, a narrative emerges of hackers as a class of computer attack-dogs. Their primary characteristics become aggression and amorality. How to guard against them? How, indeed, to round out the traditional good-versus-evil narrative? Well, naturally, with a class of poacher-turned-gamekeepers. And so we find the construction of "white-hat" hackers, protective and upstanding computer wizards for the public good.

Here is where the second form of corruption begins to emerge. The construct of the "good hacker" has paid off in unexpected ways, because in our computerized world we have also seen the emergence of a huge, aggressively competitive technology industry with a serious innovation obsession. This is the realm of startups, venture capitalists, and shiny corporate research and development departments. And, it is here, in subcultures such as Silicon Valley, that we find a rebel spirit succumbing to perhaps the only force that could destroy it: gentrification.

Gentrification is the process by which nebulous threats are pacified and alchemized into money. A raw form—a rough neighborhood, indigenous ritual or edgy behavior such as parkour (or free running)—gets stripped of its otherness and repackaged to suit mainstream sensibilities. The process is repetitive. Desirable, unthreatening elements of the source culture are isolated, formalized and emphasized, while the unsettling elements are scrubbed away.

Key to any gentrification process are successive *waves* of pioneers who   20 gradually reduce the perceived risk of the form in question. In property gentrification, this starts with the artists and disenchanted dropouts from mainstream society who are drawn to marginalized areas. Despite their countercultural impulses, they always carry with them traces of the dominant culture, whether it be their skin color or their desire for good coffee. This, in turn, creates the seeds for certain markets to take root. A WiFi coffeeshop appears next to the Somalian community center. And that, in turn, sends signals back into the mainstream that the area is *slightly less alien* than it used to be.

If you repeat this cycle enough times, the perceived dangers that keep the property developers and yuppies away gradually erode. Suddenly, the tipping point arrives. Through a myriad of individual actions under no one person's control, the exotic *other* suddenly appears within a safe frame: interesting, exciting and cool, but not threatening. It becomes open to a carefree voyeurism, like a tiger being transformed into a zoo animal, and then a picture, and then a tiger-print dress to wear at cocktail parties. Something feels "gentrified" when this shallow aesthetic of tiger takes over from the authentic lived experience of tiger. . . .

We are currently witnessing the gentrification of hacker culture. The countercultural trickster has been pressed into the service of the preppy tech entrepreneur class. It began innocently, no doubt. The association of the hacker ethic with startups might have started with an authentic countercultural impulse on the part of outsider nerds tinkering away on websites. But, like all gentrification, the influx into the scene of successive waves of ever less disaffected individuals results in a growing emphasis on the unthreatening elements of hacking over the subversive ones.

Silicon Valley has come to host, on the one hand, a large number of highly educated tech-savvy people who loosely perceive themselves as rebels set against existing modes of doing business. On the other hand, it contains a very large pool of venture capital. The former group jostle for the investor money by explicitly attempting to build network monopolies—such as those created by Facebook and Google—for the purpose of extracting windfall profit for the founders and for the investors that back them, and perhaps, for the large corporates who will buy them out.

In this economic context, curiosity, innovation and iterative experimentation are ultimate virtues, and this element of the hacker ethic has proved to be an appealing frame for people to portray their actions within. Traits such as the drive for individual empowerment and the appreciation of clever solutions already resemble the traits of the entrepreneur. . . .

Thus the emergent tech industry's definition of "hacking" as quirky- but-edgy innovation by optimistic entrepreneurs with a love of getting things done. Nothing sinister about it: it's just on-the-fly problem-solving for profit. This gentrified pitch is not just a cool personal narrative. It's also a useful business construct, helping the tech industry to distinguish itself from the aggressive squares of Wall Street, competing for the same pool of new graduates.

Indeed, the revised definition of the tech startup entrepreneur as a hacker forms part of an emergent system of Silicon Valley doublethink: individual startups portray themselves as "underdogs" while simultane- ously being aware of the enormous power and wealth the tech industry they're a part of wields at a collective level. And so we see a gradual strip- ping away of the critical connotations of hacking. Who said a hacker can't be in a position of power? Google cloaks itself in a quirky "hacker" identity, with grown adults playing ping pong on green AstroTurf in the cafeteria, presiding over the company's overarching agenda of network control.

This doublethink bleeds through into mainstream corporate culture, with the growing institution of the corporate "hackathon." We find financial giants such as Barclays hosting startup accelerators and finan- cial technology hackathons at forums such as the FinTech Innovation Lab in Canary Wharf in London, ostensibly to discover the "future of finance" . . . or at least the future of payment apps that they can buy out. In this context, the hacker ethic is hollowed out and subsumed into the ideology of *solutionism*, to use a term coined by the Belarusian-born tech critic Evgeny Morozov. It describes the tech-industry vision of the world as a series of problems waiting for (profitable) solutions.

This process of gentrification becomes a war over language. If enough newcomers with media clout use the hollowed-out version of the term, its edge grows dull. You end up with a mere affectation, failing to chal- lenge otherwise conventional aspirations. And before you know it, an earnest Stanford grad is handing me a business card that says, without irony: "Founder. Investor. Hacker."

Any gentrification process inevitably presents two options. Do you abandon the form, leave it to the yuppies and head to the next wild frontier? Or do you attempt to break the cycle, deface the estate-agent signs, and picket outside the wine bar with placards reading "Yuppies Go Home"?

25

The answer to this depends on how much you care. Immigrant neigh- 30
borhoods definitely care enough to mobilize real resistance movements to
gentrification, but who wants to protect
the hacker ethic? For some, the spirit of
hacking is stupid and pointless anyway,
an individualistic self-help impulse, not
an authentic political movement. What
does it matter if it gets gentrified?

> "A hack stripped of anti-
> conventional intent is not a
> hack at all. It's just a piece of
> business innovation."

We need to confront an irony here. Gentrification is a pacification
process that takes the wild and puts it in frames. I believe that hacking is
the reverse of that, taking the ordered rules of systems and making them
fluid and wild again. Where gentrification tries to erect safe fences around
things, hacker impulses try to break them down, or redefine them. These
are two countervailing forces within human society. The gentrification of
hacking is . . . well, perhaps a perfect hack. . . .

I'm going to stake a claim on the word though, and state that the
true hacker spirit does not reside at Google, guided by profit targets. The
hacker impulse should not just be about redesigning products, or creating
"solutions." A hack stripped of anti-conventional intent is not a hack at
all. It's just a piece of business innovation.

The un-gentrified spirit of hacking should be a commons accessible
to all. This spirit can be seen in the marginal cracks all around us. It's in
the emergent forms of peer production and DIY culture, in maker-spaces
and urban farms. We see it in the expansion of "open" scenes, from
open hardware to open biotech, and in the intrigue around 3D printers
as a way to extend open-source designs into the realm of manufacture.
In a world with increasingly large and unaccountable economic institutions, we need these everyday forms of resistance. Hacking, in my
world, is a route to escaping the shackles of the profit-fetish, not a route
to profit.

Go home, yuppies.

Understanding the Text

1. According to Scott, what motivated the original hackers?
2. Scott mentions the term "moral panic" as a lens through which hackers are
   perceived. Research the meaning of this term and explain how it applies to
   this particular subculture.
3. Why does Scott object to the "ideology of *solutionism*" (par. 27)?

Reflection and Response

4. According to Scott, how has "gentrification" corrupted the original hacker ethos? What exactly does he mean when he uses the term? What other subcultures have been gentrified in this way?

5. Scott calls the hacker ethic a composite of curiosity, deviance, and innovation. Make a list of examples, from both hacker subculture and mainstream culture, in which these three qualities come into play.

Making Connections

6. Research the famous hacker collective known as Anonymous. Do you believe that these hackers are performing a service to the world, as they claim? Is it necessary to challenge authority, even if it means causing damage? What is an acceptable level of damage?

7. In 1986, just before his arrest, Loyd Blankenship published the original "Hacker's Manifesto." In it he addresses the mainstream society:

> We explore . . . and you call us criminals. We seek after knowledge, and you call us criminals. We exist without skin color, without nationality, without religious bias . . . and you call us criminals. You build atomic bombs, you wage wars, you murder, cheat, and lie to us and try to make us believe it's for our own good, yet we're the criminals.

> Yes, I am a criminal. My crime is that of curiosity. My crime is that of judging people by what they say and think, not what they look like. My crime is that of outsmarting you, something you will never forgive me for.

How does the ethical position Blankenship espouses fit with what Scott has to say about hackers? (Consider his discussion of John Draper, the first phone phreaker.) In what ways does Scott cede the moral high ground to hackers? Are there counter-arguments to Blankenship's claim that "my crime is that of curiosity"?

A Street Art Culture Clash as Graffiti Goes Mainstream

Mark Stryker

Mark Stryker is a longtime arts reporter for the *Detroit Free Press* and the author of *Made in Detroit: Jazz from the Motor City*. He is the winner of several awards for arts reporting, including two ASCAP Deems Taylor Awards. In "A Street Art Culture Clash," he turns his attention to the fine line between art and vandalism, between community-building and the defacement of public space — a line that graffiti has challenged for the past generation. Now, as graffiti has entered the mainstream art world, the classical tagger subculture faces the possibility of being simultaneously embraced and disbanded.

To get to one of Detroit's most powerful and shocking pieces of street art, you have to ignore the barricades set up at the north end of the Dequindre Cut. The idyllic recreational walk way connects the riverfront with Eastern Market and turns into a construction zone below street level.

It's a dim and dank forest of industrial decay, overgrown weeds, and relentless graffiti, some of it profane. But there's also a fully realized mural on a concrete wall set deep into the west side of the Cut that will stop you in your tracks: A shadowy figure, hiding amid enigmatic calligraphy, wears a blue hooded sweatshirt and points a giant handgun right at you.

Drawing meaning and intensity from its location, the piece is a beautiful nightmare. In the midst of Detroit's nascent renaissance, the mural, by an anonymous artist, remains a disturbing reminder of the city's dangerous past and, for too many, its present reality.

"Is it illegal art? Yes," said Matt Eaton, director-curator of the Red Bull House of Art in Eastern Market and a longtime champion of street art. "Does that take away from its relevance as social commentary? No!"

Eaton spoke last week while giving a *Free Press* reporter and photographer an annotated tour of some of Detroit's street-art hotspots, though he had never seen this particular mural until the *Free Press* led him to it.

"That person who made this has an important message to convey. Who knows what value this person may have in their community. They have something to say, and they're trying any way they can to say it."

Street art — both authorized and unauthorized — is everywhere in Detroit. Hundreds of colorful murals now decorate the city, many of them highly polished works by a mix of some of the best-known street artists in the country and gifted local painters. Developments are moving so quickly that it's hard to keep up. Two weeks ago organizers announced the creation of Murals in the Market, a nine-day festival in September in which some 45 national and local artists will create dozens of large-scale, commissioned pieces in Eastern Market.

Last week, however, the world-famous street artist Shepard Fairey, who recently completed an 18-story mural at One Campus Martius at the bequest of real estate mogul Dan Gilbert and others, was arraigned on felony charges that while in town he also defaced public and private property without permission. He faces a maximum penalty of five years in jail and fines that could exceed $10,000 or more.

The rush of news and the controversy surrounding Fairey's arrest have reignited a debate over the value of street art, its connection to unauthorized graffiti and vandalism and the increasing role that public art is

Contemporary artist Shepard Fairey's mural on the Compuware headquarters building in Detroit. Though this mural was commissioned, Detroit police claimed that Fairey put up at least twenty-three unauthorized works. In 2016 a Detroit judge dismissed the case. Barcroft Media/Getty Images

playing in revitalizing and beautifying the city in myriad neighborhoods, from southwest Detroit to Eastern Market, downtown, the Grand River corridor, and elsewhere.

What's unfolding can be read as a clash of cultures: Those who see value in the complex history and tradition of street art, its connection to social protest and its outlaw roots—even as they disavow its excesses—versus those who don't. On another level, Detroit is witnessing the tension that occurs when a former subculture becomes 10 absorbed, sometimes co-opted, by the mainstream.

> "What's unfolding can be read as a clash of cultures: Those who see value in the complex history and tradition of street art, its connection to social protest and its outlaw roots — even as they disavow its excesses — versus those who don't."

It's Great if It's Legal

City officials say they're all in favor of street art—as long as it's legal.

"There is a difference between street art and illegal tagging—graffiti," said Alexis Wiley, Detroit Mayor Mike Duggan's chief of staff. "Street art is fantastic. There are places where it's added to an area. But bottom line: If you don't ask for property owners' permission you're committing a crime."

Street artists and their advocates argue that the celebration of risk and its connection to status is so deeply embedded within the DNA of street art that clear-cut distinctions between art and crime remain more elusive than the plain text of a city ordinance.

"From the perspective of a graffiti writer, the debate about whether graffiti is art or crime is pointless because, ideally, it is both," graffiti historian Eric Felisbret wrote last year in the *New York Times*.

Many street artists concede that the police have a job to do and that 15 ugly and destructive name-tagging should be punished.

But they also say that not all graffiti is created equal. In this view, artistically rendered signatures in stylized calligraphy on an abandoned building—to say nothing of a strategically placed and deftly painted hoodlum pointing a gun—are markers of identity, vanity, subversion, and commentary. They are not the cause of urban decay but reactions to it.

"Any street artist who is at a top level started somewhere by picking up a spray can, and probably worked illegally because they didn't have other options," said Freddy Diaz, a celebrated 22-year-old artist from southwest Detroit. Diaz has completed nearly 20 commissioned murals in his neighborhood and has begun to show in galleries and work overseas.

"I don't deface property," he said. "But when I was 16, I did illegal work, and I almost did jail time. That's when I learned to make money with my art, and I had mentors who helped show me the right way to do things. If you make graffiti a felony, that's clipping the wings of a kid. There won't be any opportunity to educate them."

Like Fairey, many of today's established street artists continue to do unauthorized work, partly as a way to reaffirm their street cred. But others have decided that as they've gotten older and matured, the risks are no longer worth it.

"For me, in the last 15 years, I've been trying to promote the posi- 20
tives of the genre," said the 43-year-old Detroit artist known as Fel3000ft. "Being an older guy with kids, I haven't worked illegally for some 20 years."

Many in Detroit's street art community say that Duggan's aggressive response toward graffiti—which stretches back a dozen years to his days as Wayne County prosecutor—threatens to smother Detroit's reputation as a haven for artistic creativity. They point to the stiff charges Fairey faces, a crackdown on local offenders, and an episode last year in which dozens of building owners were mistakenly ticketed for blight violations because of murals they approved.

Detroit artist Kobie Solomon, best known for his authorized gargantuan mural of a mythical beast on the side of the Russell Industrial Center, which is visible from I-75, said that he wouldn't be surprised if Fairey's case caused some national and local artists who have been doing authorized work in Detroit to reconsider their allegiance to the city. "The eyes of the international art world are on Detroit right now, and it's a bigger and more delicate situation than people are aware of," said Solomon. "How it's all handled could determine whether we're viewed as a progressive city or an archaic place."

City officials say the penalties are part of trying to change the culture of a city anxious to leave behind its reputation for lawlessness. For decades graffiti artists had their run of the streets. [But] Wiley resisted suggestions that art was under attack. She noted that of 30 people arrested for graffiti in the last year, fewer than 10 were Detroit residents.

Three Grosse Pointe teens were sentenced to 60 hours of community service for defacing two buildings on Michigan Avenue and Griswold Street last summer in downtown Detroit.

A few weeks later, residents applauded when Detroit Police Chief 25
James Craig announced the arrests of five young men for spray-painting a couple of buildings on Detroit's west side.

"If they believe there's such a right to do street art, then they should start tagging their own homes," Wiley said.

"If you wouldn't do it on your own house, why is it OK to come to Detroit and do it on a building and believe that it's some sort of social protest?"

Many residents near where vandalism occurs worry that graffiti can lead to neighborhood decline.

Gail Dorsey, a University District neighborhood block captain in northwest Detroit, said that she enjoys the murals she's seen around town that have been carefully planned and well-executed, but she draws the line at unauthorized work, especially in or near residential communities.

"When I see the cans come out and it's scribbles and bad language, I 30 don't see anything artistic about that," she said.

"There are empty buildings on Livernois, and I don't want to see people come out and put up stuff without permission, because there's no way to count on people putting up something good."

Vibrant Cultural Scene

. . . Detroit's exploding street art scene is among the most visible signs of the way the arts are infusing energy into the city. Culture is improving quality of life, attracting suburbanites and tourists, and providing the fodder for a regular stream of national media stories highlighting Detroit's comeback.

The legions of artists and young creatives who have been pouring into the city, the renewed relevancy of institutions like the Detroit Symphony Orchestra and Detroit Institute of Arts, and homegrown masterpieces like Tyree Guyton's Heidelberg Project are all also part of the excitement.

Culture has become a magnet for investment with the foundation world, particularly the Kresge Foundation and John S. and James L. Knight Foundation of Miami, pouring more than $50 million into the city's cultural scene since 2006. (And that's not counting the more than $366 million that foundations gave to the grand bargain to protect the DIA and shore up pensions during the city's bankruptcy.)

Last week, a family of three from Montreal strolled through the Belt, 35 the exuberant, art-filled alley, curated by the Library Street Collective, in the middle of the Z parking garage, which itself houses 24 murals, including those by leading national figures such as Revok, Hense and Maya Hayuk.

On their way to Chicago, the French-Canadian threesome stopped in Detroit for the day because they had heard about the city's rebound and that art was leading the charge.

"We're seeing all of this beautiful street art, and all of the life at Cadillac Square," said Marie-Josee Dufour. "We can see the effort people are making, but the art was a surprise. We thought we'd spend all day at the museums, but instead we're just walking around and looking. We'll come back, and we'll talk about Detroit as a place to go on vacation."

Graffiti Art's History

The history of contemporary graffiti art begins in the late '60s and early '70s in rough neighborhoods in Philadelphia and New York. Kids began simple name-tagging, and soon subway cars were being covered with spray paint. By the end of the decade graffiti was assimilated into early hip-hop culture. Certain kinds of tagging also became identified with gang activity, though graffiti had already been used for decades in some circles to mark territory.

By the '80s, a more mature kind of street art began to emerge, spreading to walls around American cities and around the world. Artists moved beyond text to more complex imagery. Keith Haring's cartoon-like figures and social and political themes began to cross over into mainstream culture. Haring and the gifted Jean-Michel Basquiat transcended their graffiti roots to become art-world stars. And graffiti and street-art styles began to influence advertising, fashion, and commercial graphic design.

In the last decade the mainstreaming of street art took a great leap 40 forward with the increasing celebrity of two artists—the anonymous Brit known as Banksy, the subject of the Academy Award-nominated documentary *Exit Through the Gift Shop* (and who bombed the abandoned Packard Plant in 2010 with two murals), and Fairey, who skyrocketed to fame in 2008 on the wings of his ubiquitous "Hope" poster of Barack Obama.

These days many street artists also show in galleries, where their works can sell for tens of thousands of dollars or more. A Banksy street mural, excavated from London, sold for $1.1 million at auction in 2013. Fairey is a one-man conglomerate, selling prints, books, skateboards and lines of clothing and accessories outfitted with his calling-card imagery like the Obey logo and Andre the Giant face.

"All things that are subcultures and successful eventually become part of the larger culture and end up having a dollar value put on them," said Roger Gastman, co-author of *The History of American Graffiti* . . . and a co-curator of "Art in the Streets," a high-profile 2011 exhibition of street art at the Museum of Contemporary Art, Los Angeles.

The proliferation of mural festivals, commissions, gallery shows, and celebrity have made it possible for many street artists to expand their creative horizons and earn a living. But it has also led to commodification and evidence that the genre has lost its edge. Gastman said that street art hasn't necessarily been sapped of all its energy and creativity but that it has been "diluted."

"More people become interested, more people become fans and less people know the true history," he said. "It also creates a lot of artists who don't have the true respect of the streets."

A Street-Art Showplace

The Dequindre Cut, which runs below street level for a little more than 45 a mile, parallel to St. Aubin Street, has become one of the most satisfying spots to see street art in Detroit.

The Detroit Riverfront Conservancy, which manages the path, has commissioned a dozen exemplary Detroit artists to do murals on the concrete bridge supports and walls along the way. The varied works include Fel3000ft's marriage of outer-space imagery and pro-Detroit text; the two-person Hygienic Dress League's enigmatic figures (one wears a gasmask and holds a bird); and the meticulously rendered, ominous and purple bird-like creature painted by the artist called Malt.

The Conservancy has also left many more examples of illegal graffiti and street art undisturbed alongside the commissioned work. It's a savvy move, allowing a sense of urban grit to remain part of the experience. Still, context matters. Nothing in the completed part of the Cut — amid the joggers, bicyclists, dog walkers, and strollers — captures the raw expression and anxious jolt of coming across the mural of the gunman on the other side of the barricade.

Will the new Detroit allow such a provocative reminder of the city's troubled history to remain? Marc Pasco, director of communications for the conservancy, said a decision about whether the work would ultimately be removed before the northern extension of the Cut opens would be made on whether the mural was deemed offensive for what he called a "family venue."

It's hard to imagine the mural surviving such a threshold, and maybe it shouldn't even be an issue. Street art by definition is ephemeral. But justified or not, something of value will disappear when that mural gets whitewashed.

Understanding the Text

1. What does Stryker mean when he writes that street art draws "meaning and intensity from its location" (par. 3)?

2. One of the block captains mentioned in the article objects to "unauthorized work" by taggers. What exactly does it mean to be "authorized"? How is the word related to both authority and authorship?

Reflection and Response

3. After considering Detroit's response to taggers, how do you define "street art"? What is the line between vandalism and artistic creation? What happens to the art form when the "criminal" label is removed?

4. Is it true, as Stryker claims, that "not all graffiti is created equal" (par. 16)? Discuss in depth.

5. In regard to a particular piece of wall art in Detroit, Stryker writes that "something of value will disappear when that mural gets whitewashed" (par. 49). Although he is referring to a specific work, show how this claim could also be interpreted as a metaphor for what happens when street art goes mainstream.

Making Connections

6. Go online and find a graffiti image that you particularly admire, and analyze it as a work of art. Consider the use of color, form, scale, contrast, and content. Will this image stand the test of time as an artwork?

7. Investigate the assimilation of graffiti into hip-hop subculture in the early 1980s, discussing the common roots of both communities. What conditions gave rise to — and closely linked — these two subcultures?

8. Stryker suggests that the street-art subculture is traditionally defined by risk, even criminality. Choose another subculture that depends on risk-taking to define its identity and discuss what would happen to the group if its activities were no longer dangerous or criminal.

How the Internet Transformed the American Rave Scene

Michaelangelo Matos

Author of *The Underground Is Massive: How Electronic Dance Music Conquered America*, Michaelangelo Matos is a longtime contributor to *Rolling Stone*, *Pitchfork*, and other magazines. Matos makes his home in Minneapolis, so it's not surprising that he has also written extensively about the late pop-music icon Prince. In this essay, originally aired by National Public Radio, Matos examines what happens when a subculture that thrives by "flying under the radar" embraces the most public of all forums, the internet.

Rave was America's last great outlaw musical subculture: created by kids, for kids, designed to be impenetrable to adults. American rave formed its own mutant funhouse approach to existing looks, sounds and ideologies. In the early-to-mid-1990s, it was driven not by stars but a sudden collective sense that, as the Milwaukee rave zine *Massive* put it in every issue above the masthead, "The underground is massive."

What better place for such a subculture to flourish than on the Internet?

Rave's rise mirrors the Web's in many ways. Both mixed rhetorical utopianism with insider snobbery. Both were future-forward "free spaces" with special appeal to geeks and wonks. (It can't be a coincidence that dance music's instruments of choice are referred to by their model numbers: 303, 606, 808, 909.) Both took root through the '80s and emerged in fits and starts through the mid-'90s, at which point both became part of the social fabric. Indeed, one of electronic dance music's key genres, IDM, was named after an email list devoted to "intelligent dance music."

"Part of the explosion of the whole electronic music scene has been totally tied to the Internet, and the way we can communicate over vast distances," says Richie Hawtin, who as Plastikman was an early rave icon.

"The Midwest—and maybe national—scene wouldn't have become 5 so interconnected without the rise of the Web circa 1994–95," agrees Matt Massive (born Matt Bonde, though we'll identify him here by his pen name), the publisher of *Massive*.

The British started raving before Americans did, but they got the idea in Ibiza. In the summer of 1987, a quartet of English DJs (Paul Oakenfold, Danny Rampling, Johnny Walker and Nicky

> "American rave formed its own mutant funhouse approach to existing looks, sounds and ideologies."

293

Holloway) vacationed on the Mediterranean island, absorbing both the expansive playing style of one DJ Alfredo—who spun everything from Cyndi Lauper to tracks made in underground electronic scenes in Chicago and Detroit to thousands, seven nights a week—and the readily available drug ecstasy (MDMA). They went back to England and—contra to the ultra-cool style long associated with London clubbing—began emulating the parties they'd witnessed on the island, pushing house and techno as the new sound of the future and ecstasy-fueled bonhomie as the new attitude, creating a communal sensibility that, by 1989, led to raves in fields with more than 10,000 revelers at a time.

In 1989, a popular Brooklyn DJ named Frankie Bones went to England and played a party called Energy, going on at 6 a.m. in front of 25,000 people. Inspired, Bones decided to start throwing parties of his own, bringing raves to the warehouses of Brooklyn. Soon after, scenes in L.A. and San Francisco began to sprout. Once the coasts adapted the new party style, things went inland, as loose regional congregations began to make themselves into a unified scene. Like drops in a pond, eventually their ripples began to touch.

At first, the connections were done the old-fashioned way. "By 1994, there was already kind of an established network of party-throwers and partygoers [in Detroit]," says Rob Theakston, a Detroit rave veteran. "At that point, the scene was maybe 200 kids max. Everything was very phone-based. [You'd] call the phone lines the day of to get directions, and even then, a lot of the direction lines would just give the vicinity because you would already know: 'Oh, Harper and Van Dyke—that's the old theater. We know where the party's going to be.' They wouldn't give you the exact address for the authorities to find out."

Many times, ravers had good reason for such secrecy. "I worked so much overtime trying to talk about how the rave scene wasn't all about drugs," says Ariel Meadow Stallings, who published and edited the rave zine *Lotus* in Seattle during the late '90s. "It was very noble of me, and I still do believe it wasn't all about drugs. But it is a drug culture. Even if you're not on drugs, the culture of the party is determined by the fact that there are people there who are."

As a style whose digital nature was encoded into its very name, techno 10 is the music of early adopters. Rather than the smoothly homogenous World Wide Web of today, cyberspace was fragmented, and whether you were on Compuserve or AOL,° the codes differed. "When [I] first signed up for the Internet in the early '90s, [I was] assigned a username, by first

---

Compuserve and AOL: early Internet service providers.

and last name," says Richie Hawtin. "Mine was RH199." Whomever next signed on that shared his initials, then, would be RH200. Presuming that numbering system kept its pace, Hawtin says that today, "a number assigned anyone would be in the millions and billions. Having a two- or three-digit number dates you as early."

Many early technology adopters became acquainted with bulletin board services (BBS) and proto-instant-messenger services such as V-Rave (the "V" is for "virtual"). "I got involved with BBS back in 1992," says Stallings. "It wasn't even the Internet. You were calling someone's hard drive, essentially, and typing messages back and forth."

"There was no World Wide Web," says Cleveland-born techno DJ and producer Jeff Samuel, whose experience typifies a lot of the local-leaning early BBS culture. "I was hanging around on music boards with [early dialup service provider] Prodigy. There was this thing called Cleveland Freenet, by Case Western Reserve University, a private college. Cleveland, of all places, was one of the first places [where] you could do real-time chat. You couldn't have Joe Schmoe getting on the Internet at that point. It just didn't happen."

"I was working in a computer lab all through college," says Damian Higgins, a.k.a. Dieselboy, one of America's top drum & bass DJs, who went to school in Pittsburgh from 1990 to 1995. "[In] my spare time, I'd go to the lab. I was addicted to the Internet—like these Korean kids at the 24/7 Internet cafes playing World of Warcraft, that was me talking about music and raves on V-Rave."

During the mid-'90s, says incoming George Washington University media professor Nikki Usher, "The big shift was [to] smaller [forums]. You had AOL kind of in the background, where you have social networking happening on a big public forum. USENET° groups allowed people to build groups around things that were of common interest. In this time, you start to see the smart communities of people who are really interested in tech, and really interested in identity politics. Those are kind of the first groups to come to social media."

A number of rave-centric mailing lists were a key ingredient in connecting dispersed partiers. In spring of 1992, M.I.T. student John Adams founded NE-Raves, covering the Northeast and/or New England, while at UC Berkeley, Brian Behlendorf began SFRaves through Hyperreal.° Within a week of its launch, Behlendorf told Mike Brown in 2000, he "went to a party [he] found out about through the list." Soon came a 15

USENET: online news-group forum established in 1980.
Hyperreal: email list promoting rave culture.

succession of lists dedicated to specific cities (313, the Detroit list) and regions: MW-Raves for the Midwest, NW-Raves for the Pacific Northwest.

Early rave thrived on anonymity, from the multiple aliases of a producer like Hawtin—who went, variously, as F.U.S.E., Plastikman, Circuit Breaker, Concept 1 and Xenon—to the white-label 12-inch, a format whose lack of artist or track information gave it a cultish mythos. Information was scarce. "Other than at raves, there was no environment to talk about [the music]," says Samuel, who was active on MW-Raves and PB-CLE-Raves (Pittsburgh-Cleveland). "When someone put out a new mixtape, it was all over the lists."

"Part of the experience of contextualizing or processing what had happened at that party was sitting down on Monday and typing out my review," says Stallings. "It was sort of the digital water cooler for the ravers. I stalked people in classes whose name I'd seen on Hyperreal because I knew they were involved in the rave scene. There was definitely a lot of back and forth between the virtual world and the reality of rave."

"NE-Raves had these get-togethers," says Higgins. "There was no Facebook or anything nearly like that back then. We'd have getting-together picnics. We were always trying to interact with one another in the real world."

Of course, there couldn't be computer-facilitated discussion without some trolls hanging around. Brandon Ivers, who was a drum & bass DJ in the Minneapolis rave scene, recalls of one such list irritant, "It added this kind of anarchistic element," he says. But they didn't kick him out. "There was still enough of an ideal of, 'Why don't we make this all work?' and 'Let's not censor ourselves.' The Internet in general at that point [was] influenced by that WELL-style, '60s-hippie, let-information-be-free type of thing."

"These were not particularly moderated discussions," says Usher. "If 20 you recall all the very early worries about AOL, you can have people posing like Internet predators in these chat rooms. These were not really regulated forums."

Or at least not completely regulated: "I remember talking to the guy who moderated MW-Rave, Chad Sponholz, about it," says Ivers. "He did take out messages that were blatant drug references. Everyone was convinced that the FBI or whatever was monitoring the mailing lists by '97. But even before that, [it] was all pretty codified."

The web had grown rapidly in the mid-'90s—it wasn't just the province of university students anymore—and raves started showing up on the mainstream's radar. The U.S. major labels began pushing "electronica" as music that could be consumed in album form by rock fans. It worked, sort of —Prodigy went to #1 with *The Fat of the Land*—and acts like The Chemical Brothers, Roni Size/Reprazent and Fatboy Slim did well.

Even Barbara Walters took notice. "They call it a rave, and it's the latest kid craze," she said on *20/20* in 1997. "Millions of youngsters, as young as age 10, flock to secret locations to party and dance through the night—that's all night long—often 'till eight or nine in the morning."

"I think a lot of [paranoia] went with increased media coverage," says Dan Labovitch, a Chicago teenager during rave's heyday and the founder of the website Rave Archive. "It wasn't so much of a feeling within the scene as external pressures. Your parents would [see] some scare news piece [and] be like, 'Oh, so that's the stuff you've been going to on weekends.'"

But the rave scene also used the Internet to circle the wagons and pro- 25 tect its members from those external pressures. Jeff Samuel recalls the stir caused by one early website. "These email lists were constantly talking about whatever new pill was there that week," he says. "And quickly there would become these copycat pills. Everybody was trying to figure out, 'Which one is the real peace-sign ecstasy pill that's *really* MDMA?' The first ecstasy-test website was a huge deal. You could suddenly see photos of the pills: 'This is the real one, and this is the bunk one that came two weeks later.' It was pretty beneath the public eye at that point—the Internet alone was beneath the public eye at that point."

The tone of MW-Raves, says Labovitch, "was very collegial. People were giving each other rides to parties and helping people out. You could be a 16-year-old kid and say, 'Hey, can somebody pick me up from my parents' house?' And somebody would drive out, pick you up from your parents' house, take you to a party, and return you. There were no thoughts like, 'Something bad's going to happen to me.'"

The mailing lists' emphasis on region—"It was NW-Raves, not Seattle-Raves," says Stallings—fueled rave's road-trip culture.

"There weren't always amazing shows in your city all the time," says Higgins. "If you were hardcore into hearing cool DJs and acts and music, you had to travel to hear that stuff."

"Any trip was an excuse to go to a rave," says Stallings. "Whatever city I was in, a rave was the best way of putting a dipstick into a community. 'Oh, the German ravers love whistles. They're breathing through whistles. Everyone has a whistle in their mouth. They won't stop whistling. Thank god there's no whistles on the West Coast.'"

It wasn't just fans who went road-tripping. "A lot of people really built 30 their names and connections by being early adopters—Dieselboy most prominently," says Massive. "He got a lot of early bookings around the country from the connections he was building on the rave lists."

"I'd see the post on alt-rave about a party five, six, seven hours away," explains Higgins. "It'd say, 'Plus more DJs to be announced.'" That's when he'd make his move: "I'd call the info line and be like, 'Hi, I'm Dieselboy from Pittsburgh. I will play for gas money if you book me at your party.' I was so small-time at the time that no one was going to fly me. So I drove around all over the place. I remember I drove 11 hours to play in Rhode Island."

Established promoters found the lists useful in other ways. "We were using the Internet in 1994–95 to communicate to our fans in the Midwest about our events," says Hawtin. "We stopped doing flyers and were able to announce events in the mid and late '90s one day before—even hours before—and get hundreds [or] thousands of people."

Not all of those pop-up parties—in a sense, the first flash mobs—were smashing successes. Jeff Samuel recalls a Cleveland party announced the same day online: "They basically piled us into a U-Haul truck, closed the door—we had no idea where we were going. We ended up in some really not-safe warehouse in a really not-safe area. There was broken glass everywhere. There was no heat. It was the middle of winter. They had lined the stairs with candles so that we could see where we were going. I was miserable—it was just freezing. I think I was the only person not on drugs there. They had one kerosene heater. I actually burned a hole through my shoe, getting all the way to my foot, trying to warm my feet up." . . .

In 1995, two audio file-compression systems debuted. Though the MP3 would eventually change the music business (and the world) as we know it, the first format to gain favor—particularly among ravers—was RealAudio.

"RealAudio was the only plug-in that could broadcast live audio," says 35
Richie Hawtin, who began using it to play audio from his parties live online in 1996. Even bigger, and more consistent, was Beta Lounge, a San Francisco website that streamed live DJ mixes.

It was manna° for dance music lovers now hooked into the World Wide Web. "I thought I was in heaven when I found Beta Lounge," says Jeff Samuel. "I'd sit around listening to mixes. They had great taste. And they presented it pretty professionally."

DJ and journalist Philip Sherburne, who cut his DJ teeth at Beta Lounge, remembers the site's HQ in late-'90s tech-bubble San Francisco. "The space was basically a big warehouse," he says. "There was obviously a lot of processing power going on, and there was often someone in the back fiddling with some obscure black box. Someone from the crew

manna: unexpected benefit; spiritual nourishment.

would always get on the mike to announce the DJ, which reinforced the idea of broadcasting out to the world. They were really pioneers of the whole podcast revolution."

By the end of the '90s, when Fatboy Slim's "Rockafeller Skank" featured in every third movie trailer and U2's arena-tour opening act was DJ Paul Oakenfold, electronic dance music wasn't nearly as scarce as it had once been. And the web helped get it up to speed. "It was communicating and reaching out to people who were into what we were doing," says Richie Hawtin. "The scene on a worldwide level is huge. [But] compared to other scenes, it's still such a small little microcosm in the world of music and entertainment. So we always, then and now, need to reach out and connect with like-minded individuals and bring them into electronic music."

Understanding the Text

1. In what sense were the original raves "future forward 'tree spaces'" (par. 3)?
2. Why did the ravers maintain such secrecy about their activities?

Reflection and Response

3. What might be the reasons that the rave scene flourished initially on the coasts before moving inland?
4. In what ways did the media's attention to the nascent rave subculture initiate changes in the subculture?
5. MP3 audio technology was adopted early on by the rave community. In your opinion, have the transformations in the way in which music is distributed and consumed been generally positive or negative for our culture?

Making Connections

6. As Matos points out, the rave scene was defined partly by the use of drugs, especially MDMA. Which other subcultures are defined by particular drugs? How does a particular drug both shape the subculture's practices and reflect the subculture's values?
7. What makes "techno" music technological? Investigate how the style of music depends on innovative technological methods. What does the relationship between technology and artistic creation tell us about turn-of-the-twenty-first-century society?

The State of Black Subcultures in 21st Century America

Brittany Julious

In this short selection from 2014, Brittany Julious touches on important issues of racial performance and identity as she traces the brief life of GHE20 GOTH1K ("ghetto gothic"), a monthly party founded in 2009 by DJ Venus X. Julious is a journalist, essayist, and oral storyteller. Her work has been featured in the *New York Times*, the *Guardian*, *Vice*, and many other periodicals. She also writes the local music column for the *Chicago Tribune* and hosts *The Back Talk*, an award-winning podcast featuring stories from women of color.

Earlier this year, DJ and party organizer Venus X announced she was ending her long-running club night, GHE20 GOTH1K, partly because mainstream public figures like Rihanna had manipulated and discredited her creation. This wasn't the first time someone accused Rihanna of stealing a subculture. Two years earlier, she appropriated the seapunk° microculture, but her dedication to seapunk, which really only included an aqua-celestial backdrop during a performance of "Diamonds" on *Saturday Night Live,* was as short-lived as the aesthetic movement's lifespan. GHE20 GOTH1K proved to be a completely different—and long lasting—subcultural source for the singer. Once Rihanna embraced the subculture, she kept embracing it.

Long before Rihanna began adopting the GHE20 GOTH1K aesthetic in her numerous, and fabulous, Instagram photos, GHE20 GOTH1K existed as a life force in New York City nightlife. Most importantly, it was a sustainable and physical life existing in an actual nightclub. Hundreds, if not thousands, of young people—especially young people of color—embraced the club night's aesthetic.

In an interview with *The Fader*, Venus X described GHE20 GOTH1K as encompassing art, fashion, music, and nightlife. Aesthetically, she noted, "It's a combination of what people consider to be very white and very black. There are staples: North Face jackets, Timberlands. And then staples of the traditional punk and goth." It was a mix—or rather, a birthing—of something born out of her two distinct interests: the ghetto of where she grew up and the aesthetics of goth. "GHE20 GOTH1K is extremely political. It's not about expensive clothes," she told *The Fader* in the same interview. "GHE20 GOTH1K was one of the first places that successfully created nightlife around music that was just on the internet,

---

seapunk: aquatic-themed subculture that originated on Tumblr in 2011.

DJ Venus X photographed in New York City for *Lurve Magazine*. Barcroft Media/ Getty Images

like alternative rap music from gay people and a lot of different club and bass music that didn't have a home in mainstream, house, or disco."

The subculture was more than something of their own, something that helped define their multifaceted interests and identity as young people of color—it was a response to mainstream culture's ideas. Like GHE20 GOTH1K, hood futurism, another subculture, was also a response to the images and sounds of the mainstream. Hip-hop and R&B musicians developed hood futurism in the 90s. In a Tumblr post by the creator of a hoodfuturism.tumblr.com, a popular blog documenting the style, the author writes that Afro Futurism inspired hood futurism, which "is centered around contemporary black artistry combined with themes like sci-fi, science, and other components that have futuristic elements." Think spaceship-like rooms with sleek lines and coppery bodysuits that feel at home in our predictions of the future. The most definitive image of this is Michael and Janet Jackson's "Scream" video, which literally takes place on a hospitable, livable space ship.

Although hood futurism is more driven by aesthetics, its sound—a 5
clinking, clattery array of sounds and samples that shouldn't make sense,
sounds that seem as contemporary now as they did ten years ago—can
be traced back to its biggest purveyors: Missy Elliott, Aaliyah, and
Timbaland. The aesthetic felt like the first visual response to hip-hop's
mainstream imagery and aesthetics. If hip-hop was the mainstream and
the storytelling of "right now" in the 90s, hood futurism was the musical
landscape of a future that was—cheesy as it sounds—out of this world.
Today, both small rappers (Azealia Banks) and large artists (Nicki Minaj)
embrace hood futurism, proving the subculture's relevancy as a viable
alternative to the mainstream.

Hood futurism and *ghetto* goth's names connect them to black culture.

Linguistically, these terms are most frequently shared through the
prism of rap and hip-hop, if we can embrace the terms *hood* and *ghetto* as
terms of places—and not just as derogatory terms employed in times of
insults.

In a series of essays for *Vulture* about the current state of hip-hop, The
Roots' Questlove° broke down the mainstreaming and dominance of
hip-hop culture: "Once hip-hop culture is ubiquitous, it is also invisible.
Once it's everywhere, it is nowhere," he writes. "What once offered resistance to mainstream culture (it was part of the larger tapestry, spooky-
action style, but it pulled at the fabric) is now an integral part of the
sullen dominant."

Stealing from and commodifying these subcultural movements feel
especially wrong. If these are movements By Outsiders and For Outsiders
(or by The Other and for the Other), taking them from people of color
is cruel. In some ways, despite an art-
ist's race, mainstream success begins to
deteriorate a performer's racial identity.
A celebrity can transcend the limitations
and community inherent in racial and
cultural identity. For many people, to live within the experience of race
or a minority status is to actively and automatically embrace people who
are like *us*. To appropriate without citing a source is a slap in the face to
traditional solidarity. A black or brown celebrity becomes nothing more
than another cog in the machine of capitalism, another person buying
and selling back to us the things we created in the first place.

> "To appropriate without cit-
> ing a source is a slap in the
> face to traditional solidarity."

In her book *Implications and Distinctions: Format, Content and Context* 10
in Contemporary Race Film, conceptual entrepreneur Martine Syms writes

---

The Roots' Questlove: professional name of Ahmir Khalib Thompson (b. 1971), percus-
sionist for Philadelphia-based hip hop ensemble The Roots (formed 1987).

about the visuals and visibility of blacks in images. In the last chapter, Syms asks, "Why not subvert the charge of being Black into an identity that we own and explore the possibilities of such a platform?" And soon after she writes, "For these possibilities to exist, the Black viewer/spectator must sit comfortably with the tension of 'bad' portrayals, 'unrealistic' experiences, and/or a non-diasporic stylistic approach. Black audiences are also complicit in constructing race . . . because the viewer/spectator is instructed to read the images and situate them in reality."

Although Syms speaks about blacks in films, this theory translates to many aspects of black culture — in particular, black identity. Creators and members of subcultures have wrestled with the experiences of the limiting mainstream and have created something that speaks to their individual interests and needs. Syms explains how she too has embarked on this cultural journey on an individual basis: "As a child nerd, a teenage punk, an art student, and beyond, I've always had eclectic interests. Somehow my parents created the perfect symbiosis between forcing me to be a token — introducing me to disparate sounds, styles, and conventions — and rooting me in Blackness," she says. "I learned who 'we' are, what 'we' eat, how 'we' talk, but I was encouraged to renegotiate that construction to better fit me."

The ubiquitousness of hood futurism as a viable alternative to the mainstream, and the end of GHE20 GOTH1K, reminds me of other subculture movements. On my Tumblr dashboard, I'm often treated to a number of surprising yet enjoyable images and ideas: black people shrouded in flowers on Black with Flowers, young black women riding bicycles on Bicycles and Melanin, and the sort of raw vulnerability and pursuit of connections otherwise known as Black Girl Feels. All offer alternatives to many ideas of blackness and black culture; they are at once feminine and joyful. Although they don't specifically talk about responding to the stereotypes and limitations of hip-hop culture, I see them as pursuits of alternatives and multiples. Maybe all of these can exist together. As one subculture ends, people give birth to other ideas and images — waiting for new voices to embrace them and a celebrity to copy their look at an award show.

Understanding the Text

1. What is GHE20 GOTH1K? What is "hood futurism"?
2. Why does Julious object so strongly to Rihanna's appropriation of GHE20 GOTH1K? Why does she open the essay with the Rihanna narrative?

Reflection and Response

3. How does the black nerd challenge ideas of racial or ethnic solidarity?

4. Identify places in the text which could benefit from more extensive discussion. What, specifically, could be added?

5. How have social media sites, especially those mentioned in the article, contributed to the appearance of new subcultures? Do you think that social media support subcultural boundaries and identities? Does a true subculture require a presence in the physical world?

Making Connections

6. In paragraph 9, Julious says that "[a] celebrity can transcend the limitations and community inherent in racial and cultural identity." Find examples from your research and your own experience to support Julious's claim.

7. Julious points out that subcultures often give birth to new subcultures. Trace the genealogy of one such daughter subculture.

8. Discuss other black/white hybrid subcultures of the kind identified by Julious, and then make a prediction about the future of such hybrids.

Wake Up, Geek Culture. Time to Die

Patton Oswalt

Patton Oswalt is a writer, comedian, and actor best known for his role as Spence on the television show *King of Queens* and as the voice of Remy in the Pixar film *Ratatouille*. As a staff writer, Oswalt helped launch the fourteen-year run of the late-night comedy show MADtv. Like many of his entertainment-business contemporaries, Oswalt identifies with the ultimate high-school outsider subculture: nerds. In this essay, he laments the ways in which mainstream culture has subsumed the values and interests he once shared with a small group of like-minded individuals, arguing that popular American culture has evolved into a near-meaningless mishmash of superficial references.

I'm not a nerd. I used to be one, back 30 years ago when nerd meant something. I entered the '80s immersed, variously, in science fiction, Dungeons & Dragons, and Stephen King. Except for the multiple-player aspect of D&D, these pursuits were not "passions from a common spring," to quote Poe.

I can't say that I ever abided by nerd stereotypes: I was never alone or felt outcast.

I had a circle of friends who were similarly drawn to the exotica of pop culture (or, at least, what was considered pop culture at the time in northern Virginia)—Monty Python,° post-punk music, comic books, slasher films, and videogames. We were a sizable clique. The terms *nerd* and *geek* were convenient shorthand used by other cliques to categorize us. But they were thin descriptors.

In Japan, the word *otaku* refers to people who have obsessive, minute interests—especially stuff like anime or videogames. It comes from a term for "someone else's house"—otaku live in their own, enclosed worlds. Or, at least, their lives follow patterns that are well outside the norm. Looking back, we were American otakus. (Of course, now all America is otaku—which I'm going to get into shortly. But in order to do so, we're going to hang out in the '80s.)

I was too young to drive or hold a job. I was never going to play sports, 5 and girls were an uncrackable code. So, yeah—I had time to collect every *Star Wars* action figure, learn the Three Laws of Robotics,° memorize Roy

---

Monty Python: British surreal sketch-comedy group (1969–1983).
Three Laws of Robotics: set of rules devised by science-fiction author Isaac Asimov to govern relations between robots and humans.

Batty's speech from the end of *Blade Runner*, and classify each monster's abilities and weaknesses in TSR Hobbies' *Monster Manual*. By 1987, my friends and I were waist-deep in the hot honey of adolescence. Money and cars and, hopefully, girls would follow, but not if we spent our free time learning the names of the bounty hunters' ships in *The Empire Strikes Back*. So we each built our own otakuesque thought-palace, which we crammed with facts and nonsense—only now, the thought-palace was nicely appointed, decorated neatly, the information laid out on deep mahogany shelves or framed in gilt. What once set us apart, we hoped, would become a lovable quirk.

Our respective nerdery took on various forms: One friend was the first to get his hands on early bootlegs of Asian action flicks by Tsui Hark and John Woo, and he never looked back. Another started reading William Gibson and peppered his conversations with cryptic (and alluring) references to "cyberspace." I was ground zero for the "new wave" of mainstream superhero comics—which meant being right there for Alan Moore, Frank Miller, and Neil Gaiman.° And like my music-obsessed pals, who passed around the cassette of Guns n' Roses' *Live ?!*@ Like a Suicide* and were thus prepared for the shock wave of *Appetite for Destruction*, I'd devoured Moore's run on *Swamp Thing*° and thus eased nicely into his *Watchmen*.° I'd also read the individual issues of Miller's *Daredevil: Born Again* run, so when *The Dark Knight Returns* was reviewed by the *New York Times*, I could say I saw it coming. And I'd consumed so many single-issue guest-writing stints of Gaiman's that when he was finally given *The Sandman* title all to himself, I was first in line and knew the language.

Admittedly, there's a chilly thrill in moving with the herd while quietly being tuned in to something dark, complicated, and unknown just beneath the topsoil of popularity. Something about which, while we moved *with* the herd, we could share a wink and a nod with two or three other similarly connected herdlings.

When our coworkers nodded along to Springsteen and Madonna songs at the local Bennigan's, my select friends and I would quietly trade out-of-context lines from *Monty Python* sketches—a thieves' cant, a code language used for identification. We needed it, too, because the essence of our culture—our "escape hatch" culture—would begin to change in 1987.

Alan Moore, Frank Miller, Neil Gaiman: Moore (b. 1953), English comic-book author; Miller (b. 1957), American comic-book author; Gaiman (b. 1960), English comic-book author.
Swamp Thing: American comic-book creature.
Watchmen: 1986 comic book series; 2009 American film adaptation.

That was the year the final issue of *Watchmen* came out, in October. After that, it seemed like everything that was part of my otaku world was out in the open and up for grabs, if only out of context. I wasn't seeing the hard line between "nerds" and "normals" anymore. It was the last year that a T shirt or music preference or pastime (Dungeons & Dragons had long since lost its dangerous, Satanic, suicide-inducing street cred) could set you apart from the surface dwellers. Pretty soon, being the only person who was into something didn't make you outcast; it made you ahead of the curve and someone people were quicker to befriend than shun. Ironically, surface dwellers began repurposing the symbols and phrases and tokens of the erstwhile outcast underground.

Fast-forward to now: Boba Fett's helmet emblazoned on sleeveless 10 T-shirts worn by gym douches hefting dumbbells. The *Glee* kids performing the songs from *The Rocky Horror Picture Show*. And Toad the Wet Sprocket, a band that took its name from a *Monty Python* riff, joining the permanent soundtrack of a night out at Bennigan's. Our below-the-topsoil passions have been rudely dug up and displayed in the noonday sun. *The Lord of the Rings* used to be ours and *only ours* simply because of the sheer goddamn thickness of the books. Twenty years later, the entire cast and crew would be trooping onstage at the Oscars to collect their statuettes, and replicas of the One Ring would be sold as bling.

The topsoil has been scraped away, forever . . . In fact, it's been dug up, thrown into the air, and allowed to rain down and coat everyone in a thin gray-brown mist called the Internet. Everyone considers themselves otaku about something—whether it's the mythology of *Lost* or the minor intrigues of *Top Chef. American Idol* inspires—if not depth, at least in length and passion—the same number of conversation as does *The Wire*. There are no more hidden thought-palaces—they're easily accessed websites, or Facebook pages with thousands of fans. And I'm not going to bore you with the step-by-step specifics of how it happened. In the timeline of the upheaval, part of the graph should be interrupted by the words "the Internet." And now here we are.

The problem with the Internet, however, is that it lets anyone become otaku about anything *instantly*. In the '80s, you couldn't get up to speed on an entire genre in a weekend. You had to wait, month to month, for the issues of *Watchmen* to come out. We couldn't BitTorrent the latest John Woo film or digitally download an entire decade's worth of grunge or hip hop. Hell, there were a few weeks during the spring of 1991 when we couldn't tell whether Nirvana or Tad would be the next band to break big. Imagine the terror!

But then reflect on the advantages. Waiting for the next issue, movie, or album gave you time to reread, rewatch, reabsorb whatever you loved,

"Waiting for the next issue, movie, or album gave you time to reread, rewatch, reabsorb whatever you loved, so you brought your own idiosyncratic love of that thing to your thought-palace."

so you brought your own idiosyncratic love of that thing to your thought-palace. People who were obsessed with *Star Trek* or the *Ender's Game* books were all obsessed with the same object, but its light shone differently on each person. Everyone had to create in their mind unanswered questions or what-ifs. What if Leia, not Luke, had become a Jedi? What happens after Rorschach's journal is found at the end of *Watchmen*? What the hell was *The Prisoner* about?

None of that's necessary anymore. When everyone has easy access to their favorite diversions and every diversion comes with a rabbit hole's worth of extra features and deleted scenes and hidden hacks to tumble down and never emerge from, then we're all just adding to an ever-swelling, soon-to-erupt volcano of trivia, re-contextualized and forever rebooted. We're on the brink of Etewaf: Everything That Ever Was—Available Forever.

I know it sounds great, but there's a danger: Everything we have today 15 that's cool comes from someone wanting more of something they loved in the past. Action figures, videogames, superhero movies, iPods: All are continuations of a love that wanted more. Ever see action figures from the '70s, each with that same generic Anson Williams° body and one-piece costume with the big clumsy snap on the back? Or played Atari's° *Adventure*, found the secret room, and thought, that's it? Can we all admit the final battle in *Superman II* looks like a local commercial for a personal-injury attorney? And how many people had their cassette of the *Repo Man*° soundtrack eaten by a Walkman?°

Now, with everyone more or less otaku and everything *immediately* awesome (or, if not, just as immediately rebooted or recut as a hilarious YouTube or Funny or Die spoof), the old inner longing for more or better that made our present pop culture so amazing is dwindling. *The Onion's*° A.V. Club—essential and transcendent in so many ways—has a

---

Anson Williams: American actor (b. 1949) best known for his role as Potsie on the television show "Happy Days."
Atari: American video-game developer (1972–1984).
Repo Man: 1984 science-fiction comedy film.
Walkman: Sony-branded portable tape player marketed in the 1970s.
The Onion: satirical newspaper featuring national and global "reports."

weekly feature called *Gateways to Geekery*, in which an entire artistic subculture—say, anime, H. P. Lovecraft, or the Marx Brothers°—is mapped
out so you can become otaku on it but avoid its more tedious aspects.

Here's the danger: That creates weak otakus. Etewaf doesn't produce a
new generation of artists—just an army of sated consumers. Why create
anything new when there's a mountain of freshly excavated pop culture
to recut, repurpose, and manipulate on your iMovie? *The Shining* can be
remade into a comedy trailer. Both movie versions of the Joker can be
sent to battle each another. The Dude is in *The Matrix*.

The coming decades—the 21st-century's '20s, '30s, and '40s—have
the potential to be one long, unbroken, recut spoof in which everything
in *Avatar* farts while *Keyboard Cat* plays eerily in the background.

But I prefer to be optimistic. I choose hope. I see Etewaf as the Balrog,
the helter-skelter, the A-pop-alypse that rains cleansing fire down onto
the otaku landscape, burns away the chaff, and forces us to start over
with only a few thin, near-meatless scraps on which to build.

In order to save pop culture future, we've got to make the present pop 20
culture suck, at least for a little while.

How do we do this? How do we bring back that sweet longing for
more that spawned Gears of War, the Crank films, and the entire Joss
Whedon° oeuvre? Simple: We've got to speed up the process. We've got
to stoke the volcano. We've got to catalog, collate, and cross-pollinate.
We must bring about Etewaf, and soon.

It has already started. It's all around us. VH1 list shows. *Freddy vs. Jason*.

Websites that list the 10 biggest sports meltdowns, the 50 weirdest
plastic surgeries, the 200 harshest nut shots. *Alien vs. Predator*. Lists of
fails, lists of boobs, lists of deleted movie scenes. Entire TV seasons on
iTunes. An entire studio's film vault, downloadable with a click. Easter
egg scenes of wild sex in *Grand Theft Auto*. Hell, *Grand Theft Auto*, period.
And yes, I know that a lot of what I'm listing here seems like it's outside
of the "nerd world" and part of the wider pop culture. Well, I've got news
for you—pop culture *is* nerd culture. The fans of *Real Housewives of Hobo-
ken* watch, discuss, and absorb their show the same way a geek watched
Dark Shadows° or obsessed over his eighth-level half-elf ranger character

---

H.P. Lovecraft, the Marx Brothers: Lovecraft, American horror fiction writer
(1890–1937); Marx Brothers, family comedy act in both vaudeville and the movies
(1905–1949).
Gears of War, the Crank films, and the entire Joss Whedon: Gears of War, third-per-
son-shooter video game released in 2006; Crank films, American black-comedy action
films by Mark Neveldine and Brian Taylor; Joss Whedon (b. 1964), American screen-
writer and director best known for the television series *Buffy the Vampire Slayer*.
***Dark Shadows*:** American gothic television soap opera (1966–1971).

in Dungeons & Dragons. It's the method of consumption, not what's on the plate.

Since there's no going back—no reverse on the out-of-control loco-motive we've created—we've got to dump nitro into the engines. We need to get serious, and I'm here to outline my own personal fantasy: We start with lists of the best lists of boobs. Every Beatles song, along with every alternate take, along with every cover version of every one of their songs and every alternate take of every cover version. *Goonies* vs. *Saw*. Every book on your Kindle. Every book *on* Kindle on every Kindle. *The Human Centipede* done with the cast of *The Hills* and directed by the Coen brothers.

That's when we'll reach Etewaf singularity. Pop culture will become 25 self-aware.

It will happen in the *A.V. Club* first: A brilliant Nathan Rabin column about the worst Turkish rip-offs of American comic book characters will suddenly begin writing its own comments, each a single sentence from the sequel to *A Confederacy of Dunces*. Then a fourth and fifth season of *Arrested Development*, directed by David Milch of *Deadwood*, will appear suddenly in the TV Shows section of iTunes. Someone BitTorrenting a *Crass* bootleg will suddenly find their hard drive crammed with Elvis Presley's "lost" grunge album from 1994. And everyone's TiVo will record *Ghostbusters III*, starring Peter Sellers, Lee Marvin, and John Candy.°

This will last only a moment. We'll have one minute before pop cul-ture swells and blackens like a rotten peach and then explodes, sending every movie, album, book, and TV show flying away into space. Maybe tendrils and fragments of them will attach to asteroids or plop down on ice planets light-years away. A billion years after our sun burns out, a race of intelligent ice crystals will build a culture based on dialog from *The Princess Bride*. On another planet, intelligent gas clouds will wait for the yearly passing of the "Lebowski"° comet. One of the rings of Saturn will be made from blurbs for the softcover release of *Infinite Jest*, twirled for-ever into a ribbon of effusive praise.

But back here on Earth, we'll enter year zero for pop culture. All that we'll have left to work with will be a VHS copy of *Zapped!*, the soundtrack to *The Road Warrior*, and Steve Ditko's eight-issue run on *Shade: The*

Peter Sellers, Lee Marvin, John Candy: Sellers (1918–2002), British comedy actor; Marvin (1924–1987), American dramatic actor; Candy (1950–1994), Canadian comedy actor.
"Lebowski": *The Big Lebowski*, 1998 comedy film by the Coen Brothers.

Changing Man. For a while—maybe a generation—pop culture pastimes will revolve around politics and farming.

But the same way a farmer has to endure a few fallow seasons after he's overplanted, a new, richer loam will begin to appear in the wake of our tilling. From *Zapped!* will arise a telekinesis epic from James Cameron. Paul Thomas Anderson° will do a smaller, single-character study of a man who can move matchbooks with his mind and how he uses this skill to pursue a casino waitress. Then the Coen brothers° will veer off, doing a movie about pyrokenesis° set in 1980s Cleveland, while out of Japan will come a subgenre of telekinetic horror featuring pale, whispering children. And we'll build from there—precognition, telepathy, and, most radically, normal people falling in love and dealing with jobs and life. Maybe also car crashes.

The Road Warrior soundtrack, all Wagnerian strings and military snare 30 drums, will germinate into a driving, gut-bucket subgenre called waste-rock. And, as a counterpoint, flute-driven folk. Then there'll be the inevitable remixes, mashups, and pirated-only releases. A new Beatles will arise, only they'll be Iranian.

Shade: The Changing Man will become the new *Catcher in the Rye.* Ditko's thin-fingered art will appear on lunch boxes, T-shirts, and magazine covers. Someone will write an even thinner, sparser, simpler version called *Shade.* Someone else will write a 1,000-page meditation about Shade's home planet. Eventually, someone will try to kill the Iranian John Lennon with a hat, based on one panel from issue 3. A whole generation of authors under 20 will have their love—or disgust—of these comics to thank for their careers.

So the topsoil we're coated in needs to wash away for a while. I want my daughter to have a 1987 the way I did and experience the otaku thrill. . . . I'd like her to share a secret look with a friend, both of them hip to the fact that, from Germany, there's a bootleg MP3 of a group called Dr. Cali-gory, pioneers of super-violent line-dancing music. And I want her to enjoy that secret look for a little while before Dr. Cali-gory's songs get used in commercials for cruise lines.

Etewaf now!

James Cameron, Paul Thomas Anderson: Cameron (b. 1964), film director best known for *Titanic* and *Avatar*; Anderson (b. 1970), film director best known for *Boogie Nights* and *Magnolia.*
Coen Brothers: American film-makers, Joel (b. 1954) and Ethan (b. 1957).
pyrokinesis: alleged psychic ability to create and control fire with the mind.

Understanding the Text

1. Explain how the Japanese word "otaku" is applied to American geek culture.
2. What does Oswalt mean by "Etewaf"?
3. How does Oswalt propose to bring about the death of geek culture? Is he serious? How do you know?

Reflection and Response

4. Although Oswalt does not explicitly identify individuals, to whom might we attribute the wide acceptance of geek/nerd subculture by mainstream culture?
5. Do you agree with Oswalt's claim that the internet has been a disaster for geek culture by allowing for instant expertise?
6. What attitude does Oswalt convey? What language and tone does he use to do so? Find specific examples from the essay to support your claims.

Making Connections

7. Name some of the admired individuals in contemporary mainstream culture who would have been scorned as geeks or nerds thirty years ago.
8. Which other subculturists define themselves at least partly by the extreme depth of their specialized knowledge?

The Death and Life of Punk, The Last Subculture

Dylan Clark

Dylan Clark is the director of the Contemporary Asian Studies Program at the University of Toronto. Trained in ethnographic field research, Clark brings a professional anthropologist's eye to the subject of punk and subcultural resistance, about which he has written extensively. He is a longtime advocate for children's rights and poverty-alleviation programs, putting into practice his commitments to those who are on the margins of power. More of his written work can be found in *Ethnology*, *Peace Review*, and *The Journal of Thought*.

Punk had to die so that it could live.

With the death of punk, classical subcultures died. What had, by the 1970s, emerged as 'subcultures' were understood to be groups of youths who practiced a wide array of social dissent through shared behavioral, musical, and costume orientations.[1] Such groups were remarkably capable vehicles for social change, and were involved in dramatically reshaping social norms in many parts of the world. These "classical" subcultures obtained their potency partly through an ability to shock and dismay, to disobey prescribed confines of class, gender, and ethnicity. But things changed. People gradually became acclimatized to such subcultural transgressions to the point that, in many places, they have become an *expected* part of the social landscape. The image of rebellion has become one of the most dominant narratives of the corporate capitalist landscape: the "bad boy" has been reconfigured as a prototypical *consumer*. And so it was a new culture in the 1970s, the punk subculture, which emerged to fight even the normalization of subculture itself, with brilliant new forms of social critique and style.

But even punk was caught, caged, and placed in the subcultural zoo, on display for all to see. Torn from its societal jungle and safely taunted by viewers behind barcodes, punk, the last subculture, was dead.

The classical subculture "died" when it became the object of social inspection and nostalgia, and when it became so amenable to commodification. Marketers long ago awakened to the fact that subcultures are expedient vehicles for selling music, cars, clothing, cosmetics, and everything else under the sun. But this truism is not lost on many subcultural youth themselves, and they will be the first to grumble that there is nothing new under the subcultural sun.

In this climate, constrained by the discourse of subculture, deviation 5 from the norm ain't what it used to be. Deviation from the norm seems,

313

well, normal. It is allegedly common for a young person to choose a pre-fab subculture off the rack, wear it for a few years, then rejoin with the "mainstream" culture that they never really left at all.[2] Perhaps the result of our autopsy will show that subculture (of the young, dissident, cos-tumed kind) has become a useful part of the status quo, and less useful for harboring discontent. For these reasons we can melodramatically pro-nounce that subculture is dead.

Yet still they come: goths, neo-hippies, and '77-ish mohawked punk rockers. And still people find solidarity, revolt, and individuality by inhabiting a shared costume marking their membership in a subculture. And still parents get upset, people gawk, peers shudder, and selves are recreated. Perhaps it is cruel or inaccurate to call these classical motifs dead, because they can be so very alive and real to the people who occupy them. Like squatters in abandoned buildings, practicing subcultists give life to what seem to be deceased structures.

Or is subculture dead? The death of subculture—that is, the death of subcultural autonomy and meaningful rebellion—did not escape the notice of many. For decades people have decried the commercialization of style, the paisley without the politics. But such laments have not failed to produce strategies. There is something else—another kind of subcul-ture, gestating and growing far below the classical subcultural terrain. For two decades a secret was kept by thousands: *punk never died*. Instead, punk had, even in its earliest days, begun to articulate a social form which anticipates and outmaneuvers the dominance of corporate-capitalism. And as the Cold War finally disappears from decades of habit, and as the political and cultural hegemony of corporate-capitalism seems unrivaled, it suddenly becomes clear that the anarchist frameworks of punk have spread into all sorts of social groupings. The social forms punks began to play with in the early 1970s have penetrated subcultures across the spec-trum. After the death of the classical subculture we witness the birth of new practices, ideologies, and ways of being—a vast litter of anarchism.

For tribes of contemporary people who might be called *punk* (and who often refuse to label themselves), their subculture is partly in revolt from the popular discourse of subculture, from what has become, in punk eyes, a commercialized form of safe, affected discontent—a series of consumed sub-jectivities, including pre-fabricated "Alternative" looks. Punk is, ironically, a subculture operating within parts of that established discourse, and yet it is also subculture partly dedicated to opposing what the discourse of subcul-ture has become. As the century rolls over, punk is the invention of not just new subjectivities but, perhaps, a new kind of cultural formation. The death of subculture has in some ways helped to produce one of the most formida-ble subcultures yet: the death of subculture is the (re)birth of punk.

Classical Punk: The Last Subculture

At the heart of early punk was calculated anger. It was anger at the establishment and anger at the allegedly soft rebellion of the hippie counterculture; anger, too, at the commodification of rock and roll (Cullen 1996: 249). Its politics were avowedly apolitical, yet it openly and explicitly confronted the traditions and norms of the powers-that-be. Describing the cultural milieu for young people in 1975, Greil Marcus° notes the centrality of cultural production: "For the young everything flowed from rock 'n' roll (fashion, slang, sexual styles, drug habits, poses), or was organized by it, or was validated by it" (Marcus 1989: 53). But by the early 1970s, with commodification in full swing, with some artists said to have compromised their integrity by becoming rich stars, and with "rock" having been integrated into the mainstream, some people felt that youth subcultures were increasingly a part of the intensifying consumer society, rather than opponents of the mainstream. Punk promised to build a *scene* which could not be taken. Its anger, pleasures, and ugliness were to go beyond what capitalism and bourgeois society could swallow. It would be untouchable, undesirable, unmanageable.

Early punk was a proclamation and an embrace of discord. In England 10 it was begun by working-class youths decrying a declining economy and rising unemployment, chiding the hypocrisy of the rich, and refuting the notion of reform. In America, early punk was a middle-class youth movement, a reaction against the boredom of mainstream culture (Henry 1989: 69). Early punk sought to tear apart consumer goods, royalty, and sociability; and it sought to destroy the idols of the bourgeoisie.°

At first punk succeeded beyond its own lurid dreams. The Sex Pistols created a fresh moral panic fueled by British tabloids, Members of Parliament, and plenty of everyday folk. Initially, at least, they threatened "everything England stands for": patriotism, class hierarchy, "common decency," and "good taste." When the Sex Pistols topped the charts in Britain, and climbed high in America, Canada, and elsewhere, punk savored a moment in the sun: every public castigation only convinced more people that punk was *real*.

Damning God and the state, work and leisure, home and family, sex and play,
the audience and itself, the music briefly made it possible to experience all those
things as if they were not natural facts but ideological constructs: things than
had been made and therefore could be altered, or done away with altogether.

Greil Marcus: American music journalist and cultural critic (b. 1945).
bourgeoisie: middle class.

It became possible to see these things as bad jokes, and for the music to come forth as a better joke. (Marcus 1989: 6)

Punk was to cross the Rubicon° of style from which there could be no retreat. Some punks went so far as to valorize anything mainstream society disliked, including rape and death camps; some punks slid into fascism. When the raw forces and ugliness of punk succumbed to corporate-capitalism within a few short years, the music/style nexus had lost its battle of Waterloo. Punk waged an all-out battle on this front, and it wielded new and shocking armaments, but in the end, even punk was proven profitable. Penny Rimbaud traces its coöptation: "within six months the movement had been bought out. The capitalist counter-revolutionaries had killed with cash. Punk degenerated from being a force for change, to becoming just another element in the grand media circus. Sold out, sanitized and strangled, punk had become just another social commodity, a burnt-out memory of how it might have been"[3] (1998: 74).

Profits serve to bandage the wounds inflicted by subcultures, while time and nostalgia cover over the historical scars. Even punk, when reduced to a neat mohawk hairstyle and a studded leather jacket, could be made into a cleaned-up spokesman for potato chips. Suddenly, the language of punk was rendered meaningless. Or perhaps—perhaps—the meaningless language of punk was made meaningful. Greil Marcus (1989:438) records the collapse of punk transgression: "the times changed, the context in which all these things could communicate not pedantry but novelty vanished, and what once were metaphors became fugitive footnotes to a text no longer in print."

Like their subcultural predecessors, early punks were too dependent 15 on music and fashion as modes for expression; these proved to be easy targets for corporate coöptation. "The English punk rock rhetoric of revolution, destruction, and anarchy was articulated by means of specific pleasures of consumption requiring the full industrial operations that were ostensibly were the objects of critique" (Shank 1994: 94). Tactically speaking, the decisive subcultural advantage in music and style—their innovation, rebellion, and capacity to alarm—was preempted by the new culture industry, which mass-produced and sterilized punk's verve. With the collapse of punk's stylistic ultimatum, what had been the foundations for twentieth-century subcultural dissent were diminished—not lost, but never to completely recover the power they once had in music and style.

Rubicon: boundary that when crossed commits a person to a course of action.

The Triumph of the Culture Industry

Having ostensibly neutralized early punk, the culture industry proved itself capable of marketing any classical youth subculture. All styles, musics, and poses could be packaged: seemingly no subculture was immune to its gaze. So leveled, classical subcultures were deprived of some of their ability to generate meaning and voice critique. . . .

With its capacity to designate all subcultures, all youth, under a smooth frosting of sameness, the culture industry was capable of violating the dignity of subcultists and softening their critique. Implied in the culture industry's appropriation of subcultural imagery was the accusation of sameness, of predictability, of a generic "kids will be kids." To paste on any group a label of synchronic oneness, is to in some way echo colonial tactics. "Youths" or "kids," when smothered with a pan-generational moment of discontent, are reduced to a mere footnote to the dominant narrative of corporate-capitalism. Trapped in nostalgia and commercial classifications, subcultures and youth are merged into the endless, amalgamated consumer culture.

No wonder, then, that subcultural styles no longer provoke panics, except in select small towns. Piercings and tattoos might get their owner rejected from a job, but they generally fail to arouse astonishment or fear.[4] Writes Frederic Jameson (1983: 124): ". . . there is very little in either the form of the content of contemporary art that contemporary society finds intolerable and scandalous. The most offensive forms of this art—punk rock, say . . . are all taken in stride by society." So too, ideas of self-gratification are no longer at odds with the status quo. In the "Just Do It" culture of the late-twentieth century, selfish hedonism dominates the airwaves. Says Simon Reynolds: "'Youth' has been co-opted, in a sanitized, censored version . . . Desire is no longer antagonistic to materialism, as it was circa the Stones' "Satisfaction."' Instead young people often relate to the alienation of The Smiths or R.E.M., who seem to lament that 'everyone is having fun except me'; the sense of failure at not having the "sex/fun/style" of the young people in the mass media (1988: 254). Indeed, long before "satisfaction" became hegemonic the commodity promised to satisfy. But because it cannot satisfy it leaves a melancholy satisfiable only in further consumption. So notes Stacy Corngold who concludes that "Gramsci's general point appears to have been confirmed: all complex industrial societies rule by non-coercive coercion, whereby political questions become disguised as cultural ones and as such become insoluble" (1996: 33). Youth subcultures, after the triumph of the culture industry, may perpetually find themselves one commodity short of satisfaction, and trapped by words that were once libratory. . . .

We can say, too, that the economy for subcultural codes suffers from hyper-inflation. In other words, the value of subcultural signs and meanings has been depleted: an unusual hairstyle just can't buy the outsider status it used to. Stylistic transgressions are sometimes piled on one another like so many pesos, but the value slips away almost instantly. Thus, by the 1990s, dissident youth subcultures were far less able to arouse moral panics (Boëthius 1995: 52) despite an accelerated pace of style innovation (Ferrell 1993: 194). In the 2000s, subcultural style is worth less because a succession of subcultures has been commodified in past decades. "Subculture" has become a billion dollar industry. Bare skin, odd piercings, and blue jeans are not a source of moral panics these days: they often help to create new market opportunities. Even irony, indifference, and apathy toward styles and subculture have been incorporated into Sprite and OK Cola commercials: every subjectivity, or so it may seem, has been swallowed up by the gluttons of Madison Avenue (Frank 1996, 1997a, 1997b).

Long Live Punk: New Ways of Being Subcultural

Looking back at the 1980s one has to ask whether punk really died at 20 all. Perhaps the death of punk symbolically transpired with the elections of Margaret Thatcher in England (1979) and Ronald Reagan in America (1980). The Sex Pistols broke up (1978), Sid Vicious died (1979), and—most damningly—too many teeny boppers were affecting a safe, suburban version of "punk." For many people, spiked hair and dog collars had become a joke, the domain of soda pop ads and teevee dramas. But did punk disappear with the utter sell-out of its foremost corporate spokesband, the Sex Pistols? Did punk vanish when pink mohawks could be found only on pubescent heads at the shopping mall? If the spectacular collapse of punk was also the collapse of spectacular subcultures, what remained after the inferno? What crawled from the wreckage? In what ways can young people express their unease with the modern structure of feeling? A new kind of punk has been answering these questions.

After shedding its dog collars and Union Jacks, punk came to be: (1) an anti-modern articulation, and (2) a way of being subcultural while addressing the discursive problems of subcultures. In fact, these two courses prove to be one path. That is, the problems of contemporary punk subcultures, after the "death" of classical subcultures, prove to be intimate with the characteristics of recent modernity. Punk, then, is a position from which to articulate an ideological position without accruing the film of mainstream attention.

Contemporary punk subcultures may therefore choose to avoid spectacle-based interaction with dominant culture. Gone too is the dream of toppling the status quo in subcultural revolution. The culture industry not only proved louder than any subcultural challenge, it was a skilled predator on the prowl for fresh young subcultures. The power to directly confront dominant society was lost also with the increasing *speed* with which the commodification of deviant styles is achieved. It may be only a matter of months between stylistic innovation and its autonomous language of outsider-ness, and its re-presentation in commercials and shopping malls.

Even the un-style of 1990s grunge (an old pair of jeans and a flannel shirt) was converted to the religion of the consumer; baptized and born-again as celebrations of corporate-capitalism. With such history in mind, new social movements such as punk attempt to forego style, shared music, and even names for themselves, for fear of being coöpted by the market democracy. Tom Frank, speaking at a convention of zinesters addressed precisely this aspect of the structure of feeling in the 1990s.

The real thing to do is get some content. *If you don't want to be coöpted, if you don't want to be ripped off, there's only one thing that's ever going to prevent it and that's politics. National politics, politics of the workplace, but most importantly politics of* culture. *Which means getting a clue about what the Culture Trust does and why, and saying what needs to be said about it. As culture is becoming the central pillar of our national economy, the politics of culture are becoming ever more central to the way our lives are played out. Realize that what the Culture Trust is doing is the greatest obscenity, the most arrogant reworking of people's lives to come down the pike in a hundred years. Be clear from the start: what we're doing isn't a subculture; it's an* adversarial *culture.* (Frank 1996)

To a certain extent, punk means post-punk—a nameless, covert 25 subculture re-formed after punk. To recap: early punk was, in part, simulated "anarchy"; the performance of an unruly mob. So long as it could convince or alarm straight people, it achieved the enactment. For its play to work, punk needed a perplexed and frightened "mainstream" off which to bounce. But when the mainstream proved that it needed punk, punk's

> "But when the mainstream proved that it needed punk, punk's equation was reversed: its negativity became positively commercial."

equation was reversed: its negativity became positively commercial. As mainstream style diversified, and as deviant styles were normalized, punk had less to act against. Punk had gambled all its chips on public outcry, and when it could no longer captivate an audience, it was wiped clean. Post-punk, or contemporary punk, has foregone these performances of anarchy and is now almost synonymous with the practice of anarchism.

Long after the "death" of classical punk, post-punk and/or punk subcultures coalesce around praxis. For contemporary punks subcultural membership, authenticity, and prestige are transacted through action internal to the subculture.

Greil Marcus' idea of punk's greatness is that the Sex Pistols could tell Bill Grundy to "fuck off" on television. The real greatness of punk is that it can develop an entire subculture that would tell Bill Grundy and safe, boring television culture as a whole to fuck off directly, establishing a parallel social reality to that of boring consumerism. (Van Dorston 1990)[5]

Stripped nude, ideologies developed in the early years of punk continue to provide frameworks for meaningful subculture. Against the threatening purview of mass media and its capacity to usurp and commodify style, punk subcultures steer away from symbolic encounters with the System and create a basis in experience.

Punks, in my work among the anarchist-punks of Seattle, don't call themselves punks. Instead they obliquely refer to the *scene* in which they "hang out." They deny that they have rules, and claim that they are socially and ideologically porous. After three decades, here is what has become of many of the CCCS' spectacular subcultures. And yet, in their stead, vibrant, living subcultures remain, with sets of regulations, norms, and their own ideological turfs. Seattle's anarchist-punks, for example, disavow an orthodox name, costume, or music; yet in many ways they continue to live, or perhaps squat, within the classical structure of subculture. Although today's punks refuse to pay the spectacular rent, they find that a new breed of subculture offers them ideological shelter and warmth.

From whence did these latter-day punks come? In contemporary 30 America, the relentless commodification of subcultures has brought about a crisis in the act of subcultural signification. Punk is today, in part, a careful articulation in response to the hyper-inflationary market for subcultural codes and meanings, an evasion of subcultural commodification, and a protest against prefabricated culture; and punk is a subculture which resists the hegemonic discourse of subculture. The public coöptation of punk has led some punks to disclaim early punk, while preserving its more political features. Having been forced, as it were, out of a costume and music-based clique, punk is evolving into one of the most powerful political forces in North America and Europe, making its presence felt in the Battle of Seattle (1999), Quebec City (2001), EarthFirst!, Reclaim the Streets, and in variety of anti-corporate movements.

Like the spectacular subcultures so aptly described by the CCCS in the 1970s, current punks are partly in pursuit of an authentic existence. However, now that stylistic authenticity has been problematized by the "conquest of cool" (Frank 1997), punks have found that the ultimate authenticity lies in political action. Where subcultures were once a steady source of freshly marketable styles for corporations, they now present corporations with a formidable opponent. *Punk* marks a terrain in which people steadfastly challenge urban sprawl, war, vivisection, deforestation, racism, the exploitation of the third world, and many other manifestations of corporate-capitalism. The threatening pose has been replaced with the actual threat.

Perhaps that is one of the great secrets of subcultural history: *punk faked its own death.* Gone was the hair, gone was the boutique clothing, gone was negative rebellion (whatever they do, we'll do the opposite). Gone was the name. Maybe it had to die, so as to collect its own life insurance. When punk was pronounced dead it bequeathed to its successors—to itself—a new subcultural discourse. The do-it-yourself culture had spawned independent record labels, specialty record stores, and music venues: in these places culture could be produced with less capitalism, more autonomy, and more anonymity. Punk faked its own death so well that everyone believed it. Many people who were still, in essence, punk did not know that they were inhabiting kinds of punk subjectivity. Even today, many people engaged in what might be called punk think of punk only in terms of its classical archetype. Punk can be hidden even to itself.

Punk had to die so that it could live. By slipping free of its orthodoxies—its costumes, musical regulations, behaviors, and thoughts—punk embodied the anarchism it aspired to. Decentralized, anti-hierarchical, mobile, and invisible, punk has become a loose assemblage of guerrilla militias. It cannot be owned, it cannot be sold. It upholds the principles of anarchism, yet is has no ideology. It is called punk, yet it has no name.

References

Boëthius, U. (1995), "Youth, the Media and Moral Panics," in J. Fornäs and G. Bolin (eds.), *Youth Culture in Late Modernity*, London: Sage.

Corngold, S. (1996), "The Melancholy Object of Consumption," in R. Bogue and M. Cornis-Pope, (eds.), *Violence and Mediation in Contemporary Culture*, Albany, NY: State of New York Press.

Cullen, J. (1996), *The Art of Democracy: A Concise History of Popular Culture in the United States*, New York: Monthly Review Press.

Ferrell, J. (1993), *Crimes of Style: Urban Graffiti and the Politics of Criminality.* NY: Garland Publishing.

Frank, T. (1996), "Zines and the Global Economy," talk given and tape recorded at the Center of Contemporary Art, Seattle, WA, 13 January 1996.

_____. (1997a), *The Conquest of Cool: Business Culture, Counterculture, and the Rise of Hip Consumerism*, Chicago, IL: University of Chicago Press.

_____. (1997b), (Untitled). Talk and book reading for *The Conquest of Cool*, from personal tape recording, Left Bank Books, Seattle, WA.

Henry, T. (1989), *Break All Rules! Punk Rock and the Making of a Style*, Ann Arbor, MI: UMI Research Press.

Jameson, F. (1983), "Postmodernism and Consumer Society" in H. Foster (ed.) *The Anti-Aesthetic: Essays on Postmodern Culture.* Seattle, WA: Bay Press.

Marcus, G. (1989), *Lipstick Traces: A Secret History of the Twentieth Century*, Cambridge, MA: Harvard University Press.

Reynolds, S. (1988), "Against Health and Efficiency: Independent Music in the 1980s," in A. McRobbie (ed.), *Zoot Suits and Second-Hand Dresses: an Anthology of Fashion and Music*, Boston, MA: Unwin Hyman.

Rimbaud, P. (1998), *Shibboleth–My Revolting Life*, San Francisco, CA: AK Press.

Shank, B. (1994), *Dissonant Identities: The Rock'N'Roll Scene in Austin, Texas*, Hanover, NH: Wesleyan University Press.

Van Dorston, A. S. (1990/2001), "A History of Punk." Fast N' Bulbous Music Webzine, http://www.fastnbulbous.com/punk.htm.

Notes

1. Though subculture has far broader meanings, it has come to signify the twentieth century category for youth groups who possess some sort of marked style and shared affiliations. And while sociologists use the term to describe an infinitely wider array of groups—sport fishermen, West Texas Baptists, or toy train hobbyists—'subculture' is more popularly used to characterize groups of young people. From the flappers of the 1920s to the Chicano cholos of the 1970s, 'subculture' is above all a container which attempts to hold various groups of young people whose affect, clothing, music, and norms, deviate from a mythological center. That these subcultures are often 'White' in their ethnic composition is regularly unmarked in academic discussions, despite its enormous import. I should add that my research focuses on the United States, though people from many nations may recognize similar trends.

2. 'Mainstream' is used to denote an imaginary hegemonic center of corporatized culture. It is used here as it is used by many people in dissident subcultures: to

denote hegemonic culture. It is, in this sense, an archetype, rather than something with a precise location and character. It serves to conveniently outline a dominant culture for purposes of cultural critique and identity formation.

3. Penny Rimbaud is one of the founding members of Crass, an English punk band that helped to revitalize, de-stylize, organize, and politicize punk in the 1980s. In some ways latter-day punk is a direct outcome of the movement led by Crass and other self-described 'anarcho-punks.'

4. Subcultures arouse no fear, that is, so long as their members are 'White.' 'Gangs,' a term which often refers to any gathering of young brown-skinned people (especially boys and young men) can frighten, alarm, and threaten straight society. The danger sometimes associated with non-White youth is the last vestige of subcultural fear. And that is one reason why 'White' youths are increasingly following the subcultural lead of their 'Black' agemates, and consuming and affecting what they believe to be is 'Black' culture.

5. Van Dorston is responding to Marcus (1989). Penny Rimbaud (1998: 79) makes much the same point: 'The pundits who now claim that punk grew out of bands like the New York Dolls, and then found its true expression in the Sex Pistols, have totally missed the point . . . The bands were secondary to an attitude, an attitude born on the street rather than manufactured in Tin Pan Alley.'

Understanding the Text

1. What does Clark mean when he claims that "punk had to die so that it could live" (pars. 1 and 33)?

2. Where does the term "cultural hegemony" (par. 7) mean? How does Clark connect the idea of hegemony to "commodification" and "consumerism"?

Reflection and Response

3. As Clark suggests, England after World War II has been a hotbed of subcultures. Why do you think this is the case?

4. Identify ways in which punk style and culture have been mainstreamed into American life. Consider especially how the original meaning of certain symbols and behaviors has changed, moving from the margins to the "unnoticed" middle of American culture.

5. Clark's writing serves as a good example of academic discourse. Choose two paragraphs from the article and rewrite them in everyday language. How do the stylistic choices that you make alter the way the reader understands punk?

Making Connections

6. Where does the word "punk" come from? In what other contexts is this word used? How are the different usages of the word "punk" connected? How are they distinct?

7. After doing some research, compare the British punk movement of the 1970s described in Clark's article to the American punk movement that came shortly after. What do these two subcultures have in common? How—and why—do they differ?

8. Throughout the article, Clark joins the conversation about punk by quoting and paraphrasing the work of others. Specifically, what kind of quotations does he use? Why? How does he decide whether to paraphrase the original sources or to quote from them?

B eing a college student means being a college writer. No matter what field you are studying, your instructors will ask you to make sense of what you are learning through writing. When you work on writing assignments in college, you are, in most cases, being asked to write for an academic audience.

Writing academically means thinking academically — asking a lot of questions, digging into the ideas of others, and entering into scholarly debates and academic conversations. As a college writer, you will be asked to read different kinds of texts; understand and evaluate authors' ideas, arguments, and methods; and contribute your own ideas. In this way, you present yourself as a participant in an academic conversation.

What does it mean to be part of an *academic conversation*? Well, think of it this way: You and your friends may have an ongoing debate about the best film trilogy of all time. During your conversations with one another, you analyze the details of the films, introduce points you want your friends to consider, listen to their ideas, and perhaps cite what the critics have said about a particular trilogy. This kind of conversation is not unlike what happens among scholars in academic writing — except they could be debating the best public policy for a social problem or the most promising new theory in treating disease.

If you are uncertain about what academic writing *sounds like* or if you're not sure you're any good at it, this booklet offers guidance for you at the sentence level. It helps answer questions such as these:

How can I present the ideas of others in a way that demonstrates my understanding of the debate?

How can I agree with someone, but add a new idea?

How can I disagree with a scholar without seeming, well, rude?

How can I make clear in my writing which ideas are mine and which ideas are someone else's?

The following sections offer sentence guides for you to use and adapt to your own writing situations. As in all writing that you do, you will have to think about your purpose (reason for writing) and your audience (readers) before knowing which guides will be most appropriate for a particular piece of writing or for a certain part of your essay.

The guides are organized to help you present background information, the views and claims of others, and your own views and claims — all in the context of your purpose and audience.

Academic Writers Present Information and Others' Views

When you write in academic situations, you may be asked to spend some time giving background information for or setting a context for your main idea or argument. This often requires you to present or summarize what is known or what has already been said in relation to the question you are asking in your writing.

SG1 Presenting What Is Known or Assumed

When you write, you will find that you occasionally need to present something that is known, such as a specific fact or a statistic. The following structures are useful when you are providing background information.

As we know from history, _____.

X has shown that _____.

Research by X and Y suggests that _____.

According to X, _____ percent of _____ are/favor _____.

In other situations, you may have the need to present information that is assumed or that is conventional wisdom.

People often believe that _____.

Conventional wisdom leads us to believe _____.

Many Americans share the idea that _____.

_____ is a widely held belief.

In order to challenge an assumption or a widely held belief, you have to acknowledge it first. Doing so lets your readers believe that you are placing your ideas in an appropriate context.

Although many people are led to believe X, there is significant benefit to considering the merits of Y.

College students tend to believe that _____ when, in fact, the opposite is much more likely the case.

SG2   Presenting Others' Views

As a writer, you build your own *ethos*, or credibility, by being able to fairly and accurately represent the views of others. As an academic writer, you will be expected to demonstrate your understanding of a text by summarizing the views or arguments of its author(s). To do so, you will use language such as the following.

X argues that _____.

X emphasizes the need for _____.

In this important article, X and Y claim _____.

X endorses _____ because _____.

X and Y have recently criticized the idea that _____ .

_____ , according to X, is the most critical cause of _____ .

Although you will create your own variations of these sentences as you draft and revise, the guides can be useful tools for thinking through how best to present another writer's claim or finding clearly and concisely.

SG3 Presenting Direct Quotations

When the exact words of a source are important for accuracy, authority, emphasis, or flavor, you will want to use a direct quotation. Ordinarily, you will present direct quotations with language of your own that suggests how you are using the source.

X characterizes the problem this way: " . . ."

According to X, _____ is defined as " . . ."

" . . . ," explains X.

X argues strongly in favor of the policy, pointing out that " . . ."

Note: You will generally cite direct quotations according to the documentation style your readers expect. MLA style, often used in English and in other humanities courses, recommends using the author name paired with a page number, if there is one. APA style, used in most social sciences, requires the year of publication generally after the mention of the source, with page numbers after the quoted material. In *Chicago* style, used in history and in some humanities courses, writers use superscript numbers (like this[6]) to refer readers to footnotes or endnotes. In-text citations, like the ones shown below, refer readers to entries in the works cited or reference list.

MLA	Lazarín argues that our overreliance on testing in K-12 schools "does not put students first" (20).
APA	Lazarín (2014) argues that our overreliance on testing in K-12 schools "does not put students first." (p. 20)
Chicago	Lazarín argues that our overreliance on testing in K-12 schools "does not put students first."[6]

Many writers use direct quotations to advance an argument of their own:

Standardized testing makes it easier for administrators to measure student performance, but it may not be the best way to measure it. Too much testing wears students out and communicates the idea that recall is the most important skill we want them to develop. Even education policy advisor Melissa Lazarín argues that our overreliance on testing in K-12 schools "does not put students first" (20).

Student writer's idea

Source's idea

SG4   Presenting Alternative Views

Most debates, whether they are scholarly or popular, are complex—often with more than two sides to an issue. Sometimes you will have to synthesize the views of multiple participants in the debate before you introduce your own ideas.

> On the one hand, X reports that _____, but on the other hand, Y insists that _____.
>
> Even though X endorses the policy, Y refers to it as " . . . "
>
> X, however, isn't convinced and instead argues _____.
>
> X and Y have supported the theory in the past, but new research by Z suggests that _____.

Academic Writers Present Their Own Views

When you write for an academic audience, you will indeed have to demonstrate that you are familiar with the views of others who are asking the same kinds of questions as you are. Much writing that is done for academic purposes asks you to put your arguments in the context of existing arguments—in a way asking you to connect the known to the new.

When you are asked to write a summary or an informative text, your own views and arguments are generally not called for. However, much of the writing you will be assigned to do in college asks you to take a persuasive stance and present a reasoned argument—at times in response to a single text, and at other times in response to multiple texts.

SG5 Presenting Your Own Views: Agreement and Extension

Sometimes you agree with the author of a source.

X's argument is convincing because _____.

Because X's approach is so _____, it is the best way to _____.

X makes an important point when she says _____.

Other times you find you agree with the author of a source, but you want to extend the point or go a bit deeper in your own investigation. In a way, you acknowledge the source for getting you so far in the conversation, but then you move the conversation along with a related comment or finding.

X's proposal for _____ is indeed worth considering. Going one step further, _____.

X makes the claim that _____. By extension, isn't it also true, then, that _____?

_____ has been adequately explained by X. Now, let's move beyond that idea and ask whether _____.

SG6 Presenting Your Own Views: Queries and Skepticism

You may be intimidated when you're asked to talk back to a source, especially if the source is a well-known scholar or expert or even just a frequent voice in a particular debate. College-level writing asks you to be skeptical, however, and approach academic questions with the mind of an investigator. It is OK to doubt, to question, to challenge—because the end result is often new knowledge or new understanding about a subject.

Couldn't it also be argued that _____?

But is everyone willing to agree that this is the case?

While X insists that _____ is so, he is perhaps asking the wrong question to begin with.

The claims that X and Y have made, while intelligent and well-meaning, leave many unconvinced because they have failed to consider _____.

A Note about Using First Person "I"

Some disciplines look favorably upon the use of the first person "I" in academic writing. Others do not and instead stick to using third person. If you are given a writing assignment for a class, you are better off asking your instructor what he or she prefers or reading through any samples given than *guessing* what might be expected.

First person (*I, me, my, we, us, our*)

I question Heddinger's methods and small sample size.

Harnessing children's technology obsession in the classroom is, I believe, the key to improving learning.

Lanza's interpretation focuses on circle imagery as symbolic of the family; my analysis leads me in a different direction entirely.

We would, in fact, benefit from looser laws about farming on our personal property.

Third person (names and other nouns)

Heddinger's methods and small sample size are questionable.

Harnessing children's technology obsession in the classroom is the key to improving learning.

Lanza's interpretation focuses on circle imagery as symbolic of the family; other readers' analyses may point in a different direction entirely.

Many Americans would, in fact, benefit from looser laws about farming on personal property.

You may feel as if not being able to use "I" in an essay in which you present your ideas about a topic is unfair or will lead to weaker statements. Know that you can make a strong argument even if you write in the third person. Third person writing allows you to sound more assertive, credible, and academic.

 SG7 **Presenting Your Own Views: Disagreement or Correction**

You may find that at times the only response you have to a text or to an author is complete disagreement.

X's claims about _____ are completely misguided.

X presents a long metaphor comparing _____ to _____;
in the end, the comparison is unconvincing because _____.

It can be tempting to disregard a source completely if you detect a piece
of information that strikes you as false or that you know to be untrue.

Although X reports that _____, recent studies indicate that is
not the case.

While X and Y insist that is _____ so, an examination of their
figures shows that they have made an important miscalculation.

SG8   Presenting and Countering Objections to Your Argument

Effective college writers know that their arguments are stronger when
they can anticipate objections that others might make.

Some will object to this proposal on the grounds that _____.

Not everyone will embrace _____; they may argue instead that
_____.

Countering, or responding to, opposing voices fairly and respectfully
strengthens your writing and your *ethos*, or credibility.

X and Y might contend that this interpretation is faulty; however,
_____.

Most _____ believe that there is too much risk in this
approach. But what they have failed to take into consideration is
_____.

Academic Writers Persuade by Putting It All Together

Readers of academic writing often want to know what's at stake in a particular debate or text. Aside from crafting individual sentences, you must,
of course, keep the bigger picture in mind as you attempt to persuade,
inform, evaluate, or review.

SG9   Presenting Stakeholders

When you write, you may be doing so as a member of a group affected by the research conversation you have entered. For example, you may be among the thousands of students in your state whose level of debt may change as a result of new laws about financing a college education. In this case, you are a *stakeholder* in the matter. In other words, you have an interest in the matter as a person who could be impacted by the outcome of a decision. On the other hand, you may be writing as an investigator of a topic that interests you but that you aren't directly connected with. You may be persuading your audience on behalf of a group of interested stakeholders—a group of which you yourself are not a member.

You can give your writing some teeth if you make it clear who is being affected by the discussion of the issue and the decisions that have or will be made about the issue. The groups of stakeholders are highlighted in the following sentences.

Viewers of Kurosawa's films may not agree with X that _____.

The research will come as a surprise to parents of children with Type 1 diabetes.

X's claims have the power to offend potentially every low-wage earner in the state.

Marathoners might want to reconsider their training regimen if stories such as those told by X and Y are validated by the medical community.

SG10   Presenting the "So What"

For readers to be motivated to read your writing, they have to feel as if you're either addressing something that matters to them or addressing something that matters very much to you or that should matter to us all. Good academic writing often hooks readers with a sense of urgency—a serious response to a reader's "So what?"

Having a frank discussion about _____ now will put us in a far better position to deal with _____ in the future. If we are unwilling or unable to do so, we risk _____.

Such a breakthrough will affect _____ in three significant ways.

It is easy to believe that the stakes aren't high enough to be alarming; in fact, _____ will be affected by _____.

Widespread disapproval of and censorship of such fiction/films/art will mean _____ for us in the future. Culture should represent _____.

_____ could bring about unprecedented opportunities for _____ to participate in _____, something never seen before.

New experimentation in _____ could allow scientists to investigate _____ in ways they couldn't have imagined _____ years ago.

SG11   Presenting the Players and Positions in a Debate

Some disciplines ask writers to compose a review of the literature as a part of a larger project—or sometimes as a freestanding assignment. In a review of the literature, the writer sets forth a research question, summarizes the key sources that have addressed the question, puts the current research in the context of other voices in the research conversation, and identifies any gaps in the research.

Writing that presents a debate, its players, and their positions can often be lengthy. What follows, however, can give you the sense of the flow of ideas and turns in such a piece of writing.

_____ affects more than 30% of children in America, and signs point to a worsening situation in years to come because of A, B, and C. Solutions to the problem have eluded even the sharpest policy minds and brightest researchers. *[Student writer states the problem.]* In an important 2003 study, W found that _____, which pointed to more problems than solutions. [. . .] *[Student writer summarizes the views of others on the topic.]* Research by X and Y made strides in our understanding of _____ but still didn't offer specific strategies for children and families struggling to _____. [. . .] When Z rejected both the methods and the findings of X and Y, arguing that _____, policy makers and health-care experts were optimistic. [. . .] Too much discussion of _____, however, *[Student writer presents her view in the context of current research.]* and too little discussion of _____, may lead us to solutions that are ultimately too expensive to sustain.

Appendix: Verbs Matter

Using a variety of verbs in your sentences can add strength and clarity as you present others' views and your own views.

When you want to present a view fairly neutrally

acknowledges	observes
adds	points out
admits	reports
comments	suggest
contends	writes
notes	

X points out that the plan had unintended outcomes.

When you want to present a stronger view

argues	emphasizes
asserts	insists
declares	

Y argues in favor of a ban on _____; but Z insists the plan is misguided.

When you want to show agreement

agrees
confirms
endorses

An endorsement of X's position is smart for a number of reasons.

When you want to show contrast or disagreement

compares	refutes
denies	rejects
disputes	

The town must come together and reject X's claims that _____ is in the best interest of the citizens.

When you want to anticipate an objection

admits
acknowledges
concedes

Y admits that closer study of _____, with a much larger sample, is necessary for _____.

Acknowledgments (continued from page iv)

Tristan Ahtone. "Why Gangs?" and "Boys in the Woods" from *Native American Gangs* by Tristan Ahtone. Al Jazeera America, January 19, 2015. Reprinted by permission of Tristan Ahtone.

Scott Anderson. "Polygamists: A sect that split from the Mormons allows multiple wives, expels 'lost boys,' and heeds a jailed prophet" from *National Geographic Magazine*, February 2010. Reprinted by permission of Scott Anderson/National Geographic Creative.

G. Beato. "The Lords of Dogtown" from *Spin Magazine*, March 1999. Reprinted by permission of SpinMedia Group.

Sinclair Bolden. "The Real Real: The Five Ways Subcultures Self-Police Themselves Online" from *The Alchemist*, February 6, 2015. Reprinted by permission of Sylvain Labs.

Anatole Broyard. "A Portrait of the Hipster" from *Partisan Review*, June 1948. Reprinted by permission of the Estate of Anatole Broyard.

Sue-Ellen Case. Excerpts from "Making Butch: An Historical Memoir" from *Butch/Femme: Inside the Lesbian Gender*, edited by Sally R. Munt (Cassell, 1998). Reprinted by permission of the author.

Dylan Clark. "The Death and Life of Punk, The Last Subculture" from *Post-Subcultures Reader*, by David Muggleton and Rupert Weinzierl. Copyright © David Muggleton and Rupert Weinzierl 2003. Published by Berg Publishers, an imprint of Bloomsbury Publishing Plc. Used by permission of the publisher.

Ariel Climer. "Riding to Resist: L.A. Bicyclists Brave Death to Empower Communities." Reprinted by permission of the author.

Lydia Crafts. "Muhammad Rocked the Casbah" from *Texas Observer*, December 14, 2007. Reprinted by permission of the *Texas Observer*.

Travis Hugh Culley. Excerpts from *The Immortal Class: Bike Messengers and the Cult of Human Power* by Travis Hugh Culley, copyright © 2001 by Travis Hugh Culley. Used by permission of Villard Books, an imprint of Random House, a division of Penguin Random House LLC. All rights reserved. Any third party use of this material, outside of this publication, is prohibited. Interested parties must apply directly to Penguin Random House LLC for permission.

Cody C. Delistray. "Commercializing the Counterculture." *Pacific Standard* by Miller-McCune Center for Research, Media, and Public Policy Reproduced with permission of Miller-McCune Center for Research, Media and Public Policy in the format Republish in a book via Copyright Clearance Center.

Edward Dolnick. Excerpts from "Deafness as Culture" from *The Atlantic Monthly*, September 1993, pp. 37–53. Reprinted by permission of the author.

James Dowd and Laura Dowd. Excerpts from "The Center Holds" in *Teaching Sociology*, January 2003, (vol 31 no 1), 20–37. Reprinted by permission of the American Sociological Association and the authors.

William Finnegan. Excerpts from "The Unwanted" from *The New Yorker*, December 1, 1997. Reprinted by permission of the author.

Alex Forman. "San Francisco Style: The Diggers and the Love Revolution" excerpted from Freedom Press publication, *Anarchy 77* (vol 7 no 7), July 1967. Reprinted by permission of Freedom Press.

Bob Frost. "Low and Slow: The History of Lowriders" from *The History Channel Magazine*, 2002. © A+E Networks, Reprinted by Permission.

BJ Gallagher. "Military BRATS = Bright. Resilient. Active. Talented. Successful." from *Huffington Post*, December 1, 2014. Reprinted by permission of the author.

Glendenb. "Femininity and Toughness: What Rodeo Queens Tell Us About America." Courtesy of *Daily Kos*.

Dana Goodyear. Excerpts from "Raw Deal" from *The New Yorker*, April 30, 2012. Reprinted by permission of the author.

Teresa Gowan. "Moorings" from *Hobos, Hustlers, and Backsliders: Homeless in San Francisco*. Copyright © 2010 by the Regents of the University of Minnesota. Used by permission of the University of Minnesota Press.

George Gurley. Excerpts from "Pleasures of the Fur" from *Vanity Fair*, March 2001. Reprinted by permission of the author.

Douglas Haddow. "Hipsters: The Dead End of Western Civilization." July 29, 2008. Reprinted by permission of the Adbusters Media Foundation.

Ross Haenfler. "Hip Hop—Doing Gender and Race in Subcultures" from *Goths, Gamers, & Grrrls*, Third Edition (2015): 4,161 words (pp. 47–65). By permission of Oxford University Press USA.

Leslie Heywood. Excerpts from "Building Otherwise: Bodybuilding as Immersive Practice" in *Critical Readings in Bodybuilding*, Routledge. Reproduced with permission of Routledge in the format Book via Copyright Clearance Center.

Immy Humes. Excerpts from "A Life Apart: A Brief Introduction to Hasidim"—a PBS series produced by Menachem Daum and Oren Rudavsky and funded by the National Endowment for the Humanities and is available at http://firstrunfeatures.com/lifeapartdvd.html and on Amazon. Used by permission of Oren Rudavsky Films.

Brittany Julious. "The State of Black Subcultures in 21st Century America" from VICE Media, July 13, 2014. Reprinted by permission of the author.

Bruce Levine. "Why Anti-Authoritarians Are Diagnosed as Mentally Ill." February 23, 2012 (http://brucelevine.net/why-anti-authoritarians-are-diagnosed-as-mentally-ill-and-how-this-helps-america%E2%80%99s-illegitimate-authorities-stay-in-charge/). Reprinted by permission of the author.

Michaelangelo Matos. © 2011 Michaelangelo Matos for National Public Radio, Inc. Excerpts from NPR news report titled "How The Internet Transformed The American Rave Scene" by Michaelangelo Matos were originally published on NPR.org on July 11, 2011, and is used with the permission of NPR. Any unauthorized duplication is strictly prohibited.

Elisa Melendez. Excerpts from "Cosplay Is Creative, Not Crazy: An Open Letter to the *New York Post*" from *Miami New Times*, August 7, 2013. Reprinted by permission of the *Miami New Times*.

Kim Murphy. "The American Redoubt: Where Survivalists Plan to Survive" from the *Los Angeles Times*, February 8, 2012. Reprinted by permission of the *Los Angeles Times*.

Patton Oswalt. "Wake Up, Geek Culture, Time to Die" from *Wired*, December 27, 2010. Reprinted by permission of Condé Nast Publications.

Kristen Schilt. Excerpts from "'A Little Too Ironic': The Appropriation and Packaging of Riot Grrrl Politics by Mainstream Female Musicians" from *Popular Music and Society*, Vol 26, No 1, 2003. Reprinted by permission of the Taylor & Francis Ltd., www.tandfonline.com.

Brett Scott. Excerpts from "The Hacker Hacked" (https://aeon.co/essays/how-yuppies-hacked-the-original-hacker-ethos). Reprinted by permission of the author.

Linda Stasi. "Syfy Looks at World of Make-believe Reality in 'Heroes of Cosplay'" from the *New York Post*, August 5, 2013. © 2013 New York Post. All rights reserved. Used by permission and protected by the Copyright Laws of the United States. The printing, copying, redistribution, or retransmission of this Content without express written permission is prohibited.

Arlene Stein. "The Stranger Next Door" by Arlene Stein. Copyright © 2001 by Arlene Stein. Reprinted by permission of Beacon Press, Boston.

Richard A. Stevick. *Growing Up Amish: The Rumspringa Years*, Second Edition. pp. 47–66. © 2007, 2014. Johns Hopkins University Press. Reprinted with permission of Johns Hopkins University Press.

Nina Strochlic, "American Gypsies Are a Persecuted Minority That Is Starting to Fight Back" from *The Daily Beast*, December 22, 2013, © 2013 The Daily Beast Company. All rights reserved. Used by permission and protected by the Copyright Laws of the United States. The printing, copying, redistribution, or retransmission of this Content without express written permission is prohibited.

Mark Stryker. "A Street Art Culture Clash as Graffiti Goes Mainstream." Reprinted by permission of *Detroit Free Press*.

Hunter S. Thompson. Excerpts from *Hell's Angels: A Strange and Terrible Saga*, 1966, 1967. Used by permission of Random House, an imprint and division of Penguin Random House LLC. All rights reserved. Any third party use of this material, outside of this publication, is prohibited. Interested parties must apply directly to Penguin Random House LLC for permission.

Index of Authors and Titles